#202263073   4/25/06   LF

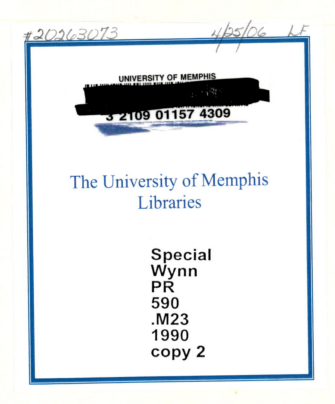

READING ROMANTICS

READING ROMANTICS

Texts and Contexts

PETER J. MANNING

New York   Oxford
OXFORD UNIVERSITY PRESS
1990

Oxford University Press

Oxford   New York   Toronto
Delhi   Bombay   Calcutta   Madras   Karachi
Petaling Jaya   Singapore   Hong Kong   Tokyo
Nairobi   Dar es Salaam   Cape Town
Melbourne   Auckland

and associated companies in
Berlin   Ibadan

Published by Oxford University Press, Inc.,
200 Madison Avenue, New York, New York 10016

Library of Congress Cataloging-in-Publication Data
Manning, Peter J., 1942–
Reading romantics : texts and contexts / Peter J. Manning.
p.   cm.
ISBN 0–19–505787–2
1. English poetry—19th century—History and criticism.
2. Wordsworth, William, 1770–1850—Criticism and interpretation.
3. Byron, George Gordon Byron, Baron, 1788–1824—Criticism and
interpretation.   4. Romanticism—England.   I. Title.
PR590.M23   1990
821'.709—dc20   89–38917   CIP

2 4 6 8 9 7 5 3 1

Printed in the United States of America
on acid-free paper

Acknowledgments

I wish to thank that community of scholars from whose encourage-
ment and genial criticism the following essays draw their strength:
James Chandler, John Clubbe, Jerome Christensen, Alan Grob,
Michael Hancher, Al Hutter, Kenneth Johnston, William Keach,
Terry Kelley, Melvin Lansky, Morton Paley, Arden Reed, Jeffrey
Robinson, Gene Ruoff, Leon Waldoff, and Jonathan Wordsworth.
All but the first of the essays were written since I came to Los
Angeles, welcomed by Paul Sheats; to him, to Anne Mellor, and to
the other members of the generously inclusive UCLA Romantics
Study Group, I owe the best kind of professional exchange. The
queries of my students at the University of Southern California
sharpened my thinking, and Leo Braudy, Jim Kincaid, Hilary Schor,
and Max Schulz have been enviable colleagues, prodding and fostering. I do not forget what I owe to a former colleague, Marjorie
Perloff, and to Jerome McGann, who during his time in Los Angeles
added the stimulus of his presence to the force of his writing. I am
also beholden to Karl Kroeber and Don Reiman, who gave support
when they could not know how much it was needed. For aid of a
more material kind, I am happy to acknowledge the American Coun-
cil of Learned Societies, the American Philosophical Society, and
the John Simon Guggenheim Memorial Foundation.

Susan Wolfson deserves at the least a paragraph by herself. My
work would be poorer without her provocative suggestions and
scrupulous attention, and her hand can be traced in whatever is

pointed or eloquent in these pages. Without her this book would not have been.

Several of the essays have appeared in earlier forms. I am grateful to the following for permission to reprint: Johns Hopkins University Press, for "Wordsworth at St. Bees: Scandals, Sisterhoods, and Wordsworth's Later Poetry," *English Literary History* 52 (1985): 33–58; *Studies in English Literature, 1500–1900,* for "Wordsworth and Gray's Sonnet on the Death of West," *SEL* 22 (1982): 505–18; University of Chicago Press, for "The Hone-ing of Byron's *Corsair,*" in *Textual Criticism and Literary Interpretation,* ed. Jerome McGann (1985); University of Illinois Press, for "Wordsworth's Intimations Ode and Its Epigraphs," *Journal of English and Germanic Philology* 82 (1983): 526–40; the University of Salzburg, for "Tales and Politics: *The Corsair, Lara,* and *The White Doe of Rylstone,*" in *Byron: Poetry and Politics,* ed. E. A. Sturzl and James Hogg, *Salzburger Studien Zur Anglistik und Amerikanistik* 13 (1981): 204–30; Wayne State University Press, for *"Michael,* Luke, and Wordsworth," *Criticism* 19 (1977): 195–211; and the Trustees of Boston University for four articles published in *Studies in Romanticism*— "Wordsworth, Margaret, and The Pedlar," 15 (1976): 195–220; "Reading Wordsworth's Revisions: Othello and the Drowned Man," 22 (1983): 3–28; *"Don Juan* and Byron's Imperceptiveness to the English Word," 18 (1979): 207–33, and "Placing Poor Susan: Wordsworth and the New Historicism," 25 (1986): 351–69.

Contents

READING
ROMANTICS

Introduction

Reading Romantics: Texts and Contexts consists of thirteen essays, some previously published and some appearing for the first time. The published pieces range from 1976 to 1986; the talks from which the unpublished ones were developed were first given in 1985 (that on *The Solitary Reaper*), 1986 (that on *The White Doe of Rylstone*), and 1987 (that on *Beppo*). Though the essays were written over more than a decade, they are united by a continuing endeavor to join formalism with wider concerns. They seek to reconnect literature with the motives from which it springs and the social relations within which it exists. The tactics have evolved, but the aim of the project— the reconceiving of the literary object as New Criticism defined it— has been constant. Bringing the essays together has afforded the occasion to revise, to eliminate some awkwardness (if surely not all) and indulge in second thoughts, to lessen redundancies and clarify ongoing themes. The resulting book contributes to the study of the Romantics by its fusion of psychoanalytic insight, textual criticism, and historical scholarship, but I aim less to stake a claim than to explore the territory jointly traced by the primary works that continue to inspire our readings and the literary theories by which we try to explain our engagements to ourselves and others.

Psychoanalysis, in its Freudian formulation and in the post-Freudian critique to which it gave rise, offers a means of approaching literary-critical problems resistant to traditional methods. The first group of essays in the volume, devoted to Wordsworth, was written under the sign of a methodology recognizably kin to that in my *Byron and His Fictions* (1978). Each essay concentrates on a canonical, representative work, drawing from the complex surfaces and still more from the gaps of the texts an animating subtext, an underlying image of the self both concealed and revealed by the poet's conscious fictions. Taken together, the four essays mark successive stages of Wordsworth's development between the 1790s and 1815, the year of his collected *Poems.* They are critical in intent, however, rather than psychobiographical. The latter pair of the group, exploring Wordsworth's relations to two of his precursors, Gray and Virgil, exemplify the necessary convergence of the personal and the literary-historical in the study of Wordsworth's language.

The broad spectrum of relations into which literary texts enter includes as well their temporal development. Compositional history, understood as itself a question needing to be thought, occupies a prominent place in the volume. The essays in the second group focus on the particular problems of reading texts composed over many years, under diverse circumstances, and with various intentions still visible in the laminations of the final published version. The wide import of these questions is made clear by analyses of *The Prelude* and *Don Juan,* a juxtaposition that complicates the polarity between Wordsworth's seemingly end-driven autobiography, which demands that he find his life "[a]ll gratulant if rightly understood" (1805, XIII, 385), and Byron's improvisatory manner, what Karl Kroeber has recently wonderfully termed its "open-sided" quality.[1] An essay on *Beppo* which exposes the process of exchange between author and public upon which the self depends draws into scrutiny the actual readership both Byron and Wordsworth imagined as they wrote.

In their mutual detestation, Byron and Wordsworth have long been taken as the antipodes of English Romanticism; Longfellow, writing in the *North American Review,* voiced a nineteenth-century commonplace when he rejoiced that the "pure and gentle philosophy" of Wordsworth was gaining ascendancy over the "noxious influence" of Byron's "unhealthy imagination."[2] Our terminology is less moralistic, but the contrasts have proved no less compelling: the Whig radical as against the Tory reactionary; the free-thinking aristocrat as against the earnest Protestant; the sensationally popular figure, one of whose works sold ten thousand copies on the day of publication, as against a poet for whom an edition of fifteen hundred copies represented success; the erratic genius who died dramatically at thirty-six in the cause of Greek freedom as against the eighty-year-old sage of Rydal Mount. To study them together through the lens of reception is one goal of *Reading Romantics*. The overtly materialist essays of the third section—on *Lara, The Corsair* (illuminated by consideration of Hone's hitherto neglected pirated edition), and *The White Doe of Rylstone*—disclose much about the institution of literature in the Romantic period and the interaction between the ideal of originality which the Romantics fostered and the means of production through which they found expression.

That the heading of the third section, "Text and Context," is merely an organizational marker should be apparent to anyone who has proceeded thus far in the book, just as the difference between sections should not obscure the continuities that link them. *Subtext* (the second term of the first division) and *context* alike suggest realms lying beyond the words of the text itself; with increasing explicitness the essays argue a contrary proposition, that those terrains are mapped in the text itself. Or, more accurately, in the encounter between the texts resituated in their world and a present-day reader. The heading of the last section, "Texts and History," describes the critical trajectory of the volume as a whole.

The first essay in the final group rereads *The Solitary Reaper*, the lyric with which Geoffrey Hartman epitomizes the thesis of *Wordsworth's Poetry 1787–1814*, still the most influential study of its subject. The critique of his transcendentalizing is staged by reconstructing the circumstances of Wordsworth's 1803 Scots tour, the writing of the poem in 1805, and the sequences in which Wordsworth placed the poem upon publication in the 1807 *Poems, in Two Volumes*. From this setting there emerges a Wordsworth quite different from Hartman's vision of "the most isolated figure among the great English poets." "Wordsworth at St. Bees: Scandals, Sisterhoods, and Wordsworth's Later Poetry" is a specimen demonstration of the vital connections of Wordsworth's ignored later verse to a host of pressing contemporary issues, religious, political, and social. Altering the sense of its conclusion alters the conception of Wordsworth's entire career, casting new perspectives on the earlier work on which his reputation rests. To suggest, moreover, that Wordsworth's late poetry is not simply a decline from his greatest achievements but can fruitfully be apprehended in relation to such Victorian writers as Keble and Tennyson is to reopen the categories of genre and period which limit understanding of other writers besides Wordsworth.

After such arguments it may seem puzzling to conclude with a troubled meditation on the New Historicism. It is, however, the argument of the book come full circle: if the New Criticism risked the diminution of poems by removing them from contexts, the New Historicism risks their diminution by collapsing them too quickly into their presumed ideological matrices. I have kept a distance from a method that has taught me a great deal in order to keep open the vitality of the poems and our discussion of them: the quest to comprehend poems in their historical difference from us and their silence before the very questions that enliven them never ends.

Notes

1. *British Romantic Art* (Berkeley: University of California Press), p. 223.
2. *North American Review* 34 (1832): 76, quoted in *Byron: The Critical Heritage,* ed. Andrew Rutherford (New York: Barnes and Noble, 1970), p. 18.

I

Texts and Subtexts

1

Wordsworth, Margaret, and The Pedlar

"On the whole poets are known by the best versions of their works: Wordsworth is almost exclusively known by his worst." So wrote Jonathan Wordsworth, provocatively; to diminish such misrepresentation, he published in 1969 MS. D of the poem which later became Book I of *The Excursion*.[1] In that middle stage the poet separated the two parts that had been together in MS. B (printed by de Selincourt and Darbishire in the notes to Volume V of the *Poetical Works*) and were to be rejoined in *The Excursion,* the narrative of Margaret's misfortunes and the character study of the narrator; the first we know as *The Ruined Cottage,* the second as *The Pedlar.* The division is beneficial to both parts, Jonathan Wordsworth suggests, because the description of the Pedlar, the product of Wordsworth's excitement at "new philosophical ideas," chiefly that of the One Life, "has almost no bearing on *The Ruined Cottage* proper," Wordsworth's "first great poem" (*The Music of Humanity,* p. xiii).

Praise for the compassion Wordsworth shows in *The Ruined Cottage,* his "insight into emotions not his own," had been anticipated by F. R. Leavis, who commented in *Revaluation* that the tale of Margaret was "the finest thing that Wordsworth wrote."[2] This view of the merit and, as it were, the detachability of the narrative has enjoyed wide acceptance; indeed, with its endorsement by both the *Oxford Anthology of English Literature* and the *Norton Anthology of English Literature,* it has become virtually canonical, at least for American readers. The editors of the *Oxford Anthology* print

The Ruined Cottage alone, declaring that it "is by common scholarly agreement now considered the most effective" version of the poem.[3] The editors of the *Norton Anthology* do likewise and observe in their headnote:

> This is a shorter and better poem than the one reprinted in *The Poetical Works* (MS. B). The latter lacks the great concluding passage, lines 493–538, and includes in Part I more than 250 lines describing the youthful development of the peddler that are extraneous to the narrative proper and soften the hard naturalism of the story by introducing into it, at considerable length, the peddler's faith that nature teaches "deeply the lesson deep of love."

Book I of *The Excursion,* "longer still," is said to dilute the impact of Margaret's sufferings even more.[4]

Curiously enough, the subtlest criticism that *The Ruined Cottage* has received comes from a position implicitly antithetical to the view that the bare story is the source of its strength. Geoffrey Hartman's analysis concludes:

> Instead of one dangerously static point two centers now appear: the "I" and the "alien" (place). This division is repeated as the "I" generates together with its persona (the Pedlar) the relation of a second person (Margaret) to a central place (the garden). . . . The middle ground of the spectrum, however, is occupied by the Pedlar and his attitude toward nature, and there "All things shall speak of Man." Human filters are made to intervene between the strange imagination and its strange object: poet→ pedlar→ (Margaret→cottage)→the ruin. . . . Ultimately poet and pedlar still stare at a ruin which stares at itself.[5]

Although he gives some further attention to Margaret in his discussion of *The Excursion,* this passage is representative of Hartman's treatment. The diagram and especially the parentheses are significant: in his concern with the metamorphoses of the apocalyptic imagination, Hartman is comparatively uninterested in the particular contents of the materials on which it works. The poet and not his tale, the bleak ruin and not the woman, engage him.

We have one group of readers for whom Wordsworth's strengths are those of impersonal but compassionate observation and another for whom his poetic self-consciousness is paramount; the two agree only in their equal neglect of the crucial relationship between the story of Margaret and the imagination of the poet. A review of the compositional history of Book I of *The Excursion* can show us how profoundly intertwined are the stories of Margaret and the Pedlar, suggest a motive for Wordsworth's impulse to separate them, and reveal the underlying coherence of the longer text with which he began and to which he returned.

I

The germ of *The Ruined Cottage* lies in the fragments of blank verse de Selincourt and Darbishire printed under the title *Incipient Madness*. The first of these begins:

> I crossed the dreary moor
> In the clear moonlight: when I reached the hut
> I entered in, but all was still and dark,
> Only within the ruin I beheld
> At a small distance, on the dusky ground
> A broken pane which glittered in the moon
> And seemed akin to life. There is a mood
> A settled temper of the heart, when grief,
> Become an instinct, fastening on all things
> That promise food, doth like a sucking babe
> Create it where it is not. From this time
> That speck of glass was dearer to my soul
> Than was the moon in heaven.
>   (*PW*, I, 314–15)[6]

The passage then describes a second experience at the hut "at another time," and this phrase, like the beginning which seems to presuppose that "the hut" is already familiar, suggests a series of visits. The fixation on the broken pane and the phrase "grief / Become an instinct, fastening on all things / That promise food" strike an obsessive note.

The simile of the sucking babe forges a link stronger than mere juxtaposition with a second fragment on the same sheet:

> I have seen the Baker's horse
> As he had been accustomed at your door
> Stop with the loaded wain, when o'er his head

Smack went the whip, and you were left, as if
You were not born to live, or there had been
No bread in all the land. Five little ones,
They at the rumbling of the distant wheels
Had all come forth, and, ere the grove of birch
Concealed the wain, into their wretched hut
They all returned. While in the road I stood
Pursuing with involuntary look
The wain now seen no longer, to my side
[   ] came, a pitcher in her hand
Filled from the spring; she saw what way my eyes
Were turned, and in a low and fearful voice
By misery and rumination deep
Tied to dead things, and seeking sympathy
She said: "that waggon does not care for us"—
                                                    (*PW*, I, 315–16)

Jonathan Wordsworth relates this scene to a dialogue between Margaret and the Pedlar in *The Ruined Cottage* (MS. D, 423–26), and the connection between the fragment and the poem, reinforced by the metrical fit of "Margaret" with the lacuna where a name should be in the fragment, is clear enough. Yet by linking these fragments to *The Ruined Cottage,* we have only begun to explore their relationship to each other.

When we consider the dying woman and her children in *An Evening Walk* (1793, 241–300), Martha in *The Thorn,* the "female vagrant" in the poem finally published as *Guilt and Sorrow, The Complaint of a Forsaken Indian Woman,* and the maiden betrayed by Clifford in *The Borderers,* "the poor tenant of that ragged homestead" (568),[7] to cite just a few of the works of this period, the recurrence of the abandoned, suffering woman is intriguing. The frequency is too great to be accounted for by popular taste or literary convention, and one is tempted to adduce in explanation guilt on Wordsworth's part over the separation from Annette Vallon. Certain repeated features, however, suggest that prior conflicts stemming from the death of Wordsworth's mother shortly before his eighth birthday are also invested in the creation of these dramatic characters, although the poetic fictions stand in complex relation to the biographical fact. The paradigm for these poems is *The Mad Mother* (retitled *Her Eyes Are Wild* in 1815) who is preserved from the despair that engulfs her only by the infant boy nursing at her breast.[8] The poem ends on a fantasy of unending happiness: "Now laugh and be gay, to the woods away! / And there, my babe; we'll live for aye." The mother saved by her son and retreating with him to live forever in nature probably corresponds with Wordsworth's desire to have saved his mother by the intensity of his love and thus to have maintained the intimacy recorded in the "Blessed Babe" passage of Book II of *The Prelude* (written by 1799). The extraordinary harmony of that tableau is the positive measure of Wordsworth's tender union with his mother; no less persuasive are these poems elaborating the pathos of the disruption of the mother-child bond. The woman in the second fragment is one in this series of sorrowing mothers in Wordsworth's poetry of the 1790s. Her particular closeness to Wordsworth is hinted at by the number of her offspring: there were also five Wordsworth children.

A second connection grows from the pitcher carried by the woman in the fragment, for this too is a common feature. In classical psychoanalytic theory, pitchers are often interpreted as displaced symbols of the maternal breast, an equation to which the Wordsworthian instances give increasing credibility. Margaret is associated with the well where the Pedlar and the poet find refreshment. The dying woman in *An Evening Walk,* is, like Margaret, married to an absent soldier, and brings a pitcher in her train of associations:

> [She] bids her soldier come her woes to share,
> Asleep on Bunker's charnel hill afar;
> For hope's deserted well why wistful look?
> Chok'd is the pathway, and the pitcher broke.
> (1793, 253–56)

In itself this pitcher is emblematic and unremarkable; in conjunction with the overgrown well and its broken bowl in *The Ruined Cottage* (MS. B, 312–41), it acquire heightened interest. De Selincourt and Darbishire print in the *apparatus criticus* of *Guilt and Sorrow* a passage from MS. 2 in which the mother of the beaten child explains to the sailor and the soldier's wife more fully than in the published poem the brutal incident that shocks them:

> Yet still she told that on the covered earth
> At breakfast they were set, their child their joy and mirth.
> Her husband for that pitcher rose; his place
> The infant took, as true as heaven is the tale,

And when desired to move, with smiling face
For a short while did in obedience fail.
He was not five years old, and him to trail
And bruise, as if each blow had been his last,
She knew not what for life his brain might ail.

(PW, I, 119)

The episode seems nakedly oedipal: the son seeks to supplant his father, who punishes him violently for his presumption while his mother tries helplessly to defend him. The absence in the manuscript of the introduction implied by the phrase "that pitcher" magnifies the psychological significance of this object in the episode.[9]

The scene has strong links with one that Wordsworth narrates of himself, the Penrith Beacon "spot of time" in Book XI of the 1805 *Prelude*.[10] Richard J. Onorato calls this moment "the truest memory of early childhood," and his discussion of it illuminates the episode in MS. 2 of *Guilt and Sorrow* and is in turn illuminated by it.[11] The boy Wordsworth, "then not six years old" (1805, XI, 280), strays from his guide James while on a horseback expedition, testing his capacity to assert his independence, much as the boy in *Guilt and Sorrow* does. Like that boy, he is brought up short: he finds himself lost and fearfully alone in the landscape. He stumbles on a gibbet where, the 1799 *Prelude* tells us, "in former times / A man, the murderer of his wife, was hung"; both the detail itself and its subsequent deletion reveal the anxious family dynamics at work in the scene (1799, 306–7).[12] The terrifying isolation is ended not as expected, by the rediscovery of James, but by the sudden appearance of a woman:

> forthwith I left the spot
> And, reascending the bare common, saw
> A naked Pool that lay beneath the hills,
> The Beacon on the summit, and more near,
> A Girl who bore a Pitcher on her head
> And seem'd with difficult steps to force her way
> Against the blowing wind.

(1805, XI, 302–8)

Onorato suggests that this scene is a screen memory, invested with memories of the mother; that plausible interpretation is corroborated by the other instances and is the clue to them all.

This survey discloses the seeds from which *The Ruined Cottage* germinates and suggests that the second fragment, the description of the sorrowing woman with five children who eventually becomes Margaret, draws on Wordsworth's feelings of despair surrounding the death of his mother. Since the hut of the first fragment and the hut of the second are the same—and the drafts of MS. A printed by de Selincourt and Darbishire show that the hut of the first corresponds to that of *The Ruined Cottage* (*PW*, V, 377)[13]—we can appreciate the essence of the "grief" that envelops the speaker of the first. He compares the grief to a "sucking babe," a simile that points straight to the heart of the situation: the speaker's obsessive return to the hut where the woman dwelt plays out a fantasy of reunion with the mother, recovering the vanished security of the infant nursing at her breast.

A third element in the situations of Wordsworth's suffering women should also be noted: the absence, for one reason or another, of their children's fathers. The "mad mother" ultimately finds solace—even joy—in her infant, but Margaret declines and dies when abandoned by Robert. The woman left alone with her children may simply reflect Wordsworth's recollection of his early childhood: his father was frequently away from home. The occupation of a soldier— on service to the king—may be an echo of John Wordsworth's sojourns on business for Sir James Lowther.[14] When, as in *The Ruined Cottage,* the children's presence cannot console the mother, that helplessness may express both an overriding consciousness of the hard fact that Ann Wordsworth died and a continuing sense of personal inadequacy (as opposed to the fantasy of infant power in *The Mad Mother*); the separation from Annette would have reinforced the latter. In *The Ruined Cottage* the situation is simultaneously doubled and condensed in the Pedlar, whose wandering occupation is analogous to soldiering and stewardship and who is also unable to help Margaret. This is a secondary aspect of the Pedlar to which I shall return.

While recognizing our conjectures as conjectures, we may speculate that in the story of Margaret, Wordsworth depicted the trauma to which he was repeatedly driven back by the perplexity of his life in the late 1790s. In the Pedlar he adumbrated what was to be his characteristic response to his loss: the transformation of the fantasy of reunion into the vision of himself as the solitary man communing with nature. The relationship of these two parts is a rich strand of his poem, perhaps its central element.

II

We have Wordsworth's own word for the role of the Pedlar. He told Isabella Fenwick in 1841–1843 "that the character I have represented in his person is chiefly an idea of what I fancied my own might have become in his circumstances" (*PW,* V, 373). The hypothetical cast of this confession rather understates the consanguinity of the poet and his creation. Two of the most resonant passages of MS. B describing the Pedlar's childhood (238–56 and 276–300) reappear in the first-person account Wordsworth gives of himself in Books II and III of *The Prelude* (1805, II, 416–34 and III, 124–67). Writing of himself in the guise of another, however, released Wordsworth from the censorship the conscious mind imposes on painful circumstances of the past; as a result, the childhood he ascribes to the Pedlar may map the inner contours of his own experience more faithfully than that of the autobiographical poem in which he was struggling to demonstrate that his vicissitudes had been "All gratulant if rightly understood" (1805, XIII, 385).

Even in his youth the Pedlar is a solitary figure. In MS. B we never see him amidst his family: his father is mentioned perfunctorily, his mother not at all. He attends school, but, in marked contrast to Books I and II of *The Prelude,* no schoolfellows appear. The lack of human contact fosters a compensatory receptivity to nature, although that is to phrase the matter more baldly than the poem admits. A new position in the family strengthens the boy's intimacy with nature:

> Ere his ninth summer he was sent abroad
> To tend his father's sheep, such was his task
> Henceforward till the later day of youth.
> Oh! then what soul was his when on the tops
> Of the high mountains he beheld the sun
> Rise up and bathe the world in light. He looked,
> The ocean and the earth beneath him lay
> In gladness and deep joy. The clouds were touched
> And in their silent faces did he read
> Unutterable love. Sound needed none
> Nor any voice of joy: his spirit drank
> The spectacle. Sensation, soul and form
> All melted into him. They swallowed up
> His animal being; in them did he live
> And by them did he live. They were his life.
>   (MS. B, 119–33)[15]

The moment in the life of his character at which Wordsworth locates this grand climax is significant. Ann Wordsworth died in March 1778; that is, just before William's "ninth summer." In the boy's being "sent abroad" we may see a figurative, greatly moderated reflection of the disruption caused by Wordsworth's mother's death.

Two other concurrences suggest that there is more than coincidence here. This "high hour / Of visitation from the living God" (134–35), of "blessedness and love" (141), bears many resemblances to the Dawn Dedication in Book IV of *The Prelude:*

> Magnificent
> The morning was, a memorable pomp,
> More glorious than I ever had beheld.
> The sea was laughing at a distance; all
> The solid Mountains were as bright as clouds
> Grain-tinctured, drench'd in empyrean light;
> And, in the meadows and the lower grounds,
> Was all the sweetness of a common dawn,
> Dews, vapours, and the melody of birds,
> And Labourers going forth into the fields.
> —Ah! need I say, dear Friend, that to the brim
> My heart was full; I made no vows, but vows
> Were then made for me; bond unknown to me
> Was given, that I should be, else sinning greatly,
> A dedicated Spirit. On I walk'd
> In blessedness, which even yet remains.
>   (1805, IV, 330–45)

These two scenes, as Jonathan Wordsworth remarks, seem "clearly based on the same memory" (*The Music of Humanity,* p. 221); if so, Wordsworth's placement of it first in a character of precisely his age at the death of his mother and then in his own person but at the age of eighteen on his first summer vacation from Cambridge is revelatory. The date of the first placement links Wordsworth's responsiveness to nature obliquely but firmly with the loss of his mother; by transferring the emotions to his late adolescence, he redefines them as part of his increasingly self-conscious consecration to poetry. A similar desire to neutralize the anxieties that originally contributed to his feelings underlies his blurring of the reference to the boy's age in the published text of *The Excursion,* discussed below. The two changes are poignant instances of the process by which Wordsworth reshaped the trauma of his early years into his adult identity as a poet.

In *The Prelude,* Wordsworth records with impressive restraint that the death of his mother left her children "destitute, and as we might / Trooping together" (1805, V, 259–60). The happy childhood he invents for the Pedlar excludes such pain. The feelings not acknowledged in his character "ere his ninth summer," however, return later. "But now, before his twentieth year was pass'd," Wordsworth says of the Pedlar:

> Accumulated feelings press'd his heart
> With an encreasing weight; he was o'er power'd
> By Nature, and his mind became disturbed,
> And many a time he wished the winds might rage
> When they were silent: from his intellect,
> And from the stillness of abstracted thought
> In vain he sought repose
>
> (MS. B, 221–28)

The violence of this passage is surprising. Nothing in the poem prepares us to understand this sudden disquiet, nor is it easy to comprehend how nature can cause "the fever of his heart" (MS. B, 237) that troubles the Pedlar. The personification of "Nature and her overflowing soul" (MS. B, 238) suggests that perhaps unresolved tensions caused by the loss of the mother have resurfaced. Finding that "the wandrings of his thought were then / A misery to him" (*PW,* V, 385), the Pedlar abandons the schoolmastership his father has recommended,[16] resolves to "quit his native hills (MS. B, 260), and sets out on his restless existence. In the finished text of Book I of *The Excursion* Wordsworth situates this crisis in his character's eighteenth year (I, 280), and the conjunction of this moment with the time of the Dawn Dedication in *The Prelude* indicates the parallelism of Wordsworth's turn to poetry and the Pedlar's briefly avowed malaise.

The second element associating the Pedlar's formative childhood experience with the death of Wordsworth's mother is in the actual language of his vision. The typically Wordsworthian oral imagery—the verbs of swallowing, drinking, and melting—recalls the fusion of mother and nursing infant: the shattered union with the mother is succeeded by communion with nature. Compare further Wordsworth's description of himself in *The Prelude,* when "a Babe, by intercourse of touch, / I held mute dialogues with my Mother's heart" (1805, II, 228–83), with "The clouds were touched / And in their silent face did he read / Unutterable love." The Pedlar's memory of Margaret echoes the original situation: "Many a passenger / Has blessed poor Margaret for her gentle looks / When she upheld the cool refreshment drawn / From that forsaken well" (MS. B, 348–51).

The Pedlar, as F. R. Leavis remarks, is "very much in the nature of an idealized self-portrait," what Wordsworth "would have liked to be." "That he should have needed to wish it is the great difference between himself" and the Pedlar, Leavis continues, acutely recognizing that the Pedlar "emerges out of Wordsworth's urgent personal problem," is born out of "his great need" (*Revaluation,* pp. 178–79). His adolescent crisis passed, no disturbances are allowed to ruffle the tranquility of the Pedlar's later existence among the hills:

> there he kept
> In solitude, and solitary thought,
> So pleasant were those comprehensive views,
> His mind in a just equipoise of love.
> Serene it was, unclouded by the cares
> Of ordinary life, unvexed, unwarped
> By partial bondage. In his steady course
> No piteous evolutions had he felt,
> No wild varieties of joy or grief,
> Unoccupied by sorrow of its own
> His heart lay open and by nature tuned
> And constant disposition of his thoughts
> To sympathy with Man, he was alive
> To all that was enjoyed where'er he went,
> And all that was endured and in himself
> Happy and quiet in his chearfulness
> He had no painful pressure from within
> Which made him turn away from wretchedness
> With coward fears. He could afford to suffer
> With those whom he saw suffer.
>   (MS. B [*PW,* V, 386–87])

Throughout these lines we feel across the praise of the Pedlar's calm the contrasting spiritual weariness of the speaker which leads him to extol it, much as the apostrophe to the Babe in *The Prelude*—"No outcast he, bewilder'd and depress'd" (1805, II, 261)—unveils Wordsworth's dejection at the moment of writing.[17] The printing of *The Ruined Cottage* alone, as in MS. D, sacrifices this indirect but telling self-characterization; moreover, by disjoining it from Mar-

garet, the division prevents us from gaining a full understanding of
"the great need" to which the Pedlar is the response.

The Pedlar's narration of Margaret's decline is an exemplum
intended to illustrate the proper attitude to human suffering. Wordsworth gives the story to a disengaged speaker who is free of "passion
over-near ourselves, / Reality too close and too intense" (to borrow
a phrase he used later for his political disillusionments, 1805 *Prelude*,
X, 641–42), and places himself as auditor within the poem. His responses are thus controlled by the Pedlar's explicit commentary,
which offers a philosophical stance that transforms sadness into consolation. As it is presented in Book I of *The Excursion* in 1814 and
thereafter, the problem is a general one of unmerited distress, but in
the 1790s its pressing personal nature is apparent: the story of Margaret that Wordsworth hears is his own story.

Though the Pedlar is nominally related to Margaret only by
compassion, he is profoundly involved in the story that pours out of
him. Beneath the surface of the ideally detached mediator, traces of
the original connection of tale and teller are visible. Despite the time
that has elapsed since Margaret's death, the Pedlar can yet "feel /
The story linger in my heart" (MS. B, 612–13). "My spirit clings /
To that poor woman," he tells the poet,

> so familiarly
> Do I perceive her manner and her look
> And presence, and so deeply do I feel
> Her goodness . . .
>   (MS. B, 614–18)

The seasonally recurring visits the Pedlar pays to Margaret as he
pursues his occupation are the obsessive returns to the hut of the
speaker of *Incipient Madness* carefully shorn of their neurotic component. Still the initial impulse is not entirely concealed: "The day
has been," he remembers,

> When I would never pass this road but she
> Who lived within these walls, when I appeared,
> A daughter's welcome gave me, and I loved her
> As my own child.
>   (MS. B, 342–46)

The father-daughter relationship is the mother-son relationship at
the core of the poem inverted: through the imagined figure of the

Pedlar with whom he identifies himself, Wordsworth transforms his position from that of the child bereft of his mother's support into that of the adult, benign father figure so imperturbably self-sufficient that he "could afford to suffer / With those whom he saw suffer." The original situation is not wholly effaced, however. "She is dead," the Pedlar repeats elegiacally:

> she is dead,
> And nettles rot and adders sun themselves
> Where we have sate together while she nursed
> Her infant at her bosom.
>   (MS. B, 358–61)

This vignette, pairing Pedlar and infant about the central figure of the mother, anticipates the still more symmetrical grouping Wordsworth was to make of the despairing Vaudracour, Julia, and their child in the tale that bears signs of his feelings about Annette Vallon:

> oftener was he seen
> Propping a pale and melancholy face
> Upon the Mother's bosom, resting thus
> His head upon one breast, while from the other
> The Babe was drawing in its quiet food.
>   (1805 *Prelude*, IX, 810–14)[18]

Behind both these disguised self-portraits lies Wordsworth's yearning at moments of crisis for the irretrievably lost harmony of mother and son, a fantasy that expresses the deepest source of his uncertainties.

The incompletion the Pedlar suffers when cut off from the nurturing woman is denied by *The Ruined Cottage* at the level of overt statement; only glimpses persist, and the grief of Margaret deserted by her husband is the ostensible subject of the poem. The latter, however, is a fictional vehicle which carries emotions denied direct expression in the former. Already afflicted by economic hardship, Margaret begins her fall into dejection when her husband Robert enlists and then vanishes. "Five tedious years / She lingered in unquiet widowhood," the Pedlar tells the poet, and it is his intimacy with her during that period which for the reader clothes the Pedlar with something of the aura of a surrogate for her absent man.[19] Margaret cannot bring herself to accept that Robert is gone forever:

> yet ever as there passed
> A Man whose garments shewed the Soldier's red
> Or crippled Mendicant in Sailor's garb
> The little child who sate to turn the wheel
> Ceased from his toil, and she with faltering voice
> Expecting still to learn her husband's fate,
> Made many a fond enquiry . . .
>
> (MS. B, 712–18)

Unable to reconcile herself to her loss, Margaret becomes trapped in the past, her dwindling commitment to life manifesting itself in the slow disintegration of her surroundings. Her emotional distress numbs her physically:

> Yet still
> She loved this wretched spot, nor would for worlds
> Have parted hence, and still that length of road
> And this rude bench one torturing hope endeared,
> Fast rooted at her heart; and here, my friend,
> In sickness she remained, and here she died,
> Last human tenant of these ruined walls.
>
> (MS. B, 736–42)

Margaret's hope of Robert's return becomes torturing because it ties her to place and past, and to understand the connection between Margaret's hope and fixity and the Pedlar's bond with nature and his unfettered movement, we must look closely at a conversation between them.

The Pedlar learns of Robert's decampment only when he visits her cottage and, instead of the "usual greeting," Margaret turns from him, sits, and weeps bitterly:

> Poor wretch! at last
> She rose from off her seat, and then, Oh Sir!
> I cannot *tell* how she pronounced my name
> With fervent love and with a face of grief
> Unutterably helpless, and a look
> That seemed to cling upon me, she inquired
> If I had seen her husband.
>
> (MS. B, 506–12)

The verbal echoes in this passage signal one component in the meaning of Book I of *The Excursion*. Margaret's "look / That seemed to cling" to the Pedlar is the reciprocal of the tenderness with which in memory his "spirit clings" to her (MS. B, 614); the repetition binds the figures together, and in Margaret's seeking through the Pedlar for her lost husband we can discern a reversed and slightly displaced version of the original situation: the son deprived of his mother. The echoes are more revealing still, because the "unutterably helpless" look that Robert's disappearance produces in Margaret, the fervent *love* the Pedlar sees in the *face* of grief caused by his absence, the voice whose affect the Pedlar "cannot *tell*," are counterparts of his great vision: "The clouds were touched / And in their silent faces did he read / Unutterable love" (MS. B, 126–28).[20] The comments already suggested by the oral imagery of the entire passage are extended and confirmed by this repetition: Wordsworth imbues his feelings for nature with the bonds of affection broken at his mother's death. To see the Pedlar's vision and Margaret's blankness at her desertion together is to witness the process by which Wordsworth healed himself.

The conjunction of Margaret and the Pedlar confirms much of what we know only by inference and speculation from Wordsworth's other poems about the special quality of his feeling for nature. The Pedlar's reverie of Margaret's reawakening, the beginning of which has previously been quoted, is revelatory:

> so familiarly
> Do I perceive her manner and her look
> And presence, and so deeply do I feel
> Her goodness that a vision of the mind,
> A momentary trance comes over me
> And to myself I seem to muse on one
> By sorrow laid asleep, or borne away,
> A human being destined to awake
> To human life or something very near
> To human life, when he shall come again
> For whom she suffered.
>   (MS. B, 615–25)

Jonathan Wordsworth finds this fantasy "strange and beautiful" but "unWordsworthian" (*The Music of Humanity,* pp. 138–39); it is nonetheless provocative. The Pedlar's vision of Margaret, coming upon him after her death, is literally concerned with that death, redefining it as a sleep to be ended by Robert's return. "One / By sor-

row laid asleep," however, seems figuratively to apply as well to the
five moribund years of Margaret's widowhood, passed in futile expectation. Margaret's death-in-life is a bleaker version of the joy-
lessness that Wordsworth expresses in his own voice in the roughly
contemporary *Tintern Abbey,* and the moment of insight in that
poem is suggestively similar to this passage:

> that blessed mood,
> In which the burthen of the mystery,
> In which the heavy and the weary weight
> Of all this unintelligible world
> Is lighten'd:—that serene and blessed mood,
> In which the affections gently lead us on,
> Until, the breath of this corporeal frame,
> And even the motion of our human blood
> Almost suspended, we are laid asleep
> In body, and become a living soul:
> Where with an eye made quiet by the power
> Of harmony, and the deep power of joy,
> We see into the life of things.
>
> (38–50)[21]

What is apparently uncharacteristic in the Pedlar's reverie is its
Chinese-box structure: in a trance he has a vision of Margaret in a
trance. On its surface the poem makes a firm distinction between
Margaret's attachment to Robert and the Pedlar's attachment to nature, but if we accept that Margaret and the Pedlar both dramatize
Wordsworth's feelings about the loss of his mother, we realize that
at the deepest level the two trances are identical or, rather, that it
is proper that the Pedlar's include Margaret's. The Pedlar's vision
of her is co-ordinate with his vision of the joy of nature, and the
co-ordination suggests that just as he sees Margaret "laid asleep"
until she shall be reunited with her husband, so exactly is one element of Wordsworth's own response to nature the fantasy of reunion
with the lost mother. The Lucy poems are germane here, for their
view of death as a going-into the larger life of nature opens the door
to such fantasies of rejoining the beloved through nature. Wordsworth uses the same phrase—"laid asleep"—to describe both the
Pedlar's vision of Margaret awaiting Robert to be reborn into life
and his own moment of selflessness in *Tintern Abbey,* the sublime
vision of "the life of things." This recurrence points to a strand in

Wordsworth's view of nature that he was unable to acknowledge and, indeed, in the distance he placed between Margaret and the Pedlar, sought to deny. The "presence that disturbs me with the joy / Of elevated thoughts" which he records in *Tintern Abbey* (95–96) is animated by the memories of the mother figure disclosed in the haunting of the Pedlar by Margaret's "Manner and her look / And presence."[22]

The relationship of Margaret and the Pedlar that I suggest illuminates many details of the poem. The Pedlar, for example, learns that Margaret's son has been sent from her to work:

> While on the board she spread our evening meal
> She told me she had lost her elder child,
> That he for months had been a serving boy
> Apprenticed by the parish.
>
> (MS. B, 599–602)

Jonathan Wordsworth objects: "The overstatement 'lost' at first seems to imply that the child is dead, and if this usefully suggests Margaret's own extreme reaction, it also draws attention to the real state of affairs." Though "not a very serious fault," he says, "it is doubtful whether the moment of pathos [Wordsworth] creates is worth the consequences" (*The Music of Humanity,* p. 134). The emphatic verb is significant, however, if the feelings of a son separated from his mother and alone in the world are the center of the poem. The collapse of Luke in *Michael,* which Wordsworth wrote at approximately the same time, may express a boy's—or man's—fear that he cannot stand without the support of his parents, and the contrasting portrait of himself Wordsworth implicitly presents in lauding the Babe of *The Prelude* as "No outcast he, bewilder'd and depress'd," tends to the same conclusion.[23] It is this "lost" son of Margaret's that enables us to ponder the full weight of Wordsworth's praise of the Pedlar, of the question that precedes it, "Why should he grieve? he was a chosen son" (MS. B, 272), and of Wordsworth's use of the line again to characterize himself in *The Prelude:* "Why should I grieve? I was a chosen Son" (1805, III, 82).

In the Pedlar, whom he renamed the Wanderer when *The Ruined Cottage* appeared as Book I of *The Excursion,* Wordsworth delineated his response to the feelings of mourning and arrest that he voiced through Margaret. The common condition of Margaret and the Pedlar is their solitariness, and in him we witness Words-

worth's attempt to convert the desertion that afflicts her into affirmation. Against Margaret, reduced to stasis, staring down a "length of
road (MS. B, 738), "her eye . . . busy in the distance, shaping
things / Which made her heart beat quick" (MS. B, 705–7), he set
another version of himself as the unengaged spectator leading a
"way-wandering life" (MS. B, 304), uninvolved with others and
hence free of the sorrow that inevitably accompanies mortal affections. "He from his native hills / Had wandered far, much had he
seen of men" (MS. B, 59–60) is the positive view of the Pedlar's
mobility, a curiously Wordsworthian cosmopolitanism, but other instances of the verb *to wander* betray the darker connotations of root-
lessness and aimlessness which Wordsworth tried to combat with
the figure of the Pedlar. We have already encountered the "wandering thoughts" that make the Pedlar miserable; even "the wandering
gypsey in a stormy night" (MS. B, 33) shuns the dilapidated hut
that means so much to him; Margaret, rambling afield when he pays
his unexpected visit, confesses to him: "in good truth I've wandered
much of late; / And sometimes, to my shame I speak, have need /
Of my best prayers to bring me back again" (MS. B, 596–98). Earlier Margaret has explained to the Pedlar that Robert enlisted in
secret because "he feared / That I should follow with my babes,
and sink / Beneath the misery of that wandering life" (*PW,* V,
31).[24] These recurrences are the powerful minor chord that swells
the resonance of Wordsworth's initial presentation of himself in
The Ruined Cottage. In the opening lines he introduces himself
through a contrast between the ease of a man resting on the cool,
shaded grass and his own difficult traveling:

> Other lot was mine;
> Across a bare wide Common I had toiled
> With languid feet which by the slippery ground
> Were baffled still; and when I stretched myself
> On the brown earth, my limbs from very heat
> Could find no rest, nor my weak arm disperse
> The insect host which gathered round my face
> And joined their murmurs to the tedious noise
> Of seeds of bursting gorse which crackled round.
>   (MS. B, 18–26)

The sense of frustration, of being beset, of endless journeying, is
only fully explicated by the remainder of the poem, imaginatively

perceived. The Pedlar is a partial self-portrait; the poem which became Book I of *The Excursion,* taken whole, is a multifaceted one,
and we need to have it whole to understand Wordsworth.

III

As Book I of *The Excursion* now stands, the tale of Margaret's decline is contained within a structure of exquisitely varied distances,
its effect modulated first by the Wanderer and then by Wordsworth's
responses as the auditor within the work. The Wanderer breaks
off his narrative before its sad end, unwilling to endure the recollection of Margaret's woe: "Why should we thus, with an untoward
mind . . . disturb / The calm of nature with our restless thoughts?"
(I, 599–604). Wordsworth, however, has been affected and, in
words we can now adequately appreciate, admits that "In my own
despite, / I thought of that poor Woman as of one / Whom I had
known and loved" (I, 612–14). "A heart-felt chillness crept along
my veins" (I, 619), he says, begging the Wanderer to resume his
story "for my sake" (I, 624). The evident turmoil the outcome
causes in him prompts the Wanderer at the end to try to assuage the
emotions he has raised:

> Why then should we read
> The forms of things with an unworthy eye?
> She sleeps in the calm earth, and peace is here.
> I well remember that those very plumes,
> Those weeds, and the high spear-grass on that wall,
> By mist and silent rain-drops silvered o'er,
> As once I passed, into my heart conveyed
> So still an image of tranquillity,
> So calm and still, and looked so beautiful
> Amid the uneasy thoughts which filled my mind,
> That what we feel of sorrow and despair
> From ruin and from change, and all the grief
> That passing shows of Being leave behind,
> Appeared an idle dream . . .
>   (I, 939–52)

In the assimilation of Margaret to the larger harmony of nature, we
recognize the completed tragic rhythm of engagement, arousal, and
catharsis, but Wordsworth had not always been able to round off
the story of Margaret so serenely.

As de Selincourt and Darbishire print it, MS. B ends on a note of unrelieved distress: "The End" is written at the close of the Pedlar's tale: 'here, my friend, / In sickness she remained, and here she died, / Last human tenant of these ruined walls" (MS. B, 740–42). Wordsworth told Isabella Fenwick that this original conclusion (MS. B, 696–742) was the first part of the poem to be written, and in June 1797 Coleridge sent the last thirty-seven lines of it in a letter to J. P. Estlin.[25] That Wordsworth should initially have ended his poem in this stark fashion reveals that it was precisely as a story of unmerited suffering, untransformed by any mitigating philosophical context (though distanced through the Pedlar), that he first conceived the story of Margaret. Given the origins of Margaret in his own experience it is not surprising that that should have been so, nor, given those origins, should it be surprising that to find a comforting resolution for her story was a matter of urgent personal concern.

To preserve his own equanimity, Wordsworth had somehow to resolve the contradiction between the benevolent nature and integrated self affirmed in the picture of the Pedlar and the overwhelming effect of Margaret's decline and death, increased by its climactic final position. The manuscripts bear out what we might have expected, that Wordsworth could not immediately surmount his dilemma. There were at least three attempts, to be dated February–March 1789, before he found in the reconciling image of the speargrass the agent of transformation he required (*PW*, V, 400–404). Even then Wordsworth could not lay his work aside. The reason customarily advanced for the division of the poem in MS. D is that Wordsworth had become uneasy about the double-barreled form it had taken, but since he subsequently reunited the two parts and placed the resulting poem at the head of the gravest and most substantial work he ever published, the formal reason alone is insufficient. It seems likely that one motive in Wordsworth's decision to separate the extended portrait of the Pedlar from the story of Margaret was his recognition that despite the asserted consolation of the new ending, the barren narrative overshadowed the joy in the One Life declared through the Pedlar. Wordsworth may also have felt that the conjunction of Margaret and the Pedlar, as the poem then stood, too transparently betrayed their interrelationship and hence his own troubled state of mind. The division of MS. D was radical surgery that preserved the poem by depriving it of its psychological complexity: the gain in narrative concentration entailed the reduction of perspectives. The subtle manipulation of distance which is the distinctive success of the finished poem is Wordsworth's brilliant resolution of the troubling meditation on which he had embarked.

The process of detachment Wordsworth began when he made the first-person fragments of *Incipient Madness* into a tale told him by another continued. In rough-draft addenda to MS. D and in MS. E of 1801–1802, he altered the Pedlar's birthplace from his own northern England background to Scotland.[26] Moreover, he transformed the anonymous Pedlar of MS. B who had become the fictional "Armytage" of MS. D into "Patrick Drummond," who, as Wordsworth later told Isabella Fenwick, was in part a picture of James Patrick, a pedlar he had known in his youth and to whom he was soon to become distantly related by marriage. The slight mask and the disguising of his imagined alter ego as a real person seem briefly to have encouraged a half-cloaked revelation: we hear now that the Pedlar has lost a parent. By the final version, however, this detail is deleted, and in the Wanderer only the transformed background remains:

> Among the hills of Athol he was born;
> Where, on a small hereditary farm,
> An unproductive slip of rugged ground,
> His parents, with their numerous offspring, dwelt;
> A virtuous household, though exceeding poor!
> Pure livers were they all, austere and grave,
> And fearing God; the very children taught
> Stern self-respect, a reverence for God's word,
> And an habitual piety, maintained
> With strictness scarcely known on English ground.
>
> (I, 108–17)

In this course of emancipating his poem from biography, Wordsworth's rehandling of even minor details often proves significant. "She is dead," the Pedlar laments for Margaret in MS. B,

> And nettles rot and adders sun themselves
> Where we have sate together while she nursed
> Her infant at her bosom.
>
> (358–61)

In the final text of *The Excursion* Wordsworth excised this memory and replaced it with a much more conventional image, removing the important link between Margaret, the infant, and the Pedlar:

> She is dead,
> The light extinguished of her lonely hut,
> The hut itself abandoned to decay,
> And she forgotten in the quiet grave.
>   (I, 507–10)[27]

As he had done in reducing the number of Margaret's children from five to two, Wordsworth continued to change the numbers in his poem and thus further to free it from his life. The "five tedious years" of Margaret's widowhood, parallel to the length of time Wordsworth's father outlived his mother, are altered to "Nine tedious years" (I, 871); the Pedlar's being "sent abroad" to tend his father's sheep "ere his ninth summer" is given a milder and less revealing form: "From his sixth year, the Boy of whom I speak, / In summer, tended cattle on the hills" (I, 18–19). Most important, the vision of nature which in MS. B immediately follows the statement of the boy's being sent abroad is now separated from it by seventy-five lines and an implied passage of time between "the Boy" and "the growing Youth" (I, 197) who has the revelation of nature's "unutterable love" (I, 205). Thus, Wordsworth obscured the foundations of the exalted insight in the experience of the child.

We may hypothesize that these alterations, by breaking the specific links between Wordsworth and his characters, along with the consolation the Pedlar affords in the revised ending, made possible a contrary diminution of distance between him and his creator. Prior to MS. B, the Pedlar and the poet are chance acquaintances; in February–March 1798 Wordsworth made them friends, but through MS. D their meeting at Margaret's cottage is still accidental. In the final text of *The Excursion,* the poet meets the Wanderer at the hut "by appointment" (I, 50); "I looked round, / And to my wish and to my hope espied / The Friend I sought" (I, 31–33). These changes bring the Pedlar and his tale closer to the poet, as if to acknowledge the fateful quality of the experience he is about to have.

The net effect of these changes, however, is safely to withdraw Wordsworth from his tale, and they mark the evolution of his stance in another way as well. The severe piety of the upbringing Wordsworth finally imagines for the Pedlar makes him very like the Leech-Gatherer of *Resolution and Independence,* whose "stately speech" seems to the poet "Such as grave livers do in Scotland use, / Religious men, who give to God and man their dues" (96–

98). The gradual emergence of these stern and monitory figures in Wordsworth's work is a tacit admission that nature alone could not fulfill the demands he had placed on her. The reshaping of the Pedlar in effect belies the consolation he offers. The shift in the depiction of him from one fostered almost wholly by nature to one reared within the discipline of the Scots church is an especially poignant illustration of Wordsworth's spiritual progress from the celebration of maternal nature to the patriarchal virtues of patience and fortitude enforced by his later poetry. The explicitly Christian additions of 1845, presenting Margaret as a believer in "the unbounded might of prayer," her "soul / Fixed on the Cross" (I, 936–37), and softening the human tragedy of the conclusion still more by an invocation of "the breast of Faith" (I, 955), are recognizably continuous with the stoicism to which Wordsworth had already turned by 1804.

The development of Book I of *The Excursion* provides us a view of Wordsworth's inner life as moving as it is revealing. Its value, however, is more than documentary: to follow Wordsworth as he refashions his narrative is to observe the maturing of the characteristic lineaments of his art. If the bane of psychoanalytic criticism is reductivism, its potential boon is to alert us to the energies that inform literature. The atmosphere of helplessness that enshrouds Wordsworth's story suggests the unchangeable fact of loss from which his fiction grew. "I stood," the poet says at the conclusion of the Wanderer's tale,

> and leaning o'er the garden wall
> Reviewed that Woman's sufferings; and it seemed
> To comfort me while with a brother's love
> I blessed her in the impotence of grief.
>
> (I, 921–24)

In this desolate inability to redeem what is past we recognize the feelings invested in the tale, and in the poet's fraternal sympathy we contemplate a muted and displaced echo of the son's filial despair. In giving a life history to the Pedlar Wordsworth may have elaborated him beyond what his story alone required, but story for its own sake was never Wordsworth's concern: Margaret, the Pedlar in all his fullness, and the poet as auditor form a complete unit.

Notes

1. *The Music of Humanity* (New York: Harper, 1969). In addition to the works later cited, I have made use of the following: Helen Darbishire, *"The Ruined Cottage* and *The Excursion,"* in *Essays Mainly on the Nineteenth Century* (London: Oxford University Press, 1948), pp. 1–13; John Alban Finch, *"The Ruined Cottage* Restored: Three Stages of Composition," *Bicentenary Wordsworth Studies,* ed. Jonathan Wordsworth (Ithaca: Cornell University Press, 1970), pp. 29–49; Judson S. Lyon, *The Excursion: A Study,* Yale Studies in English, No. 114 (New Haven: Yale University Press, 1950); Thomas M. Raysor, "Wordsworth's Early Drafts of *The Ruined Cottage* in 1797–98," *Journal of English and Germanic Philology* 55 (1956): 1–7; Paul D. Sheats, *The Making of Wordsworth's Poetry, 1795–98* (Cambridge, Mass.: Harvard University Press, 1973). In " 'Finer Distance': The Narrative Art of Wordsworth's 'The Wanderer,' " *English Literary History* 39 (1972): 87–111, Reeve Parker argues that "the strength of Wordsworth's poem lies in his resourcefulness in projecting his manifest personal and psychological involvement through a complex artistic structure"; our conclusions coincide, but I have tried to explore more fully the nature of that involvement.

2. F. R. Leavis, *Revaluation* (1947; rpt. New York: Norton, 1963), p. 179. Leavis reconsiders and amplifies his essay in "Wordsworth: The Creative Conditions," *Twentieth-Century Literature in Retrospect* (Cambridge, Mass.: Harvard University Press, 1971), ed. Reuben A. Brower, pp. 323–41. He there argues for Book I of *The Excursion* as "the form in which *The Ruined Cottage* ought to be current" because of its "dramatic mode of presentation": "while the tale is told by the Pedlar, the poet himself (William Wordsworth) is so insistently and effectively a presence for us that the sensibility *we* share is felt as very personally his."

3. Harold Bloom and Lionel Trilling, eds., *The Oxford Anthology of English Literature: Romantic Poetry and Prose* (New York: Oxford University Press, 1973), p. 130.

4. M. H. Abrams et al., eds., *The Norton Anthology of English Literature,* 3d ed. (New York: Norton, 1974), II, 145.

5. *Wordsworth's Poetry 1787–1814* (New Haven: Yale University Press, 1964), p. 140.

6. Quotations from Wordsworth's poetry are taken from *The Poetical Works of William Wordsworth,* ed. E. de Selincourt and Helen Darbishire (Oxford: Clarendon, 1940–1949). Abbreviated *PW.*

7. Compare the lines that initially concluded *The Ruined Cottage:* "and here, my friend, / In sickness she remained, and here she died, / Last human tenant of these ruined walls" (MS. B, 740–42).

8. Martha Ray of *The Thorn* offers a similar example. Pregnant and deserted, she goes temporarily mad, but "the unborn infant wrought / About its mother's heart, and brought / Her senses back again" (139–41).

9. The full text of MS. 2, *Adventures on Salisbury Plain,* is now available in *The Salisbury Plain Poems of William Wordsworth,* ed. Stephen Gill (Ithaca: Cornell University Press, 1975).

10. Quotations from *The Prelude* are taken from the edition by E. de Selincourt, 2d ed., rev. by Helen Darbishire (Oxford: Clarendon, 1959).

11. *The Character of the Poet: Wordsworth in THE PRELUDE* (Princeton: Princeton University Press, 1971), pp. 205–19.

12. This "spot of time" is one of the two moved from Part I of the *Two-Part Prelude* (1799) to Book XI in 1805. As the second concerns the death of Wordsworth's father (1805, XI, 345–89), it seems plausible to connect this episode with the mother as Onorato does. The text of the *Two-Part Prelude* is that given in the *Norton Anthology of English Literature*, II, 197–218. See Chapter 5 for a discussion of these reshapings.

13. Jonathan Wordsworth follows T. M. Raysor in placing MS. A of *The Ruined Cottage* before "Incipient Madness"; de Selincourt and Darbishire and John Alban Finch place MS. A later; Mark Reed, in Appendix XIII of *Wordsworth: The Chronology of the Early Years* (Cambridge, Mass.: Harvard University Press, 1967), concludes: "The two MSS. must be regarded as dating from about the same time."

14. "Owing to his constant preoccupation with business," Mary Moorman writes in *William Wordsworth: A Biography* (1957; rpt. London: Oxford University Press, 1968), John Wordsworth "was not intimately known" to his children (I, 70).

15. This first extended quotation from MS. B is the proper occasion to repeat Jonathan Wordsworth's strictures upon it: "[Miss Darbishire's] comments unfortunately give an impression that the manuscript represents a single stage in the poem's development, when in fact it consists partly of fair copy in Dorothy's hand and partly of the poet's working drafts" (*The Music of Humanity*, p. 16). I have chosen to quote from it nonetheless because it best illustrates the matrix from which Wordsworth's poem emerged.

16. In MS. B, the father suggests the schoolmastership; in Book I of *The Excursion,* it is the mother (312ff.). The change may well be part of Wordsworth's attempt to give the Pedlar the maternal support of which the character was originally deprived.

17. The praise of the Pedlar as one who does not "turn away from wretchedness / With coward fears" becomes especially resonant in contrast to Wordsworth's judgment in *The Prelude* on his own delay in offering assistance to the discharged soldier whom he meets in Book IV: "Without self-blame / I had not thus prolong'd my watch; and now, / Subduing my heart's specious cowardise . . ." (1805, IV, 432–34). The passage is the earliest stratum of *The Prelude,* and drafts of it are found in the Alfoxden and Christabel notebooks and MS. 18A, together with MS. D of *The Ruined Cottage.*

18. The echo sounded by "propping" in this passage connects it with a childhood memory. Immediately following the description of the Blessed Babe in his mother's arms, Wordsworth indirectly alludes to his mother's death: "For now a trouble came into my mind / From obscure causes: I was left alone / Seeking this visible world, nor knowing why. / The props of my affections were removed . . ." (1799, 321–24).

19. Though he judges it a "mere coincidence" (p. 127), F. W. Bateson observes in *Wordsworth: A Re-Interpretation,* 2d ed. (London: Longmans, 1956), that "in 1797 when the first draft of *The Ruined Cottage* was com-

pleted five years had elapsed since Wordsworth had left Annette 'A wife and widow.' " Robert's desertion of Margaret is perhaps a reenactment of Wordsworth's separation from Annette Vallon. If so, it is significant that Wordsworth palliates Robert's conduct by stressing the economic constraints of the times and the benevolence of his motive, to provide money for his family. The doubling of Robert and the Pedlar, Wordsworth's chief figure of himself, thus counters the defection of the one with the imaginative solicitude of the other, whose returns to the cottage would thus express the poet's own anxieties and fantasies about Annette.

20. This reading is supported by another echo: the phrase "unutterable love" occurs in connection with parental devotion in Book VIII of *The Prelude*. Disturbed by London, Wordsworth is cheered by the sight of a father who brings his "sickly babe" into the sun and "eye[s] it with unutterable love" (1805, VIII, 837–59).

21. Text from *Lyrical Ballads: Wordsworth and Coleridge,* ed. R. L. Brett and A. R. Jones (London: Methuen, 1965).

22. Compare the twice-repeated reference to the mother as a "beloved Presence" in the "Blessed Babe" passage of *The Prelude*. To interpret Margaret as a mother figure thus closely tied to Wordsworth may here provoke the rejoinder that in her grief she ignores her children. In his essay "The Poetry of Wordsworth," De Quincey facetiously insists on Margaret's responsibility for the decline of her family and half-seriously charges that her child died "of neglect" through her "criminal self-indulgence." *De Quincey's Writings* (Boston: Ticknor and Fields, 1856), IX, 18. Children often interpret the death of a parent as an abandonment of them; some such ensuing resentment on Wordsworth's part may well have contributed to the portrait De Quincey detects of a bad mother who is carefully not said to be one. Compare, for example, Wordsworth's praise of the swans in *An Evening Walk:* "Ye ne'er, like hapless human wanderers, throw / Your young on winter's winding sheet of snow" (1793, 239–40). The lines are followed by the description of the suffering woman cited in Part II, and the conjunction suggests a conscious denial of a felt maternal inadequacy.

23. See Chapter 5.

24. In both MS. B and MS. D the line reads "Beneath the misery of a soldier's life"; this reading is that of Book I of *The Excursion* (681), one of the few examples in which the final text is the most suggestive.

25. Earl Leslie Griggs, ed., *Collected Letters of Samuel Taylor Coleridge* (Oxford: Clarendon, 1956), I, 327–28.

26. Following Professor James Butler, Mark Reed, in Appendix VI of *Wordsworth: The Chronology of The Middle Years* (Cambridge, Mass.: Harvard University Press, 1975), now assigns MS. E to 1803–1804.

27. For the filiations between Wordsworth's recurrent depictions of the breaking of dwellings and the family life they once contained, compare this final image with that of the ruin of Michael's cottage, whose "Light was famous in its neighbourhood, / And was a public symbol of the life, / The thrifty Pair had liv'd" (136–38): "The Cottage which was nam'd The Evening Star / Is gone, the ploughshare has been through the ground / On which it stood" (485–87).

2

Michael, Luke, and Wordsworth

I

Michael is one of the most warmly praised of Wordsworth's poems; few will dissent from the verdict of Karl Kroeber in his *Romantic Narrative Art* that it is "the high point of Wordsworth's narratives."[1] To account for the moving power of the story, however, is not easy: the final effect on us is greater than analysis of its naturalistic texture can explain. "Unimpressive detail" and a "paucity of notable incident," in Kroeber's words, yield a poem that yet engages our deepest feelings. This chapter seeks the source of the engagement in the unspoken emotional tension underlying the narrative, generated in particular about the figure of Luke and by the major silences of the poem. That tension is not resolved, but it is at last circumscribed through Wordsworth's multifaceted self-presentation. From the Wordsworth in Michael and the Wordsworth in Luke comes the Wordsworth in the narrator-poet of the prologue.

Michael is a tale of broken covenants told by a narrator apparently aloof from it:

> It was the first,
> The earliest of those tales that spake to me
> Of Shepherds, dwellers in the vallies, men
> Whom I already lov'd, not verily
> For their own sakes, but for the fields and hills
> Where was their occupation and abode.
>
> (21–26)[2]

Acknowledging the tale's limitations and proffering only modest claims for its worth, the poet safely encloses its power:

> And hence this Tale, while I was yet a boy
> Careless of books, yet having felt the power
> Of Nature, by the gentle agency
> Of natural objects led me on to feel
> For passions that were not my own, and think
> At random and imperfectly indeed
> On man; the heart of man and human life.
>
> (27–33)

The self-deprecation is beautifully controlled: the speaker who emerges is a man grown into sophistication, familiar with books, and able to look tolerantly upon his juvenile philosophizing. But this asserted distance between teller and tale may be a form of evasion, as are the poem's silences—evasion because the issues raised by the tale are crucial. *Michael* is a structure through which Wordsworth asks questions central to his life. Curiously, but not unusually for him, the poetic fiction is a means whereby through self-evasion Wordsworth manages an extraordinary act of self-exploration. The questions concern the "Cheerful faith" he had announced in *Tintern Abbey* that "Nature never did betray / The heart that loved her" (123–24) and the meaning of the affirmation he had expressed by his return to Grasmere just a year before. The silences lead us to the questions.

The poem is named after Michael, but he is not the only figure to feel the strain on the "domestic affections" that Wordsworth singled out as a central theme: the dilemma of "parents . . . separated from their children, and children from their parents,"[3] falls equally upon Luke. Wordsworth's handling of the sources of the poem also directs our attention to Luke. Dorothy Wordsworth's journal for October 11, 1800, makes plain that the inception of the poem was a physical object, a straggling heap of stones: "After Dinner we walked up Greenhead Gill in search of a sheepfold. . . . The sheepfold is falling away it is built nearly in the form of a heart unequally divided."[4] In 1836 Wordsworth told Mr. Justice Coleridge that *"Michael* was founded on the son of an old couple having become dissolute and run away from his parents; and on an old shepherd having been seven years in building up a sheepfold in a solitary valley." In this account we can see that the two components of

Michael, the old shepherd and the corrupted son, were originally independent. To Isabella Fenwick Wordsworth imparted another detail: "the character and circumstances of Luke were taken from a family to whom belonged, many years before, the house we lived in at Town-End."[5] The sheepfold, with its suggestive unequal division, the old man and the profligate son in whose place Wordsworth found himself when he moved into Town-End less than a year before he began to write—these are the elements of *Michael,* but it is Wordsworth who joined them into the whole we now have.

What it was that led Wordsworth to develop his story as he did is a matter in which no absolute knowledge is possible, and yet his creation of a plot in which an old man suffers the loss of his beloved land and his hope of the future because of the defection of a son arouses our curiosity. Wordsworth's own financial prospects were uncertain, and the thirty-year-old poet who had resisted family pressure to take orders or to find regular employment as a schoolteacher may well have seen in Luke's failure, as in Michael's plight, an ominous analogy to his own unsettled future.[6] What is clear is that, in Mary Moorman's words, the composition of *Michael* was a "toilsome advance."[7] Dorothy's journal entries for the two months it took to finish the poem are filled with evidence of the pain it cost Wordsworth to continue:

> *Saturday [18th October]* . . . William worked all the morning at the Sheep-fold but in vain. He lay down in the afternoon til 7 o'clock but could not sleep. . . .

> *Tuesday 21st* . . . Wm had been unsuccessful in the morning at the Sheepfold. . . .

> *Wednesday Morning [22nd]* . . . Wm composed without much success at the Sheepfold. . . .

> *28th October, Monday* . . . Wm could not compose much fatigued himself with altering.

Intermittently occurring among these laments are notes that William is "not well" (indeed, both Dorothy and Coleridge were also ill during this period); finally, Dorothy records completion of the poem on December 9, 1800.

The story of Michael and Luke is a node from which crucial doubts radiate, doubts that Wordsworth explored through his fiction.

The specter of Luke's collapse bears hard on Wordsworth's own projects: the inability of Luke's ideal training to sustain him outside the valley suggests a parallel uncertainty in his creator. *The Prelude,* already begun, required that he incorporate the disappointments of his own experience beyond the valley into an affirmative structure in which all was "gratulant if rightly understood" (1805, XIII, 385), and the original basis of the affirmation was Wordsworth's trust in the values whose weakness Luke exposes; the philosophical poem Coleridge was pressing on him was also unthinkable until the doubts were resolved.

II

We may briefly recapitulate the crisis of Michael's—and Luke's— life. Years before the time of the poem, Michael had been bound as surety for another; the unexpected failure of this man leaves Michael in his old age obligated for a sum "but little less / Than half his substance" (226–27). At first, the only recourse seems to be "to sell / A portion of his patrimonial fields" (233–34); unable to bring himself to act upon this resolve, Michael devises a second plan, which he then relates to his wife:

> Our Luke shall leave us, Isabel; the land
> Shall not go from us, and it shall be free,
> He shall possess it, free as is the wind
> That passes over it.
>
> (254–57)

The hope that inspires Michael is that by working for a kinsman Luke shall earn enough to quit the debt, but the succinct parallel construction of "Our Luke shall leave us / The land shall not go from us" says with the characteristic understated power of Wordsworth's language the nature of the choice forced upon Michael.

One form of the silence in the poem is the unemphatic way in which Wordsworth treats this determining event. The conflict at the dramatic heart of the plot between the shepherd's love of his son and his love for his property is curiously unstressed; as Kroeber observes, "Wordsworth minimizes that conflict, and, finally, in Michael's last address to Luke blurs the two motives together." From the outset Wordsworth asserted that the birth of his child intensified Michael's attachment to the land:

> why should I relate
> That objects which the Shepherd loved before
> Were dearer now? that from the Boy there came
> Feelings and emanations, things which were
> Light to the sun and music to the wind;
> And that the Old Man's heart seemed born again.
>
> (208–13)

Luke's rejuvenating effect is mentioned throughout the poem. "A child," the narrator remarks, "more than all other gifts, / Brings hope with it, and forward-looking thoughts" (154–55). In two lines Michael sums up their life among the hills: "in us the old and young / Have play'd together" (364–65). This statement defines the joy Luke brought. He offered Michael the promise of continuity: through him the inevitable mutability of mortal life was to have been offset, the saving contact with youthful freshness maintained. Luke seemed to promise a rescue from flux like that Michael already experiences from the mountains, "Which like a book preserv'd the memory" of his acts and past (70). So long as the two means of preservation—the boy and the land—were in harmony, one could deepen the other: the crisis of *Michael* comes when nature and the human are driven apart.

Readers of Wordsworth are familiar with the dialectical relationship between human emotion and landscape that exists in his poetry. Throughout most of *The Prelude,* the resource that steadies Wordsworth against overwhelming blankness is the "forms distinct" of his native region, the "real solid world / Of images" provided by his childhood experience in nature (1805, VIII, 594–605). These underpin the continuity of the self and in turn make possible human relationships: Love of Nature leads to Love of Mankind. But Michael is trapped by circumstance at that critical point at which human affections and attachment to the land no longer co-operate but instead pull in opposite directions. The situation in which Wordsworth places Michael is a radical test of his own consciously elaborated myth of healthful being in the world.

When Isabel assents to Michael's plan, he concludes:

> —Make ready Luke's best garments, of the best
> Buy for him more, and let us send him forth
> To-morrow, or the next day, or to-night:
> If he could go, the Boy should go to-night.
>
> (289–92)

If Luke, though eighteen, is not consulted about the course of his future—a feature indicative of the patriarchal structure that permeates *Michael*—Michael's disposition of his son is not unaccompanied by second thoughts. The sleepless nights ensuing upon his decision prompt Isabel to urge Luke to remain:

> Thou must not go,
> We have no other Child but thee to lose,
> None to remember—do not go away,
> For if thou leave thy Father he will die.
> (305–8)

Luke makes light of his mother's fears, and when the kinsman's letter offering him employment arrives there is no "prouder heart than Luke's" (325). Hence, though Luke seems at first the passive instrument of his father's decision, he is subsequently shown as a willing participant in it.

There is nonetheless a stratum of the poem that complicates our sense of Luke's relationship to Michael. On the evening before Luke's departure, Michael brings him to the sheepfold he has begun to build. The occasion marks the introduction of the sheepfold into the poem, and the long delay of the chief symbol heightens the solemnity of the scene. Michael recounts to Luke his birth, Michael's solicitude for him, and their intertwined life together, with that combination of strength and tenderness that readers recognize as distinctively Wordsworthian and which causes Luke to sob aloud. Through the words just quoted—"in us the old and young / Have play'd together"— Michael articulates the self-perpetuation he desires from his son, and as he reaches forward to the next generation, so he extends backward to the last:

> —Even to the utmost I have been to thee
> A kind and a good Father: and herein
> I but repay a gift which I myself
> Receiv'd at others' hands, for, though now old
> Beyond the common life of man, I still
> Remember them who lov'd me in my youth.
> Both of them sleep together: here they liv'd
> As all their Forefathers had done, and when
> At length their time was come, they were not loth
> To give their bodies to the family mold.
> (371–80)

"I wish'd that thou should'st live the life they liv'd" (381), Michael continues, and that sentence epitomizes the meaning of the ritual he is about to perform: Luke is to be ceremonially initiated into the changeless pattern of his family. By a shared formal gesture, Michael seeks to guarantee the continued integrity of his family:

> I knew that thou could'st never have a wish
> To leave me, Luke, thou hast been bound to me
> Only by links of love, when thou art gone
> What will be left to us!—But, I forget
> My purposes. Lay now the corner-stone
> As I requested, and hereafter, Luke,
> When thou art gone away, should evil men
> Be thy companions, let this Sheep-fold be
> Thy anchor and thy shield; amid all fear
> And all temptation, let it be to thee
> An emblem of the life thy Fathers liv'd.
>
> (410–20)[8]

The ritual is an assertion, against the destructive possibilities of change, of patriarchal values so constant as to become virtually trans-historical. Beneath the surface, however, are traces of doubt: the unconscious "links of love" must be reinforced by transforming them into a conscious "emblem" if they are to suffice against the pressure of temptation and evil men.

The positive affirmations of *Michael* resonate with undertones of troubling character. The tableau of the dignified elderly father and his beloved only son performing a "covenant" (424) at a sheepfold inevitably releases associations of the intended sacrifice by Abraham of Isaac, associations deepened by the patriarchal structure and the biblical echoes of the passage.[9] This does not mean that we are to interpret Michael as an oppressive father dooming his child, al-though, as I shall propose more fully, Wordsworth's portrayal of his decision and his readiness to dispatch Luke hints at a certain resent-ment buried in the poem.[10] Other scriptural echoes cluster about this scene, enriching rather than restricting its meaning. The sacrifice of Isaac had long since been taken by exegetes as a type of the sacrifice of Christ, and Michael's address to his son—"thou art the same / That wert a promise to me ere thy birth" (343–44)—recalls the prophecies of the coming of Christ. Immediately before the scene at the sheepfold occurs a simile of the family sitting together "like happy people round a Christmas fire" (313), a phrase that makes its own muted preparatory contribution to this delicate casting of Luke in the role of Christ. But if Wordsworth thus quietly draws an analogy between the hope Michael has of Luke's aid and the hope in the Savior, there are less auspicious notes as well: Michael's warnings of future temptations that may beset his son remind us that Luke is the Gospel containing the parable of the Prodigal Son (15:11–31).

The convergence of these echoes of differing tenor is puzzling but not inexplicable. Their common ground is their focus on the role of the son: Michael acts out a ritual he understands as a renewal of the faith of the fathers, but the echoes direct us rather to the moral dilemma in which the son is placed. We may think of them as so many alternative possibilities confronting Luke, so many various futures latent in his position: the sacrificed son? the prodigal son? the redeeming son? The poem even puts forward its own desired ending to the experience on which Luke is about to embark: Isabel decides to give her consent to Michael's plan because of the memory of Richard Bateman, a parish boy in the neighborhood who went up to London, entered overseas trade, and "grew wond'rous rich," building a chapel at his birthplace with his wealth (268–80). Isabel's "looking back into past times" (267) is itself an assertion of continuity, and the true story incarnates the fantasy that animates both Michael and Luke, whose "heart . . . has been beating fast / With many hopes" (408–9).

Our sense of the relationship between Michael and Luke is amplified by the fate of a passage present in the manuscripts from which *Michael* emerged but which Wordsworth did not incorporate in any poem he published. The "Matron's Tale" now found in Book VIII of the 1805 *Prelude* (222–311) was, in de Selincourt's words, "originally written as an incident in the life of Michael and Luke."[11] As with the example of Richard Bateman, Wordsworth's customary matter-of-fact narration almost disguises an emblematic function: the story of the strayed sheep is kin to the parable of the Lost Sheep which precedes that of the Prodigal Son in Luke (15:3–7). Wordsworth's story warrants dwelling upon. A father and son have been searching in vain for more than a day for a straggler from their flock when the boy suddenly remembers a piece of folk wisdom and exuberantly cries, "I know where I shall find him" (252). Separating from his father, the boy intently pursues his search even through a rainstorm. At last, he spies the sheep on an island in the midst of a brook:

> Before the Boy knew well what he had seen
> He leapt upon the island with proud heart
> And with a Prophet's joy. Immediately
> The Sheep sprang forward to the further Shore
> And was borne headlong by the roaring flood.
> At this the Boy look'd round him, and his heart
> Fainted with fear; thrice did he turn his face
> To either brink; nor could he summon up
> The courage that was needful to leap back
> Cross the tempestuous torrent; so he stood,
> A Prisoner on the Island, not without
> More than one thought of death and his last hour.
>   (278–89)

It is not difficult to see what in this scene justifies the excited language in which the discovery of the sheep is conveyed. The acumen
and dedication of the boy are the proof of his capacity for independence: he locates what eludes his father and thus establishes his own
ability. No sooner is the goal achieved, however, than the achievement is blasted: the sheep is not saved by the boy's action, but destroyed, and the boy himself is reduced from prideful rescuer to
fearful victim. The happy ending to which the story comes is not
unambiguous. The worried father sets forth in search of his son as the
son set off in search of the sheep, and locates him in the middle of
the roaring brook:

> The Shepherd heard
> The outcry of his Son, he stretch'd his Staff
> Towards him, bade him leap, which word scarce said
> The Boy was safe within his Father's arms.
>   (308–11)

Here the father's intervention accomplishes for the boy what the boy
could not for the sheep, but in its symmetry his success is the precise
index of the boy's failure. The power of the father sets off the weakness of the son.[12]

"It is possible," R. S. Woof remarks of this sequence, "that the
poem has lost something by its exclusion, since the episode establishes in a rich and dramatic fashion the relation between father and
son."[13] In addition to the obvious gain in compactness, it is possible
to discern another reason that might have led Wordsworth to forgo
the elaboration. The tale depicts the rescue of a son by his father, and
the crisis of *Michael* turns on precisely the opposite: the necessity

imposed on a son to rescue his father. Events have thrust Luke out of the world in which saving fathers will always afford timely aid to bewildered sons, and the conjunction of the episode and the fate of Luke would too nakedly have reduced his dilemma to that of a boy deprived of the paternal benevolence the episode illustrates.

The subsequent fortunes of the "Matron's Tale" enlarge our understanding of the implications of its removal from *Michael*. It reappears in Book VIII of the 1805 *Prelude*, "Retrospect," which marks a second beginning within the *Prelude* itself. After the dismaying recital of his London residence in Book VII, Wordsworth returns his poem to Helvellyn and his formative childhood experience in nature, as if in the midst of his current uncertainties drawing sustenance from the memory. In this framework it is virtually unavoidable to see in the lost sheep, an "Adventurer" (275), an analogy to the poet, and to apply the Matron's words concerning the animal to his own imaginative course in his "retrospect":

> 'For take note,
> Said here my grey-hair'd Dame, that tho' the storm
> Drive one of those poor Creatures miles and miles,
> If he can crawl he will return again
> To his own hills, the spots where, when a Lamb
> He learn'd to pasture at his Mother's side.'
>
> (252–57)

We may therefore speculate that when, after having transferred the episode from *Michael* to the story of his own life, Wordsworth eliminated it from the later versions of *The Prelude*, the renewed omission represents his firm decision to turn his back on the fantasy of parental rescue embedded in the tale. Perhaps the mature poet, revising his work more than ten years after the completion of the 1805 *Prelude*, no longer wished to acknowledge the appeal the fantasy had once held for him; perhaps it was merely that the role of the son needing to be rescued was one that had become foreign even in imagination to the established poet and the almost fifty-year-old father of five children.

The bringing into the narrative of his own life a story initially kept at slight distance by its connection to one of his characters, and the widening circles of meaning given the story of the lost being by the structure of the 1805 *Prelude*, enable us to see the dilemma at the heart of *Michael*. Deep in the texture of the poem but illuminated by the imbricated biblical allusions surrounding Luke we can descry a boy's—or man's—doubts that he can stand alone in the world without the support of his parents and home. The plot rapidly brings about the worst of the alternatives suggested by the allusions and parallel stories, and Luke falls with terrifying swiftness:

> Meantime Luke began
> To slacken in his duty, and at length
> He in the dissolute city gave himself
> To evil courses: ignominy and shame
> Fell on him, so that he was driven at last
> To seek a hiding-place beyond the seas.
>
> (451–56)

The question that this outcome puts to the adequacy of the tradition in which Michael has raised Luke applies both to them, as characters within the poem, and to the poet himself, who in the introductory lines described the story as one entwined with his own childhood and nascent consciousness. The coolly external treatment Wordsworth gives to Luke's decline, the affectless manner in which he refuses any tragic resonance to the boy's fate, seem deliberately designed to muffle the significance of the collapse.

Throughout the latter part of the poem Wordsworth engages in a suggestively bipartite strategy: Luke is kept from the foreground, but the dimensions of the catastrophe for which his failure is responsible are made abundantly clear. "If thou leave thy Father he will die," Isabel has told Luke (308), and Michael's final words to his son as he lays the first stone of the sheepfold redouble the weight upon him: " 'whatever fate / Befall thee, I shall love thee to the last, / And bear thy memory with me to the grave' " (425–27). The covenant on which Luke defaults is a covenant of emotional trust as well as of ongoing values; the consequences of his failure are to destroy the rejuvenation Michael has found in him and to bring to an end the patriarchal tradition of the family. Michael is crushed, and the dissolution of the changeless world follows:

> There, by the sheep-fold, sometimes was he seen
> Sitting alone, with that his faithful Dog,
> Then old, beside him, lying at his feet.
> The length of full seven years from time to time
> He at the building of this Sheep-fold wrought,

And left the work unfinished when he died.
Three years, or little more, did Isabel,
Survive her Husband: at her death the estate
Was sold, and went into a Stranger's hand.
The Cottage which was nam'd The Evening Star
Is gone, the ploughshare has been through the ground
On which it stood; great changes have been wrought
In all the neighbourhood, yet the Oak is left
That grew beside their Door; and the remains
Of the unfinished Sheep-fold may be seen
Beside the boisterous brook of Green-head Gill.

                                            (476–91)

And so the poem comes full circle, returning us to the "tumultuous brook" where our quest began (2), but the closed circle belies a tension: so far from serving as the guarantor of human continuity, nature, as represented by the brook, seems in its energy and abundance almost hostile to the transient human projects whose emblem is the unfinished sheepfold.

The bare ending calls forth a series of linked observations. Michael endures his fate in silence: " 'tis believ'd by all," Wordsworth says, "That many and many a day he thither went, / And never lifted up a single stone" (473–75). The stark scene draws its power from its wordlessness, but we may pause for a moment over this distinct absence of any attempt to articulate the impact of Luke's collapse, to define and name it as opposed to merely witnessing its force. Luke, too, departs from the poem without a word, hastily dismissed as if Wordsworth were determinedly deflecting attention from the remorse that his failure might well be thought to have caused in him. Most important of all, Wordsworth *in propria persona* makes no appearance at the conclusion of his poem; any expectation created by the framing introduction that the tale would end with a symmetrical concluding meditation in the poet's own voice goes unfulfilled. What are we to make of the reticence of the narrator?

Though consideration of this feature of the poem must be tentative, it seems apparent that the impulses that first led Wordsworth to combine two independent local traditions in such fashion as to make Luke the agent of disaster are present in the finished work. A curious doubling heightens the sense the poem exudes of mutual betrayal between youth and its elders: the man for whom he has been bound surety and whose misfortunes pull Michael down in his wake is Michael's "Brother's Son" (221). The poem repeats with variations the failure of the younger generation to meet its obligations to its seniors: Luke defrauds not only his parents' hope but also that of the generous kinsman who befriends him. The austere tones struck softly but more than once in the presentation of Michael may proceed from resentment of a responsibility imposed before the bearer could sustain it. By the conclusion of the poem the humorous vignette of the five-year-old Luke trying to act as "a Watchman" over the flock acquires deeper resonance. "To his office prematurely call'd," as the narrator notes, Luke is capable only of serving as "something between a hindrance and a help," and "for this cause," he continues, "not always, I believe, / Receiving from his Father hire of praise" (190–201): the combination of resentment and guilt is pervasive. The very abruptness of Luke's departure from the poem, puzzling to generations of Wordsworth's readers, alerts us to its importance. The guilt not enunciated by Luke is everywhere woven into the structure of the poet's fiction, which throughout ignores causal relations to dwell rather on the feelings aroused by the central situation, slowing and shaping linear narrative into contemplation.

The significance *Michael* had for Wordsworth is part of its significance for us because it is built into the narrative. Through the constellation of doubts that surround Luke we can approach the mysterious silence of the narrator. It is not news to observe that Wordsworth's poetic power arises from understatement, but it is fruitful to specify what it is that Wordsworth here understates. The heart of *Michael* is a network of implications. Again and again, the poem circles about the figure of the failed son without ever releasing into clarity the weight of Wordsworth's involvement, but we are moved rather than baffled because the reticulated structure of the poem makes us aware of what remains unspoken. By keeping the richly implicating pattern in the background or beneath the surface (we may choose either metaphor), Wordsworth enables it to work on us like the half-submerged intuitions of our own inner lives.

It is not only behind Luke that we feel the presence of Wordsworth. The failure of Luke is first the failure of Michael, who chooses to disjoin father and son and to dispatch Luke from the harmonious world of the valley. Michael's goodness as a father is not here in question, but only the sundering of the continuity represented by his assertion that "in us the old and young / Have play'd together" (364–65). The distance between the consciousness of youth and that

of the perhaps wiser but surely more constrained adult is a recurrent
theme of the *Lyrical Ballads:* one need only name *Anecdote for
Fathers* and *We Are Seven,* or consider the pains of loss Matthew
expresses in *The Two April Mornings* and *The Fountain.* These
poems embody dramatically the interior division into "two conscious-
nesses" Wordsworth describes in *The Prelude* (1805, II, 32). The
configuration is given its most severe form in *There Was a Boy,*
where Wordsworth stands transfixed in mourning over the grave of
his own lost intimacy with nature.[14] *Michael,* the concluding poem of
the second volume of *Lyrical Ballads,* seems most like the concluding
poem of the first volume: *Tintern Abbey.* In both, the assertions of
continuity are ringed by doubt: in Michael's exhortations to Luke we
seem to encounter again Wordsworth's address to Dorothy, a conscious intent to pass on values to, and be remembered by, the next
generation, mingling with a more urgent need to recapture through it
the speaker's own former self.[15] In this final poem of the collection,
Michael, living on, a broken figure, discloses a Wordsworth who fears
that his development has betrayed his childhood integration.

The complementary pair of Michael and Luke, however, is only
one part of Wordsworth's multifaceted self-presentation in *Michael;*
his other, more recognizable face is visible in the introduction. The
breaking of the union of old and young, and of human affections and
the land, is repaired, as it were, by the stance Wordsworth adopts in
the prologue. The shattered covenant between the eighty-year-old
Michael and the eighteen-year-old Luke is succeeded by the compact
between the narrator and his heirs:

> Therefore, although it be a history
> Homely and rude, I will relate the same
> For the delight of a few natural hearts,
> And with yet fonder feelings, for the sake
> Of youthful Poets, who among these Hills
> Will be my second self when I am gone.
>   (34–39)

Above the anxious images of the failed son and the grieving adult,
Wordsworth places the vision of himself as the intrepid and trust-
worthy guide of his readers, the sage father of future poets. The prologue sets against the fallings-away of Michael's brother's son and of
Luke the poet's own pious action of transmitting a tale from his
childhood. Appearing only as the communal spokesman of what is

"believ'd by all" (473), he assumes the burden of memorializing the traditions overset in the narrative, perpetuating them more successfully than Michael and more eloquently than the enigmatic stones by themselves.[16] The transition from Michael's covenant in the land to the poet's covenant implies a recognition that continuity must be sought not in the forms of nature alone but in the products of imagination.

Michael's intimate communion with the mountains exists now only in the artful fictions of the "Poets . . . among these Hills" who self-consciously choose to write of the ideal intimacy and dignity he symbolizes: *Michael,* as Wordsworth declares in the subtitle, is "A Pastoral Poem," a literary landscape, a creation of the mind. Wordsworth began *Michael* immediately after completing the *Preface* to the *Lyrical Ballads,* and the prologue reflects his new thoughtfulness about his art and his audience.[17] The half-apologetic, half-challenging introduction to the narrative echoes the scornful remarks of the *Preface* about the debasement of public taste, and after that pithy review of poetic theory and history it it not surprising to hear in the statement through which Wordsworth defines his audience in *Michael* as "a few natural hearts" (36) a domesticated version of Milton's invocation in *Paradise Lost* of "fit audience . . . though few" (VII, 31).[18] In *Michael* as in the prose, Wordsworth steps forward as the assured poet, discoursing wisely on the essence of his art. The voice of the prologue is so measured as already almost to have become impersonal; soon it will lose all connection with Wordsworth's personal history. Once under way, this disembodied voice renders *Michael* seemingly independent of its author. As Wordsworth himself recedes from view, the Wordsworthian myth can be constituted and set free from private psychological vicissitudes.

In the celebration of the timeless world of the valley and the shepherd's patriarchal life, Luke remains as the irreducible element that summons the myth into being. The division between man and nature he brings about, a catastrophe to the actors within the story, marks for the poet the always fateful birth of self-consciousness. The reminiscence of *Paradise Lost,* minor in itself, links with the biblical echoes of the narrative to mark not only Wordsworth's ample, informed voice but also his theme. Together they reinforce the sense that the journey up the mountain the poet asks us to take to the hidden valley, to repeat for ourselves the ritual of Michael and Luke, is a journey to a place of revelation. The outcome shows the revelation to be the insufficiency of nature, or perhaps one should say only its inaccessibility to those who have been cast out of the vale. It is not fortuitous that the poem should memorialize the pastoral world at the moment of its supersession, for only the dispossessed appreciate what has been lost. Divorced from it as present from past, prologue from story, the imagination sings over the death of the natural: Wordsworth and his readers meet to share in an elegy for the securities we all no longer know.

Notes

1. Quotations are taken from Chapter 6 of *Romantic Narrative Art* (Madison: University of Wisconsin Press, 1960).

2. Unless otherwise indicated, all quotations from the *Lyrical Ballads* are taken from the text of the first editions edited by R. L. Brett and A. R. Jones, *Lyrical Ballads* (1963; rpt. London: Methuen, 1968).

3. This is the context in which Wordsworth places *Michael* in the letter to Charles James Fox accompanying a presentation copy of the second edition of *Lyrical Ballads; The Letters of William and Dorothy Wordsworth*, ed. Ernest de Selincourt, 2d ed., rev. by Chester L. Shaver (Oxford: Clarendon, 1967), I, 312–15. My interpretation of this letter was suggested by that of Stephen Parrish in *The Art of the Lyrical Ballads* (Cambridge, Mass.: Harvard University Press, 1973), pp. 182–83, but the disjunction between letter and poem is striking. In the letter, Wordsworth attributes the recent "rapid decay of the domestic affections among the lower orders of society" to "the spreading of manufactures through every part of the country . . . the heavy taxes upon postage . . . workhouses, Houses of Industry, and the invention of Soup-shops &c. &c. superadded to the encreasing disproportion between the price of labour and that of the necessaries of life," but these causes are absent from the poem. For Marjorie Levinson ("Spiritual Economics: A Reading of 'Michael,' " Chapter 2 of her *Wordsworth's Great Period Poems* [Cambridge: Cambridge University Press, 1986]) and David Simpson (" 'By conflicting passions pressed': 'Michael' and 'Simon Lee,' " Chapter 5 of his *Wordsworth's Historical Imagination: The Poetry of Displacement* [New York and London, Methuen: 1987]), the suppressions are the key to the contradictions of Wordsworth's own social position, and the substitutions and emphases they entail are the heart of his characteristic poetic practices. Our readings are alike suspicious in seeking to disclose a suppressed but animating complex of motives; theirs grant priority to (Wordsworth's evasion of) the materialist conditions to which the letter alerts us, whereas mine implicitly treats the correspondence with a Member of Parliament as a strategic rationalization of a text whose originating impulses were personal (not private) and remained hidden. As the later chapters in this book suggest, I would now try to synthesize the two fields of interpretation.

4. *Journals of Dorothy Wordsworth*, ed. Mary Moorman (London: Oxford University Press, 1971), p. 44.

5. Both quotations from *The Poetical Works of William Wordsworth*, ed. Ernest de Selincourt and Helen Darbishire (1944; rev. ed. Oxford: Clarendon, 1952), II, 478.

6. The alleviation provided by the legacy of Raisley Calvert was by itself inadequate, complicated as it had been by the need to repay loans extended by Josiah Wedgwood during the stay in Germany and by the unreliability of Basil Montagu in paying monies due Wordsworth.

7. *William Wordsworth: A Biography* (1957; London: Oxford University Press, 1968), I, 498.

8. In the final text, as printed by de Selincourt in *PW*, II, the last lines of this passage read:

> should evil men
> Be thy companions, think of me, my Son,
> And of this moment; hither turn thy thoughts
> And God will strengthen thee: amid all fear
> And all temptation, Luke, I pray that thou
> May'st bear in mind the life thy Fathers lived,
> Who, being innocent, did for that cause
> Bestir them in good deeds.
>
> (405–12)

The expansion is significantly different in spirit from the original conception of *Michael* and suggests the religious consolation to which Wordsworth turned only after the failure of nature's support recorded by the poem.

9. A second scriptural parallel is the "heap" of stones that serves to mark the "covenant" between Jacob and Laban (Genesis 31:43–55). This pact is the resolution of the hostility between son and father-in-law, made after Jacob's surreptitious departure. If recognized in *Michael*, the echo deepens the hints of generational tension in the poem. For verbal echoes, see Psalm 90:4, "His truth shall be thy shield and buckler," and other such doublets; Psalm 118:22, "The stone which the builders refused is become the head stone of the corner," cited by Jesus (Luke 20:17) and of him by Peter (Acts 4:11 and I Peter 2:7).

10. The negative aspects of Michael's fathering are argued by Sheldon Halpern, *"Michael:* Wordsworth's Pastoral of Common Man," *Notre Dame English Journal* 8 (1972): 22–23.

11. *The Prelude*, ed. E. de Selincourt, 2d ed., rev. by Helen Darbishire (Oxford: Clarendon, 1959), p. 578.

12. In his discussion of *The Prelude*, this incident is similarly treated by Richard J. Onorato, *The Character of the Poet: Wordsworth in THE PRELUDE* (Princeton: Princeton University Press, 1971), pp. 307–10. The likelihood of identification between the poet and the boy, suggested below, is increased by a passage Onorato prints from the Dove Cottage papers in which Wordsworth describes himself endangered by a swollen river in the Alps.

13. "John Stoddart, 'Michael,' and *Lyrical Ballads*," *Ariel* 1 (1970): 7–22.

14. MS. JJ, printed by de Selincourt, reveals that the boy of the poem was originally Wordsworth himself (*The Prelude*, p. 639). See also Chapter 5.

15. A common cluster of images draws the two poems together. Compare "from the Boy there came / Feelings and emanations, things which were / Light

to the sun and music to the wind; / And . . . the Old Man's heart seemed born again," in *Michael* (210–13), to Wordsworth seeing in Dorothy "My former pleasures in the shooting lights / Of thy wild eyes" and his prayer that "the misty mountain winds be free / To blow against" her, making her memory "a dwelling-place / For all sweet sounds and harmonies" (*Tintern Abbey*, 119–20 and 137–43). Compare also Wordsworth in *Tintern Abbey*, "well pleased to recognize / In nature and the language of the sense, / The anchor of my purest thoughts, the nurse, / The guide, the guardian of my heart, and soul / Of all my moral being" (108–12), with the function Michael intends the sheepfold to serve for Luke: "let this Sheep-fold be / Thy anchor and thy shield: amid all fear / And all temptation, let it be to thee / An emblem of the life thy Fathers liv'd, / Who, being innocent, did for that cause bestir them in good deeds" (417–22). The passage from nature in *Tintern Abbey* to the emblem in *Michael* is indicative of Wordsworth's development between 1798 and 1800, see also n. 8 above.

16. See Geoffrey H. Hartman, "Wordsworth, Inscriptions, and Romantic Nature Poetry," *From Sensibility to Romanticism*, ed. F. W. Hilles and Harold Bloom (New York: Oxford University Press, 1965), pp. 389–414. Hartman also discusses *Michael* in his *Wordsworth's Poetry 1787–1814* (New Haven: Yale University Press, 1964), pp. 261–66.

17. Mark Reed, in *Wordsworth: The Chronology of the Middle Years* (Cambridge, Mass.: Harvard University Press, 1975), assigns the composition of the *Preface* to the period June 29–September 27, 1800, with revisions in the first week of October (p. 19); the visit to the sheepfold occurred October 11.

18. Some lines above the description of the audience as "a few natural hearts," Wordsworth describes the tale itself as "not unfit, / I deem, for the fire-side, / Or for the summer shade" (20–21).

3

Wordsworth and Gray's
Sonnet on the Death of West

If, despite all demonstrations of continuity with the eighteenth century, the *Preface* to the *Lyrical Ballads* (1800) is still taken as a
turning point in English literary history, it is largely because Wordsworth presents himself as making such a rupture with the past.
Thomas Gray figures largely in his act of self-definition. Concerned
to advance the view that there "neither is nor can be any essential
difference" between the language of prose and that of good poetry,
Wordsworth embodies its opposite in Gray, whom he describes as
"more than any other man curiously elaborate in the structure of his
own poetic diction."[1] Having placed his predecessor "at the head of
those who by their reasonings have attempted to widen the space of
separation betwixt Prose and Metrical composition," Wordsworth
then quotes in its entirety Gray's "Sonnet on the Death of Mr. Richard
West" in order to show that Gray's own best practice belies these
"reasonings":

> In vain to me the smiling Mornings shine,
> And redd'ning Phoebus lifts his golden fire:
> The birds in vain their amorous descant join;
> Or chearful fields resume their green attire:
> These ears, alas! for other notes repine,
> *A different object do these eyes require.*
> *My lonely anguish melts no heart but mine;*
> *And in my breast the imperfect joys expire.*
> Yet Morning smiles the busy race to chear,

And new-born pleasure brings to happier men:
The fields to all their wonted tribute bear:
To warm their little loves the birds complain:
I fruitless mourn to him, that cannot hear,
And weep the more, because I weep in vain.[2]

The five lines he has italicized, Wordsworth asserts, "will easily be perceived [to be] the only part of this Sonnet which is of any value," and the language of those lines, he proclaims in conclusion, "does in no respect differ from that of prose."

Coleridge spoke for many since when he observed in the *Biographia Literaria* that Wordsworth has "taken for granted rather perhaps too easily" the "reader's sympathy with his praise or blame of the different parts" of the sonnet.[3] He had little difficulty in showing that the rejected lines were stylistically consistent with those praised. Subsequent critics, seeking to provide for Wordsworth the "argumentative anlysis" Coleridge found wanting, have usually speculated on Wordsworth's objections to the Latinate word order, the formulaic adjective-plus-noun pattern, and the personification in the censured lines.[4] Wordsworth's half-praising, half-dismissing attitude to Gray, however, has remained puzzling. Generations of readers have sensed that the issue of poetic diction to which Wordsworth confines the discussion does not adequately explain the handling of the poem. In limiting his argument to formal considerations Wordsworth both announces and veils the opposition between the mode of his own poetry and that of the sonnet.

In trying to understand Wordsworth's polemic it is useful to remember that the *Preface* renders diction contingent upon another term: feeling. As his 1802 *Appendix on Poetic Diction* makes clear, Wordsworth approves of heightened language when it arises spontaneously from affecting situations. "The earliest Poets of all nations generally wrote from passion excited by real events; they wrote naturally, and as men," he there says; "feeling powerfully as they did, their language was daring, and figurative." "In succeeding times," Wordsworth's primitivistic history continues, "men ambitious of the fame of Poets, perceiving the influence of such language, and desirous of producing the same effect, without having the same animating passion, set themselves to a mechanical adoption of those figures of speech, and . . . applied them to feelings and thoughts with which they had no natural connection whatsoever" (p. 314). Because Wordsworth derides poetic diction when he judges the connection between the figures and the presumed originating passion to be either mechanical or, to use the word of the *Preface,* "arbitrary," his objections to style lead quickly to questions of content. In this light, it becomes significant that the poem on which Wordsworth rests his case centers on the death of a loved one. Wordsworth's discussion of Gray's treatment of his grief is cryptic, its grounds unarticulated, even as Gray depicts himself as blocked from utterance. This reserve in the face of death is shared by the poems in the 1800 second volume of *Lyrical Ballads.* Consider the understatement of "and Oh! / The difference to me." The gaps in Wordsworth's discursive prose match what is left powerfully unsaid in his poetry; together they suggest a shift in the poetic decorum of bereavement.

James Swearingen has noted that the lines of Gray's sonnet that Wordsworth stigmatizes describe nature, whereas those in italics convey the poet's inward state.[5] Indeed, all but one of the poem's personal pronouns are found in the italicized portions. Yet Swearingen draws conclusions that are at best arguable:

> The poetic responsiveness that [Wordsworth] demands assumes that mysterious spiritual bond between nature and the man that he regards as metaphysically true; but the sonnet assumes that men and nature are fundamentally different. The lines seem artificial to him because in the poem Gray is estranged from nature by the fact of death: he cannot enter joyfully into the renewal of a world in which he, like West, is perishing. Historically, it is Gray's sense of estrangement, not Wordsworth's synthesis, that has prevailed in our poetry.

Swearingen's comments about Gray's "alienation from nature" seem unexceptionable, but his sense of Wordsworth's metaphysical affirmation is challenged by the haunting reticence of a poem like *A Slumber Did My Spirit Seal.* The differences between the two poems involve something other than a difference between the poets' "beliefs" about nature.

To read Gray's poem is to experience a complete stasis: the paralysis of imagination by grief. The sonnet is distinguished by an unusual massiveness built upon what Gray's recent editor, Roger Lonsdale, summarized as "relentless rhyming (the sestet half-rhyming with the octave),"[6] a Miltonic elevation of diction,[7] and, most important, the numerous repetitions. Chief of these is the return at the close of the poem of the phrase with which it opens: the sonnet begins and ends with the declaration "in vain" and so suggests, as Lonsdale comments, the "fruitless circling" of the poet's sorrow. The stability of the formal pattern, moreover, is joined to a sentence pattern of equal regularity. The sonnet consists of three units, two of six lines each flanking the central distich: "My lonely anguish melts no heart but mine; / And in my breast the imperfect joys expire."

This stasis is the outward evidence of Gray's declared emotional paralysis; the sonnet is constructed on not one but two motionless figures, for the death of West is doubled in the changeless grief of speaker. Without West to share his burden of grief, Gray is driven back into a solitary death-in-life: his joys "expire" in his breast, his mourning is "fruitless."[8] Gray's grief feeds on itself and perpetuates its own condition: he weeps the more because he weeps in vain. Gray becomes the tomb of his loss, his immobility the counterpart and representation of West's death. Death in Gray's poem institutes an absolute break in time: even as the world of natural process moves onward, the speaker's grief resists the progress of life.[9]

Wordsworth aims his scorn not at the lines in which Gray voices his sorrow but at those that theatrically station the grieving figure in the midst of a busy world. The eighteenth century recognized this quality in Gray as "melancholy," a sensibility different from the tradition of philosophical melancholy descending from Milton's *Il Penseroso*. Older critical studies, such as those by Amy Louise Reed, John W. Draper, and Eleanor Sickels, amply explored Gray's relation to this tradition and the changes wrought in it by the popularity of his *Elegy Written in a Country Churchyard*.[10] The kindred distinction at stake in the title of one of Freud's most important essays, "Mourning and Melancholia," sheds further light on Gray's response to West's death.[11] Freud characterized melancholia in part as that inability to detach oneself from lost objects which Gray's poem epitomizes, and distinguished it from the "work of mourning," the complex and arduous process in which one gradually acknowledges loss yet paradoxically gains the strength to begin life anew through identification with the lost object. This distinction suggests differences between Wordsworth's and Gray's means of confronting loss which illuminate the enigmatic judgments passed by the *Preface*.

A Slumber Did My Spirit Seal has little of the evident artifice of Gray's sonnet:

> A slumber did my spirit seal,
> I had no human fears:

> She seem'd a thing that could not feel
>   The touch of earthly years.
>
> No motion has she now, no force
>   She neither hears nor sees
> Roll'd round in earth's diurnal course
>   With rocks and stones and trees!
>   (p. 154)

Yet, upon examination, the unassuming quatrains disclose a structure as exact as the patterns of Gray. As Paul de Man observed, the blank space between the stanzas marks a pivotal moment dividing the unselfconsciousness of the speaker before Lucy's death from his recognition of mortality after it.[12] Wordsworth's first stanza describes himself asleep in his former illusion of Lucy's immortality: "A slumber did my spirit seal." And the thoughtlessness he imputes to himself, his failure to have the "human fears" proper to a full recognition of one's own mortal humanity, affects also his image of Lucy: she, too, appears, if the line break is given weight, "a thing that could not feel."

If the shift from the first stanza to the second marks the moment of Lucy's death, it marks still more powerfully the shift in the consciousness of the speaker. The progression from the past tense to the present instigates a countermovement to Lucy's death that has no equivalent in Gray's poem. The stopping of West's life was the stopping of Gray's; for Wordsworth, the death of Lucy is the occasion of his own awakening. While "she" now has "no motion" and "no force," her death releases the speaker's formerly sealed spirit and propels him from error to self-knowledge. Similarly, if the "she" in the emphatic position in the sixth line "neither hears nor sees," the speaker implicitly does both, understanding for the first time both Lucy's and his own mortality. The second stanza corrects the first: the accumulated negatives attached to Lucy suggest by inversion Wordsworth's own mental activity.

Printed immediately before *A Slumber Did My Spirit Seal* in the 1800 *Lyrical Ballads* is *She Dwelt Among Th' Untrodden Ways,* a poem that further illustrates this paired death and awakening:

> She dwelt among th' untrodden ways
>   Beside the springs of Dove,
> A Maid whom there were none to praise
>   And very few to love.

A Violet by a mossy stone
  Half hidden from the Eye!
—Fair, as a star when only one
  Is shining in the sky!

She *liv'd* unknown, and few could know
  When Lucy ceas'd to be;
But she is in her Grave, and Oh!
  The difference to me.

(p. 154)

If Lucy in this poem is said to have *"liv'd* unknown" so that "few could know / When Lucy ceas'd to be," her death has nonetheless made a deeply felt "difference" to the speaker himself. The poem passes from the opening "she," Lucy's obscure past life, to its closing "me," the reflective consciousness of the speaker in which the memory of Lucy is preserved. These twin movements, from past to present and from the dead beloved to the continuing self, characterize the process of mourning and radically differentiate Wordsworth's poem from Gray's. Wordsworth most poignantly expressed this difficult double view of an object as simultaneously admitted to be lost but present to the mind in his late sonnet *Surprised by Joy,* in which the poet's impulsive turning to share his transport with his daughter Catharine is checked by the realization that she is "deep buried in the silent tomb." The poem reveals the cleaving to loss and the guilt over forgetting that tinge the "faithful love" that so vividly, if deceptively, recalled Catharine's image to life, and these remain in tension with the sober conclusion, the poet's renewed awareness that "neither present time, nor years unborn / Could to my sight that heavenly face restore."[13] In an 1802 addition to the *Preface* to the *Lyrical Ballads* Wordsworth described the poet as a man "affected more than other men by absent things as if they were present." This interplay of absence and presence, as in *Surprised by Joy* or the Lucy poems, gives energy to his representation of loss and death.

Because the process of mourning involves the relinquishing of a beloved object as well as the internalizing of it, psychoanalysts often speak of mourning as a second death, a psychic murder. This phenomenon helps to explain the notorious conflict of interpretations that rages over the final lines of *A Slumber Did My Spirit Seal.*[14] The half-heard resonance of "urn" in "diurnal" suggests a funeral ceremony, a ritual *division* of the dead from the living.[15] Lucy is dismissed into a realm of nature that has the cosmic energy of "earth's diurnal course" but lacks the distinctively human self-consciousness that now belongs to the speaker. It is to the survivor that Lucy appears "roll'd round," part of, but subjected to, a cycle from which he for the moment stands apart. The Lucy poems thus do not record Wordsworth's recognition that his poetic object never was, as Frances Ferguson put it.[16] Rather, they dramatize his acknowledgment that the object has been lost and his consequent ambivalent withdrawal from it.

It is tempting to judge Wordsworth's return to himself self-centered in comparison with Gray's bereavement, but the effect is that Wordsworth keeps Lucy alive in imagination in a way that has no equivalent in Gray's poem. Gray's unchanging sorrow freezes the image of West departed, incorporating it within the poet's own arrested development. There is, properly speaking, no image of West at all, only that of the narcissistically suffering speaker. The action on which *A Slumber Did My Spirit Seal* is founded, the change in Wordsworth's self-awareness, revises the image of Lucy, too. She is no longer "a thing that could not feel." What that state truly means is all too powerfully revealed in the second stanza, when her death joins Lucy to the "rocks and stones and trees." But her death makes her a fully mortal, hence human, figure in the poet's now enlightened imagination. As her physical body is assimilated to the nonhuman world, the poet endows her in retrospect with the humanizing "touch of earthly years." In coming to see his previous views as mistaken, Wordsworth alters and unfixes the past: even as Lucy's physical death is admitted, her image is animated by being absorbed into fresh contemplation. The "now" of the second stanza is therefore a full moment, as opposed to the empty "now" in which Gray is imprisoned. Deprived of the real presence of West, Gray becomes moribund; in contrast, Wordsworth dramatizes an ongoing evolution in his understanding of his relationship with Lucy.

The process of internalizing Lucy and the "silence and the calm / Of mute insensate things" with which she is associated is explicit in the closing lines of another poem from the second volume of *Lyrical Ballads*. If *A Slumber Did My Spirit Seal* manifests traces of the numbing that is an initial response to loss, *Three Years She Grew* is recuperative:

> She died and left to me
> This heath, this calm and quiet scene,

The memory of what has been,
And never more will be.

(p. 199)

The speaker of this poem faces the blankness of "what has been" but "never more will be." He is saved from emptiness by his "memory," which can retain what has been lost in reality.[17] Gray, it might be said (invoking another of Freud's central distinctions),[18] repeats his anguish over West's death, repeats and acts it out forever in his rigid pose; Wordsworth, on the other hand, works through the grief that would tie him to Lucy's death to a quiet memory that acknowledges loss. His epitaphs—and Coleridge, sent *A Slumber Did My Spirit Seal* in a letter, immediately recognized is as a "sublime Epitaph" (quoted by Brett and Jones, p. 301)—are memorials not only to lost objects but also to his past mistakes of understanding, now rectified by painful experience. The Lucy poems trace the passage from the naive faith in immortality that Wordsworth confessed was his own childhood conviction to a chastened adult recognition of mortality. It is death that leads Wordsworth to appreciate Lucy, that ends his delusion, that guides him outside himself to the natural world of which he now realizes she was a part; it is death that brings the bequest of "this heath, this calm and quiet scene." Wordsworth joins with the nature from which Gray is alienated, not because he feels a joyful spiritual bond, as Swearingen would have it, but because he sees nature as the very emblem of man's mortality: the bleak landscape of "rocks and stones and trees" is the nature to which he too will one day have to return. Gray, beholding cyclical renewal, withdraws from nature; Wordsworth, beholding nature as the world into which Lucy dies, accepts the "touch of earthly years" which nature bodes as his own condition. The ambiguity of the antecedent for "she" in the third line of the first stanza of *A Slumber Did My Spirit Seal* is fully exploited. Reading the poem from the beginning, one may take the pronoun as referring to "my spirit," and it is only when the second stanza is reached that the "she" can be understood to refer to someone other than the poet. This revision, this splitting of the "I" from the "she" which is caused by death and recognized by the speaker (and brought home to the reader), is precisely the work accomplished by mourning. Yet the shock is to the poet's own spirit as well: Lucy's death betrays the inadequacy of his confidence, and it is by this negative route that his solipsism is overcome.[19]

The awakening of self-consciousness in *A Slumber Did My Spirit Seal* paradoxically culminates in the elimination of the "I" from the second stanza. The perspective from which it is uttered transcends the single "I": the voice (scarcely belonging anymore to a human speaker) seems to proceed from an otherworldly height looking down upon "earth's diurnal course." From this cosmic vantage, the death of Lucy and the changes undergone by the speaker are alike shorn of their terror. Ego is here suspended, while the fear that usually accompanies such self-abolition is understated, modulated toward "calm and quiet." Wordsworth has been forever stamped by Keats's memorable phrase as the poet of the "egotistical sublime," yet all readers recognize this movement too as characteristically Wordsworthian. The two modes are not so much contradictory as complementary, halves of a binary pair. If the death of Lucy is a narcissistic wound, one protective response is to strip the self until it is as minimal as the world shorn of its beloved object, to reduce it until it approximates the admired peace of mute, insensate things. Through deprivation Wordsworth reaches an impersonal detachment and sounds the voice of a gnomic wisdom.

This movement beyond the self contrasts markedly with Gray's sonnet, which registers the magnitude of West's loss through the prominent self-concentration of the speaker. Years later, in the third *Essay on Epitaphs,* Wordsworth criticized the conclusion of Gray's epitaph on his mother— "she was the careful tender Mother of many Children, one of whom alone had the misfortune to survive her"—for "withdraw[ing] the attention of the Reader from the Subject to the Author of the Memorial" by "permanently and conspicuously" recording a "transitory and poignant" despair as a "fixed feeling." What it the regret, Wordsworth demanded, "but lurking and sickly selfishness?"[20] The accusation parallels Freud's insight that in melancholia there is a "conflict due to ambivalence" toward the lost object. Wordsworth would have known from the biographies that Gray had been intensely attached to his mother and remained so after her death. The life in Anderson's *Works of the British Poets,* for example, comments that Gray "cherished the remembrance of his loss with a melancholy pleasure."[21] Wordsworth singled out that suppressed resentment in Gray because it was a quality of his own temperament. The sole reference in *The Prelude* to the death of his mother when he was eight ends, "She left us destitute, and as we might / Trooping together" (1805, V, 259–60). Wordsworth combated his sense of

abandonment and nostalgia by a lifelong process of mourning, difficult and perhaps by its very nature impossible to complete. As *The
Prelude,* already begun, was to show (like the *Ode: Intimations of
Immortality*), he struggled throughout his career to convert memories of loss into aspirations for the future.

The speakers of Gray's and Wordsworth's poems can be compared in another way as well. The imagery of the sonnet is drawn
from adult activity: Gray stands surrounded by the "busy race" of
"happier men." Lonsdale points out that the governing contrast
between abounding nature and the withered speaker in the sonnet
derives from the conventions of Italian Renaissance love poetry in
which the lover mourns the loss of his beloved. The adaptation of
heterosexual conventions for a lament over a friend is striking, and
it supports the propriety of Gray's usage in the second-to-last line of
"fruitless" for "fruitlessly," which Wordsworth declared "a defect"
because he did not see that the word functions as an adjective as well
as an adverb, intensifying the sense of the sexual sterility to which
Gray has been reduced: "I fruitless."[22] Insofar as these sexual figures
suggest West's role as a nurturing, mirroring other, the traditional
pastoral expressions have a function in conveying the meaning of
West's death that Wordsworth's contempt for the lines fails to recognize.

The nurturing relationship appears in *A Slumber Did My Spirit
Seal,* too, but more boldly. Wordsworth's poem seems to begin in
earliest experience, as if the speaker were a babe slumbering in the
protection of a mother envisioned as omnipotent and immortal. It is
not only the similarities between the first stanza and the Blest Babe
passage of the *Two-Part Prelude,* written not long afterward, that call
up this maternal tableau: the ambiguous referent of the pronoun
"she" is appropriate to the dual unity of mother and infant, insofar
as an infant does not distinguish between himself and his mother.
Lucy's death provokes a crisis of separation, but the identity it would
establish gains no more substance than the blank between the two
stanzas before it too is subsumed by the transmortal perspective of
the last lines. The vision of an archaic bareness, of primal exposure,
in the last line threatens the tranquillity the voice suggests. Wordsworth's poem thus runs the gamut of man's senses of himself, from
infantile peace and security through a vulnerable growth into a re-
flectiveness founded on acknowledged loss.

This sequence unfolds in a virtual simultaneity within the brevity
and epigrammatic symmetry of *A Slumber Did My Spirit Seal.* Past

and present, death and birth, infancy and age, self and other, exaltation and lament are drawn by the compact structure of the poem into
a perpetual entwining and untwisting, so that it is interpretation itself
that is vitally "roll'd round." It is perhaps less important to reach a
comprehensive interpretation of the poem, a stable distribution of
these categories, than it is to note how thoroughly the poem inter-
twines them, so that each term immediately evokes its opposite and
sends the reader through the cycle again. The unsettled, disturbing
quality permits a summary comparison with Gray and suggests some
general differences between eighteenth-century and romantic modes.
The signs that I have thus far been reading chiefly in terms of Gray's
own responses are shaped by traditional elegiac conventions. Gray's
poem is a solidly constructed monument rigidly dividing before and
after—the representation of an unchanging figure, the emblem of an
eternal absence. Gray immortalizes West and his own bereavement
by halting time, with West forever lost, himself forever grieving. Had
Wordsworth understood the elaborate artifice of the poem—its sonnet
form (announced in the title), in itself an allusion to tradition, its
rhymes and repetition, its conventional language—as he understood
the value of meter, he might have found it appropriate. Meter provides, he noted in the *Preface,* "an intertexture of ordinary feeling"
that tempers and restrains passions that have "an undue proportion
of pain," and so makes it possible for the reader (and the writer) to
confront "distressful" materials (p. 264).

But there is more to the artifice than that. Gray's sonnet recalls
West's *Ad Amicos,* a poem that West had sent him in 1737, in which
he anticipated his death.[23] Gray's work appears in this light as an
intimate gesture, carrying on West's words to build that tomb within
the breasts of friends which West wished to have built. Moreover,
West's poem is itself an imitation of several originals: an elegy by
Tibullus, a famous letter by Alexander Pope (recorded in Lonsdale's
notes, p. 65). Once heard, these and the other literary echoes place
Gray's lament within the exchanges of a circle of men of letters, and
so modify one's sense of the sonnet. The reader who recognizes the
allusions is urbanely complimented, drawn into the band of initiates.
Even as Gray presents the reader with a gallery of funerary sculptures
(Gray, West, Pope, Tibullus), an infinite regress of markers of a
common loss, he achieves social affirmation. The endless chain of the
same neatly embodies a universal, timeless condition: against the
cyclical rhythms of natural renewal Gray sets the particularly human
rhythm of repeated loss.

Such graceful echoing generalizes the meaning beyond the poet's personal situation. However caught up he may be in his grief, Gray looks out through the stylized gestures of his poem, in the lines Wordsworth dismissed, to a world unspoiled by his sorrow,[24] and to other men who have known similar suffering. The poetic devices that presumably caused Wordsworth to reject most of the poem are the means through which Gray articulates his grief, at once declaring their inability to provide consolation and employing their expressive potential.[25] Gray draws upon literary history—the accumulated resources of men conscious of their place in a social and historical network—to erect an art both witty and statuesque against the pains of time and death to which his poem attests. The decorum of the poem is both a matter of art and a manner of being in the world, a style and a means of meeting grief. Gray transforms himself into artifice, an unchanging image given meaning by a cultural code of which the decrease in currency is shown by Wordsworth's praising only those lines that seem most nakedly "sincere." Wordsworth, in contrast, attains impersonality by reduction and sets in motion a ceaseless metamorphosis that witnesses the inseparability of life and death in "this *active* universe" and in the most intimate reaches of the single self.

Wordsworth's condemnation of Gray's moving work thus points to a central characteristic of his own poems, although the issue of poetic diction that is the occasion for introducing the sonnet into the *Preface* does not by itself explain the prominence accorded it. In *A Slumber Did My Spirit Seal* and its companions man is deprived of the traditional supports Gray can still invoke, and the resonance of conventional elegiac properties like the violet and the star shrink almost to nothing. Alone amid the ambiguously signifying "permanent forms of nature," man must learn to surmount the bafflement of death without other men. Wordsworth's disparaging treatment of the sonnet is a cryptic but genuine signpost of the demarcation between the elegiac mode it still exploits and the epitaphs of the *Lyrical Ballads*.

Notes

1. All quotations from the *Lyrical Ballads* are taken from the edition of R. L. Brett and A. R. Jones (1963; rpt. and rev. London: Methuen, 1968). The quoted portions of the *Preface* appear on pp. 252–53.

2. I print the text as it appeared on its first publication, in William Mason's

The Poems of Mr. Gray, to Which Are Prefixed Memoirs of His Life and Writings (York, 1775), p. 60. Wordsworth's text, with full stops only at the twelfth and fourteenth lines, obscures the formal elegance of the sonnet. It does not correspond to any of the eighteenth-century versions that I have seen, but its source may lie in a customary indifference to punctuation rather than in a particular printing. Even after the appearance of the sonnet in Mason's *Memoirs,* it was often omitted from editions of Gray and collections; it is not to be found in Johnson's *Works of the English Poets* (London, 1790), nor even in the expansion by Chalmers (London, 1810). The sonnet is absent from the poems printed as the Gray section in Anderson's *Works of the British Poets* (London, 1795), which Wordsworth had with him in Grasmere in 1800, but it is printed there twice, once in the prefatory biography of Gray, where it is characterized as "exceedingly tender and mournful," and once on the title page of the section of West's poems, immediately following, with different accidentals each time. For the importance to Wordsworth of Anderson's collection, see William Heath, *Wordsworth and Coleridge: A Study of Their Literary Relations in 1801–1802* (Oxford: Clarendon, 1970), pp. 22–24.

3. *Biographia Literaria,* ed. George Watson (New York: Dutton, 1965), p. 212. I have slightly rearranged the sentence.

4. See, for example, Skrikumar Banerjee, *Critical Theory and Poetic Practice in the "Lyrical Ballads"* (London: Williams and Norgate, 1931); and W. J. B. Owen, *Wordsworth's Preface to Lyrical Ballads, Anglistica* IX (Copenhagen: Rosenkild and Bagger, 1957).

5. James Swearingen, "Wordsworth on Gray," *Studies in English Literature* 14 (Autumn 1974): 489–509; the quoted passage is on p. 509. Several critics have commented on the seeming counterpoint of voices in the sonnet. The observations of F. Doherty, "The Two Voices of Gray," *Essays in Criticism* 13 (July 1963): 222–30, are extended and refined by Patricia Meyer Spacks, "Statement and Artifice in Thomas Gray," *SEL* 5 (Summer 1965): 519–32.

6. Roger Lonsdale, ed., *The Poems of Thomas Gray, William Collins, Oliver Goldsmith* (London: Longman, 1969), p. 67.

7. The Miltonic echoes are most fully studied by Joseph Foladare, "Gray's 'Frail Memorial' to West," *Publications of the Modern Language Association* 75 (March 1960): 61–65.

8. The loss of West means the loss of the only fit audience for the poem, a fact reflected in Gray's having left it unpublished during his lifetime. See Dustin Griffin, "Gray's Audience," *EIC* 28 (July 1978): 208–15.

9. Gray's sonnet thus partakes of the tradition of the spring elegy, which Wordsworth was to take up and transform in 1802 with "Resolution and Independence" and the Intimations Ode; see Heath, *Wordsworth and Coleridge,* pp. 123–41.

10. Amy Louise Reed, *The Background of Gray's Elegy* (New York: Columbia University Press, 1924); John W. Draper, *The Funeral Elegy and the Rise of English Romanticism* (1929; rpt. New York: Octagon, 1967): Eleanor Sickels, *The Gloomy Egoist: Moods and Themes of Melancholy from Gray to Keats* (New York: Columbia University Press, 1932).

11. *The Standard Edition of the Complete Psychological Works of Sigmund*

Freud, 24 vols. (London: Hogarth Press, 1957), XIV, 239–58. Hereafter cited as *SE.*

12. Paul de Man, "The Rhetoric of Temporality," in *Interpretation: Theory and Practice,* ed. Charles S. Singleton (Baltimore: Johns Hopkins University Press, 1969), pp. 173–209.

13. *The Poetical Works of William Wordsworth,* 5 vols., ed. E. de Selincourt and Helen Darbishire, 2d ed. (Oxford: Clarendon, 1954), III, 16.

14. The earliest stages of the controversy (F. W. Bateson, Cleanth Brooks, and others) are examined by Michael Hancher, "The Science of Interpretation and the Art of Interpretation," *Modern Language Notes* 85 (December 1970): 791–802; see also Appendix I, "Objective Interpretation," of E. D. Hirsch's *Validity in Interpretation* (New Haven: Yale University Press, 1967). J. Hillis Miller presents the oppositions of the poem as the source of its strength in "On Edge: The Crossways of Contemporary Criticism," *Bulletin of the American Academy of Arts and Sciences* 32 (1979): 13–32. In *Wordsworth's Poetry 1787–1814* (New Haven: Yale University Press, 1964), Geoffrey Hartman briefly considers "A Slumber" in connection with mourning (pp. 157–62); see also his essay "Wordsworth, Inscriptions, and Romantic Nature Poetry," in *From Sensibility to Romanticism,* ed. F. W. Hilles and Harold Bloom (New York: Oxford University Press, 1965), pp. 389–413. Hartman returns to the poem in "Words and Wounds," Chapter 5 of his *Saving the Text: Literature/Derrida/Philosophy* (Baltimore: Johns Hopkins University Press, 1981), to comment that the second stanza is "tonally unreadable" (pp. 147–48).

15. The resonance of "urn" in "diurnal" is noted by Norman Holland, "Literary Interpretation and Three Phases of Psychoanalysis," *Critical Inquiry* 3 (Winter 1976): 221–33, which takes *A Slumber* as its example. Holland's third phase, however, almost completely shifts the critical emphasis from the text to his own experience of reading.

16. Frances Ferguson, "The Lucy Poems: Wordsworth's Quest for a Poetic Object," *English Literary History* 40 (Winter 1973): 532–48, rpt. as Chapter 6 of her *Wordsworth: Language as Counter-Spirit* (New Haven: Yale University Press, 1977).

17. A bleaker view of *Three Years She Grew* is put forward by Alan Grob, *The Philosophic Mind* (Columbus: Ohio State University Press, 1973), pp. 202–4.

18. "Remembering, Repeating and Working Through," *SE,* XII, 145–56.

19. Hugh Sykes Davies was the first to point out that the "she" of the third line appears grammatically to have "my spirit" as its antecedent, *EIC* 15 (April 1965): 135–61, but he failed to see that it was the ambiguity of the referent that is its most important feature; I have tried to preserve it by an account of the temporal experience of reading the poem. Roman Jacobson's concept of the pronoun as a "shifter" is helpful in seeing the connection of the change the poem narrates to both the "I" and the "she."

20. *The Prose Works of William Wordsworth,* 3 vols., ed. W. J. B. Owen and Jane Worthington Smyser (Oxford: Clarendon, 1974), III, 87–88.

21. This sentence occurs immediately after Gray's epitaph on his mother; though it actually refers to another loss, it indicates a general characteristic of Gray's temperament emphasized in the biography.

22. Johnson's *Dictionary* gives "having no offspring" as the third definition of "fruitless." Although one would not wish to make too much of it because of the wide difference in tone, the phrase "imperfect joys" in the eighth line of the sonnet echoes a Restoration subgenre of erotic poetry concerned with sexual impotence and frustration; Rochester's *The Imperfect Enjoyment* is the best-known example. See Richard E. Quaintance, "French Sources of the Restoration 'Imperfect Enjoyment' Poem," *Philological Quarterly* 42 (April 1963): 190–99.

23. West's *Ad Amicos* (printed in part by Lonsdale, p. 65) includes the lines:

> though this face be seen no more,
> The world will pass as cheerful as before,
> Bright as before the day star will appear,
> The fields as verdant, and the skies as clear
>
> . . . .
>
> Unknown and silent will depart my breath,
> Nor nature e'er take notice of my death.
> Yet some there are (ere spent my vital days)
> Within whose breasts my tomb I wish to raise.

24. Noted by Donald C. Mell, *A Poetics of Augustan Elegy* (Amsterdam: Rodopi, 1974), p. 68.

25. Because Gray makes use of the stock phrases as well as revealing their limitations it is inaccurate to speak of his dramatized "rejection" of them, as does Geoffrey Tillotson, *Augustan Poetic Diction* (London: Athlone Press, 1964), p. 88.

4

Wordsworth's Intimations Ode and Its Epigraphs

At the outset of his essay "The Immortality Ode," Lionel Trilling observes:

> Criticism, we know, must always be concerned with the poem itself. But a poem does not always exist only in itself: sometimes it has a very lively existence in its false or partial appearances. These simulacra of the actual poem must be taken into account by criticism and sometimes in its effort to come at the poem as it really is, criticism does well to allow the simulacra to dictate at least its opening moves.[1]

Trilling was concerned with the tradition of critical interpretations that comes to encase a canonical text, but with the *Ode* the encasing begins with Wordsworth himself. Who now can read the poem without an intervening consciousness of the poet's own glosses on his work, those later simulacra of its meaning: the Isabella Fenwick note of 1842–43, with its invocation of Enoch, Elijah, and Platonic myth, and its reminiscences of childhood trances of idealism, also recorded by R. P. Graves and Bonamy Price; or the 1815 letter to Catherine Clarkson explaining the poem? And who can separate the poem from the three lines from *My Heart Leaps Up* which became its epigraph only in 1815, or from its title, also added in that year, habitually shortened (as in Trilling's essay), with unexamined consequences upon our understanding, to *The Immortality Ode?*[2]

In 1807, however, when the poem we know as *Ode: Intimations of Immortality from Recollections of Early Childhood* first appeared as the last work in *Poems, in Two Volumes,* it was headed simply *Ode,* and its epigraph was "Paulo maiora canamus," taken from Virgil's fourth eclogue. If, as Wordsworth later asserted, "to the attentive and competent reader the whole sufficiently explains itself," the first reviewers appear to have been, at least by Wordsworth's standards, neither attentive nor competent. One critic thought that the poem was a second *Ode to Duty;* another complained that "the reader is turned loose into a wilderness of sublimity, tenderness, bombast, and absurdity, to find out the subject as well as he can"; and Jeffrey proclaimed in the *Edinburgh Review* that the *Ode* was "beyond all doubt, the most illegible and unintelligible part of the publication. We can pretend to give no analysis or explanation of it."[3] Jeffrey noted the Virgilian motto as the "title," but noticing did not lessen his bafflement. That introduction, however, provided an interpretive signal that might have led readers to recognize the genre of the poem. I should like in this chapter to explore the continuities and contrasts suggested by reading the *Ode* in the light cast by Virgil's poem, and to consider the effects Wordsworth brought about when he replaced the original epigraph with lines from *My Heart Leaps Up.*

Virgil's fourth eclogue is an account of the birth of a wonder child ushering in a new golden race and age, with a famously provocative elision of exact historical reference. The theme appealed to Wordsworth, whose own poem offers a mythic paean to the child he once was, incorporating a nativity within it as well. The appearance of Virgil's "let's sing a nobler song" at the head of Wordsworth's poem shows, too, that the mixture of pastoral and prophetic modes accorded with the *Ode*'s thematic interests.[4] The allusion to the eclogue, and to the rich tradition that arose from its interpretive crux of the babe as either a particular real child or a mythic symbol, announces the puzzles of the *Ode* as deliberate and rooted in convention. Even the hyperbolic praise of the infant in the eighth stanza ("Thou best Philosopher . . .") that so troubled Coleridge is prepared for in the tender, comic exaggeration of Virgil's mode.

But if the eclogue was in many ways suitable to Wordsworth's purposes, he rejected its most distinctive feature. Though miraculous, Virgil's babe realizes his identity in mortal life and matures by modeling himself on his father. Beneath the extravagance is visible a familiar pattern of psychological growth, the stages of which Virgil clearly marks:

> But first, child, earth's uncultivated gifts
> Will spring up for you . . .
> Your crib itself will shower you with flowers . . .
> But when heroic praise, parental deeds
> You read and come to know what manhood is,
> Plains slowly will turn gold with tender grain . . .
> Later, when strengthening years have made you man,
> Traders will leave the sea, no sailing pine
> Will barter goods: all lands will grow all things.

The prophesied golden age is concomitant with the achievement of manhood in the paternal image: the child will rule "the world calmed by his father's hand."

The son's relationship with his mother is equally untroubled. The poem concludes with a striking image:

> Come now, sweet boy: with smiling greet your mother
> (She carried you ten long and tedious months)
> Come now, sweet boy: who smiles not on a parent
> Graces no god's carouse nor goddess' bed.

This tableau, its ceremonial function underlined by the repetition of "incipe, parve puer," harmoniously unites the generations and blends the familial and the divine. The infant's smile is the meet repayment of his mother's labor in his own birth, an acknowledgment of the inextricably dependent status of his origin; in turn, however, the smile is the passport to the world of adult sexuality, the ground that will make possible his later active participation in the erotic life of "gods" and "goddesses" (and so the adults appear to the child).

In affording the child such an optimistic plot and such providential models, Virgil was actually rewriting his own precursors. As Renato Poggioli pointed out, in placing the golden age in the future, "Virgil had already paradoxically reinterpreted the most important of all pastoral myths. While the whole of antiquity . . . had relegated the dream of mankind's happy state to the beginning of time, Virgil here projected that dream into the age to come."[5] Wordsworth's *Ode* restores the myth of antiquity, once again placing paradise at the origin, Heaven "in our infancy."[6] This alteration is perhaps not as absolute as it first appears, for a paradise located in the past is the mirror image of one projected into the future.[7] The reversal, however, alters the representation of the family and the child's development within it.

Indeed, Virgil's idyllic portrait of a fulfilled adulthood following easily from the child's position within the family triangle is quite different from the tensions that pervade the situation of the child in Wordsworth's *Ode*. The "growing Boy" finds himself enclosed by the "Shades of the prison-house"; the "Youth" who still is "Nature's Priest" is succeeded by the "Man" who perceives his "vision splendid" die away. Wordsworth's mythic account of the stages of human decline is followed in the seventh stanza by a satiric portrayal that is its bitter complement.[8] The "light upon him from his Father's eyes" inadequately recompenses the playing child for the loss of the "celestial light"; adult roles appear only as "parts" on a " 'humourous stage,' " his emulation of them no more than a self-debasing "imitation," not a process of genuine growth. His mother's love disturbs rather than comforts: he is "Fretted by sallies of his Mother's kisses."

Such a satiric dismissal of the parents, however, is enfranchising: it frees the child from any obligation to them. The previous stanza of the *Ode,* by defining the child's alienation as that of a "Foster-child," degrades his parents into mere foster parents. The true home of the child is not the prisonhouse of mundane existence but "elsewhere."[9] This family romance, however, entails its own problems, because the child is "blindly with [his] blessedness at strife," eager to assimilate into the world whose authority Wordsworth derogates. The absent, lost heritage with which he aligns himself intensifies his unease: his "Immortality" "broods" over him, "a Master o'er a Slave, / A Presence which is not to be put by."

Through its vision of transformation Virgil's poem effortlessly reconciles the roles of son and parents, pastoral harmony and heroic glory, and this world with the divine. In Wordsworth's poem these pairs are split apart, and the son is torn between two allegiances. "Oh evil day! if I were sullen / While the Earth herself is adorning," the poet confesses in the fourth stanza, and the conditional seems intended to disguise his state, and his responsibility for it, from himself: it is his own myth of otherworldly origin that converts the earth into a mere "homely Nurse."

The ninth stanza brings the attempted resolution:

> Not for these I raise
> The Song of thanks and praise;
> But for those obstinate questionings
> Of sense and outward things,
> Fallings from us, vanishings;
> Blank misgivings of a Creature
> Moving about in worlds not realiz'd,
> High instincts, before which our mortal Nature
> Did tremble like a guilty Thing surpriz'd

If these childhood recollections are, as Wordsworth claimed, the core of the *Ode,* the attempted recuperation is brilliant: the child's uncertainties are reinterpreted by the adult as "the fountain light of all our day, / . . . a master light of all our seeing." The "Fallings from us, vanishings; / Blank misgivings," however, are traces of the home elsewhere and the original abandoned self, betrayed by the child's own avid maturation. Behind Wordsworth's "High instincts, before which our mortal Nature / Did tremble like a guilty Thing surpriz'd" lies Horatio's description of Hamlet's father's ghost—"it started like a guilty thing / Upon a fearful summons"—hinting at the oedipal contest of Shakespeare's play, the son's obligation to his absent father, his duty to punish his "foster" father/uncle and his derelict mother, his allegiance to a home in comparison to which the present one is a prison, even as Wordsworth's allegiances make the world a prison-house. "Mortal nature" would repress those allegiances but remains troubled by the "high instincts" that are a problematic parallel to Virgil's "higher things."

The crisis the poem explicitly describes, that of the fading of the celestial light, thus discloses itself as a myth concealing another conflict, between resistance to the everyday adult would that the transformative myth reduces to sterility and assimilation to that same world.[10] "Listlessness" and "mad endeavour" are the alternate, depressive and manic, phases of this unresolved dilemma. The child who cooperates with his own absorption by the everyday world is not simply "blindly with [his] blessedness at strife" but seeking to escape the conflict of loyalties by burying the self in "custom" "Heavy as frost, and deep almost as life!" Willful blinding is preferable to continued division.

The question "Whither is fled the visionary gleam? / Where is it now, the glory and the dream?" had forced the breaking-off of the poem in 1802. The myth of the universally vanishing vision is the first response formulated by the 1804 resumption, which approaches the question of where the vision has fled by asking where it originated. A deterministic myth, with its generalized picture of decline from infancy to manhood, thus comes into being as a consoling formulation.[11] The lament contains a comfort: it places the vision safely in the past and represents its dissolution as an inevitability rather than as a matter of individual fallibility. It is the Child, the Youth, the Man who experiences these losses, not the first-person narrator of the beginning and the very end of the poem: the "I" of the 1802 opening yields to the inclusive "he," "we," and "our" of the 1804 continuation. Thus doubly distanced—by time and by generalization—from a personal crisis, the narrator can declare his fidelity to the vision while remaining removed from its demands. Trilling's avowedly "naturalistic" interpretation of the *Ode* invokes a version of Freud to legitimate Wordsworth's account of maturing: for all three figures the loss is an ineluctable one. Yet before we accept as merely "true" or "natural" this movement from the "eagerness of infantine desire" to "duty and to truth," in the words of *The Prelude* (1805, II, 25–26),[12] we might ask what purposes this presentation serves in the psychic economy of the poem.

One advantage, surely, is that the poet may mourn the loss of vision in experience but secure it in the mind by an act of memory:

> O joy! that in our embers
> Is something that doth live,
> That nature yet remembers
> What was so fugitive!

Abrupt transitions, like this one from the melancholy prospect of the eighth to the ninth stanza, reversing bare or gloomy narratives into revelations of strength, are not uncommon in Wordsworth and always signal moments of particular intensity. Such a discontinuity, a characteristic formal feature of the sublime ode, here manifests those urgent grounds of his imagination that remain unspoken in, otherwise effaced by, the discourse of the *Ode*. The last of the 1802 stanzas concluded as the Tree and the Field "speak of something that is gone" and the Pansy "Doth the same tale repeat"; in 1804, that tale of absence is redefined as memory, as the tale of the knowledge of absence, as it were. As Kenneth Johnston observed some time ago, "what Wordsworth gives thanks for in his memories of childhood is something that even then he experienced as a loss, a 'vanishing.' "[13]

It is memory alone that stabilizes this experience of disappearance, which is to say that in the poem Wordsworth reconstitutes himself as a historical being. The mythic history of decline from an ahistorical origin is in turn replaced by the history of the individual, the unique experience already anticipated by the *single* tree, the *one* field, the specific Pansy. Even while declaring that "nothing can bring back the hour / Of splendour in the grass, of glory in the flower," Wordsworth affirms continuity by a transference of his own memorial powers to a nature that at once provides an external ground for the self and seems to include it: it is "nature [that] yet remembers / What was so fugitive." What vanished can now be interpreted as the human beginning of a deepening life in time that offsets both the sublime claims of infancy and youth and the guilt of falling away.

Wordsworth thus survives to speak the elegy over his own youthful narcissism, to record the chastening of the grandiose childhood "indisposition to bend to the law of death as applying to our own particular case" that he recalled to Catherine Clarkson in the letter referred to at the beginning of this chapter (*LMY*, p. 189). He survives, in fact, by speaking that elegy, by defining himself as the elegist of that narcissism. Nativity and elegy are not unrelated forms, as Milton's *On the Morning of Christ's Nativity* and still more his *Lycidas* had shown: the drowned shepherd of *Lycidas* is reborn "In the blest Kingdoms meek of joy and love." Wordsworth, through the image of life continuing in its own ashes,[14] is reborn as the poet of "the human heart by which we live," committed to the songs of his own loss, the Virgilian "puer" become the Virgil of "sunt lacrimae rerum."

The union with the past is not only consoling, it is also fecundating: "The thought of our past years in me doth *breed* / Perpetual benedictions" (emphasis added). The poet appears as a mother, inseminated by thoughts of the past and thus able to "see the Children sport upon the shore." This parent is not a foster parent, a deceptive homely nurse, or an exigent master brooding over a slave, but a true cherisher. Wordsworth counters the sense of a killing truancy from the past by mothering it, thus converting its monitory power into beneficence: as he preserves them, so the thoughts of the past now "uphold" and "cherish" him. The vision of the babe leaping up on its mother's arm that provoked the poet's fears of alienation in the fourth stanza is now internalized, and so becomes sustaining; hence the innocent brightness of a newborn day will be lovely yet.[15]

The contrast between this image of self-begetting fertility, however, and the sexuality of the conclusion of Virgil's poem forcefully indicates how private is the world of the *Ode*. Virgil's poem, addressed to a consul, looks through an image of adult sexuality to the renovation of an entire social and natural order; Wordsworth's turns inward. Absent from this tableau is the world of action and of mature sexuality of Virgil's poem—the figure of the father. Manhood appears in Wordsworth's poem only through the narrator as a figure of contemplation, caught between the myth of pre-existence he imagines and the future promised by "the faith that looks through death." His position in this world remains threatened by anxiety: "And oh ye Fountains, Meadows, Hills, and Groves, / Think not of any severing of our loves!" In that line invocation yields immediately to supplication, and in the next to assertions of loyalty: "Yet in my heart of hearts I feel your might; / I only have relinquish'd one delight / To live beneath your more habitual sway." Wordsworth seems in the ambiguities of that last phrase to accommodate himself to the two conflicting demands upon him: the sense of an imperious immortality brooding over him like a master over a slave and the "custom" of ordinary adult existence. Able to join the pastoral world before him only "in thought," Wordsworth strives to make of such "Thoughts that do often lie too deep for tears" the source of his final power. The "eye / That hath kept watch o'er man's mortality" can give a "sober colouring" to the landscape to set against the lost visionary gleam. So, too, in the fourth eclogue the poet's own prayer briefly reveals the mortal conditions that make the vision of a golden age precious: "O that a remnant of long life be mine, / Giving me breath to celebrate your deeds. . . ." In both poems this separation of speaker and vision provides the deepening that in Wordsworth becomes the poetry of the "philosophic mind."

Yet Virgil's poem is a celebration that largely steps outside of time. From the beginning, in which the foretold birth of the babe is hailed as a return, through the description of the stages of his growth, which in the lines quoted above suspends the question of agency (making uncertain whether the babe is the cause of the golden age or its emblem), to this glimpse of the mortal poet and the final lines of the poem in which the babe is yet to be born, Virgil creates out of the political conditions of contemporary Rome a prophetic vision, a wish, independent of ordinary chronology. Wordsworth's *Ode* is linear, or at best chiastic, combating loss only by human understanding.

Wordsworth celebrates, too, but what he celebrates, as he moves toward the "Thoughts that do often lie too deep for tears" that are the final words of his poem, is mourning. Deeper things, rather than Virgil's higher things, are his concern. "The soothing thoughts that spring / Out of human suffering" are the emblems of his choice: the suffering is the penalty of his renunciation and the badge of his authenticity, the soothing quality from the presentation of this choice as an inevitability.[16]

A brief look at another of the *Ode*'s contexts illuminates this situation. The first mention of the poem comes in Dorothy Wordsworth's journal entry of March 27, 1802: "At Breakfast Wm wrote part of an Ode."[17] As Paul Magnuson has observed, the form of the poem was fixed from the outset, well before Wordsworth had worked out its argument.[18] Even as Virgil began his eclogue by announcing a more exalted subject, so Wordsworth from the beginning elevated pastoral to the gravity of an ode. Some of the sublime connotations of that form for him may be seen on another, contemporary occasion on which Wordsworth employed the term. In the Arab Dream portion of Book V of *The Prelude,* on which Wordsworth was working at about the time he completed the *Ode* in March 1804, the narrator, acknowledged in the 1850 text to be Wordsworth himself, hears "An ode in passion uttered, which foretold / Destruction to the children of the earth / By deluge now at hand" (1805 *Prelude,* V, 97–99). The stone that utters this apocalyptic ode, however, is also "a god, yea many gods, / Had voices more than all the winds, and was / A joy, a consolation, and a hope" (107–9). This paradoxical joining of destruction and consolation is only one of the many doublings that mark the scene: Wordsworth and his "studious friend"; the Arab who is and is not Don Quixote; the stone and shell, which are both also books, and which must seemingly be buried in order to be preserved; the desert and the ocean; the bond between the Arab and the narrator, who finds that "A wish was now engendered in my fear / To cleave unto this man, and I begged leave / To share his errand with him" (115–17). The Arab travels onward while looking behind him at the approaching deluge:

> And looking backwards when he looked I saw
> A glittering light, and asked him whence it came.
> "It is," said he, "the waters of the deep
> Gathering upon us." Quickening then his pace
> He left me: I called after him aloud;

He heeded not, but with his twofold charge
Beneath his arm—before me in full view—
I saw him riding o'er the desert sands
With the fleet waters of the drowning world
In chace of him; whereat I waked in terror,
And saw the sea before me, and the book
In which I had been reading at my side.

(128–39)

The ambivalence of the moment, already attested by the numerous splittings, reaches such intensity as to disrupt the narrator's sleep.

Several features of this passage recur in the *Ode:* the glittering light that is also the engulfing flood matches, at one end of the poem, the "celestial light" of Wordsworth's myth of otherworldly origin, and, at the other, the "immortal sea / Which brought us hither." The linking of these two images thus makes evident the tension between the visionary world and ordinary human experience that the *Ode* seeks to reconcile. Wordsworth's uneasy position is revealed in the narrator's mixture of "wish and fear" toward the Arab knight, whose abandonment of him despite his call parallels the fading of the visionary gleam lamented in the Ode. At the same time, in this dream where all the split, reversed, and merged identities are fantasies of a single mind, one might read this abandonment as Wordsworth's relinquishment of the dangers of commitment to the visionary quest, self-protectively represented by its opposite: the knight's heedlessness of him.

The continuing fascination exerted by the "semi-Quixote," to whom Wordsworth acknowledges returning "Full often" in thought, epitomizes the temptations that the *Ode* is concerned to discipline:

And I have scarcely pitied him, have felt
A reverence for a being thus employed,
And thought that in the blind and awful lair
Of such a madness reason did lie couched.
Enow there are on earth to take in charge
Their wives, their children, and their virgin loves,
Or whatsoever else the heart holds dear—
Enow to think of these—yea, will I say,
In sober contemplation of the approach
Of such great overthrow, made manifest
By certain evidence, that I methinks

> Could share that maniac's anxiousness, could go
> Upon like errand.
>
> (149–61)

The cost in human connectedness required by this identification must have been apparent to Wordsworth in the spring of 1804, when his wife was pregnant with their second child. The questing knight whose grandeur is inseparable from his ode foretelling "destruction to the children of the earth" writes at large the dilemma the child faces in the *Ode*. That child experiences "A Presence" (eighth stanza) which is less like the benign "beloved presence" of the Blest Babe passage (1805 *Prelude,* II, 255) than like the sublime "presence" of *Tintern Abbey,* which *"disturbs* . . . with the joy / Of elevated thoughts" (94–95, emphasis added); it is a presence, in the words of the *Ode,* "which is not to be put by." Wordsworth chooses to forgo the quest, to place himself at a remove from the brooding Master and the haunted child, rather than to endure their demands.

The resolving image of the ninth stanza precisely stations the poet:

> Hence, in a season of calm weather,
> Though inland far we be,
> Our Souls have sight of that immortal sea
> Which brought us hither,
> Can in a moment travel thither,
> And see the Children sport upon the shore,
> And hear the mighty waters rolling evermore,

"Calm" here is to temperament as "inland" is to geography: calm because inland, because safe from the apocalyptic ocean that wells up before the dreamer of *Prelude* V, the "eternal deep" of the *Ode*. This watcher, merely traveling to see and hear the ocean, is in no danger of being swept away by it. In his influential analysis of these lines in "The Structure of Romantic Nature Imagery" William Wimsatt noted that in logic the children do not belong on the seashore: "they are not strictly parts of the traveler-space vehicle, but of the soul-age-time tenor, attracted over, from tenor to vehicle."[19] This "imposition of image upon image," as Wimsatt termed it, is a metaleptic transformation that marks Wordsworth's freedom from the regressive impulses risked by the *Ode*'s lament for the past. The children become only figures generated within the poet's tropes, creatures of metaphor and myth. The immediacy urged in the third stanza—"Shout round me, let me hear thy shouts, thou happy Shepherd Boy!"—and the intimate address of the eighth stanza to "Thou little Child" give way to the mere seeing of children on the shore; the child who reads the eternal deep in the eighth stanza is himself read in the ninth, and that the children of the latter stanza can be said to "sport" marks the allaying of anxiety won by the tactic of distancing. Unlike Virgil's, sung to an approaching rejuvenation, Wordsworth's "song of thanks and praise" in the ninth stanza arises in, and is made possible by, the space left by the lost immediacy of vision. Like the Arab, Wordsworth looks backward in order to travel forward and buries in order to preserve.

This stance gains an aura from another aspect of the allusion to the fourth eclogue, the way traditional interpretation had seen the poem as prophesying the birth of Christ.[20] Wordsworth later suggested to Miss Fenwick that "the fall of man presents an analogy in . . . favour" of the notion of pre-existence, and the preservation of the past in memory emerges as a private spiritual analogue to the Christian's keeping alive the presence of Christ in his heart: the kingdom of God is within you. The Christian resonance accords with the language of transcendence running throughout the poem; it strengthens, for example, the echoes in "Another race hath been, and other palms are won" of I Corinthians 9:24–25: "Know ye not that they which run in a race run all, but one receiveth the prize? So run, that ye may obtain. And every man that striveth for the mastery is temperate in all things. Now they *do it* to obtain a corruptible crown; but we an incorruptible."

I would argue nonetheless that the indirectness of the reference to scripture is as important to the success of the poem as the reference itself. To introduce the poem with an epigraph from the fourth eclogue is to recall a poet whose "Christian" allusions are always subject to debate; the Christianity of Wordsworth's language is also ambiguous. It is noteworthy that although the *Ode* is replete with declarations of the "truths that wake, / To perish never," such assertions are absent from the final stanza. If the concluding movement of elegy is consolation, then it is the restraint of Wordsworth's final affirmations that is remarkable. The inclusive self-portrait that emerges from the disparate pictures of the *Ode* is that of "A meditative, oft a suffering man," to borrow the contemporaneous words of the *Prelude*,[21] "temperate in all things," as in the Pauline exhortation. The closing emphasis is on the continuing "joys and fears" of this meditative mind and not on a heavenly resolution. The poem exploits the resonance of Christian faith without committing itself to belief, to the conviction that would lessen its human uncertainty.[22] Virgil, the virtuous pagan moving toward revelation but never vouchsafed it, thus makes a poignant figure for Wordsworth.

It is just such strong ambiguities that the alterations to the poem between 1807 and 1815 reduce. Dismayed by the reviews, urged by Crabb Robinson to provide a title for the *Ode* "to guide the reader to a perception of its drift," and seeking more urgently for consolation himself, Wordsworth replaced the merely formal heading of *Ode* with *Ode: Intimations of Immortality from Recollections of Early Childhood.*[23] The change, like the earlier conversion of *The Leech-gatherer* upon publication into *Resolution and Independence,* was an act of interpretation, a subsequent "clarification" by the poet that limited the rich equivocations of his original text. In the *Ode,* immortality is a concept inseparably linked to experiences of mortality; the title shifted the emphasis to the former.[24] The substitution of three lines from *My Heart Leaps Up* for "Paulo maiora canamus" had similar effects. The Virgilian epigraph, as we have seen, was appropriate in signaling an interpretive complexity and infelicitous in the contrast it brings forward between the discords of Wordsworth's own work and Virgil's prophecy of a general fertility based on an infant in a harmonious family. The assertion that "The Child is Father of the Man" tries to complete the family romance, obliterating the strains of dependency that the poem witnesses. The unambivalent celebration of the child as father in the lyric does not betray the cost of such a backward-facing gesture, whereas the original epigraph pointed to the loss of the active paternal model in Virgil's eclogue, the man who marks the emergence of a new civic order. The political hopes of Wordsworth's earlier years are not to be found in the *Ode.*[25] The conditional form of "I could wish" is the only trace in the lyric of the gaps between the sublime self and the world around him in the *Ode:* the celebration of "natural piety," with its double allegiances to the natural order and the complex of paternal, social, and religious values contained in the concept of *pious,* places such piety above the hints of rebellion that the poem illustrates.[26] The new epigraph, taken from a poem "more confident"[27] than the *Ode* itself, evades in its epigrammatic density the conflicts acted out by the *Ode.* The *Ode* proceeds from pastoral elegy in 1802 to an elegy for pastoral in 1804; the lyric reinstalls at the head of the text the constant relation of man and nature, affirming at the outset the continuity that the poem must labor to establish. The man's heart leaps up to the rainbow in the same phrase and hence as certainly, joyfully, and naturally as the babe leaps up on his mother's arm.

To begin the *Ode* with "The Rainbow" is, moreover, to write in the language of divine sanction rather than of nature, to throw the emphasis on the enduring presence of that covenant against destruction rather than on the *Ode*'s experience that "The Rainbow comes and goes." In the unbroken sequence "So was it . . . So is it . . . So be it" that his new epigraph summons up, Wordsworth underrepresents the pathos of change and separation in the *Ode* itself, the difficulty of its progress from the irregular lines and abrupt transitions of the beginning of his poem to the steadily meditative blank verse of the conclusion.[28] In placing as the epigraph to the final poem of his collection an excerpt from the poem that stood first in the collection, Wordsworth sought to impose on his writings a closure, a completeness that obscures the powerful tensions within the *Ode*.[29] If in 1807 the Virgilian epigraph raised the question of career, of Wordsworth's further poetic growth toward "higher things," the symmetry established by the substitution of "The Rainbow" in 1815 suggested rather that the canon was now closed. The history of the poem mediates the debate between Trilling and Raysor over its meaning: whereas the *Ode* may have begun in 1802 as a poem about growing up, it is completed in 1815 as a poem about the possibilities of immortality. The acts of giving a title to the poem and changing the epigraph shed light on what is most moving in the poem: Wordsworth's need continually to interpret himself, to try yet again to rewrite into permanence the self he had written into being from that primary "forgetting," those elemental "vanishings."

Notes

1. "The Immortality Ode," in *The Liberal Imagination* (1950; rpt. Garden City, N.Y.: Doubleday Anchor, n.d.), p. 125.

2. Alan Grob, in *The Philosophic Mind* (Columbus: Ohio State University Press, 1973), endorses the opinion of Thomas M. Raysor ("The Themes of Immortality and Natural Piety in Wordsworth's Immortality Ode," *Publications of the Modern Language Association* 69 [1954]: 861–75) that the later views "reinforce rather than conflict with views already present in the poem in 1804" (p. 275), but even a "reinforcement" can constitute a significant alteration in balance.

3. Donald R. Reiman, ed., *The Romantics Reviewed* (New York: Garland, 1972), Part A, 1:20; A, 1:337; and A, 2:436, respectively.

4. In January 1816 Wordsworth wrote to Wrangham that "The Eclogues of Virgil appear to me, in that in which he was most excellent, polish of style and harmony of numbers, the most happily finished of all his performances." *The Letters of William and Dorothy Wordsworth, The Middle Years, Part II, 1812–1820,* ed. Ernest de Selincourt, 2d ed., rev. by Mary Moorman and Alan G. Hill (Oxford: Clarendon, 1970), p. 276; hereafter cited as *LMY*. Three years later, he repeated the praise: "I think I mentioned to you that these Poems of Virgil have always delighted me much; there is frequently in them an elegance and a happiness which no translation can hope to equal" (*LMY,* 523). I have made use of the translation and interpretation of the eclogues by Paul Alpers, *The Singer of the Eclogues: A Study of Virgilian Pastoral* (Berkeley: University of California Press, 1979). For an astute discussion linking Wordsworth's ambivalence to pastoral with his attitudes toward the past, see Thomas McFarland, "Creative Fantasy and Matter-of-Fact Reality in Wordsworth's Poetry," *Journal of English and Germanic Philology* 75 (1976): 1–24.

5. Renato Poggioli, *The Oaten Flute* (Cambridge, Mass.: Harvard University Press, 1975), p. 19.

6. The text of the *Ode* cited throughout is from *Poems, in Two Volumes, and Other Poems, 1800–1807,* ed. Jared Curtis (Ithaca: Cornell University Press, 1983).

7. On the link between elegy and prophecy, see Michael Cooke, "Elegy, Prophecy, and Satire in the Romantic Order," in his *Acts of Inclusion* (New Haven: Yale University Press, 1979), pp. 1–54.

8. Helen Vendler contrasts "the Child in his immensity of soul" in the eighth stanza with the satiric portrait of "the Child wholly in exterior semblance" of the seventh stanza in her finely detailed "Lionel Trilling and the *Immortality Ode,*" *Salmagundi* 47 (1978): 66–86.

9. In the fullest psychoanalytic study of Wordsworth's poetry, *The Character of the Poet: Wordsworth in THE PRELUDE* (Princeton: Princeton University Press, 1971), Richard J. Onorato examines the recurrent conflict between the "opposed demands on child and man of the external world and its reality, on the one hand, and of a greater inner reality being sought regressively, on the other" (p. 69).

10. This interpretation accords roughly with David Ferry's account of Wordsworth divided between "mystic" and "sacramental" visions (*The Limits of Mortality* [Middletown, Conn.: Wesleyan University Press, 1959]), and Geoffrey Hartman's antithesis of apocalypse and akedah (*Wordsworth's Poetry 1787–1814* [New Haven: Yale University Press, 1964]).

11. The source of this myth may well have been suggested to Wordsworth already in 1802, however, by conversations with Coleridge about Proclus and other philosophers. See John D. Rea, "Coleridge's Intimations of Immortality from Proclus," *Modern Philology* 26 (1928): 201–13; and Herbert Hartman, "The 'Intimations' of Wordsworth's *Ode,*" *Review of English Studies* 6 (1930): 129–48.

12. All quotations from *The Prelude* are from *The Prelude 1799, 1805, 1850,* ed. Jonathan Wordsworth, M. H. Abrams, and Stephen Gill (New York: Norton, 1979).

13. "Recollecting Forgetting: Forcing Paradox to the Limit in the 'Intimations Ode,' " *The Wordsworth Circle* 2 (1971): 59–64.

14. On the possible alchemical sources of this image, see John D. Rea, "Wordsworth's Intimations of Palingenesis," *Review of English Studies* 8 (1932): 82–86.

15. I am uncertain precisely how much weight should be attached to the suggestion of the poet as mother carried by the imagery; certainly the metaphor should not be forced into a rigid identification. I do believe, however, that in regarding his potentially terrifying otherworldly allegiances with tenderness instead of suppressing them, Wordsworth endeavors to incorporate the powers represented in his earlier work as belonging to a maternal Nature (see the sixth stanza of the *Ode*). The description of those powers as including "Severer interventions" (1805 *Prelude*, I, 370) indicates the disquieting aspects that must be (re)interpreted into beneficence. I note, too, that the famous lines on the "obscure sense / Of possible sublimity" in the 1805 *Prelude* (II, 331–41) come in the verse paragraph immediately following lines that seem to allude to the death of the poet's mother: "I was left alone / Seeking the visible world, nor knowing why" (II, 292–93). The language of the former passage—"I deem not profitless those fleeting moods / Of shadowy exultation; not for this, / That they are kindred to our purer mind / And intellectual life, but that the soul . . ."—is echoed in the ninth stanza of the *Ode:* "Not for these I raise / The song of thanks and praise; / But for those obstinate questionings / Of sense and outward things, / Fallings from us, vanishings; / Blank misgivings of a Creature / Moving about in worlds not realiz'd. . . ." The parallels suggest a sequence: the *Prelude* (and here *1805* is mostly unchanged from *1799*) marks the loss of the mother as the "cause" that "now to Nature's finer influxes / My mind lay open" (II, 297–99); the *Ode* traces the internalization of such a past relationship with nature, itself the successor of the world made harmonious for the Blest Babe by the mother's presence (I, 237–80).

16. In "Resonances of Joy," Chapter 4 of *Wordsworth and the Human Heart* (New York: Columbia University Press, 1978), John Beer suggestively compares these lines to Oswald's speech in *The Borderers:* "Suffering is permanent, obscure and dark, / And shares the nature of infinity." The conjunction underlines the progress made in the *Ode:* it is suffering, as much as joy, that links man to man and discloses infinity, suffering that gives the philosophic mind its sublime authority.

17. *Journals of Dorothy Wordsworth,* ed. Mary Moorman (London: Oxford University Press, 1971), p. 106.

18. Paul Magnuson, "The Genesis of Wordsworth's Ode," *The Wordsworth Circle* 12 (1981): 23–30.

19. William Wimsatt's essay, originally published in 1949, is reprinted in his *The Verbal Icon* (Lexington: University of Kentucky Press, 1954).

20. John Ogilby's translation of Virgil, which Wordsworth owned, places this "Argument" at the head of the fourth eclogue: "Here Sibil is apply'd to Pollio's son, / Her Prophesies his Genethliacon: / But Christs birth by happy errour sings, / The Prince of Poets crowns the King of Kings." Frances Ferguson touches on the relation of the *Ode* to "the Christianized Pollio tradition" and also discusses its relation to the canon in *Wordsworth: Language as Counter-Spirit* (New Haven: Yale University Press, 1977), pp. 96–125.

21. 1805 *Prelude* XIII, 126. According to Mark Reed (*Wordsworth: The Chronology of the Middle Years* [Cambridge, Mass.: Harvard University Press, 1975]), this part of XIII was composed during the interval of January to March 1804 (p. 15); the last seven stanzas of the *Ode* were "probably composed, and the poem completed, probably early 1804, by 6 Mar." (p. 27).

22. Harold Bloom observes that "the logic of the *Ode* only *plays* at being a logic of concepts" (*The Visionary Company* [Garden City, N.Y.: Anchor Doubleday, 1963], p. 183). In *A Map of Misreading* (New York: Oxford University Press, 1975) Bloom contrasts the ending of the *Ode* with that of *Lycidas:* "The Wordsworth of the Ode will not present himself as an 'uncouth swain,' and the sober coloring imparted by his mature eye substitutes for the blue of the Miltonic mantle" (p. 149). Though Bloom's emphasis on this non-pastoral conclusion is fruitful, his restriction of the poem to "a misprision or powerful misreading of *Lycidas*" (p. 144) narrows its concerns.

23. Robinson claimed his influence in the affixing of a title in 1861. *The Correspondence of Henry Crabb Robinson with the Wordsworth Circle 1808–1866,* ed. E. J. Morley (Oxford: Clarendon, 1927), II, 838–39.

24. On the linking of immortality to mortality, see Kenneth R. Lincoln, "Wordsworth's Mortality Ode," *Journal of English and Germanic Philology* 71 (1972): 211–25.

25. Compare the role of the fourth eclogue in the *Ode* with the political implications of the echoes of it in Wordsworth's 1793 *Descriptive Sketches,* as noted by M. H. Abrams in "English Romanticism: The Spirit of the Age," in *Romanticism Reconsidered,* ed. Northrop Frye (New York: Columbia University Press, 1963), pp. 50–51. In Chapter 3 of her *Wordsworth's Great Period Poems* (Cambridge: Cambridge University Pres, 1986), "The Intimations Ode: A Timely Utterance," Marjorie Levinson argues that it is precisely the function of the *Ode* "to transfer ideologically *possessed* material from public to private domain" (p. 83). Wordsworth recovered the political weight of the *Ode* when in *The Convention of Cintra* (1809) he quoted lines 5–7 to celebrate the Spanish uprisings in the spring of 1808 against the forces of Napoleon. *The Prose Works of William Wordsworth,* 3 vols., ed. W. J. B. Owen and Jane Worthington Smyser (Oxford: Clarendon, 1974), I, 297. See also Chapter 8.

26. On "piety" in the *Ode* see also Paul Fry, *The Poet's Calling in the English Ode* (New Haven: Yale University Press, 1980), pp. 133–61.

27. The phrase is Raysor's; see n. 2 above.

28. I owe to Paul Sheats this observation on the significance of the changes in the verse.

29. Yet note how already in 1807 the Virgilian motto of the *Ode* seems to complete the epigraph on the title page of Vol. I: "Posterius graviore sono tibi Musa loquetur / Nostra: dabunt cum securos mihi tempora fructus." In Chapter 12 of his provocative study *Radical Literary Education: A Classroom Experiment with Wordsworth's "Ode"* (Madison: University of Wisconsin Press, 1987), "The History of Revision in the 'Ode': From 'Untam'd Pleasure' to 'Heaven-born Freedom,' " Jeffrey C. Robinson revealingly analyzes Wordsworth's changes to his text.

II

Texts and
Textual History

5

Reading Wordsworth's
Revisions: Othello
and the Drowned Man

I

After telling in *The Two-Part Prelude* of his discovery of the Drowned Man, Wordsworth observes:

> I might advert
> To numerous accidents in flood or field,
> Quarry or moor, or 'mid the winter snows,
> Distresses and disasters, tragic facts
> Of rural history, that impressed my mind
> With images to which in following years
> Far other feelings were attached—with forms
> That yet exist with independent life,
> And, like their archetypes, know no decay.
> (1799, I, 279–87)[1]

Shifts from the recounting of childhood experience as if from the child's perspective to the commenting voice of the adult narrator in *The Prelude* usually mark Wordsworth's attempt to achieve closure of the recalled incident, his declaration of its meaning for him. The confident, detached tone of this passage, which moves easily from consideration of narrative alternatives to the concluding affirmation of "know no decay," seems to perform the same function. Yet its rhythm and its syntax remain curiously at odds with each other, for the long single sentence depends from a conditional that is never resolved. "I might advert" if such and such conditions obtained or if it were necessary, but perhaps they don't, or it isn't; "I might advert," but I choose not to, though the grounds are unexplained. Here, as in *Tintern Abbey,* an irresolution in expected syntax creates an opening in which the imagination hovers. Accidents, distresses, disasters, and tragic facts are glimpsed but suspended. The all too plain sight of death in the Drowned Man shades off into a mode in which mortality is only uncertainly seen, the more easily then to be transformed into evidences of "independent life" and permanent archetypes.

This conclusion may interest us less than Wordsworth's act of evoking but occluding what he evokes. The gesture is the more striking because, as the Norton editors note, Wordsworth's phrase, "I might advert / To numerous accidents in flood or field," echoes Othello's description of his wooing of Desdemona: "Wherein I spake of most disastrous chances, / Of moving accidents by flood and field" (I, iii, 133–34). The text within the text opens a recess within Wordsworth's words, another puzzle to interpretation. The disappearance of this passage after 1799 piques one's curiosity about the role of Othello here, for the echo, virtually canceled before it appears by an adverting that is never fulfilled and then fully canceled in revision, nonetheless participates in a web of significant associations in Wordsworth's work. These in turn bring to prominence questions of the temporal dimensions of *The Prelude* and of our understanding of how to read its successive stages.

II

The narrator's declaration, "the moving accident is not my trade," in the roughly contemporary *Hart-Leap Well* (1800) is the best known of Wordsworth's afterimages of Othello.[2] The line, which opens the second part of the poem by dismissing the sorts of appeal exemplified by the tale of the first part, touches a central strain in Wordsworth's imagination, his attraction to, and chastening of, stories that arouse the passions.[3] In an evocation of tales left untold, like that of *The Two-Part Prelude,* Wordsworth recalls toward the end of *Home at Grasmere* (1800–1806) the "wild appetites and blind desires, / Motions of savage instinct" that were his childhood delight (706–7), and his continuing engagement with accounts of martial valor:

> Yea, to this hour I cannot read a Tale
> Of two brave Vessels matched in deadly fight

> And fighting to the death, but I am pleased
> More than a wise man ought to be; I wish,
> Fret, burn, and struggle, and in soul am there.
> But me hath Nature tamed and bade to seek
> For other agitations or be calm
>
> (721–27)[4]

This rehearsal of repudiated passions and impulses to "disobey" (713) climaxes in lines echoing Othello's cry when he comes to doubt Desdemona's chastity. Othello:

> O now, for ever
> Farewell the tranquil mind! Farewell content!
> Farewell the plumed troops, and the big wars
> That make ambition virtue—O, farewell!
> Farewell the neighing steed, and the shrill trump,
> The spirit-stirring drum, th'ear-piercing fife,
> The royal banner and all quality,
> Pride, pomp, and circumstance of glorious war!
>
> (III, iii, 344–51)[5]

So Wordsworth:

> Then farewell to the Warrior's schemes, farewell
> The forwardness of Soul which looks that way
> Upon a less incitement than the cause
> Of Liberty endangered, and farewell
> That other hope, long mine, the hope to fill
> The heroic trumpet with the Muse's breath!
>
> (745–50)

As critics have long remarked, the theological and the psychological run tandem in Othello's cherishing of the woman who integrates his universe.[6] In his reliance on her perfection, Othello is not dissimilar to Wordsworth sustained by a maternal presence in nature. It is Desdemona, too, to whom Wordsworth often turns in his reminiscences of *Othello*. In the sonnet sequence *Personal Talk* (1802–1804) he declares, "Dreams, books, are each a world; and books we know, / Are a substantial world," and he continues:

> Two shall be named, pre-eminently dear,—
> The gentle Lady married to the Moor;

> And heavenly Una with her milk-white Lamb.
> (33–34, 40–42)

Wordsworth opposes these "gentle" and "dear" heroines and the imaginative realms they inhabit to the everyday intercourse of the world. The nature of the "personal themes" (37) he finds in these works is indicated by his statement that *Othello* was one of the three "most pathetic of human compositions."[7] As the heroic warrior yields to the dupe and his murdered innocent, Shakespeare's play powerfully joins the sublime and the pathetic.

Othello describes "the story of [his] life" to Desdemona and Brabantio:

> I ran it through, even from my boyish days
> To th' very moment that he bade me tell it:
> Wherein I spake of most disastrous chances,
> Of moving accidents by flood and field,
> Of hair-breadth scapes i' th'imminent deadly breach
> (I, iii, 131–35)

Though Othello first told this story at Brabantio's request, making of it a means to win him membership in the Venetian community, its disruptive power is revealed by the circumstances in which he now speaks: the irate father charges him before the Venetian Senate with having used "spells and medicines bought of mountebanks" (I, iii, 61) to charm away his daughter. Othello's exploits, the source of his appeal, also mark him as an outsider, one who since his arms "had seven years' pith" (I, iii, 83) has lived in the male world of the tented field, among cannibals, in slavery—a romance kin to Wordsworth's Gothic elaborations of his own childhood, glanced at in the lines from *Home at Grasmere* quoted above, lightly mocked in *The Prelude* (1805, VIII, 525–41, 610–16), and presented at length in such early works as *The Vale of Esthwaite* (1786–1788). Desdemona, whose attention to Othello's stories is distracted by household chores, would "ever as she could . . . come again," eagerly demanding that Othello complete his story. "I did consent," he now recalls,

> And often did beguile her of her tears
> When I did speak of some distressful stroke
> That my youth suffered. My story being done,
> She gave me for my pains a world of sighs
> (I, iii, 154–58)

"She loved me for the dangers I had passed," Othello concludes, "And I loved her, that she did pity them" (I, iii, 166–67). Words transform the youthful hardships into a "pitiful" tale that finds the ideally sympathizing womanly listener—and perhaps one should observe here, with Freud, that such a finding is always a refinding. Yet this success encounters prohibitions: we hear the story of this story as Othello defends himself before the Venetian Senate for having "ta'en away this old man's daughter" (I, iii, 78). As Othello wooed Desdemona by repeating his broken, interrupted story, so now he must repeat it again before the "Most potent, grave and reverend signors" (I, iii, 76). Once again the power of his narrative is confirmed: "I think this tale would win my daughter too," assents the Duke (I, iii, 170).

The structure of the third scene of *Othello* thus discloses through its layers of repetition a single scene: the excluded child united with the loving woman, his authority sanctioned by the reigning patriarchal figure. Light is shed on this scene, and Wordsworth's echo of it in *The Prelude,* by another image of it in *The Borderers* (1796–1797; 1842). Marmaduke explains to Oswald how he has come to respect Herbert, the father of his beloved Idonea:

> Though I have never seen his face, methinks,
> There cannot come a day when I shall cease
> To love him. I remember, when a Boy
> Of scarcely seven years' growth, beneath the Elm
> That casts its shade over our village school,
> 'Twas my delight to sit and hear Idonea
> Repeat her Father's terrible adventures,
> Till all the band of playmates wept together;
> And that was the beginning of my love.
> And, through all converse of our later years,
> An image of this old Man still was present,
> When I had been most happy.
>
> (87–98)

This idyll systematically inverts the original scene. In place of the seven-year-old Othello, already swept up in the world of man's wars, there is the seven-year-old Marmaduke, tranquilly surrounded by his friends; instead of the divisive effect of Othello's narration, there is a "band of playmates" in shared sympathy; instead of Desdemona found later, there is Idonea present already in childhood; instead of a threatening Brabantio, there is an absent father, loved for his sufferings. The most forceful inversion is the placing of Marmaduke in Desdemona's role of the pitying hearer, and this is the key to them all; the harmony of the scene, free of rivalries of any sort, is achieved only at the cost of making the hero feminine and passive. The tableau of *The Borderers* is that of *Othello* shorn by fantasy of all its conflicts. Yet even this extraordinarily benign re-seeing of *Othello* cannot control the conflicts between father, suitor, and daughter: Herbert, returned, forbids the relationship of Marmaduke and Idonea, and in the words of the Iago-like Oswald, "that another in his Child's affection / Should hold a place, as if 'twere robbery, / He seemed to quarrel with the very thought" (56–58); Marmaduke in the end "unintentionally" abandons Herbert to die without food on the waste and collaterally inflicts great pain on the ostensibly beloved Idonea.[8]

The final eruptions of violence even from the peaceful triangle initially presented in *The Borderers* suggest the murderous potential carried in *Othello*. In the heroic stories that Wordsworth abandons in *Home at Grasmere,* in the tragic facts to which he does not advert in *The Two-Part Prelude,* there lurks the image of the storyteller he does not wish to become and the question of what sorts of story he will tell instead. For if Othello is the outsider who can convert his stories of death into tales of love, he also becomes the murderer who kills the wife his tales have won. These echoes reverberate through *The Two-Part Prelude,* uncannily suggesting a story lying just beyond the one being told.

III

"Ere I had seen / Eight summers," Wordsworth begins:

> —And 'twas in the very week
> When I was first transplanted to thy vale,
> Beloved Hawkshead; when thy paths, thy shores
> And brooks, were like a dream of novelty
> To my half-infant mind—I chanced to cross
> One of those open fields which, shaped like ears,
> Make green peninsulas on Esthwaite's lake.
>   (1799, I, 258–65)

Unsaid here is the cause of Wordsworth's relocation in Hawkshead, the death of his mother in March 1778. Although "transplanted" carries a sense of "uprooted," the metaphor softens the disruption, and the harmony of self and natural world is extended by the intimate address to the paths and shores. This first sentence teases, however, for the certainty with which Wordsworth locates the incident "in the very week" of his arrival in Hawksnead seems unexplained by the casual description of his having "chanced to cross" a field.[9]

The suggestiveness of the narrative increases in the next section:

> Twilight was coming on, yet through the gloom
> I saw distinctly on the opposite shore,
> Beneath a tree and close by the lake side,
> A heap of garments, as if left by one
> Who there was bathing. Half an hour I watched
> And no one owned them; meanwhile the calm lake
> Grew dark with all the shadows on its breast,
> And now and then a leaping fish disturbed
> The breathless stillness.
>
> (266–74)

Striking in this crepuscular scene is the conjunction of gloom and distance with clarity. Wordsworth insists that he saw "distinctly on the opposite shore" the heap of garments that he places so precisely "Beneath a tree and close by the lake side." Here, as in the first section, the narrative doubles and repeats itself, for just as the young boy gazes to fix the garments across a darkening space, so the adult poet looks back across twenty years of memory. *"As if left by one / Who there was bathing"* (emphasis added) holds off definite causal explanation, shifting the emphasis to the prolonged and breathless act of attention. Our own sense of narrative logic asks for a justification of this suspense, a reason why the scene has been remembered and narrated, but the text continues to withhold one.

At last it comes:

> The succeeding day
> There came a company, and in their boat
> Sounded with iron hooks and with long poles.
> At length the dead man, 'mid that beauteous scene
> Of trees and hills and water, bolt upright
> Rose with his ghastly face.
>
> (274–79)

Even here the narrative obscures the action it presents. The passage of time to the succeeding day is recorded, but the announcement is made in a matter-of-fact manner quite different from the intense half-hour watching of the day before and elides the time between. "There came a company" also refuses explanation, especially of any possible connection between the boy's watching and their coming.[10] This narrative reticence contrasts to the activity of the men sounding "with iron hooks and long poles"; the text at once probes the past and remains aloof from it. The most startling suppression is in Wordsworth's bland announcement of "the dead man," as if his death were a fact known all along and not a surprising revelation. And indeed it has been known all along, probably inferred by the child, certainly known by the remembering narrator. So that, the reader can now say, is why the scene was remembered. Wordsworth's language perfectly catches the way in which traumatic incidents are known in the mind but kept from full articulation. Moreover, even before the "ghastly fact" manifests itself, Wordsworth prevents it from functioning as a radical break by presenting it as a repetition: the rising of the corpse amidst the beauteous scene merely repeats more darkly the leaping fish disturbing the stillness.

This erosion of primacy precludes reading the episode as a simple displacement of the death of Wordsworth's mother. Death, it seems, was already there, although not recognized. The corpse rises from the water as the incident as a whole rises in memory, and together they show the narrator a death that for the moment is the center of his landscape. The clarity of this rising to the surface intrigues; compare, for example, the far more elusive account given by the obsessively staring narrator of a slightly earlier poem, *The Thorn* (1798):

> Some say, if to the pond you go,
> And fix on it a steady view,
> The shadow of a babe you trace,
> A baby and a baby's face,
> And that it looks at you;
> Whene'er you look on it, 'tis plain
> The baby looks at you again.
>   (214–20)

The components of this scene are similar: the intense look, the body of water, the face of the dead. But what the scene gives back is a reflection of the onlooker's overheated imagination, and the whole is relegated by the introductory phrase "Some say" to a realm of superstition.[11] No such distance between poet and narrator, which Wordsworth sought to increase in his note to the poem, is possible in *The Two-Part Prelude*. What rises to the surface in the narrative is indubitably there, just as it is indubitably rising within memory here.

Still more interestingly, what the boy sees is not the face of a child like himself but that of a man. This figure, rising phallically "bolt upright" (278), invites psychoanalytic readings, oedipal and pre-oedipal: a vengeful paternal image disrupting the son's intimacy with his mother, a figure of separation, divorcing the boy from his maternal surroundings. But such interpretations do not exhaust the episode, which confronts the boy with his own mortality, forcing him into the heightened self-consciousness of that protracted stare at the abandoned garments for a significance that is not disclosed, and then disclosed too clearly. In thus recounting the boy's passage from a chance crossing to an event of particular meaning the episode does seem to mark a transition from the thoughtless "half-infant mind" (263) of the child to the reflective consciousness of the adult; in that sense, the face the boy confronts is his own.

Already in the beginning of *The Two-Part Prelude* it is the boy himself who has been "a fell destroyer," provoking by his bird hunting "Low breathings coming after [him]" (I, 33–49), whose stealing of a shepherd's boat unleashes a huge cliff which, like the corpse, "Upreared its head" (I, 110) to chastise him. No wonder, if the death that looms up before him images his own obscure guilt, that the narrator should turn away from the incident with such studied nonchalance:

> I might advert
> To numerous accidents in flood or field,
> Quarry or moor, or 'mid the winter snows,
> Distresses and disasters, tragic facts
> Of rural history, that impressed my mind
> With images to which in following years
> Far other feelings were attached—with forms
> That yet exist with independent life,
> And, like their archetypes, know no decay.
>
> (I, 279–87)

The echo of *Othello* now shows its filiations to the incident, connecting itself both to the young Wordsworth as the disrupter of a womanly peace, appropriately punished for his transgressions, the Wordsworth who, in the words of *Home at Grasmere*, must be "tamed" and made

"calm" as the lake is calm, and the Wordsworth who now tells this
story, the destructiveness of his younger self transformed. The close
of the passage sets against the death in the episode the undecaying,
preserving "life" of memory, while the introduction to the incident
insists that its effect was to teach "the growth of mental power / And
love of Nature's works" (I, 257–58). The power to work such transformation is the power of narrative, the freedom "in following years"
to attach "Far other feelings" to the original scenes, so that what
"know[s] no decay" is rewritten from the monitory to the consoling,
as this calm conclusion itself suggests (I, 284–87).

The statements of unconstrained choice, to advert or not as the
poet chooses, are somewhat belied, however, by the actual narrative
sequence of *The Two-Part Prelude*. The incident of the Drowned
Man is followed by the brief characterization of the "spots of time"
(I, 288–96) and then by the Penrith Beacon episode (I, 296–327).
Many critics have remarked upon the similarities of the two narra-
tions. In the second, the adventuring Wordsworth is by "some mis-
chance / Disjoined" from his guide and, frightened and alone, stumbles upon another image of death, a gibbet. Wordsworth here conflates
two murder stories and superimposes upon the recent murder of a
butcher an earlier crime in which "A man, the murderer of his wife,"
was hanged. The fitness of the detail is enhanced by its consonance
with the story of Othello glimpsed in the preceding episode. It is as if
the outlines of a plot at first only shadowily glimpsed had been delayed, split off, and had now begun to emerge.[12] The lake of the first
incident is replicated in the "naked pool" of the second, and just as
the Drowned Man with "his ghastly face" erupts in the first, so the
second incident releases a spectral figure: "A girl who bore a pitcher
on her head / And seemed with difficult steps to force her way /
Against the blowing wind" (I, 317–19). The repetitions from episode
to episode are reinforced by the numerous repetitions within this episode, which a second time describe "The woman and her garments
vexed and tossed / By the strong wind" (I, 326–27). The wind is a
familiar trope for Wordsworth's imagination; the woman's struggle
against it suggests how the figure is seen but remains inaccessible, perhaps is kept inaccessible.

Richard Onorato's conjecture that the Penrith Beacon episode is
a screen memory for Wordsworth's later separation from his mother
is strengthened by the subsequent spot of time, which is explicitly
about the death of his father.[13] Again, details recur: the horses of the

Beacon episode reappear as the horses for which Wordsworth waits to take him home from school; the intense looking across the water in the Drowned Man episode, echoed in the pool and the search for James, is paralleled by a Wordsworth who "watched / With eyes intensely straining, as the mist / Gave intermitting prospects of the wood / And plain beneath" (I, 346–49). The Drowned Man and the phantom murdered wife and "visionary" (I, 322) woman are succeeded by the death of Wordsworth's father, a seeming actualization of those "indisputable shapes" the boy saw advancing in the mist. "The event," Wordsworth writes,

> With all the sorrow which it brought, appeared
> A chastisement; and when I called to mind
> That day so lately passed, when from the crag
> I looked in such anxiety of hope,
> With trite reflections of morality,
> Yet with the deepest passion, I bowed low
> To God, who thus corrected my desires.
>
> (I, 353–60)

This final chastisement completes a movement begun in the hinted allusion to Othello, because it is Wordsworth's own "desires" that must be corrected, the assertiveness that carries with it associations of murdered wives and dead fathers that must be renounced.

In 1804–1805, when Wordsworth revised and expanded his poem, this sequence was broken. The Penrith Beacon episode and the Waiting for the Horses were placed in the new Book XI, and the Drowned Man in Book V. Othello disappears from the new conclusion to the episode. After describing the rising of the corpse Wordsworth now writes:

> And yet no vulgar fear,
> Young as I was, a child not nine years old,
> Possessed me, for my inner eye had seen
> Such sights before among the shining streams
> Of fairyland, the forests of romance—
> Thence came a spirit hallowing what I saw
> With decoration and ideal grace,
> A dignity, a smoothness, like the words
> Of Grecian art and purest poesy.
>
> (1805, V, 473–81)

It seems at first an immense leap from the images of nature that conclude the 1799 account to this invocation of Grecian art and purest
poesy. Yet insofar as the 1799 acount echoes *Othello,* its texture, too,
discloses a narrative already mediated by previous literature, and the
differences between the two texts are proportionately less radical. The
placing of the incident in a book now explicitly titled *Books* is a further indication of the developing theme of the relations between death
and the stories told about it.[14]

   Consider the effects Wordsworth produced by relocating the
Drowned Man after the simile he employs in Book IV to characterize his progress on *The Prelude:*

> As one who hangs down-bending from the side
> Of a slow-moving boat upon the breast
> Of a still water, solacing himself
> With such discoveries as his eye can make
> Beneath him in the bottom of the deeps,
> Sees many beauteous sights—weeds, fishes, flowers,
> Grots, pebbles, roots of trees—and fancies more,
> Yet often is perplexed, and cannot part
> The shadow from the substance, rocks and sky,
> Mountains and clouds, from that which is indeed
> The region, and the things which there abide
> In their true dwelling; now is crossed by gleam
> Of his own image, by a sunbeam now,
> And motions that are sent he knows not whence,
> Impediments that make his task more sweet;
> Such pleasant office have we long pursued
> Incumbent o'er the surface of past time—
> With like success.

                                                                    (247–64)

Several echoes, verbal and structural, tie this passage to the Drowned
Man. In both there is the prolonged gaze across or through the "breast"
of the calm water, in both the presence of "beauteous" sights, and in
both the viewer finds his gaze returns him a "gleam / Of his own image." This specular double is shocking in the Drowned Man episode,
but here in Book IV he is associated only with a "pleasant office," a
"sweet" task. It is not difficult to see the differences. The boy is con-
fronted by the abrupt rising of a literal death, and his curiosity trans-
fixes, even fixates, him. Nothing rises from the depths to challenge the
poet, who gazes only on past time: the "impediments" that prevent

the sharp distinction of past and present protect him from the eruptions of sudden power that face the boy. The simile, and because it is a simile, is subject to the remembering writer's control; otherness, and the self as other, is rendered mild, and the poet freed to move easily along. The imagination here is "solace," and the simile casts its shadow forward: to come upon the Drowned Man after reading this passage is to have the terrifying elements of that scene proleptically rewritten, past deaths reduced to brief perplexities, already enlisted in the poet's recuperative project.[15]

The reader of the 1805 *Prelude* approaches the Drowned Man through the Dedication Scene and the Discharged Soldier as well. The inherent risk of the affirmations of the Dedication Scene— "bond unknown to me / Was given, that I should be—*else sinning greatly*— / A dedicated spirit" (1805 *Prelude*, IV, 342–44; emphasis added)—seems to present itself when Wordsworth juxtaposes to this morning exaltation the evening encounter with the Discharged Soldier (1805, IV, 400–504). Though Wordsworth is walking along the public way, the imagery of "the road's wat'ry surface" (371) links the scene to the twilight Esthwaite Water of the Drowned Man. If at first what "rose as from some distant region of [Wordsworth's] soul" were "beauteous pictures" (392–94), the reverie is soon interrupted by "an uncouth shape" (402). Wordsworth is driven to prolonged and unreciprocated watch of this figure just as his boyhood self was impelled to gaze at the uncommunicative heap of garments, and the man "stiff in his form, and upright, lank and lean" (407), his mouth showing "ghastly in the moonlight" (411), anticipates how the dead man " 'mid that beauteous scene / Of trees and hills and water, bolt upright / Rose with his ghastly face" (1805, V, 470–72). We should dwell for a moment on the way in which Wordsworth's narrative sequence makes the incident from his adolescence precede one from his childhood. For the reader, the effect, again, is to give the Drowned Man in his new location a quality of déjà vu, and such an effect mitigates the abrupt intrusion of death on the child in the incident itself.

It is important also to note that though Othello vanishes from the Drowned Man in the 1805 text many of the functions he filled are accomplished by the Discharged Soldier. The former presence of Othello suggests a kinship between the poet and the military man otherwise less visible. Like Othello, the man tells "in simple words a soldier's tale" (445) of "what he had endured / From hardship, battle, or the pestilence" (470–71). Unlike Othello, however, whose

storytelling is as potent as his exploits, the Discharged Soldier has
been subdued by his experience:

> Solemn and sublime
> He might have seemed, but that in all he said
> There was a strange half-absence, and a tone
> Of weakness and indifference, as of one
> Remembering the importance of his theme
> But feeling it no longer.
>
> (473–78)

Looked at in conjunction with the echo of Othello in the 1799 *Prelude,* and the allusions that lie beyond it in *Personal Talk* and *Home at Grasmere,* the Discharged Soldier appears as a stripped version of the hero, a dismaying fantasy of the actual consequences of aggression. In his capacity as a storyteller who has forgotten the importance of his story he is equally an unwelcome double to the poet who beholds "With ill-suppressed astonishment his tall / And ghastly figure moving at my side" (467–68). If the ghostly presence figures a potential future for Wordsworth himself, then his mode of resolving the encounter is significant: to "measure back" the way they have come is to renounce that future. Wordsworth leads the soldier to a laborer's cottage, ending his isolation, restoring him to social bonds. The suffering in the soldier's narrative and the sublimity of his solitariness are both domesticated in Wordsworth's humanitarian vignette. The story ends not with the soldier, who had been "travelling to his native home" (449), but with the poet, who after accomplishing his good deed "sought with quiet heart my distant home" (504). The peaceful resonances of that concluding line mark the distance Wordsworth sought to put between himself and his own attraction to adventure. The Discharged Soldier is both a warning figure and an image of the power of renunciation and endurance that Wordsworth would claim for himself. Whether such a figure can be domesticated is a recurrent question of his poetry.

    The question rises to the philosophical level at the opening of Book V with the meditation on man surviving "Abject, depressed, forlorn, disconsolate" (1805, V, 27), deprived of his perishable books. The connection between story and death only hinted in the echo of *Othello* in 1799 becomes the explicit subject of this book on "books," introduced by the meditation and expanded in the Arab Dream. Don Quixote extends the romance implications carried by Othello, even as the Arab knight of the dream is an apocalyptic cousin of the solitary Discharged Soldier. In the strange fusions and decompositions of the dream the lakes that are the setting of the other scenes become the Deluge, "the waters of the deep" (130). Wordsworth's sympathy with the "semi-Quixote," his declaration that "Enow there are on earth to take in charge / Their wives, their children, and their virgin loves" (153–54), disrupts the harmony established at the close of Book IV. The admission that he "Could share that maniac's anxiousness, could go / Upon like errand" (160–61), places the commitment to literature of both knight and poet against domestic affections.

It is, therefore, with the logic of defense that Wordsworth turns immediately to locate literature "in the lisping time of infancy / And, later down, in prattling childhood" (169–70). The "benediction" on literature as a power "For ever to be hallowed" (219–20), the "Food for the hungry ears of little ones, / And of old men who have survived their joy" (212–13), attempts to substitute for the image hitherto evident of the storyteller as a bearer of death a benign portrait of his social usefulness. But it is almost inevitable, given the relation of story and death, that this discourse should lead Wordsworth to the only direct mention of the death of his mother in *The Prelude* (256–60). Hence, although the new sequence of the poem separates the Drowned Man from the Penrith Beacon episode and the Waiting for the Horses, it brings it adjacent to the death of the mother to which it is chronologically and thematically linked. One should note, too, that Wordsworth's praise for fairy tales and imaginative literature of all kinds on the grounds that they take the child out of himself—"The child whose love is here, at least doth reap / One precious gain—that he forgets himself" (368–69)—brings with it this poignant statement of personal loss, a hint of "blame" that must be "checked" (260–64), and the uncharacteristically vehement denunciation of contemporary education that occupies almost a hundred lines of the book (290–388).

Even as it argues for the consoling power of literature, then, Wordsworth's narrative repeatedly turns to death and loss, and against this return generates the stories and interpretations by which it grows. The diatribe against education is succeeded by the Boy of Winander, taken over from MS. JJ and transposed into the third person, and then by the Drowned Man. This juxtaposition clearly demonstrates Wordsworth's endeavor to convert his stories of death into means of connection. Like Wordsworth in the Drowned Man episode, the fictional boy into whom he has transformed himself stands by a "glimmering lake" (394). This boy's experience, however, is tranquil: he listens to the owl's shouts across "the wat'ry vale" (I, 400),

> or the visible scene
> Would enter unawares into his mind
> With all its solemn imagery, its rocks,
> Its woods, and that uncertain heaven, received
> Into the bosom of the steady lake.
>
> (409–13)

If no vision of death interrupts this scene, as it does for the boy in the Drowned Man immediately following, death nonetheless supervenes in a still more direct fashion: "This boy was taken from his mates, and died / In childhood ere he was full ten years old" (414–15). This boy is thus linked with the "child not nine years old" of the next episode, and behind him to the poet who lost his mother before he was eight. One's impulse to align these events is reinforced by the subsequent comment of the narrator:

> Fair are the woods, and beauteous is the spot,
> The vale where he was born; the churchyard hangs
> Upon a slope above the village school,
> And there, along that bank, when I have passed
> At evening, I believe that oftentimes
> A full half-hour together I have stood
> Mute, looking at the grave in which he lies.
>
> (416–22)

This "full half-hour" of watching duplicates the "Half an hour I watched" (I, 270) of the boy in the 1799 version of the Drowned Man: perhaps that is why in 1805 the phrase is changed to the indefinite "Long I watched." The narrator's fixed muteness is the counterpart to the silence in which the boy received his vision, but it is a moment of emptiness, the opposite of the plenitude that "unawares" fills the boy. The churchyard that "hangs / Upon a slope" is a funereal successor to the boy who "hung / Listening" (406–7). This temporal sequence carries the narrative from the timelessness of the boy to the stasis of the adult, confronting death as the boy in the next episode will do. Only a continuing narrative can dissolve this rigidity and set death within the context of life again: Wordsworth's own power to develop depends on his finding another "ending" to this story of lost bliss.

The lines that follow have attracted less critical attention than the visionary portions of Book V, but they are crucial to an understanding of the aims of the poem as a whole. Wordsworth continues:

> Even now methinks I have before my sight
> That self-same village church: I see her sit—
> The thronèd lady spoken or erewhile—
> On her green hill, forgetful of this boy
> Who slumbers at her feet, forgetful too
> Of all her silent neighbourhood of graves,
> And listening only to the gladsome sounds
> That, from the rural school ascending, play
> Beneath her and about her.
>
> (1805, V, 423–31)

In Book IV Wordsworth recalled seeing on his return from Cambridge to Hawkshead "the snow-white church upon its hill / Sit like a thronèd lady, sending out / A gracious look over all its domain" (13–15). The church is the symbol of the maternal presence of the vale, and Wordsworth's ascription to her of forgetfulness discloses a reproach for having been abandoned, like the memory recorded not two hundred lines above of how by his mother's death her children were left "destitute, and as we might / Trooping together" (259–60). "Forgetful," however, is not a mark of reproach only. The "thronèd lady['s]" forgetfulness contrasts strongly with the narrator's repeated gaze at the boy's grave and makes tranquillity possible. Moreover, the church has not abandoned the boy: she remains the center of her "silent neighbourhood of graves," the mother whose unobtrusive presence fosters the play of the living children who surround her.

These signs of continuity in the scene are paralleled in the narrator's own relation to it. "Even now methinks I have before my sight / That self-same village church" asserts, through the imagination's "methinks," the poet's power to recapture a lost past. The Boy of Winander episode itself, taken out of context or in the form of the *Lyrical Ballads,* is elegiac, but by placing it within this framework in Book V Wordsworth makes it restitutive.[16] As he proceeds, the reparative nature of his art becomes still clearer:

> May she long
> Behold a race of young ones like to those

With whom I herded—easily, indeed,
We might have fed upon a fatter soil
Of Arts and Letters, but be that forgiven—
A race of real children, not too wise,
Too learned, or too good, but wanton, fresh,
And bandied up and down by love and hate;
Fierce, moody, patient, venturous, modest, shy,
Mad at their sports like withered leaves in winds;
Though doing wrong and suffering, and full oft
Bending beneath our life's mysterious weight
Of pain and fear, yet still in happiness
Not yielding to the happiest upon earth.

                                              (431–44)

These lines work through the questions of loss that occupy Book V.
The resentment implicitly directed against the mother for the abandonment of her death yields to the restorative wish for her continu-
ance: "May she long behold. . . ." Criticisms are not denied but
voiced with a moderation that allows them to be "forgiven." This
generosity not only perpetuates the lost mother but also revivifies
Wordsworth's account of his childhood: the dead boy at whose grave
he could only stare is succeeded by this energetic portrait of the "race
of real children." The apocalyptic register in which Book V opens is
not more fundamental to a complete understanding of Wordsworth
than is this effort to contain the sublime attractions of "pain and fear"
within a narrative of "happiness," less immediately captivating but
more sustaining of his daily life. The 1805 *Prelude* develops at length
the project only begun in 1799.

     A pursuit of echoes half-heard in this section, as with *Othello* in
the 1799 version of the Drowned Man, may bring Wordsworth's aims
into sharper focus. The lines on the "race of real children" quoted
above suggest an oblique re-vision of Gray's *Ode on a Distant Prospect of Eton College,* of which Wordsworth owned a copy "in Gray's
own handwriting."[17] To hear Gray behind Wordsworth is to recognize the genealogy of *The Prelude,* to acknowledge its double origin,
in literary history as well as in the *facta* of Wordsworth's life. Even
more than the echo of *Othello,* this instance characterizes the speaker
of *The Prelude* as a voice amid the words of his precursors rather
than a unique and independent presence, a strand within a polyphony
that includes among others Shakespeare, Milton, and Gray.

     "Ye distant spires, ye antique towers, / That crown the watry glade," Gray's poem begins, with a landscape similar to Words-worth's, but "distant" is its key term, for the gap between the poet's present and the "fields belov'd in vain / Where once my careless childhood stray'd" remains unclosed.[18] Though Gray can summon the image of "Full many a sprightly race" of sporting children, like Wordsworth's "race of young ones," the memory of the past bestows only "a momentary bliss," and it does no more because Gray con-ceives of it as having merely the power to "sooth[e]" his "weary soul" rather than as the source of an enduring value. For Gray, moreover, the happiness of a child depends on his inevitably temporary status as "A stranger yet to pain." Wordsworth's children, "mad at their sports like withered leaves in winds," are passionately absorbed in their ac-tivities; Gray's are haunted by the disillusionment the speaker sees awaiting them: "Still as they run they look behind, / They hear a voice in every wind, / And snatch a fearful joy." Melancholically looking behind him from the vantage of the suffering that the poem insists is the condition of man, Gray sees in childhood only a fragile peace that he would extend if he could. The concluding lines are al-most too celebrated to quote again:

> Yet ah! why should they know their fate?
> Since sorrow never comes too late,
> And happiness too swiftly flies.
> Thought would destroy their paradise.
> No more; where ignorance is bliss,
> 'Tis folly to be wise.

Wordsworth's lines almost systematically reverse Gray's. Words-worth buries the Boy of Winander and his harmony with maternal nature, as if to test the strength of his childhood experience, and then revivifies the bonds through the reparative fantasy of the lady-church. For Gray thought can only "destroy" paradise, whereas for Words-worth thought ties together past and present and creates the inter-change that enables the past to survive, reconceived, as a beneficent force in the present. Wordsworth, who also looks behind as he moves forward, can imagine a process in which childhood develops into ac-tive wisdom:

> Simplicity in habit, truth in speech,
> Be these the daily strengtheners of their minds!
> May books and Nature be their early joy,

> And knowledge, rightly honored with that name—
> Knowledge not purchased with the loss of power!
>   (II, 445–49)

Gray was for Wordsworth an exemplum of the poet whose knowledge lacked power:[19] the continuum he plots between books and nature, and youth and maturity, is intended to prevent that fate.

The reader of the Drowned Man in the 1805 version of *The Prelude* thus encounters the passage as part of a family of texts sharing imagery and configuration which together mediate its violence. The sequence from the simile in Book IV (247–64) through the Moment of Dedication and the Discharged Soldier (361–504) to the dream of the Arab Knight/Don Quixote and the Deluge (V. 49–139) places the power of story against impending death. This development is of a piece with verbal changes in the Drowned Man episode:

> Well do I call to mind the very week
> When I was first entrusted to the care
> Of that sweet valley—when its paths, its shores
> And brooks, were like a dream of novelty
> To my half-infant thoughts. . . .
>   (V, 450–54)

The shift from the "thy" of 1799 to the "its" of 1805 marks the distance the poet puts between himself and nature. The poet's emphasis falls in 1805 on the shaping of his own narrative rather than on the child's spontaneous mythmaking. The "transplanted" child is now said to be "entrusted to the care": human purposiveness replaces natural harmony. Most important, although the boy still comes upon the incident when he "chanced to cross" the field, his "roving up and down alone" is similarly characterized: "seeking I knew not what" (456). If what the boy seeks is undefined, something absent or lost, still such seeking has a goal, and the goal is not the boy's alone but also the narrative's. The incident that follows loses its quality of randomness. The line gives the episode a narrative shape, presenting the discovery as a response to a desire, a fulfillment of an aroused expectation.

Wordsworth's revisions aim at lessening the shock of the scene. The smooth incorporation of the incident into the larger design of the narrative makes possible a brief heightening: whereas in 1799 the leaping fish merely "disturbed / The breathless stillness" (273–74) now it "snapped" it (V, 465). The vivid break in continuity, how-ever, attaches to the fish and not to the corpse. The most telling addi-tion follows: "The succeeding day— / *Those unclaimed garments telling a plain tale*— / Went there a company" (V, 466–68; em-phasis added). What had been enigmatic and abrupt to the boy is en-folded in the poet's acts of interpretation. The "plain tale" is his end in *The Prelude:* adventure and tragedy are demystified. The "ghastly face" of the dead man itself becomes "a spectre shape— / Of terror even" (V, 427–73). If "spectre" and "terror" appear at first to inten-sify the experience, the "spectre shape" derealizes the actual face of the corpse, and the measured evaluation "of terror even," comfort-ably fitting the apparition into its proper Gothic niche, makes the en-tire scene into familiar literature.

The lines that follow may thus be seen as building upon founda-tions laid in the earlier books of *The Prelude:*

> And yet no vulgar fear,
> Young as I was, a child not nine years old,
> Possessed me, for my inner eye had seen
> Such sights before among the shining streams
> Of fairyland, the forests of romance,—
> Thence came a spirit hallowing what I saw
> With decoration and ideal grace,
> A dignity, a smoothness, like the words
> Of Grecian art and purest Poesy.
>
> (V, 473–81)

This conclusion seeks closure by inserting into the episode a "before," thus denying that it instituted a radical break. The Drowned Man is not the first eruption of death in the 1805 *Prelude:* the reader, what-ever may have been the truth for the boy Wordsworth, has seen such sights before in the poem, and seen them integrated into the poet's development. The "inner eye" that the poet describes as already pres-ent in the boy is the power of harmonizing interpretation whose growth the poem traces, and the backward projection is the corollary of the premise that "each most obvious and particular thought" "Hath no beginning" (1805, II, 233–36).

The evidence that Wordsworth had encountered death in his childhood reading in fairy tale and romance is his subsequent ac-count of how he possessed "at that time . . . A slender abstract of the Arabian Tales" (482–84). That the assertion that the nine-year-old boy was unfrightened should be made plausible by what follows discloses the conditions governing the actual writing of *The Prelude: all* its explanations are inevitably after the fact. This citing of the *Arabian Nights* functions as well to meet the doubts raised by the chronologically later Arab Dream that has opened Book V. The language of this passage is unobtrusively but consistently solemn. Wordsworth recounts how the discovery that his book was only a part of the collection seemed "a promise scarcely earthly" (491), how he made "a league, a covenant, with a friend" (492), and "religiously" (497) preserved his vow to save money to purchase the complete set. The boys' failure to attain their object repeats in this undramatic narrative fashion the laments for the unreliability of books that begin the book, but the disquiet is remedied:

> And afterwards, when, to my father's house
> Returning at the holidays, I found
> That golden store of books which I had left
> Open to my enjoyment once again,
> What heart was mine!
>
> (1805, V, 501–5)

A reader who compares the immediate context of the Drowned Man in 1799 with that of 1805 cannot help being struck by the symmetry of Wordsworth's reversal. In 1799 the Drowned Man leads into the spots of time, including Wordsworth's waiting for the horses to take him home from school "The day before the holidays began" (331), and then into the anxiety-provoking death of the father "ere [he] had been ten days / A dweller in [his] father's house" (350–51). Removing this passage to Book XI, Wordsworth substitutes the narrative in which the father appears as the dispenser of a "golden store of books" to the enjoying child rather than as a figure of chastisement. This scene restores a benevolent image of the father and, by thus associating stories with him, validates the poet's own enterprise. Story now exists within the happy family, rather than as a sign of estrangement and rebellion.

From this vignette Wordsworth modulates into an affirmation of the power and goodness of literature, the second attribute necessary to tame the disruptive potential of the first: to be absorbed in reading is to risk "defrauding the day's glory" (512), to become separated from nature. Nonetheless, "the tales that charm away the wakeful night / In Araby" (520–21) are the means by which man may "charm away" the "woes" of humanity, as Wordsworth announced he did at the outset of Book V. In the list of works that follows, desire is transformed into comfort:

> romances, legends penned
> For solace by the light of monkish lamps;
> Fictions, for ladies of their love, devised
> By youthful squires; adventures endless, spun
> By the dismantled warrior in old age
> Out of the bowels of those very thoughts
> In which his youth did first extravagate—
> These spread like day, and something in the shape
> Of these will live till man shall be no more.
>   (521–29)

In the tales told by the squire to his love, one sees a parallel to Othello reciting his adventures to Desdemona, in the dismantled warrior a discharged soldier redeemed by the stories he tells, and in the final affirmation a resolution to the apocalyptic doubts with which Book V begins.

As it moves from the Arab Dream to the *Arabian Nights* Book V shows Wordsworth's development from the questing knight, the figure of disruption, to the poet of consolation. The new conclusion to the Drowned Man episode is a nodal point of themes visible throughout the expanded early books.[20] Not the man of action, not Othello, but Scheherezade telling tales to ward off masculine power and death becomes Wordsworth's image of the storyteller—a Desdemona with a voice. Some later changes in the passage, in 1816–1819, offer a further perspective:

> ' The succeeding day,
> Those unclaimed garments telling a plain tale
> *Drew to the spot an anxious crowd; some looked*
> *In passive expectation from the shore,*
> *While from a boat others hung o'er the deep,*
> Sounding with grappling irons and long poles.
>   (1850, V, 442–47; emphasis added)

The Norton editors comment that the additions "place the solitary experience recorded in 1799 and 1805 in an untypically social context," but such a social context is consonant with Wordsworth's endeavor to make his childhood experiences the base of his role as a public poet. The additions, moreover, introduce the concept of audience. Wordsworth distinguishes between those who look with "passive expectation" and those who actively search and grapple, a distinction like that he employed to insist upon imaginative effort from readers of his poetry. The added detail of the men who "from a boat . . . hung o'er the deep" connects this latter group with the poet's simile for his own work in Book IV—"As one who hangs down-bending from the side / Of a slow-moving boat, upon the breast / Of a still water . . ." (1850, IV, 256–58)—which paradoxically undercuts the emphasis on such imaginative struggle. Wordsworth's assertions that he was not scared at nine because of the books he had read then is the idealized double of an affirmation that he was no longer scared because of what he had written since: his revisions concealed as much as they revealed, and his imagination guarded as much as probed its depths.

This solution is not without its troubling complement, for Wordsworth rewrote, or wrote against, his previous writing rather than wholly erasing it. If the simile anticipatorily controls the episode of the Drowned Man, so too the episode of the Drowned Man, which the reader encounters later, remains to disturb the calm of the simile: the pairing resists stabilization. The lines invoking ideal grace and purest poetry at the revised conclusion of the Drowned Man episode indicate by their very excess[21] Wordsworth's desire to reach repose, in the word of the contemporary *Ode to Duty,* to write a poetry freed from the cycle of return to the disconcerting stories of loss and death that had proved his most fertile materials. Pure poetry does not draw into itself the unsettled life of the writer; such poetry, the product of a man "whose principles were made up, and so prepared to deliver upon authority a system of philosophy,"[22] was the final and self-consuming end of the poem. Wordsworth's expansions, however, defer rather than resolve this problem: *The Prelude* embodies the conflicts it strives to still. In the poem the rebelliousness of the child "not yet tamed / And humbled down" survives, as does the author's praise for that child's "friends": the "Forgers of lawless tales . . . Who make our wish our power, our thought a deed, / An empire, a possession" (V, 545–53). "Forgers" trembles at the brink of an ineluctable pun, for as Wordsworth reshaped his past into ideal forms he recast it in ways accordant not with irrecoverable experience but with his own current situation. The process by which Wordsworth made his earlier writing the matrix of his continued poetic activity was less the natural one his language describes[23] than it was a series of discrete authorial choices, widely separated in time, often discontinuous in intent. The internal dialogue of *The Prelude* exists within the final text as well as between texts: an edition such as the Norton Critical, which preserves all three texts in a single format, amplifies and clarifies, rather than creates, the conversation between the layers and versions of the poem(s).

In this textual history Othello occupies only a minuscule space, but he stands at a point critical to Wordsworth's formulation of his role as a poet.[24] The excision of Othello and the "distresses and disasters, tragic facts of rural history" from the episode of the Drowned Man is one sign of Wordsworth's determination to make over those stories of suffering and loss upon which his imagination turned. In Othello the 1799 text gives us a figure in whom death and the power of story are inextricably joined. The 1805 and 1850 texts give us a Wordsworth "hallowing what [he] saw," laboring to transform the waters of death and deluge into "the shining streams / Of fairyland" (1805, V, 476–78).[25] Discarding the echo discloses as much as did its original presence; taken together, the texts show Wordsworth's changing relationship to his own narrative and to the self constructed by it, and reveal both the disruption latent within his poetry and the solace with which he opposed it. The vicissitudes of Othello in his texts are a microcosm of the oscillations of Wordsworth's imagination.[26]

Notes

1. All quotations from *The Prelude* are taken from *The Prelude, 1799, 1805, 1850,* ed. Jonathan Wordsworth, M. H. Abrams, and Stephen Gill (New York: Norton, 1979).

2. Texts of other poems taken from William Wordsworth, *The Poems,* ed. John O. Hayden (Harmondsworth: Penguin, 1977).

3. This ambivalence is a topic prominent in recent criticism. See, for example, Andrew L. Griffin, "Wordsworth and the Problem of Imaginative Story: The Case of 'Simon Lee,'" *Publications of the Modern Language Association* 92 (1977): 392–409; and James H. Averill, *Wordsworth and the Poetry of Human Suffering* (Ithaca: Cornell University Press, 1980).

4. The text is that of MS. D, *Home at Grasmere,* ed. Beth Darlington (Ithaca: Cornell University Press, 1977).

5. *Othello,* ed. Kenneth Muir (Harmondsworth: Penguin, 1968).

6. See, for example, Arthur Kirsch, "The Polarization of Erotic Love in *Othello,*" *Modern Language Review* 73 (1978): 721–40.

7. M. L. Peacock, Jr., *The Critical Opinions of William Wordsworth* (Baltimore: Johns Hopkins University Press, 1950), p. 94.

8. This brief account of *The Borderers* draws on the interpretations advanced by Ernest de Selincourt, "Wordsworth's Preface to *The Borderers*," *Oxford Lectures on Poetry* (Oxford: Clarendon, 1934), pp. 157–79; Roger Sharrock, *"The Borderers:* Wordsworth on the Moral Frontier," *Durham University Journal* 56 (1964): 170–83; and R. F. Storch, "Wordsworth's *The Borderers:* The Poet as Anthropologist," *English Literary History* 36 (1969): 340–60. On the political radicalism embodied and rejected by the drama, see David Erdman, "Wordsworth as Heartsworth; or, Was Regicide the Prophetic Ground of those 'Moral Questions'?" in *The Evidence of the Imagination,* ed. Donald H. Reiman, Michael C. Jaye, and Betty T. Bennett (New York: New York University Press, 1978), pp. 12–14.

9. In "The Accidents of Disfiguration: Limits to Literal and Rhetorical Reading in Book V of *The Prelude*," *Studies in Romanticism* 18 (1979): 547–65, Cynthia Chase studies the relation between "accidents" in the episode and the allegorical strategies by which they are given meaning. Though my point of departure places this essay somewhat to their side, I should like to acknowledge my indebtedness also to Evelyn Shakir, "Books, Death, and Immortality: A Study of Book V of *The Prelude*," *SiR* 8 (1969): 156–68; J. Hillis Miller, "The Stone and the Shell: The Problem of Poetic Form in Wordsworth's Dream of the Arab," *Mouvements premiers: Etudes critiques offertes à Georges Poulet* (Paris: Corti, 1972), pp. 125–47; Leslie Brisman, *Romantic Origins* (Ithaca: Cornell University Press, 1978), pp. 276–361; Jonathan Arac, "Bounding Lines: *The Prelude* and Critical Revision," *Boundary* 2, 7, iii (1979): 31–48; J. R. Barth, "The Poet, Death, and Immortality: The Unity of *The Prelude,* Book V," *Wordsworth Circle* 10 (1979): 69–75; Lawrence Kramer, "That Other Will: The Daemonic in Coleridge and Wordsworth," *Philological Quarterly* 58 (1979): 298–320. An essay that I inexplicably missed when writing this piece is "The Artifice of Disjunction: Book 5, *The Prelude,*" *Papers on Language and Literature* 14 (1978): 32–50, by Michael C. Jaye, who challenges the paramount value of unity and urges that we "understand contradictions as contradictions, unresolved conflicts as unresolved, and inconsistency as inconsistency" (p. 34).

10. In a draft of the passage Wordsworth mentions but then deletes having told his "little household" of the incident. See *The Prelude,* ed. Ernest de Selincourt, 2d ed., rev. by Helen Darbishire (Oxford: Clarendon, 1959), p. 162.

11. On the specular relationships of *The Thorn,* see particularly Jerome C. Christensen. "Wordsworth's Misery, Coleridge's Woe: Reading 'The Thorn,' " *Papers on Language and Literature* 16 (1980): 268–86.

12. Theresa M. Kelley illuminatingly analyzes the "suppressions and retrievals" of Wordsworth's various accounts in "The Economics of the Heart: Wordsworth's Sublime and Beautiful," *Romanticism Past and Present* 5 (1981): 15–32.

13. Richard J. Onorato, *The Character of the Poet: Wordsworth in THE PRELUDE* (Princeton: Princeton University Press, 1971), pp. 205–19.

14. The title itself reflects Wordsworth's increasing desire to highlight his theme; it was not present in MS. M (1804).

15. In his astute essay "Fruitful Failure and Incidental Cause: The Will in *The Prelude*," Michael G. Cooke observes that the simile is "a reflective, metaphorical reprise of the rowboat episode" of Book I; the observation points to another layer in the evolving repetitions studied here. *The Romantic Will* (New Haven: Yale University Press, 1976), p. 99.

16. On their original publication in the 1800 *Lyrical Ballads* the lines break off with the death of the boy at "ten years old." The sequence from MS. JJ through to the final form of the passage in *The Prelude* shows Wordsworth absorbing the isolated memory of the past into the present and projecting into the future.

17. *The Letters of William and Dorothy Wordsworth, The Later Years,* ed. Ernest de Selincourt (Oxford: Clarendon, 1939), III, 1271. De Quincey's recollection of the then-unpublished *Prelude* increases the likelihood that Gray is relevant here: he recalls Wordsworth describing "himself as roaming, hand-in-hand, with one companion, along the banks of Esthwaite Water, chanting, with one voice, the verses of Goldsmith and of Gray" (cf. 1805, V, 575–607). Quoted in the Norton edition, p. 546.

18. Text taken from *The Complete Poems of Thomas Gray,* ed. H. W. Starr and J. R. Hendrickson (Oxford: Clarendon, 1966).

19. "Gray failed as a Poet," Wordsworth declared, "not because he took too much pains and so extinguished his animation, but because he had little of that fiery quality to begin with; and his pains were of the wrong sort." *The Letters of William and Dorothy Wordsworth, The Middle Years, Part II, 1812–20,* ed. Ernest de Selincourt, 2d ed., rev. by Mary Moorman and Alan G. Hill (Oxford: Clarendon, 1979), p. 301.

20. These patterns, generating significances unavailable in *1799*, should be weighed against the argument of Jonathan Wordsworth that the earlier text "offers in a simpler and more concentrated form much of what one thinks of as best in the thirteen-book poem," and his regret that in 1805 the Drowned Man is "exiled to the fifth (and most obviously hodge-podge) Book of the extended poem." Quotations from his "The Two-Part *Prelude* of 1799," rpt. in the Norton edition, pp. 567–85.

21. See David Perkins, *The Quest for Permanence* (Cambridge, Mass.: Harvard University Press, 1959): "The very violence of these fears may be what compels Wordsworth to assert that the incident could be blunted, the fears managed" (p. 17).

22. Coleridge's description of his hopes for *The Recluse. Table Talk,* July 31, 1832.

23. For example, his assertion that he who in his childhood "With living Nature hath been intimate" will "Receive enduring touches of deep joy / From the great Nature that exists in works / Of mighty poets" (1805, V, 612–19), or his wish that his own work "might become / A power like one of Nature's" (1805, XII, 311–12).

24. Another echo of *Othello* in *The Prelude*, pointed out to me by Jonathan Arac, further illustrates Wordsworth's return upon himself. In Book VI

Wordsworth conveys his enthusiasm for the French Revolution by recalling "the spirit-stirring sound" of "the fife at war," and his sight of "the Brabant armies on the fret / For battle in the cause of Liberty" (1805, VI, 685–92). The passage shows the displacement of the image of Othello from the agent of familial tragedy to the political hero, the Shakespearean warrior who served the state become the just revolutionary. This commitment to action disappears by the end of *The Prelude*, as Wordsworth chooses to "seek beneath the name [of Poet] / My office upon earth, and nowhere else" (1805, X, 919–20). When the same network of phrases from *Othello* recurs in *Home at Grasmere*, in the lines quoted at the outset of this chapter, it suggests less the egalitarian hopes of 1790 than the rooted Burkean patriotism of Wordsworth's later years. The repetition displays the survival of Wordsworth's political ardor and its modulation into its opposite.

25. The protracted composition of *The Prelude* leads to other contexts for the revised ending. One wonders how much the affirmation depends on the precarious transformation into encouragement of another startling encounter by the water's edge, that of "Resolution and Independence" (1802). See Peter J. Manning, " 'My former thoughts returned': Wordsworth's *Resolution and Independence*," *WC* 9 (1978): 398–405.

26. "Oscillations" is the term aptly employed by J. Hillis Miller to describe the characteristic gestures of Wordsworth's imagination, in "The Still Heart: Poetic Form in Wordsworth," *New Literary History* 2 (1971): 297–310.

6

Don Juan and Byron's Imperceptiveness to the English Word

In a famous essay which mixes praise and contempt in characteristic fashion, T. S. Eliot observed in 1937:

> Of Byron one can say, as of no other English poet of his eminence, that he added nothing to the language, that he discovered nothing in the sounds, and developed nothing in the meaning, of individual words. I cannot think of any poet of his distinction who might so easily have been an accomplished foreigner writing English.[1]

From this stigma of "imperceptiveness . . . to the English word" Byron and Byron criticism have yet wholly to recover.[2] The condemnation is best challenged by examining the assumptions on which it rests.

Eliot's privileging of the word is true to his symbolist heritage. Implicit in the negative verdict on Byron is the recommendation of an evocative poetry, one that gathers itself into a dense concentration of almost magically suggestive power, a poetry marked by moments at which meaning seems to overflow mere connotation, by nodal points at which meanings accumulated through an entire work converge and are released. The sense of an investment of meaning beyond the capacity of words creates a brief illusion of intensity and inclusiveness. A standard that invokes the word thus tends to acquire the hieratic associations of the Word, the authoritative utterance in which not only meaning but also being seem actually to reside. For

Coleridge, the most reflective theorist of this mode among the English Romantics, symbolism was, as J. Robert Barth has reiterated, intimately bound up with a sacramental view of the world.[3] At its extreme, however, Eliot's position values the single pregnant phrase, the resonant, gnomic aphorism. Keats's Grecian Urn, animated by the inquiries of its beholder, itself speaks only teasingly or remains silent. Unheard melodies can be judged sweeter than real ones because with them the gap between signifier and signified is widest, and the power of suggestion verges therefore on the infinite.

Other premises for poetry are possible, and attitudes other than awed contemplation are appropriate ends. One could sketch a poetics based not on the word but on words—that is, not on the charge granted the individual word (whether through special diction, or as the focus of an imagistic or narrative pattern, or by an aura of numinous presence), but on the relationship between words in themselves unremarkable. In contrast to Eliot's bias toward the symbolic, hence the static, one might urge the disjunctive and the dynamic; in place of Eliot's favoring of "full" speech, one might posit a discourse based on absence, one that never offers the consolations of climax or comprehensiveness, never holds forth the promise of an order suddenly made manifest. *Don Juan* exemplifies these procedures, and its richness refutes Eliot's judgment of "this imperceptiveness of Byron's to the English word" by revealing the narrowness of Eliot's criteria. I shall argue that it is precisely in proportion to his refusal to exalt the individual word that Byron is able to display the multiple functions of language itself.

I

The language of *Don Juan* can be approached through the role of language as it is conceptualized *in* the poem. The most satisfying starting point is paradoxically a scene in which language is unnecessary, Byron's depiction of the embrace of Juan and Haidée. "They had not spoken; but they felt allured, / As if their souls and lips each other beckon'd," the narrator observes (II, 187):

> They fear'd no eyes nor ears on that lone beach,
>   They felt no terrors from the night, they were
> All in all to each other: though their speech
>   Was broken words, they *thought* a language there,—
> And all the burning tongues the passions teach

> Found in one sigh the best interpreter
> Of nature's oracle—first love,—that all
> Which Eve has left her daughters since her fall.
>
> (II, 189)[4]

This characterization of Haidée's voice presents a familiar Romantic figure, at once pathetic and sublime. Voice is here an absolute presence, capable of doing without the agency of words and directly inspiring a response from its hearers. The less Haidée and Juan can talk, the more intensely they share:

> And then fair Haidée tried her tongue at speaking,
>   But not a word could Juan comprehend,
> Although he listen'd so that the young Greek in
>   Her earnestness would ne'er have made an end;
>
> (II, 161)

Freedom from language becomes the very mark of intimacy:

> And then she had recourse to nods, and signs,
>   And smiles, and sparkles of the speaking eye,
> And read (the only book she could) the lines
>   Of his fair face, and found, by sympathy,
> The answer eloquent, where the soul shines
>   And darts in one quick glance a long reply;
> And thus in every look she saw exprest
> A world of words, and things at which she guess'd.
>
> And now, by dint of fingers and of eyes,
>   And words repeated after her, he took
> A lesson in her tongue; but by surmise,
>   No doubt, less of her language than her look:
> As he who studies fervently the skies
>   Turns oftener to the stars than to his book,
> Thus Juan learn'd his alpha beta better
> From Haidée's glance than any graven letter.
>
> (II, 162–63)

Just before the return of Lambro brings it to an end Byron presents again the preternatural harmony between Juan and Haidée:

> The gentle pressure, and the thrilling touch,
>   The least glance better understood than words,

Which still said all, and ne'er could say too much;
    A language, too, but like to that of birds,
Known but to them, at least appearing such
    As but to lovers a true sense affords;
Sweet playful phrases, which would seem absurd
To those who have ceased to hear such, or ne'er heard.
                                                                      (IV, 14)

The poem puts forward two analogies to the communion that ordinary language is too clumsy to express. The first is mythical and honorific: "They were alone once more; for them to be / Thus was another Eden" (IV, 10). Byron delineates the privacy of Juan and Haidée as a mutual transparency, a vision of complete reciprocal love seemingly prior to the fall into selfhood. This formulation is co-ordinate with another of differing tenor; the poem continues, "All these were theirs, for they were children still, / And children still they should have ever been" (IV, 15). The second analogy introduces an infantile coloring into the paradisal scene.

Haidée and Juan both appear as children to the narrator enmeshed in a bewildering adult world, but within the story their roles are clearly distinguished: Haidée functions as the mother of the infantile Juan. Famished and half-drowned, Juan is reborn from the sea and nursed back to health in Haidée's warm, well-provisioned, and womblike cave. As the weakened Juan slept, Haidée "bent o'er him, and he lay beneath, / Hush'd as the babe upon its mother's breast" (II, 148); when he revived, Haidée, "who watch'd him like a mother, would have fed / Him past all bounds" (II, 158).

These similes and the narrative configuration in which they occur place the ideal wordlessness of Haidée and Juan in parallel to the symbiotic union of mother and infant, at that early stage of human development before the infant comes to see himself as separate from the mother. Language at this level is a secret and subtle bond, a process of ceaseless and delicate adjustment, of needs understood and gratified before they are expressed. The figurative identification of the erotic sublime, as it were, with the dyad of mother and infant has important consequences for the conceptualization of language in *Don Juan.*

Juan participates briefly in a state anterior to the formation of an independent identity, but this fantasy of boundaryless bliss conflicts with the continued integrity of the adult who imagines it. To aspire toward the condition of Haidée and Juan carries the threat of self-abolition: to an autonomous being the idealized fusion is equivalent to a dangerous dissolution.[5] Inevitably, the beloved Haidée is therefore also a figure of death. As many critics have remarked, ominous overtones surround her from the moment of her introduction:

> Her hair, I said, was auburn; but her eyes
>   Were black as death, their lashes the same hue,
> Of downcast length, in whose silk shadow lies
>   Deepest attraction, for when to the view
> Forth from its raven fringe the full glance flies,
>   Ne'er with such force the swiftest arrow flew;
> 'Tis as the snake late coil'd, who pours his length,
> And hurls at once his venom and his strength.
>
> (II, 117)

Even Haidée's most maternally protective gestures bear, in exact relation to their nurturing power, vampiric suggestions:

> And then she stopp'd, and stood as if in awe,
> (For sleep is awful) and on tiptoe crept
>   And wrapt him closer, lest the air, too raw,
> Should reach his blood, then o'er him still as death
> Bent, with hush'd lips, that drank his scarce-drawn breath.
>
> (II, 143)

These sinister aspects are reinforced by the two other instances of wordlessness in *Don Juan* with which the episode of Haidée and Juan is thematically connected. The first concerns the grotesque "misshapen pigmies, deaf and dumb" (V, 88), who guard Gulbeyaz's door:

> Their duty was—for they were strong, and though
>   They looked so little, did strong things at times—
> To ope this door, which they could really do,
>   The hinges being as smooth as Rogers' rhymes;
> And now and then with tough strings of the bow,
>   As is the custom of those eastern climes,
> To give some rebel Pacha a cravat;
> For mutes are generally used for that.
>
> They spoke by signs—that is, not spoke at all
>
> (V, 89–90)

Through the seemingly capricious comparison with the verse of
Samuel Rogers, Byron links "smooth" writing to muteness and death,
while the slant rhyme of "do" with "though" and "bow" makes clear
that he himself rates lithe movement above euphony.[6] The conversation between Juan and General Lascy during the battle of Ismail displays a second, but different, linking of speechlessness and death; this
exchange, like that between Juan and Haidée, is marked by linguistic
incompatibility:

> Juan, to whom he spoke in German, knew
>   As much of German as of Sanscrit, and
> In answer made an inclination to
>   The General who held him in command;
> . . . .
> Short speeches pass between two men who speak
>   No common language; and besides, in time
> Of war and taking towns, when many a shriek
>   Rings o'er the dialogue, and many a crime
> Is perpetrated ere a word can break
>   Upon the ear, and sounds of horror chime
> In like church bells, with sigh, howl, groan, yell, prayer,
> There cannot be much conversation there.
>
> (VIII, 57–58)

Byron's description of Juan's enthusiasm for battle recalls several features of the episode of Juan and Haidée and so brings the
two episodes into relationship:

> —I say not *the* first,
>   But of the first, our little friend Don Juan
> Walked o'er the walls of Ismail, as if nurst
>   Amidst such scenes—though this was quite a new one
> To him, and I should hope to *most*. The thirst
>   Of Glory, which so pierces through and through one,
> Pervaded him—although a generous creature,
> As warm in heart as feminine in feature.
>
> And here he was—*who upon Woman's breast,*
>   *Even from a child, felt like a child;* howe'er
> The man in all the rest might be confest,
>   To him it was Elysium to be there;
> And he could even withstand that awkward test
>   Which Rousseau points out to the dubious fair,

> "Observe your lover when he *leaves* your arms;"
> But Juan never left them, while they had charms,
>
> Unless compelled by fate, or wave, or wind,
>   Or near relations, who are much the same.
> (VIII, 52–54; emphasis added in 53)

The end of this sequence reminds the reader of Juan's enforced departure from Julia as well as from Haidée, and the incongruity of echoing Juan's amorous exploits in the midst of carnage is Byron's means of reinforcing the fundamental kinship of the opposites. Juan is "nursed" in battle as he is nursed by Haidée; for Juan to be alone with Haidée "was another Eden" (IV, 10), and for him to be fighting "was Elysium" (VIII, 53). Byron announces "fierce loves and faithless wars" (VII, 8) as his subject, and the reversal of Spenser is possible because at one level love and war function identically. The link between the two actions is passion, etymologically the root of passivity. Juan's much-remarked passivity might be considered as the annulment of psychological distance, the consequence of an overwhelming presence. The thirst for glory "pervades" Juan, or, to cite the *OED* definitions, it diffuses and spreads through or into every part of him, it permeates and saturates him. Common to the intensity of war and love is an obliteration of detachment, and, as the introduction of the configuration both here and in the Haidée episode insinuates, the prototype of this experience, erasing the outlines of the self, is the fusion of infant and mother.

The fantasy of fusion is situated at two poles: it is a fantasy of origins, of mother and infant, and it returns as a fantasy of prospective conclusions in sexual union, or in war and death. These become prominent in Byron's portrayal of the lustful Empress Catherine whose troops destroy Ismail. Catherine's infatuation with Juan establishes the equivalence of the "oh!" of sexual joy and the "ah!" of misery:

> Oh Catherine! (for of all interjections
>   To thee both *oh!* and *ah!* belong of right
> In love and war) how odd are the connections
>   Of human thoughts, which jostle in their flight!
> Just now *yours* were cut out in different sections:
>   *First* Ismail's capture caught your fancy quite;
> *Next* of new knights, the fresh and glorious hatch;
> And *thirdly,* he who brought you the dispatch!
> (IX, 65)

Byron began the description of Catherine by expanding upon Horace's ascription of war to sexual passion: "nam fuit ante Helenam cunnus taeterrima belli / causa" (Satire I, 3:107–8). The *doubles entendres* of that passage are not more remarkable than its insistence that the gate of life and death is one:

> Oh, thou "teterrima Causa" of all "belli"—
>   Thou gate of Life and Death—thou nondescript!
> Whence is our exit and our entrance,—well I
>   May pause in pondering how all Souls are dipt
> In thy perennial fountain:—how man *fell,* I
>   Know not, since Knowledge saw her branches stript
> Of her first fruit, but how he falls and rises
> *Since, thou* has settled beyond all surmises.
>
> Some call thee "the worst Cause of war," but I
>   Maintain thou art the *best:* for after all
> From thee we come, to thee we go, and why
>   To get at thee not batter down a wall,
> Or waste a world? Since no one can deny
>   Thou dost replenish worlds both great and small:
> With, or without thee, all things at a stand
> Are, or would be, thou Sea of Life's dry Land!
>
> Catherine, who was the grand Epitome
>   Of that great Cause of war, or peace, or what
> You please (it causes all things which be,
>   So you may take your choice of this or that)—
>
>   (IX, 55–57)

Catherine, at once aggression and sexual passion, birth and death, source and end, is an image of woman as the terrifying and engulfing force who must be resisted. The light she retrospectively casts alters the impression made by Juan and Haidée. Their intimacy offers the sole example of complete communication in *Don Juan,* and Byron's treatment of it, in itself and as part of the series culminating in Catherine, suggests how the fantasy union presses toward a lethal silence. Catherine's Russian is as foreign to Juan as Haidée's Romaic, nor does Catherine speak directly in the poem. If Haidée and Juan transcend the usual barriers of the self, the poem also delineates the limitations inherent in their ecstasy. Insofar as their love is perfect it is finished, incapable of development; "for they were children still, /

And children still they should have been" (IV, 15). Haidée and Juan reach a state of atemporal happiness, but from the human perspective such freedom from time is stasis and death. The narrator observes as Haidée and Juan join their lives on the beach that she:

> had nought to fear,
> Hope, care, nor love beyond, her heart beat *here*.

> And oh! that quickening of the heart, that beat!
> How much it costs us!

(II, 202–3)

What the illusion of the all-encompassing *here* costs is the past and still more the future, the change of the self in time.

The totality of Juan's and Haidée's passion is a fearful exclusion, but the countervailing claims of the life they sublimely reject are kept before the reader by the interventions of the narrator. He enables us to perceive that the fantasy of full speech and full understanding, with its attendant values of wholeness, presence, and atemporality, is not an isolated ideal: the thematic networks within which it exists in *Don Juan* expose its connection with silence and the death silence figures. Juan's passion annihilates him on the breast of Haidée, and an ultimate value of silence brings to an end of the role of the poet. The narrator and Juan, the poet and the character, are equally endangered: the Latin root of *infant* means "he who does not speak." The episode of Haidée and Juan is Byron's version of the *Ode on a Grecian Urn:* in Byron's meditation on his lovers, as in Keats's, the values of an encompassing symbolic, finally static imagination are set against the humbler commitments and narrative imaginings of the speaker himself. Both poets at last withdraw from the potent ideal they have imagined—the figures on the urn, Juan and Haidée—to face the imperfections of "breathing human passion." But whereas Keats throughout his career remains uncertain what language to put in place of the ennobling fictions of epic and romance that he repeatedly elaborated only to reject, Byron deploys a language that acknowledges and enacts the inescapable facts of absence and loss while affirming human vitality. "You have so many 'divine' poems," Byron vexedly exclaimed to his publisher, "is it nothing to have written a Human one?"[7] The style of *Don Juan* is co-ordinate with the role of speech in the poem: it is best studied through the plot it represents.

II

Somewhat later in his essay on Byron, Eliot turns to "a long passage of self-portraiture from *Lara*" already singled out by Charles Du Bos in *Byron et la fatalité* and declares:

> Du Bos deserves full credit for recognizing its importance; and Byron deserves all the credit that Du Bos gives him for having written it. This passage strikes me also as a masterpiece of self-analysis, but of a self that is largely a deliberate fabrication—a fabrication that is only completed in the actual writing of the lines. The reason why Byron understood this self so well, is that it is largely his own invention; and it is only the self that he invented that he understood perfectly.

Eliot here brilliantly specifies the self-creation Byron wrought in the Byronic hero, but the creation was not wholly uncontingent. If the Byronic hero was no simple transcription of Byron but a fabrication, it was nonetheless a fiction responsive to the fears and desires of its author. The role required of the Byronic hero is displayed in the relationship in *Don Juan* between Juan and Lara's descendant, Haidée's father, Lambro.

At first glance Lambro functions merely as a *senex* who intrudes upon the lovers and puts an end to their happiness. Insofar as Haidée's love imperils Juan, however, Lambro is also a savior who rescues Juan from an absorption he is too weak to withstand. Byron's two heroes are the opposing faces of a single figure (biographically, Juan embodies parts of Byron's childhood, and Lambro, returning to his shattered home, expresses aspects of Byron's response to his broken marriage).[8] *Don Juan* presents in the temporal sequence of drama the continuum of psychological strategy: the stern warrior is the protagonist Byron generates to preserve the passive child from collapsing back into his mother. Alfonso's interruption of Juan's affair with Julia in Canto I operates as a similarly providential occurrence, because Juan risks being crushed by the older women for whom he has become the pawn: his mother, Inez, who contrived the affair for her own reasons, and Julia, suddenly transformed at the end of the canto from a sympathetically self-deceiving lover into a skillfully deceitful intriguer.[9]

As the defense Julia makes on the night the lovers are discovered (I, 145–47) reaches its climax, Byron's rhetoric rises toward the sublime: "pale / She lay, her dark eyes flashing through their tears, / Like skies that rain and lighten" (I, 158). While the tide of Julia's apology breaks over Alfonso and his posse, Juan lies inert, hidden in the bed between Julia and her maid, "half-smother'd" (I, 165), in danger of "suffocation by that pretty pair" (I, 166). Here as elsewhere in *Don Juan,* the powerful speech of others is a menace to the hero.

The erotic triangle in both these episodes bears unmistakable oedipal overtones, and in both the function of the father figure as a principle of difference is apparent. By forcibly separating Juan from the mother whose love overwhelms him, Lambro, like Alfonso before him, makes possible Juan's independence. Moreover, even as the child models his identity on the father whom he cannot supplant, so Juan asserts himself in responding to this older rival. Attacked by Alfonso, Juan is driven to act: "His blood was up; though young, he was a Tartar, / And not at all disposed to prove a martyr" (I, 184). So, too, after his weakness and silence in Canto II and his position in Canto III as Haidée's consort, dependent on her wealth and status, Juan achieves a brief autonomy in his defiance of Lambro: " 'Young man, your sword;' so Lambro once more said: / Juan replied, 'Not while this arm is free' " (IV, 40). This confrontation is virtually the first time Byron presents Juan in direct discourse, and his speech is the proof of his temporary self-sufficiency.[10]

When Lambro overcomes Juan and casts him forth he sets in renewed motion the oscillating and ambiguous journey whose curves shape *Don Juan.* In his passivity Juan falls into a repetitive series at each stage of which he is almost absorbed by a dominating woman— Julia, Haidée, the "imperious" Gulbeyaz, the devouring Catherine, the "full-blown" Fitz-Fulke, and Adeline, "the fair most fatal Juan ever met" (XIII, 12); circumstances free him from her, but only to propel him toward the subsequent lapse. The journey is ambiguous because this potentially deadly woman, mother and lover, is a figure of desire and because Juan's freedom consists only of this endless chain of disruptions and losses.

Two alternatives to this dilemma would seem to exist in *Don Juan.* One is typified by Lambro, whose isolated marauding life and coolly powerful manner show him as the avatar of the hero who fills Byron's earlier works. The absolute masculine will with which Lambro crushes Juan and re-establishes his priority, however, *Don Juan* exposes as no solution at all. His contest is depicted by the narrative as more with Haidée herself than with her love object. Haidée's resistance to Lambro (IV, 44–45) is uncolored by the irony with which Byron tinges Juan's, and the extended pathetic description of her death (IV, 54–71) completes the eclipse of Juan's moment of bravery. In exerting his authority over Haidée, Lambro destroys the peace of his home: the desolate fate he brings on his island and himself (IV, 72) reveals that he too cannot exist apart from the mother figure. The second solution is embodied in the narrator, who is not so much in the story as above it, but whose words are shaped by the same exigencies as those his story witnesses.

Don Juan locates the origin of language in the Edenic harmony of mother and child: Haidée teaches Juan his "alpha beta" (II, 163). The narrator develops the myth from his own experience:

> 'Tis pleasing to be school'd in a strange tongue
>   By female lips and eyes—that is, I mean,
> When both the teacher and the taught are young,
>   As was the case, at least, where I have been;
> They smile so when one's right, and when one's wrong
>   They smile still more, and then there intervene
> Pressure of hands, perhaps even a chaste kiss;—
> I learn'd the little that I know by this
>
> (II, 164)

Language here figures as innately sexualized: talk is desire. Byron underscores the connection in writing of Italy in *Beppo:*

> I love the language, that soft bastard Latin,
>   Which melts like kisses from a female mouth,
> And sounds as if it should be writ on satin,
>   With syllables which breathe of the sweet South,
> And gentle liquids gliding all so pat in,
>   That not a single accent seems uncouth,
> Like our own harsh, northern whistling, grunting guttural,
> Which we're obliged to hiss, and spit, and sputter all.
>
> I like the women too . . .
>
> (44–45)[11]

Yet the consummation of the desire for women must be resisted, deferred, because it would annihilate the poet's voice. As the puns on death and dying in Elizabethan poetry reveal, orgasm is "the little death." It is also, as a canceled, unfinished stanza of *Don Juan* suggests, a phenomenon literally beyond language:

> But Oh! that I were dead—for while alive—
>   Would that I neer had loved—Oh Woman—Woman—
> <All that I writ> All that I write or wrote can neer revive
>   To paint a sole sensation—though quite common—
> Of those in which the Body seemed to drive
>   My soul from out me at thy single summon
> Expiring in the hope of sensation—[12]

Juan's career and the narrator's reflections thus place language between two equally dangerous termini, both of which are approached with desire yet self-protectively put off. At one extreme looms the power of erotic bliss to annul self and voice, at the other the similar threat of the fusion of infant with mother.

In this schema language exists as the unresolved middle between the states that would abrogate it. Moreover, this middle is a middle of repetitions, for the story *Don Juan* tells is of the loss of the desired object in the necessary separation from her, the yearning for her, and the fresh flight from her. Human existence, as the poem sees it, perpetually re-enacts the primary liberating catastrophe of separation. A repetition is also a re-petition, a re-asking: the repetitions of the poem set forth again and again the mournful questions "How did I become separate?" "Who am I?" Women as much as men exemplify the pattern: once begun, they too must re-enact their initiating gesture:

> In her first passion woman loves her lover,
>   In all the others all she loves is love,
> Which grows a habit she can ne'er get over,
>   And fits her loosely—like an easy glove,
> As you may find, whene'er you like to prove her:
>   One man alone at first her heart can move;
> She then prefers him in the plural number,
> Not finding that the additions much encumber.
>
> I know not if the fault be men's or theirs;
>   But one thing's pretty sure; a woman planted—
> (Unless at once she plunge for life in prayers)—
>   After a decent time must be gallanted;
> Although, no doubt, her first of love affairs

> Is that to which her heart is wholly granted;
>   Yet there are some, they say, who have had *none,*
> But those who have ne'er end with only *one.*
>   (III, 3–4)

The last stanza illustrates the ever-varying interpenetrations of the story level and the narrative commentary in *Don Juan,* the two aspects Robert Escarpit has distinguished as "le temps fictif" and "le temps psychologique."[13] This interpenetration breaks down any simple distinction between the story and its telling: there is only the modulation of language. The narrator's seemingly unmotivated generalization recalls Julia, banished to a convent a canto earlier, and her imposed constancy is the fate his fluid mode avoids. Juan vows eternal fidelity:

> And oh! if e'er I should forget, I swear—
>   But that's impossible, and cannot be—
> Sooner shall this blue ocean melt to air,
>   Sooner shall earth resolve itself to sea,
> Than I resign thine image, Oh! my fair!
>   Or think of anything excepting thee
>   (II, 19)

This protestation is notoriously interrupted by retching, and happily, for Juan's romantic dedication to a single image is the willed counterpart to Julia's unwilling stasis. Juan can go forward because he forgets and because he is prevented from ever looking back. Similarly, Byron's refusal to linger over the episode of Juan and Haidée is a refusal of fixation, a refusal of the seductions of completion and finality. He writes their story not as a self-contained heroico-pathetic romance like his own earlier tales, but as part of an ongoing narrative whose rhythms undo the authority both of its dreams of bliss and of its conclusion. Byron repudiates his own temptation by the totalizing fantasy of Juan and Haidée (IV, 52–53, 74), passionate union or faithful death, to affirm the vital multiplicity of his own independent existence: not for him the diminishing pledge not to "think of anything else, excepting thee." In so doing he restores the intermediate space in which language (and hence his poem) can continue to exist. The space is empty, and marked by absence and lack, but it is an emptiness that invites filling by the imagination of the poet.

III

At the end of the first canto of *Don Juan* Byron threatens to promulgate a definitive set of "poetical commandments": "I'll call the work 'Longinus o'er a Bottle, / Or, Every Poet his *own* Aristotle ' " (I, 204). In no respect does Byron differ more greatly from the rules than in his departure from the Aristotelean precept that a work of literature should have a beginning, a middle, and an end: *Don Juan* is all middle. The epic conventionally begins *in medias res,* but at the actual middle point of epic is a stabilizing device, a place about which the story can be organized: Odysseus narrating his adventures, Aeneas describing the fall of Troy to Dido, Raphael recounting the war in Heaven to Adam and Eve as an instructive example. In *Don Juan,* however, the condition of unfinishedness is not merely an aspect of the story, a temporary fiction exposed when the whole is complete, but one that attaches to the poet himself and influences the ongoing creation of his text.

The lines of *Don Juan* which the notion of indeterminacy perhaps first brings to mind are the melodramatic ones at the end of Canto XV:

> Between two worlds life hovers like a star,
>   'Twixt night and morn, upon the horizon's verge:
> How little do we know that which we are!
>   How less what we may be!
>
> (XV, 99)

This fundamental unsettledness speaks in other tones as well:

> Of all the barbarous Middle Ages, that
>   Which is the most barbarous is the middle age
> Of man; it is—I really scarce know what;
>   But when we hover between fool and sage,
> And don't know justly what we would be at,—
>   A period something like a printed page,
> Black letter upon foolscap, while our hair
> Grows grizzled, and we are not what we were,—
>
> Too old for youth,—too young, at thirty-five,
>   To herd with boys, or hoard with good threescore,—

> I wonder people should be left alive;
> But since they are, that epoch is a bore
>
> (XII, 1–2)

This reflection has been prepared for by the allusions to Dante in the previous cantos (e.g., X, 27), but Byron transforms the tradition that thirty-five, as the midpoint of man's allotted span of years, is a moment of decision; the era which in *The Divine Comedy* marks a crisis becomes in *Don Juan* a particularly anomalous stage in which meaningful choice seems impossible. The stanzas connect the uncertainties of middle life directly to the paradoxes of a text—"A period something like a printed page, / Black letter upon white foolscap"—and this odd conjunction recurs at the opening of the fifteenth canto, where Byron opposes the fertile indeterminacy of his text to the brevity of life and blankness of boredom:

> Ah!—What should follow slips from my reflection:
>   Whatever follows ne'ertheless may be
> As àpropos of hope or retrospection,
>   As though the lurking thought had follow'd free.
> All present life is but an Interjection,
>   An "Oh!" or "Ah!" of joy or misery,
> Or a "Ha! ha!" or "Bah!"—a yawn, or "Pooh!"
> Of which perhaps the latter is most true.
>
> But, more or less, the whole's a syncopé,
> Or a singultus—emblems of Emotion,
> The grand Antithesis to great Ennui
>
> (XV, 1–2)

Here is another form of the paradox already noted. The contradiction recurs, for the "syncopé" of emotion which combats boredom itself abolishes consciousness: a syncope is also the loss of syllables and sounds in the middle of a word, hence also the emblem of the cutting-short of the poet's voice. The sexual overtones of the "Oh!" of "joy" and their equivalence to the "Ah!" of "misery" recall the dangerous themes previously developed in the portrait of Catherine (see IX, 65, quoted above).

The intermediate position *Don Juan* occupies thus appears as a positive *modus vivendi*. The repeated suspension of the story functions on two levels. Juan is caught between infantile unconsciousness and sexual self-annihilation, and the poem's interruption of all his affairs corresponds to a refusal to allow passion its obliterating force. The narrator, yearning for both states, is also caught between his lost youth ("No more—no more—Oh! never more on me / The freshness of the heart can fall like dew" [I, 214]), and a future that must ultimately be death. His refusal to treat life according to the familiar pattern of crisis autobiography is a dissent from the notion of a fixed identity, of a life stiffening into shape once and for all, just as his refusal to precipitate a single final meaning is a mode of ensuring the inexhaustible vitality of his text. On both levels he is committed to filling the empty present, to staving off closure at any cost: "the past tense, / The dreary 'Fuimus' of all things human," which "must be declined" (XIII, 40) again links life and language by operating brilliantly in both contexts. The poem's insistence on its own indeterminacy and arbitrariness is its style of freedom: by rejecting the points of fullness—origin and end—Byron devotes himself to a discourse of absences, fragments, and losses which can yet keep the moment open.

The characteristic mode of this discourse is excursive, associative, metonymic, in contrast to the kind of metaphoric, symbolic concentration lauded by Eliot. As we have seen, Byron's resistance to such nodes of convergence is a matter both of substance and of technique: he denies the fatal power of certain meanings by continuing past them, and refuses permanence to identifications and identity. *Don Juan* is thus an anti-sublime poem, a poem that no sooner reaches a point of intensity than it undoes its own effects: the poem advances by negating the obsessions to which it returns, and then moving on, again and again.[14] Insofar as Juan represents aspects of Byron's life, for example, they are admitted only by negation: Juan's crises are Juan's, never acknowledged as the narrator's. Byron, in contrast to Coleridge and Wordsworth, deliberately stays on the surface (as much as he can), and that is why, despite the extravagantly artificial manner of *Don Juan,* he appears as a realist.[15]

The narrative of *Don Juan* seems to be set free of the constraints of purposefulness:

> I ne'er decide what I shall say, and this I call
>   Much too poetical. Men should know why
> They write, and for what end; but, note or text,
> I never know the word which will come next.
>   (IX, 41)

Don Juan abounds in this sort of confession, each a protest against a vision of complete authorial control. Byron renounces the goal of a fictitious (and factitious) unity, of a designed poem whose meaning would be thoroughly determinate, thoroughly subservient to an end. In so doing he reinstates the power of language to initiate an endless play of meanings, a range of possibilities unrestricted by the demands of an author obviously shaping, or invested in, his work. Compare, for example, the increasing pressure Wordsworth places on his narrative in the later books of *The Prelude* as he strives to make his lived experience accord with a scheme in which "All [is] gratulant, if rightly understood" (1805, XIII, 385).[16] Byron's structureless habit of proceeding enables him to combat his anxieties by playing them out; it allows him to take on as his own some of the characteristics of the women whom he has placed as the potent other, desired and feared. His characterization of his poem is suggestively similar to that which he gives of women's letters:

> The earth has nothing like a She epistle,
> And hardly heaven—because it never ends.
>   I love the mystery of a female missal,
> Which, like a creed, ne'er says all it intends,
>   But full of cunning as Ulysses' whistle,
> When he allured poor Dolon . . .
>   (XIII, 105)

The digressive manner of *Don Juan* bespeaks a relaxation of will which permits ominous material to surface: instead of repression, whose indefinite force heightens the sublime, the associative chains of *Don Juan* work toward expression and neutralization.[17] Symbolic and metaphoric poetry achieves its richness through compression and ambiguity; *Don Juan,* which, like women's letters, also "ne'er says all it intends," creates its vitality by extended meanings—inexhaustible sequences rather than pregnant points.

Eliot remarks that "if Byron had distilled his verse, there would have been nothing whatever left," but he is uninterested in the positive implications of his witticism. Byron's manner liberates his unconscious; it enables him to write a poem that can continually surprise its author. The long poem for which the Romantics strove, only to find their aspirations turn into an onerous task or poignant failure, is for Byron a spontaneous, ceaselessly proliferating process. Novelty, rather than inevitability, marks the growth of *Don Juan.* The result is a poetry of surprising conjunctions and momentary delights. Consider, for example, the last quoted stanza. "The earth has nothing like a She epistle" sounds, apart from the oddity and false literariness of "She epistle," like a cliché, but the weakly descriptive phrase acquires force when a buried comparison is released in the second line: "And hardly heaven." This in turn becomes the starting point of a brief but consistent series of religious terms: "mystery," "missal," and "creed." If, as the drafts McGann prints of this stanza suggest, Byron was trapped into "whistle" by the need to rhyme with "epistle" and "missal," he resourcefully overcame the awkwardness with the allusion to Dolon and Ulysses. The unexpected change of context, from Christian to classical, is found elsewhere, notably in the clash between epic and Christian values which Byron insists that the reader confront with the Siege of Ismail. The poem repeatedly draws on epic tradition: Ismail is the modern counterpart of Troy, and Juan's wanderings are a skewed version of Odysseus's, as the echoes of the *Odyssey* in the Haidée episode make explicit.[18] The linking of female letters to epic craftiness insinuates again the replacement in *Don Juan* of physical adventure by the greater psychological perilousness of "cruizing o'er the ocean woman" (XIII, 40). Moreover, the juxtaposition of religious terms and deception—"you had better / Take care what you reply to such a letter" ends the stanza—connects the seemingly chance allusion to the theme of hypocritical piety running throughout the poem: think of Donna Inez keeping the erotically ornamented "family Missal" for herself (I, 46). It also recalls the elaborate love letter written by the convent-bound Julia in Canto I. Byron drops the allusions at the close of the stanza, but not before they have provoked trains of association that send the reader over the whole poem. To read *Don Juan* is to encounter a succession of such tantalizing occasions, a succession that is not determined by any obvious logic, which is inconsecutive but not therefore inconsequential. The sequences begin with license but as they develop become meaningful; they are justified by what they unfold, and so rise above irrelevance. *Don Juan* is not so much "fortuitous," as Jerome McGann describes it, as it is "overdetermined"; it is because the "fortuitous" happenings can be situated in many overlapping configurations that they possess meaning.[19] The reader may explore each occasion or not, as he chooses, before the flow of the narrator's talk carries him on to the next. The poem, then, is not precisely the "grand poetic riddle" (VIII, 139) the narrator once calls it. Riddling is part of its appeal, but—to use a word that in its various forms occurs twenty-three times in the poem—it is rather a multiplicity of "puzzles." *Don Juan* asks less for comprehensive interpretation than for participation.

This range of meaning is possible only when the radically private language of mother and child represented in the relationship of Juan and Haidée is broken by the separation of the child from the mother. The taboos of the Oedipus complex send the son forth on his metonymic career, seeking satisfaction not in his mother but in a surrogate for her, not striving to usurp his father in actuality but to become like him in another setting. The Oedipus complex is thus, as Freud insisted, the foundation of culture, because it is through the Oedipus complex that the child passes from the family to his broader culture. To do so is to pass from the private language of mother and child to the pre-existent terms of the culture, to dream nostalgically of that lost transparency of communication but to feel oneself doomed to speak in the always slightly misfitting words the culture provides; at this level the ever-present allusions of *Don Juan* are the emblem of the pre-emption of the narrator's own voice by the babble of all who have preceded him. "Doomed" but also "enabled": in *Don Juan* Byron exploits this dilemma instead of concealing it by a myth of symbolic plenitude.

To illustrate the strengths of Byron's manner it may be useful to turn once more to Coleridge. Arguing in the *Biographia Literaria* against Wordsworth's assertion that the *Lyrical Ballads* were written in "the real language of men," Coleridge examines the fallacy on which the statement rests:

> Every man's languages varies, according to the extent of his knowledge, the activity of his faculties, and the depth or quickness of his feelings. Every man's language has, first, its *individualities;* secondly, the common properties of the *class* to which he belongs; and thirdly, words and phrases of *universal* use. The language of Hooker, Bacon, Bishop Taylor, and Burke, differs from the common language of the learned class only by the superior number and novelty of the thoughts and relations which they had to convey. The language of Algernon Sidney differs not at all from that, which every well-educated gentleman would wish to write, and (with due allowances for the undeliberateness, and less connected train, of thinking natural and proper to conversation) such as he would wish to talk. Neither one or the other differ half as much from the general language of cul-

tivated society, as the language of Mr. Wordsworth's homeliest composition differs from that of a common peasant. For "real" therefore we must substitute *ordinary*, or *lingua communis*. And this, we have proved, is no more to be found in the phraseology of low and rustic life than in that of any other class. . . . Anterior to cultivation the lingua communis of every country, as Dante has well observed, exists every where in parts, and no where as a whole.[20]

In the *Preface* to the *Lyrical Ballads* Wordsworth had espoused a view of language as deriving directly from objects; Coleridge exposes the mistake of this "natural" view by maintaining that the "best part of human language . . . is derived from reflection on the acts of the mind itself," and is "formed by a voluntary appropriation of fixed symbols to internal acts" (II, 54). He thus restores language to the distinctively human matrix in which it comes into being, and his formulation permits a recasting of Eliot's critique. To say that Byron "added nothng to the language" is, in Coleridge's more discriminating framework, to indicate the lack of any strongly idiosyncratic "individualities" in his style, but also to throw the emphasis on its "common properties" and "words and phrases of *universal* use."

Byron cherishes the membership of *Don Juan* in the linguistic community to which it ineluctably belongs. The words he speaks have a history of their own, meanings they carry with them from their innumerable uses outside and prior to the poem. They are his only for an instant, loaned to him only briefly for his own purposes, before they return to their larger ongoing life. "If fallen in evil days on evil tongues," Byron writes in the *Dedication* to *Don Juan,* "Milton appeal'd to the Avenger, Time," and he continues: "Time, the Avenger, execrates his wrongs, / And makes the word '*Miltonic*' mean '*sublime*'" (st. 10). Of more interest than Byron's enlistment of Milton to lambaste Southey is his highlighting of the historical process by which words acquire meaning. The allusion to *Paradise Lost* is typical of *Don Juan,* a veritable echo chamber reverberating with phrases, imitations, parodies, and half-heard fragments from Homer, Virgil, Dante, Shakespeare, Milton, Pope, and scores of lesser figures. These shadowy presences augment Byron's voice by locating him within his tradition. Even were it true, as Eliot charges, that Byron added nothing to the language, one might yet reply that through him a whole tradition is summoned and renovated. His contempt for the "insolent . . . wish," as he saw it, of Southey, Coleridge, and

Wordsworth "to supersede all warblers here below" (*Dedication,* st. 3) is the corollary of his refusal to give superordinate value to the concept of originality which, given his consciousness of, and commitment to, the public continuities of language, could only seem to him an impoverishing mystification.

Allusion is only a special case of the way in which *Don Juan* continually unmasks the illusion of its own autonomy in order to reap the benefits of acknowledging all that lies outside it. To choose words already invested with significance by their recognizability as literature—allusions—is in one respect to beg the central issue, because one of the fundamental questions raised by *Don Juan* concerns the conventional distinctions between the literary and the nonliterary. Macassar oil, Congreve's rockets, the brand names of ships' pumps, and all the other odd objects that find their way from daily life into *Don Juan,* on the one hand, and the highwaymen's slang, parodied jargons, and the mention of pox and like taboo subjects, on the other, constitute a challenge, less socially radical than Wordsworth's but kindred and no less far-reaching, to the notion of a specialized poetic diction. *Don Juan,* building on the comic precedents of the previous century,[21] demonstrates more thoroughly than does Wordsworth's own work the contention of the *Preface* to the *Lyrical Ballads* "that there neither is, nor can be, any essential difference between the language of prose and metrical composition." The conversation poem that "affects not to be poetry," that undertaking about whose implications Coleridge remained uneasy, reaches a triumphant apogee in *Don Juan.*[22]

Yet to speak, as in the title of Ronald Bottrall's essay, of "Byron and the Colloquial Tradition in English Poetry" is still somewhat to underestimate the ramifications of *Don Juan,* because the poem places itself in relation not only to a tradition *within* literary history but also to what would seem to stand outside it.[23] *Don Juan* could scarcely exist without the conventions Byron manipulates to make his meaning. If his "narration [of her genealogy] / May have suggested" (I, 59) that Julia will be the culmination, that is only because of the expectations of a pattern held by readers and writers within a given culture, their common literary competence. But Byron does not privilege these patterns, or, to put it more accurately, he privileges them by calling attention to their artificiality. To read *Don Juan* is to be made aware of the arbitrary agreements on which the making and maintaining of meaning rest. The relationship between flamboyant literariness and ostentatious anti-, or non-, literariness is a differential one: each throws the other into relief, and both together direct our attention to the functioning of language, to the conventions by which it works and the domains into which historically it has divided itself. By unveiling the artificiality of his own procedures, Byron displays the fictiveness of language generally and the delicate and complex consensus through which it is preserved. The myriad slippages and maladjustments of that social network create the gaps in which his irony and satire operate.

Don Juan, to return to the quotation from Coleridge, can imitate "the indeliberateness, and less connected train, of thinking natural and proper to conversation" because it sees conversation as an exemplary act performed in language, hence different in degree only, not kind, from literature. Byron repeatedly announces a freedom guided only by his own intelligent curiosity: "So on I ramble, now and then narrating, / Now pondering" (IX, 42). By refusing to mark itself off absolutely from everyday life, by denying that it constitutes any sort of special experience, *Don Juan* gains the power to include its opposite within itself. "This narrative is not meant for narration," the narrator comments, "But a mere airy and fantastic basis, / To build up common things with common places" (XIV, 7). Byron had chosen as the motto for the first cantos of *Don Juan* "Difficile est propria communia dicere," a phrase he had translated in *Hints from Horace* as "Whate'er the critic says or poet sings / Tis no slight task to write on common things."[24] He thereby directly connects the difficulty of his art to the prosaic nature of his medium: because his words claim no magic in themselves and because he regularly turns us outward from his words to their uses elsewhere, Byron demonstrates with remarkable clarity the basis of poetry not in "individual words," as Eliot implies, but in the relationship they mutually establish. Though seeing that Byron must be quoted at length to make his effect, Eliot does not recognize the alternative conception of language his practice successfully illustrates: individually colorless counters are transformed into a compelling series by the unexpected but self-validating connections Byron fabricates between them. The aggregative and associative mode of the poem is a virtual paradigm of Coleridge's definitions of the Fancy, but the loss of the intensity Coleridge ascribed to the Imagination only is more than offset by the revelation of the power of language itself, both within and without this particular poem. Despite Byron's evident pride in his achievement, *Don Juan* is almost less concerned with its own status as a unique *parole,* to use a Saussurean distinction, than it is with the overall function of *langue.*[25] *Don Juan* advances its claim to our interest not so much by conveying a meaning as by making its readers aware of the prior conventions on which any sharable meanings whatever depend.[26] Or, to remain with Coleridge, to read *Don Juan* is to be made aware of the characteristics of the "lingua communis [which] . . . exists every where in parts, and no where as a whole."

Despite such declarations as that of Wordsworth in the *Prospectus* to *The Recluse* that he would employ "words / Which speak of nothing more than what we are," the poetics of Romanticism habitually resorts to a language of intimation. If the period is one of Natural Supernaturalism, as a magisterial description would have it, that terminology itself betrays the very binary opposition the poetry seeks to mediate. In the *Preface* to the *Lyrical Ballads* Wordsworth sets forth his aims in a fashion that similarly maintains a distinction: he proposed, he says, "to choose incidents and situations from common life" and "to throw over them a certain coloring of imagination, whereby ordinary things should be presented to the mind in an unusual way." To see merely the object is the sign of Peter Bell's imaginative poverty: "A primrose by a river's brim / A yellow primrose was to him, / And it was nothing more" (II, 58–60). Though he insists on the "real," Wordsworth takes the object as instrumental to the transforming imagination. For Coleridge likewise, the symbol is defined by its embodiment of a realm beyond itself: it "is characterized by a translucence of the Special in the Individual, or of the General in the Especial or of the Universal in the General. Above all the translucence of the Eternal in and through the Temporal."[27] But in poetry there can be only words, and this illusion of depth and timelessness is a linguistic conjuring trick, a sleight of hand performed in language and inseparable from it. Byron's satiric and anti-sublime deconstructions strip away this illusion, insisting that we recognize that it is through our own language that we create the images that enchant us. Byron stresses not the "mystery" putatively residing in the object but the "doubt" caused by our own fallible mental activities. Paradoxically, it is by thus affirming the priority of our constructions that Byron returns us to the object world, but not as an empirical, objective given. To stretch Oscar Wilde, he too knows that it is only shallow people who do not judge by appearances: *Don Juan* shows that "the real" is the totality of our conventions, the agreed-upon social vision of reality. Here, too, Coleridge provides a useful gloss. In a footnote to Chapter IV of the *Biographia Literaria,* he discusses the evolutionary process by which synonyms initially "used promiscuously" gradually distinguish themselves from each other: "When this distinction has been so naturalized and of such general currency, that the language itself does as it were *think* for us (like the sliding rule which is the mechanic's safe substitute for arithmetical knowledge) we then say, that it is evident to *common sense*" (I, 86). *Don Juan* continually lays bare the dangers of this "common sense" by correcting delusion, attacking cant, brutally reiterating the brutal "facts" of war and death, but simultaneously calling to our attention the sway of language and social bonds on which it in turn rests. "I write the world" (XV, 60), Byron can declare, because in writing he fully enters the transpersonal medium in which "the world" represents (and misrepresents) itself to itself.

Language in *Don Juan* thus points not to a supralinguistic reality (and hence is spared the agonizing doubt of language characteristic of a Shelley) but to a community of speakers and readers in the world their language builds up. In his influential *Romantic Image* Frank Kermode showed how "inextricably associated" in the Romantic-Symbolist tradition are the beliefs "in the image as a radiant truth out of space and time, and in the necessary isolation or estrangement of men who can perceive it."[28] These views may be found throughout *Childe Harold* and occasionally in *Don Juan,* but the nature of the latter poem qualifies the statements made within it. Even as he reduced the magical image, Byron restored the poet to his fellow men. Their common habitation in language binds together the two central figures of *Don Juan:* the narrator and the reader his fiction projects. The isolation Byron-as-Juan suffers is recuperated in the affiliation of Byron-as-narrator to his audience.

Though the web of words which is *Don Juan* reveals "the class to which [Byron] belongs" and the aristocratic Whig liberalism of his principles, the poem is remarkably unprescriptive of its reader. Assent, or the maneuvering of the reader into a point of view congruent with that of the author, is only one of the many and successive aims of the poem: the implicitly dramatized responses range from shock and anger to laughter at the author's image of himself, the narrator. The most generous aspect of *Don Juan* is the depth and variety of the experiences it acknowledges: the poem solicits the reader to bring with him all the works of literature he has read, all the political controversies in which he is enmeshed, all the mundane objects through which he moves, all his conflicting passions as child, parent, and lover. The poem functions not so much centripetally, directing attention to its uniqueness (though it does so gleefully), as centrifugally, returning each reader to the complex of private and public experiences that make up his particular life.[29] The comprehensiveness of *Don Juan* and the much debated question of its status as epic are subjects that can be reformulated in terms of the inclusiveness of the response it figures but does not restrict.[30] There is no single perfect reading of *Don Juan:* the text enfranchises all that infinite series of readings, neither idiosyncratic nor stock, which the common cultural context of author and reader empowers. It earns this richness because it is shaped not by the concept of uniqueness but by the concept of difference. The narrator demonstrates that identity exists only through the roles furnished by his culture, and hence is something both his and not his. To avert a threatening alienation, an imprisonment in a role, he must continually repudiate the stances he adopts, defining himself not by fixed points but by the shifting pattern of his movement between them. At one level *Don Juan* is a prolonged elegy for the loss of the union of mother and child represented by Haidée and Juan, but the poem also deploys a tenacious and resilient resistance to the temptations of that fantasy. The attempt to master the conflict perpetuates it: the repetitions of *Don Juan* reiterate the dilemma, revealing Byron's continued subjection to, as well as his conquest of, his desires and fears. The place of language in *Don Juan* is inevitably ambiguous: the situations in which it might be superseded by transparency of communication Byron rejects as self-destructive, and so he remains trapped, his reliance on language the sign of all that he has lost. Language for Byron can never be what it briefly is for Haidée and Juan, private and innocent; every fresh employment of it further implicates him in the continuum of history and society. Caught in words, however, Byron makes the exposure and exploitation of their treacherous wealth serve his ends. By displaying the unavoidable inauthenticity of language, he liberates its fictiveness and sets in motion the self created only through it. He unmasks the illusion of full meaning dear to Eliot and the Symbolists, asking us to recognize that poetry can be made not only by saturating the individual word but also by ceaselessly uncovering the paradoxes hid in the use of ordinary words. The contradictions at the center of an existence defined by a language that is creative but inevitably con-

ventional, his but not his, a means of connection but a story of
separation, a mode of recovery but an admission of loss, a fantasy of
wholeness that is desired but resisted, Byron accepts and makes generate the elaborate play that enlarges the narrator and animates the
words of *Don Juan*.

Notes

1. "Byron," *On Poetry and Poets* (1943; rpt. New York: Noonday, 1964),
pp. 232–33.

2. I mean only to indicate that this accusation has not been rebutted, not
to underrate the excellent studies of Byron's style. In addition to the works
cited below, I would single out George M. Ridenour, *The Style of DON JUAN*
(New Haven: Yale University Press, 1960); M. K. Joseph, *Byron the Poet*
(London: Gollancz, 1964); and W. W. Robson, "Byron as Poet," rpt. in his
Critical Essays (London: Routledge, 1966), pp. 148–88. Two recent essays
of relevance are Bernard Beatty's "Lord Byron: Poetry and Precedent," in
Literature of the Romantic Period 1750–1850, ed. R. T. Davies and B. G.
Beatty (New York: Barnes and Noble, 1976), pp. 114–34; and Francis Berry's
"The Poet of *Childe Harold*," in *Byron: A Symposium*, ed. John D. Jump
(New York: Barnes and Noble, 1975), pp. 35–51, which also takes up Eliot's
critique.

3. *The Symbolic Imagination: Coleridge and the Romantic Tradition*
(Princeton: Princeton University Press, 1977).

4. All quotations of *Don Juan* are from *Lord Byron: The Complete Poetical Works*, ed. Jerome J. McGann, Vol. V (Oxford: Clarendon, 1986).

5. See on this subject Jean Laplanche, *Life and Death in Psychoanalysis*,
tr. Jeffrey Mehlman (Baltimore: Johns Hopkins University Press, 1976).

6. The variant for line 4 printed by McGann shows the original contrast
to have been between the quiet of the doors and the vitality of Byron's own
speaking voice: "The hinges being <oiled / oilier> much smoother than these
rhymes."

7. Letter of April 6, 1819, *Byron's Letters and Journals*, ed. Leslie A.
Marchand, Vol. VI (Cambridge, Mass.: Harvard University Press, 1976),
p. 105.

8. Lambro, usually said to be modeled on Ali Pacha, had autobiographical roots, too. See III, 51–52.

9. To the degree that Inez connives at the affair she and Julia converge.
Juan's affair with Julia thereby seems a displacement of maternal incest: Alfonso's intervention is thus punishment for the forbidden act and rescue from
a dangerous absorption.

10. Juan first speaks in the poem during the second canto, when his farewell is quickly cut short by seasickness (II, 18–20), and when he bars the
panicky crew from the grog (II, 36), where Byron takes his speech directly
from a scene in his sources. He is unheard during the subsequent 180 stanzas
of Canto II and throughout Canto III.

11. Quotation from *Lord Byron: The Complete Poetical Works,* ed. Jerome J. McGann, Vol. IV (Oxford: Clarendon, 1986).

12. Printed in *Don Juan,* ed. McGann, p. 660.

13. *Lord Byron: Un tempérament littéraire,* 2 vols. (Paris: Cercle du Libre, 1957), II, 58.

14. It could not, of course, repeatedly undo the sublime if it did not repeatedly strive for it. This movement is akin to that described as "desublimating" by Thomas Weiskel, *The Romantic Sublime* (Baltimore: Johns Hopkins University Press, 1976). I have not used the term because the relation between "the sublime" and "sublimation" within Weiskel's otherwise stimulating argument remains problematic.

15. Roman Jakobson proposed the relationships of metaphor to symbolism and metonymy to realism in section 5, "The Metaphoric and Metonymic Poles," of his essay, "Two Aspects of Language and Two Types of Aphasic Disturbances," in Roman Jakobson and Morris Halle, *Fundamentals of Language,* 2d rev. ed. (The Hague: Mouton, 1971), pp. 69–96.

16. The notion of free play is taken from Jacques Derrida; see, for example, "Structure, Sign, and Play in the Discourse of the Human Sciences," *The Structuralist Controversy,* ed. Richard Macksey and Eugenio Donato (Baltimore: Johns Hopkins University Press, 1972), pp. 247–65.

17. The relationship of repression and the sublime is a theme of the criticism of Harold Bloom; see *A Map of Misreading* (New York: Oxford University Press, 1975).

18. For example, III, 23, on Lambro's arrival, "An honest gentleman at his return / May not have the good fortune of Ulysses." The allusions are studied in my *Byron and His Fictions* (Detroit: Wayne State University Press, 1978).

19. "Fortuitous" is a word McGann often uses to describe the growth of the poem in *DON JUAN in Context* (Chicago: University of Chicago Press, 1976). The accretive chains, however, are often generated by the anxieties aroused by certain recurrent subjects, such as women. The motives for the resulting digressions and evasions are partly concealed from Byron himself. These gaps and switches suggest that the meaning of *Don Juan,* to use a Lacanian phrase, is not simply one that Byron speaks but one that speaks him. It is precisely such "arbitrary" links as the one the rhyme forces between epic craft and female cunning that show the connection and inscription of personal and cultural themes in the unconscious. *Don Juan* seems to me a little less rationally experimental, less scientifically instructive and more anarchic (as well as obsessive), than it appears in McGann's presentation. *DON JUAN in Context* is nonetheless the most penetrating discussion yet of the mode of the poem; that, starting from such different premises, my conclusions should often coincide with McGann's I wishfully interpret as corroboration of their general rightness.

20. James Engell and W. Jackson Bate, eds., *Biographia Literaria,* 2 vols. (Princeton: Princeton University Press, 1983), II, 55–56. Subsequent page references are incorporated in the text.

21. A. B. England has explored Byron's affinities with Butler and Swift

as well as the more commonly cited Pope and Fielding in *Byron's DON JUAN and Eighteenth-Century Literature* (Lewisburg, Penn.: Bucknell University Press, 1975).

22. See Max F. Schulz, *The Poetic Voices of Coleridge* (Detroit: Wayne State University Press, 1964), pp. 81, 179.

23. *Criterion* 18 (1939): 204–24, and rpt. in M. H. Abrams, ed., *English Romantic Poets: Modern Essays in Criticism* (New York: Oxford University Press, 1960), pp. 210–27. Bottrall answers Eliot by arguing that Byron's "interest was rather in the fundamental rhythmic movement of speech than in the word."

24. Given in the variorum *Don Juan,* IV, 4.

25. Ferdinand de Saussure, *Course in General Linguistics,* ed. Charles Bally, Albert Sechehaye, and Albert Riedlinger, tr. Wade Baskin (New York: McGraw-Hill, 1966), Chapter 3.

26. In an essay of that title, Roland Barthes locates "the structuralist activity" in the reconstruction of an object in order to show its rules of functioning (tr. Richard Howard, *Partisan Review* 34 [1967]: 82–88). The structuralist critic Barthes describes focuses not on the content of meanings but on the act of producing them: he "recreates the course taken by meaning, he need not designate it." A criticism based on these principles reveals virtues in Byron ignored by the still-prevailing organicist or apocalyptic camps.

27. "The Statesman's Manual," *Lay Sermons,* ed. R. J. White, *Collected Works of Samuel Taylor Coleridge,* Vol. VI (London: Routledge, 1972), p. 30.

28. Frank Kermode, *Romantic Image* (1957; rpt. New York: Random House-Vintage, 1964), p. 2.

29. Ruskin commented long ago on a conjunction between the proselike directness in Byron and the suggestive freedom he grants the reader. Observing that "He is the best poet who can by the fewest words touch the greatest number of secret chords of thought in the reader's own mind, and set *them* to work in their own way," Ruskin chooses as specific example a couplet from *The Siege of Corinth:*

> "'Tis midnight: on the mountains brown—The Pale round moon shines deeply down." Now the first eleven words are not poetry, except by their measure and preparation for rhyme; they are simple information, which might just as well have been given in prose—it is prose, in fact: It is twelve o'clock—the moon is pale—it is round—it is shining on brown mountains. Any fool, who had seen it, could tell us that. At last comes the poetry, in the single epithet, "deeply." Had he said "softly" or "brightly" it would still have been simple information. But of all the readers of that couplet, probably not two received exactly the same impression from the "deeply," and yet received more from that than from all the rest together. Some will refer the expression to the fall of the steep beams, and plunge down with them from rock to rock into the woody darkness of the cloven ravines, down to the undermost pool of eddying black water, whose echo is lost among their leafage; others will think of the deep *feeling* of the pure light, of the thousand memories and emotions that rise out of their

rest, and are seen white and cold in its rays. This is the reason of the
power of the single epithet, and this is its *mystery*.

Quoted in *Byron: The Critical Heritage,* ed. Andrew Rutherford (New
York: Barnes and Noble, 1970), pp. 426–27.

30. See, for example, Donald Reiman's forceful brief essay, *"Don Juan*
in Epic Context," *Studies in Romanticism* 16 (1977): 587–94.

7

The Nameless Broken Dandy and the Structure of Authorship

For Francis Jeffrey, writing in *The Edinburgh Review* in 1818 an appropriately unsigned notice of an anonymously published poem narrated by "a nameless sort of person, / (A broken Dandy lately on [his] travels" (st. 52),[1] Byron's *Beppo* was "absolutely a thing of nothing."[2] For Jerome McGann and other modern critics, it is "probably the most crucial single work in the entire canon."[3] At once trivial and critical to that trajectory of a name that we call a career, *Beppo* presents a series of paradoxes which begin and end with the authorless status of its first appearance.[4]

To set this nothing in perspective it is useful to consider an earlier instance of play between the naming *in,* and the anonymity *of,* a text: Byron's outburst of disappointment at the abdication in April 1814 of that other figure who signed himself NB, not so much his alter ego as his alter image, in whom he saw his reflection and with whom he was joined in popular view as the type of the Promethean genius.[5] The *Ode to Napoleon Buonaparte,* which Byron wrote in heat and Murray published with speed to capitalize on sensational news, opens:

> 'Tis done—but yesterday a King!
> And arm'd with Kings to strive—
> And now thou art a nameless thing
> So abject—yet alive!
> Is this the man of thousand thrones,

145

Who strew'd our Earth with hostile bones,
   And can he thus survive?
Since he, miscall'd the Morning Star,
Nor man nor fiend hath fall'n so far.

The failure of his hero nobly to have committed suicide fuels Byron's indignation: by preserving his life, Napoleon has paradoxically destroyed his name. As Lucifer was "miscalled" the Morning Star, so the judgments of those who praised Napoleon are exposed by his craven conduct. In a journal-entry Byron confessed that he was "utterly bewildered and confounded," and the threat to his own identity produced a dispersal of voices notable even in his habitually echoing prose. In the space of a page, Byron invokes Otway's *Venice Preserved;* Shakespeare's *Antony and Cleopatra, Hamlet,* and *Macbeth;* Juvenal's and Johnson's "Vanity of Human Wishes"; Milo; Sylla; Charles V; Amurath; and Dionysius at Corinth. Many of these found their way into the *Ode* (*BLJ,* III, 256–57). Byron, however, was wrong: Napoleon sought exactly the exchange of life for name Byron wished of him. Although Byron had already written his poem and did not know it, Napoleon attempted to poison himself on April 12 but survived.[6] That the apparent revelation of intrinsic character was thus based on a mistake only emphasizes the mirroring circuit in which the "name" is suspended.

   Once the *Ode to Napoleon Buonaparte* passed from the poet to his publisher the names of both Byron and Napoleon were governed by the laws, commercial and legal, of trade. Byron's instructions to Murray reveal the various conventions upon which authorship depends. Byron sent the poem as a gift on April 10, telling Murray that he "might print it or not as you please"; later the same day, he added that "if deemed worth printing" it should be *"without* a name," but admitted that he had "no objection to it's [*sic*] being *said* to be mine." The diffidence was a polite fiction: Byron knew that the topicality of the subject and the celebrity of the author ensured publication, and Murray knew that Byron wanted it, providing him proofs within a day. These Byron immediately corrected and returned, reiterating that "[i]t will be best *not* to put my name to our Ode but you may *say* openly that it is mine": speech thus permitted authorship to be known and profited from while not yet acknowledged. "[W]e will incorporate it in the first *tome* of ours that you find time or the wish to publish," Byron told Murray; as the repeated use of "our" indicates, copyright fixed authorship in the exchange of author and publisher (*BLJ,* IV, 94).[7]

Even as Byron and the *Ode* float within the *"channel* of publication" (*BLJ,* IV, 104), so within the poem the representation of Napoleon, once seated upon "The throne of the world" (*BLJ,* III, 256), was shaped by the tax code. Finding that the early editions of the *Ode* were subject to the stamp duty levied on pamphlets of less than a sheet, Murray requested further stanzas. Byron complied, furnishing three more, though displeased with them; the addition of the current fifth stanza to the third edition, however, seems to have served the purpose, and the new stanzas were never used in Byron's lifetime. Subsequently, in spite of Byron's expressed desire that they be omitted, they became the conclusion of the received text.[8] Editors and regulations motivated as much by political censorship as revenue considerations thus triumphed over Napoleon and Byron, the exemplars of Romantic will.

I begin my chapter on *Beppo* with this episode because it suggests the interplay of authorship with the conditions of production and replaces the static opposition between the proper name and anonymity with a fluid continuum. In the *Ode* Byron had loftily consigned Napoleon to Elba: "Then haste thee to thy sullen Isle, / And gaze upon the sea" (st. 14). Self-exiled from England, Byron, after a brief stay in Switzerland, made for Venice, "as it has always been (next to the East) the greenest island of my imagination" (*BLJ,* V, 129). Pleasurable as Venice was, Byron disclosed a melancholy truth in fashioning a narrator who describes himself as a nameless, broken dandy. The scandal of the separation had ended Byron's reign as the darling of Whig society, and *Manfred* and the third and fourth cantos of *Childe Harold* had won not a name but notoriety.

Beppo is anonymous in a deeper sense as well. As critics rightly observe, it marks the pivot in Byron's turn on the Romantic excesses of his generation. He repeated to Moore in 1818 what he had told Murray in 1817: "I . . . said, that I thought—except [Crabbe and Rogers]—all of *'us youth'* were on the wrong tack" (*BLJ,* VI, 10). Moore shrewdly saw this deprecation as a tactic to confirm his own eminence: "being quite sure of his own hold upon fame he contrives to loosen that of all his contemporaries, in order that they may fall away entirely from his side, and leave him unencumbered, even by their floundering."[9] Indeed, a manifesto that alludes to the ceaselessly devious Falstaff does not so much clarify as fruitfully mystify Byron's poetic program. If Byron declared "I certainly am a devil of a mannerist—& must leave off" (*BLJ,* V, 185), he sought to escape the style that had brought him fame only to devise another that would extend his grip on the public. Some reviewers, unaware of the authorship of *Beppo,* took it as a satire on Byron, which indeed it was, but the new Byron to succeed the repudiated one would be not the true voice of feeling so much as it was another modulation in the relations existing between the historical Byron, his reading, his publisher, and the audience and critics of this and his prior texts. The emerging self of *Beppo* (and subsequently of *Don Juan*) evolved within a network that enabled the expatriate Byron to remake his name even as it restricted how he could do so. *Beppo* is a text in which the issue of anonymity is primary, not accidental.

I overstate the case in order to contrast it to a biographical reading of the poem. In 1968 Jerome McGann asserted, "Everything in *Beppo* orbits around Byron; it is the figure of Byron, both as an artist and (more importantly) as a human being, which determines both the form and significance of the details."[10] In an excellent introduction to his edition of the manuscript, McGann in 1986 still argues that "The tale is [Byron's] vehicle for transmitting what is essentially a very personal poem."[11] I should like to invert the terms: the self acquires its image—not its essence—by telling tales that negotiate or, to use a more Byronic term, navigate impersonal structures.

Byron came to speak in the voice of *Beppo* by a series of mediations. He happily credited W. S. Rose and John Hookham Frere's *The Monks and the Giants* with having displayed for him the possibilities of the *ottava rima* stanza, and through them he returned to the Italian originals of the style, many of whom he knew already: Pulci, Berni, Casti.[12] If the chivalric romance that the pseudonymous Whistlecrafts had put forward was *A Prospectus and Specimen of an Intended National Work,* Byron's elaborately artificial Italian comedy might well seem its anti-national antipodes. Such stanzas as those on the suspension of Habeas Corpus (sts. 47–49) illustrate why Byron told Murray that *Beppo* had "politics & ferocity, & won't do for your Isthmus of a Journal," the conservative *Quarterly Review* (*BLJ,* VI, 9), but the poem's manner was itself read politically, as the denunciation of Byron's "cosmopolitan liberality" in the notice of *The British Review* attests. Declaring that *Beppo* came "reeking from the stews of Venice," William Roberts connected it to the growth "of a denationalizing spirit" in English society since the French Revolution, a symptom of the "decay of that masculine decency, and sobriety, and soundness of sentiment, which, about half a century ago, made us dread the contagion of French or Italian manners."[13] From the smug center of British chauvinism where he locates himself Roberts astutely specifies Byron's allegiances, and the association of suspect politics with gender impropriety is one to explore further.

Two triangles map the contours of *Beppo:* that of Laura, the Count, and Beppo *in* the poem, and that formed *outside* it by the poet, the poem, and his audience. The outer one inflects the plot which it encloses—as digression overwhelms narrative—because, as W. P. Elledge has argued in a brilliant essay, Byron's eye remains anxiously on the England from which he had parted.[14] Nothing better illustrates the apparently merely arbitrary constellations through which self-representation is composed than the treatment of William Sotheby.[15]

Byron finished a first draft of *Beppo* in eighty-four stanzas on October 10, 1817; to that matrix he added in the next two weeks five stanzas expanding his attack on "bustling Botherby" and his coterie of bluestockings. I quote the first, in which Byron cites the absence of a Botherby as a special advantage of the confinement to which Turkish women are subject:

> No solemn, antique gentleman of rhyme,
>> Who having angled all his life for fame,
> And getting but a nibble at a time,
>> Still fussily keeps fishing on, the same
> Small "Triton of the minnows," the sublime
>> Of mediocrity, the furious tame,
> The echo's echo, usher of the school
> Of female wits, boy bards—in short, a fool![16]

In his very lack of necessary relationship to the story of *Beppo* and seemingly fortuitous arrival in the text Sotheby focuses the literary dynamics that the poem exposes. The previous spring in Rome Byron had received what he called "a scurvy *anonymous* letter" together with a marginally annotated copy of the Italian edition of his *Prisoner of Chillon* volume. "The dog" might have been "right enough" to judge "that out of ten things—eight were good for nothing," Byron told Murray, but the anonymity of the letter incensed him. Such unauthored, or unauthorized, criticism Byron took to violate "all the courtesies of life & literature": "he should put his name to a note—a man may *print* anonymously—but not write letters so" (*BLJ,* VI, 24, rearranged).

The distinction Byron draws between the codes of (private) life and (public) literature, between presence and text, however, collapsed. Murray evidently mentioned the lampoon to Sotheby, who denied responsibility for the incident that produced it. "As Mr. S says that he did not write this letter &c I am ready to believe him," Byron conceded to Murray, but the statement of the man was outweighed by the evidence of the text. Byron enumerated his reasons for having believed in Sotheby's authorship:

> firstly—similarity in the handwriting . . . 2dly. the *Style*—more especially the word "Effulgence" a phrase which clinched my conjecture as decisively as any coincidence between Francis & Junius—3dly. the paucity of English *then* at Rome . . . 4thly. my being aware of Mr S[otheby]'s patronage & anxiety on such occasions which led me to the belief that with very good intentions—he might nevertheless blunder in his mode of giving as well as taking opinions—& 5thly. the Devil who made Mr. S[otheby] one author and me another.

Despite Sotheby's explicit disclaimer Byron refused to retract his stanzas, and in so persisting he made clear that acts of interpretation, not intentional origins, affix a text to an author.

Byron continued:

> As to Beppo I will not alter or suppress a syllable for any man's pleasure but my own—if there are resemblances between Botherby & Sotheby or Sotheby and Botherby the fault is not mine—but in the person who resembles—or the persons who trace a resemblance.—Who find out this resemblance?—Mr. S[otheby]'s *friends—who* go about moaning over him & laughing? Mr. S's *friends*—whatever allusions Mr. S may imagine—or whatever may or may not really exist in the passages in question—I can assure him—that there is not a literary man or a pretender to Literature—or a reader of the day—in the World of London—who does not think & express more obnoxious opinions of his Blue-stocking Mummeries than are to be found in print— (*BLJ,* VI, 35)

This disingenuous apologia re-emphasizes the location of identity outside the self: Sotheby is Botherby if his friends say so. The identification "may or may not really exist" in *Beppo:* Byron disavows his intention while affirming it. The anonymous letter, denied by its putative author; the anonymous poem, written in English in Italian style; behind the fictional Botherby, the proper name Sotheby (but how,

exactly?); behind the nameless narrator, Byron (but how, exactly?)—
the figures and texts circulate, cut off from authors, among "literary
men" and "pretenders to Literature."

Sotheby is also a point at which the triangles inside and outside
the poem touch. The links may be seen as well in the tandem development of the ten stanzas Byron added to the original eighty-four-
stanza matrix of his poem. Five are the description of Botherby, one
the description of the speaker as "a nameless sort of person, / (A
broken Dandy lately on my travels)" (st. 52), and two an expansion
in the description of Laura's lover, the Count:

> He patroniz'd the Improvisatori,
>   Nay, could himself extemporize some stanzas,
> Wrote rhymes, sang songs, could also tell a story,
>   Sold pictures, and was skilful in the dance as
> Italians can be, though in this their glory
>   Must surely yield the palm to that which France has;
> In short, he was a perfect cavaliero,
> And to his very valet seem'd a hero.
>
> Then he was faithful, too, as well as amorous,
>   So that no sort of female could complain,
> Although they're now and then a little clamorous,
>   He never put the pretty souls in pain;
> His heart was one of those which most enamour us,
>   Wax to receive, and marble to retain.
> He was a lover of the good old school,
> Who still become more constant as they cool.
>
> (sts. 33–34)

Botherby in the midst of "Blue-stocking Mummeries" and the dilet-
tante Count, whose " 'bravo' was decisive, for that sound / Hushed
'academie' sighed in silent awe" (st. 32) but who waits docilely on
Laura, are alike visions of the man of letters reduced to what Byron
calls a "supernumerary slave, who stays / Close to the lady as a part
of dress" (st. 40), a "piece of female property" (*BLJ,* VII, 28).

Byron's unease on this score is a repeated theme of his Italian
years; what particularly matters here is an unacknowledged kinship
between the Italian and English sites of the story. *Beppo* proceeds by
contrasting Italian and English society, but at the point where they
touch such binary oppositions disclose a muted equivalence. Let us
return to the added stanzas on Botherby:

A stalking oracle of awful phrase,
  The approving *"Good!"* (by no means GOOD in law)
Humming like flies around the newest blaze,
  The bluest of bluebottles you e'er saw,
Teasing with blame, excruciating with praise,
  Gorging the little fame he gets all raw,
Translating tongues he knows not even by letter,
And sweating plays so middling, bad were better.

One hates an author that's *all author,* fellows
  In foolscap uniforms turned up with ink,
So very anxious, clever, fine and jealous,
  One don't know what to say to them, or think,
Unless to puff them with a pair of bellows;
  Of coxcombry's worst coxcombs even the pink
Are preferable to these shreds of paper,
These unquenched snuffings of the midnight taper.

Of these same we see several, and of others,
  Men of the world, who know the world like men,
S[co]tt, R[oger]s, M[oo]re, and all the better brothers,
  Who think of something else besides the pen;
But for the children of the "mighty mother's,"
  The would-be wits and can't-be gentlemen,
I leave them to their daily "tea is ready,"
Smug coterie, and literary lady.

                                        (sts. 74–76)

    Botherby is savaged on two related but distinguishable grounds.
The first is that of gender: Botherby is excoriated for his effeminizing
absorption—like the Count—in a circle of women, against which
Byron sets a vision of male bonding, allying himself firmly with "all
the better brothers." The second is rather an issue of the professionalization of literature: Botherby is *all author,* a man of letters who
translates Latin and German, writes poems, produces dramas, and
publishes tours. Against this image of career Byron sets himself as
one of the aristocratic amateurs, "Men of the world, who know the
world like men."
    The two charges overlap, and their conjunction is revealing.
These stanzas merge effeminization with professionalization, and
Byron was acutely and ambivalently aware that his reputation with
women had contributed greatly to the commercial success of *Childe
Harold's Pilgrimage* and the Turkish tales. One illustration, discussed

elsewhere in this book, is the brouhaha over the publication of *Stanzas to a Lady Weeping*. On January 22, 1814, Murray reported to Byron Gifford's opinion that "you ought to slip [the verses] quietly amongst the Poems in 'Childe Harold' " rather than annex them to *The Corsair*, where Byron intended them, because the tale "is to be read by women, and it would disturb the poetical feeling."[17] Not for nothing did Murray produce engravings of his handsome poet, a lord yet exotic, for purchasers to bind into their volumes of Byron's work, or urge him "to resume my old *'Corsair* style, to please the ladies,' " as Byron told Shelley in Italy. To Shelley's warm contempt for such pecuniary considerations Byron replied: "John Murray is right, if not righteous: all I have yet written has been for women-kind: you must wait until I am forty, their influence will then die a natural death, and I will show the men what I can do."[18]

"I have not written to please the women or the common people," Byron declared in the rush of popularity after the publication of *Childe Harold*, and the convoluted connections between gender, writing, and audience animate *Beppo*. To put it schematically: if professionalization is equated with the feminine, then Byron must doubly dissemble the literary venture, the attempt to establish his name on a new basis, that *Beppo* represents. The easy conversational manner upon which every reader has remarked needs to be understood against the structures of publication that it masks. Donning the pose of one who even from Italy knows more of the sayings of the London literati than Murray or Sotheby, Byron affirms his membership in the world from which he had parted; at the same time, dismissing Botherby and the bluestockings, Byron proclaims his masculine independence and denies his implication in the motives that drive professional authors.[19]

This strategy produces complex tensions, because the chat that obscures the trial of the market upon which Byron and Murray were embarked is another term for gossip—and gossip is traditionally associated with women.[20] If to characterize the inclusiveness with which *Don Juan* surveys the Europe of Byron's times Jerome McGann titles a recent essay "The Book of Byron and the Book of a World,"[21] I might perhaps indicate the miniature world of *Beppo* with an epigram from Rousseau scornfully cited by Mary Wollstonecraft in *A Vindication of the Rights of Woman:* "The world is the book of women."[22] *Beppo* springs from a sexual anecdote, drawing us in with the fascination always exerted by "sinful doings" (st. 41), and swirling outward toward the comparative discussion of national *mores.*

In renouncing his magniloquent style in *Beppo* Byron also renounced heroism, or rather shrank it to the dimensions of the clever pun:

> Crush'd was Napoleon by the northern Thor,
>> Who knock'd his army down with icy hammer,
> Stopp'd by the *elements,* like a whaler, or
>> A blundering novice in his new French grammar;
>>>> (st. 61)

Heroism is not merely absent from the world of *Beppo* but rather thus deliberately excluded. The poem shifts from north to south, public to private, honor to shame (or at least scandal), from consolidating masculine power to the plural and the insinuating. In Canto 3 of *Childe Harold's Pilgrimage* Byron had portrayed Napoleon as the figure of antithetical extremes who disrupts the Aristotelean ethical mean; the "new French grammar" Napoleon wrote in making himself emperor, however, in turn yields to the elements not so much of nature as of Byron's own mocking linguistic facility. In place of the fatal determinism of the Byronic hero, there is the unfettered digressiveness of anecdote. This language is the weapon of the powerless, perhaps capable of achieving what masculine will cannot, perhaps only capable of reassuring those at the margins, as Byron in Italy was, of their freedom to comment. Unlike *Childe Harold's Pilgrimage* and the tales, concerned to impose on their audience the single, unique, dominant Byronic hero, the language of *Beppo*—not without, given Byron's withdrawal from England, a certain pathos—elaborates a community. The English "you" with which the narrator addresses and marks his distance from his readers plays off against integrating usages: "One of those forms which flit by us" (st. 13); "and really if a man won't let us know / That he's alive, he's *dead,* or should be so" (st. 35), "Our standing army, and disbanded seamen" (st. 49); and so forth. This presumption of agreement simultaneously creates a microcosm against the larger world and serves as the go-between of the private and public worlds.

Much as William Roberts became alarmed by the "decay of masculine decency" *Beppo* witnesses, so Francis Jeffrey, describing its style as "loquacious prattling" and "gay and desultory babbling," recognized Byron's intimate, easy language of intrigue and fashion as an appropriation from the opposite gender as society stereotypes it. The passing fancy of a pensioned "missionary author" to teach the harem-bound "poor dear Mussulwomen" "Our Christian usage of the parts of speech" (st. 77, rearranged) is one condescending imagining in the poem of a language of and for women; a richer one is the description of Laura:

> Laura, when drest, was (as I sang before)
>   A pretty woman as was ever seen,
> Fresh as the Angel o'er a new inn door,
>   Or frontispiece of a new Magazine,
> With all the fashions which the last month wore,
>   Coloured, and silver paper leav'd between
> That and the title-page, for fear the press
> Should soil with parts of speech the parts of dress.
>   (st. 57)

Byron's own similes of inn and magazine soil Laura by implicating her in the world of commerce, but at the same time they mark the milieu his writing also inhabits and turn us back to those female readers of magazines who shaped his success.

The virulence of Byron's attack on Sotheby and the bluestockings is a reflex of the anxious fantasy at play in Byron's otherwise pleasurable immersion in Venice: a fear that the male self is rendered precarious by the power of the woman-dominated society of salons and *cavaliere servente* for which Laura stands in the poem, and that of the audience of women readers outside it. Though the "nameless broken Dandy" is undeniably male, "broken" suggests a ruin beyond the financial, an impotence at once sexual and political. Consider, for instance, the proliferation of feminine rhyme (as in the stanzas on the Count [e.g., sts. 31–34]) in that self-description:

> But I am but a nameless sort of person
>   (A broken Dandy lately on my travels)
> And take for rhyme, to hook my rambling verse on,
>   The first that Walker's Lexicon unravels,
> And when I can't find that, I put a worse on,
>   Not caring as I ought for critics' cavils;
> I've half a mind to tumble down to prose,
> But verse is more in fashion—so here goes.
>   (st. 52)

Or consider the difficulty of placing Byron's praise of Italian:

> I love the language, that soft bastard Latin,
>   Which melts like kisses from a female mouth,
> And sounds as if it should be writ on satin,
>   With syllables which breathe of the sweet South,
> And gentle liquids gliding all so pat in,
>   That not a single accent seems uncouth,
> Like our harsh northern whistling, grunting guttural,
> Which we're obliged to hiss, and spit, and sputter all.
>
>   (st. 44)

If the very next stanza, beginning "I like the women too," asserts a traditional masculine identity, nonetheless Byron speaks a language throughout *Beppo* that repeatedly emulates that "[w]hich melts like kisses from a female mouth." "His heart was one of those which most enamour us," the narrator says of the Count in the added stanza quoted above, seeming momentarily to cross the border between genders and slip into identification with women and the oddly unstable sexuality of "amorous / clamorous / enamour us" (st. 34). The more Byron disguises the authorial venture through his amateurish and gossipy pose, in short, the more his narrator verges on the feminine he scorns.

Yet analysis of this persona in terms of Byron's psychology, even of the bisexuality persuasively set forth by Louis Crompton,[23] should be contained within acknowledgment of the setting of *Beppo* at the time of Carnival. As the opening stanzas repeatedly insist, Carnival is a ritual of mask and masquerade, when "you may put on whate'er you like" (st. 5), and the shifting of identities it fosters Byron brings home to his readers by likening it to "Mrs. Boehm's masquerade" (st. 56) and comparing "the Ridotto" to "our Vauxhall" (st. 58). Carnival is the privileged moment of transgression, and, as Terry Castle has recently argued, the more complexly the assumed costume disrupts the usual sexual and hierarchical roles of its wearer, the more the opportunities for equivocation multiply. The transformation of Beppo into a Turk is less salient, and less disturbing, than Byron's own travesty. William Roberts's denunciation of the poem has a long history in the moralistic condemnation of such ambiguous and promiscuous events.[24]

To argue that beneath this voice we always hear Byron the Improviser is to beg the question of why this voice at this time. I suggest instead that the peculiarly suspended quality of *Beppo,* its focus hovering in the pairing of England and Italy, its nameless, sexually evasive narrator negotiating through his own verbal skill the engulfing power of women and the male violence lurking in the allusions to Othello, Macbeth, and Odysseus returning to slaughter the suitors, corresponds to a Byron wishing to remake his poetic identity and uncertain of the forces outside him that would determine it.

At the close of the poem Byron re-establishes the traditional sexual roles he has put into play by the treatment meted out to Laura.[25] If it is the traditional place of women to be silent, obedient, and chaste, Laura is none of these; indeed, in choosing a lover she has seized the masculine prerogative and reversed the exchange of women on which society is based. Laura wards off any embarrassing conflict between returning husband and faithful *cavalier servente* by her irrepressible curiosity about Beppo's foreign experience, but such defusion by language sounds the knell of male heroism, and Byron moves swiftly to subordinate her. Beppo, the narrator says, "threw off the garments which disguised him" and is rebaptized, restoring everyone to his and her "proper" place. In a gesture that realizes the male bonding against which Botherby has been set, Beppo "borrow[s] the Count's small-clothes for a day" (st. 98), and the final vision shows Laura trivialized and the men united:

> Whate'er his youth had suffered, his old age
>   With wealth and talking made him some amends;
> Though Laura sometimes put him in a rage,
>   I've heard the Count and he were always friends.
>   (st. 99)

This tableau nonetheless leaves unsettled the tensions of the poem. Laura functions all too evidently as the necessary link between the men, a link whose necessity explains the ensuing necessity to deny her importance. The uneasy secret is still visible: the male bond passes through women. Whatever we say about Byron the man here, for Byron the poet the audience of women remains inescapable, the clear distinction between himself and Sotheby, already breached in the similarities of Botherby and the broken dandy, impossible to maintain. Within the poem Byron exits by reminding us that he stands above the "nothing" he has narrated, fixing his priority to his story in a series of first-person clauses: *"He* said that *Providence* protected him— / For my part, I say nothing" (st. 96); "trading /

With goods of various names, but I've forgot 'em" (st. 97); "dinners, where he oft became the laugh of them, / For stories,—but *I* don't believe the half of them" (st. 99); culminating in the final indifference, "I've heard the Count and he were always friends" (st. 99). The function of *Beppo* was to kindle interest in a "Byron" different from those before seen, to intrigue readers into purchasing this new mode. By such explicit concluding gestures, Byron signaled that interest was to be focused not on his tale but on him, and on "his pen at the bottom of a page" (st. 99), the material agent of translation that makes of the book we buy a passport to an imagined authorial and richly oral presence. As Ross Chambers has suggested, such embedded reminders of the situation of the storyteller are characteristic of the new nineteenth-century conditions of literature in which the writer could only speculate on his distant and unknown audience.[26] With direct communication deferred, Byron in Italy had to resort to arts of seduction uneasily like Laura's, and such wiles remain vulnerable: his aloofness to his story within *Beppo* apotropaically mimes that of the readers without, who might prove as immune to his charms.

The appeal of the name thus forms the salient question, and ir *Beppo* only Byron will possess one. Beppo gives his to the tale, but as Byron told Murray in an appropriately belittling parenthesis, it is only a common diminutive, "(the short name for Giuseppe—that is the *Joe* of the Italian Joseph)" (*BLJ*, V, 269); the Count is merely "the Count"; Laura owes her name ostensibly to Byron's metrical convenience:

> A certain lady went to see the show,
>   Her real name I know not, nor can guess
> And so we'll call her Laura, if you please,
> Because it slips into my verse with ease.
>
> (st. 21)

Despite this parade of freedom, the new name the success of *Beppo* won for Byron enmeshed him in the institution of literature that he scornfully epitomized in Botherby/Sotheby. Murray published *Beppo* in February 1818, Byron having thrown in the copyright with Canto IV of *Childe Harold* "to help you round to your money" (*BLJ*, V, 269). The sublime style and the colloquial style that inverted it were all one on Murray's ledgers. Byron's name first appeared on the fifth edition, already reached in April, but the acknowledgment reflected a weighing of commercial gain against fears of suit from Sotheby. "If you think that it will do *you* or the work—or *works* any good," Byron wrote Murray, "—you may—or may not put my name to it—*but first consult the knowing ones;*—it will at any rate shew them—that I can write cheerfully, & repel the charge of monotony and mannerism" (*BLJ,* VI, 25). Murray, no fool when it came to calculating where his interest lay, replied: "I have heard no word more from Mr. Sotheby; and as to my having ventured upon any alteration or omission, I should as soon have scooped one of my eyes out."[27]

If the reception won by his new production redefined Byron's name, so his name reciprocally guaranteed that the transformation would be noticed; in its review, the *Monthly Magazine* commented that it "should have passed over [*Beppo*] had not his lordship's signature commanded our attention."[28] Thus did Byron's publisher seal the new course of Byron's name; the aristocratic title remained implicated in, and dependent upon, the balance sheets of the book trade.

The matter does not quite end there. In a revision of the agreement for the sum to be paid for *Beppo,* Murray suggested to Byron that the copyright "cancel all former bookselling accounts between us *up* to that period" (*BLJ,* IX, 84). The transaction was a fitting one: in exchange for the books Murray had furnished Byron, the highly literary manuscript from which he made further profits. The cycle continued. "I have finished the First Canto (a long one, of about 180 octaves) of a poem in the style and manner of 'Beppo,'" Byron wrote Murray six months later, "encouraged by the good success of the same" (*BLJ,* VI, 67). Success produced success, and a new project, which would rewrite the Byronic self and extend the partnership—until, scandalized by *Don Juan* and *Cain,* Murray withdrew, and Byron's name became Hunt's. But that is another essay.

Notes

1. All quotations from Byron's poetry are from *Lord Byron: The Complete Poetical Works,* ed. Jerome J. McGann (Oxford: Clarendon, 1980–). Hereafter cited as *PW.*

2. *Edinburgh Review* 29 (February 1818), as quoted in *Byron: The Critical Heritage,* ed. Andrew Rutherford (New York: Barnes and Noble, 1970), p. 122.

3. Jerome McGann, in *Shelley and His Circle 1773–1822,* Vol. VII, ed.

Donald H. Reiman (Cambridge, Mass.: Harvard University Press, 1986), p. 247.

4. Readers will recognize here and throughout my indebtedness to Jerome Christensen, "Byron's Career: The Speculative Stage," *English Literary History* 52 (1985): 59–84.

5. One example of many, apposite here: in April 1817 Byron wrote to deny the assertion of an essay in a Venetian newspaper, purportedly translated from the Literary Gazette of Jena, that Napoleon was the protagonist of *Childe Harold III* "under a fictitious name." Byron declared that "Buonaparte is not the protagonist of the poem under any name," but the page he required to explain his attitudes suggests that if the essay was undeniably wrong, literally, it was right figuratively. *Byron's Letters and Journals*, ed. Leslie A. Marchand, Vol. V (Cambridge, Mass.: Harvard University Press, 1976), pp. 201–2. The volumes of this series, begun in 1973, are hereafter cited parenthetically in the text as *BLJ*.

6. See Felix Markham, *Napoleon and the Awakening of Europe* (New York: Collier, 1965), p. 126.

7. Not until the tenth edition did the *Ode* appear with Byron's name on it (*PW*, III, 456).

8. See *PW*, III, 456.

9. *The Journal of Thomas Moore*, ed. Wilfred S. Dowden, Vol. II (Newark: University of Delaware Press, 1985), p. 448.

10. Jerome McGann, *Fiery Dust: Byron's Poetic Development* (Chicago: University of Chicago Press, 1968), p. 288.

11. *Shelley and His Circle*, VII, 246.

12. See Peter Vassallo, *Byron: The Italian Literary Influence* (New York: St. Martin's Press, 1984).

13. *British Review* 11 (May 1818): 327–33, quoted in *The Romantics Reviewed*, ed. Donald Reiman (New York: Garland, 1972), Part B, 1:456.

14. W. Paul Elledge, "Divorce Italian Style: Byron's *Beppo*," *Modern Language Quarterly* 46 (1985): 154–64.

15. Frederick L. Beaty compactly narrates the relations of Byron and Sotheby lying behind *Beppo* in Chapter 4 of his *Byron the Satirist* (DeKalb: Northern Illinois University Press, 1985).

16. This is stanza 73 of the Clarendon text; for the compositional history of the poem, see the apparatus to that edition; Vol. VII of *Shelley and His Circle;* and T. G. Steffan, "The Devil a Bit of Our *Beppo*," *Philological Quarterly*, 32 (1953): 154–71, who first analyzed the Pierpont Morgan manuscript and from whom I take the term "matrix." The "bustling Botherby" of the manuscripts became "bustling Botherbys" in the first edition, which Byron let stand; thus, printer's errors, or publisher's caution, turn individuals to plural.

17. Samuel Smiles, *A Publisher and His Friends: Memoir and Correspondence of the Late John Murray*, 2d ed. (London: John Murray, 1891), I, 211. See Thilo von Bremen, *Lord Byron als Erfolgsautor*, Athenaion Literaturwissenschaft, Band 6 (Wiesbaden: Athenaion, 1977), p. 191.

18. *Recollections* of E. J. Trelawny, quoted in *His Very Self and Voice*, ed. Ernest J. Lovell (New York: Macmillan, 1954), p. 267. In "Women and the Romantic Author—The Case of Byron," Sonia Hofkosh observes that

Byron's "literary career is also the chronicle of a love affair," in which "the woman in the romance enacts the marketplace forces that contest the writer's exclusive claim to his work." *Romanticism and Feminism*, ed. Anne K. Mellor (Bloomington: Indiana University Press, 1988), pp. 93–114.

19. The third term of the identification "Count → Botherby," which Byron was at pains to suppress, is Byron himself, as "Presbyter Anglicanus" shrewdly pointed out in *Blackwood's Magazine* 3 (June 1818: 323–29: "We look below the disguise which has once been lifted, and claim acquaintance, not with the sadness of the princely masque, but with the scoffing and sardonic merriment of the ill-dissembling reveller beneath it. In evil hour did you step from your vantage-ground, and teach us that Harold, Byron, and the Count of *Beppo* are the same." Quoted in *Byron: The Critical Heritage*, ed. Andrew Rutherford (New York: Barnes and Noble, 1970), p. 129.

20. See Patricia Meyer Spacks, *Gossip* (New York: Knopf, 1985).

21. *The Beauty of Inflections* (Oxford: Clarendon, 1985), pp. 255–93.

22. *A Vindication of the Rights of Woman*, ed. Carol H. Poston (New York, Norton: 1976), p. 39.

23. *Byron and Greek Love* (Berkeley: University of California Press, 1985).

24. Terry Castle, *Masquerade and Civilization: The Carvivalesque in Eighteenth-Century English Culture and Fiction* (Stanford: Stanford University Press, 1986). I have also learned from Eve Kosofsky Sedgwick, *Between Men: English Literature and Male Homosocial Desire* (New York: Columbia University Press, 1985).

25. For a shrewd study of Byron's ultimately restabilizing playing with gender, see Susan J. Wolfson, " 'Their she condition': Cross-dressing and the Politics of Gender in *Don Juan*," *ELH* 54 (1987): 585–617. An instance particularly germane to *Beppo* is the "[Epistle to Mr Murray]" which follows it in Jerome McGann's Oxford Authors edition of Byron (Oxford: Oxford University Press, 1986). Written as a verse letter to Murray on January 8, 1818, its last three stanzas recall the conclusion of *Beppo* but display the relation of writing to women that Byron was concerned to establish *in propria persona*:

> Now, I'll put out my taper
> (I've finished my paper
>   For these stanzas you see on the *brink* stand)
> There's a whore on my right
> For I rhyme best at Night
>   When a C–t is tied close to *my Inkstand*.
>
> It was Mahomet's notion
> *That* comical motion
>   Increased his "devotion in prayer"—
> If that tenet holds good
> In a Prophet, it should
>   In poet be equally fair.—
>
> For, in rhyme or in love
> (Which both come from above)

I'll stand with our *"Tommy"* or *"Sammy"*)
But the Sopha and lady
Are both of them ready
And so, here's "Good Night to you dammee!"

26. Ross Chambers, *Story and Situation: Narrative Seduction and the Power of Fiction* (Minneapolis: University of Minnesota Press, 1984).
27. Smiles, *A Publisher and His Friends,* I, 394. Letter of June 16, 1818.
28. *The Romantics Reviewed,* ed. Reiman, Part B, 4:1671.

III
Texts and Contexts

8

The White Doe of Rylstone,
The Convention of Cintra,
and the History of a Career

The story of how Wordsworth delayed publishing *The White Doe of Rylstone,* finished in 1807–08, until 1815 is familiar. The received account runs like this: the poem represented Wordsworth's effort to transform materials from the north of England and the borders, the stuff of romance and ballad which Sir Walter Scott had mined so successfully, into an exemplum of imagination and faith, but the poem proved too spiritual and lacking in adventure for those who heard or read the manuscript—Coleridge, Lamb, Hazlitt, Jane Marshall—and, discouraged, Wordsworth kept it back. The recent Cornell edition by Kristine Dugas persuasively reconstructs the "lost" version of 1807–08 but tells essentially the same story about the delay.[1] These explanations are largely Wordsworth's own, and criticism has rather too quickly accepted Wordsworth's defensive claim for the superiority of his mode. Against this narrative I should like to set another one. I want to suggest that *The White Doe,* however it may transform popular narrative, was at least in inception an attempt to capitalize on that genre, and that we should not overlook the temptations to which Wordsworth, as an impecunious and badly reviewed author, was subject. The letters show that had *The White Doe* succeeded, Wordsworth intended to follow it with *Peter Bell* and *The Waggoner,* also finished this early but not published until 1819. Secondly, I want to speculate that the reasons for not publishing *The White Doe* are not wholly to be found in the poem itself but are to be sought in the political climate of 1808.

I

In June 1807, on their way back from Coleorton, the Beaumont property where they had been residing, the Wordsworths stopped at New Grange to visit with John and Jane Pollard Marshall. Jane Pollard had been Dorothy's school friend; her husband was a wealthy linen manufacturer, eventually the acknowledged head of the Leeds flax-spinning industry. A dissenter, who helped Edward Baines establish the Leeds *Mercury* as the leading organ of Whig entrepreneurial opinion, and an associate of Brougham, with whom he shared an enlightened Benthamite commitment to education, Marshall was in many ways the epitome of that new class of mill owners and international capitalists who were anathema to Wordsworth. The families nonetheless remained firm friends. Wordsworth's Irish tour of 1829 was made in the company of Marshall, who was then prospecting for new business to offset declining profits, and in 1832 Wordsworth advised him in the purchase of a magnificent estate at Derwentwater for his son. In 1807 John Marshall was already visibly embarked on the spectacular rise that won him a fortune estimated on his death in 1845 at between one and a half and two and a half million pounds and carried his children into landholding society in the Lake District and eminent marriages. New Grange, the substantial residence and profitable farm to which the Marshalls had removed from Leeds in 1805, marked the first step of this ascent.[2]

Associations like these with aristocrats like Beaumont and plutocrats like Marshall disclose the anomalies of Wordsworth's own social position and the strains in his critique of contemporary society. New Grange had formerly been the residence of another of the Wordsworths' close friends, Mrs. Thomas Clarkson. The contrasts raised between their condition and the comfortable circumstances of those dear to them sound through the letter Dorothy wrote upon her return to Grasmere to Mrs. Clarkson, expressing a wish that her husband's writing would pay for a trip to Grasmere the following summer: "Why should he not, prosperous as you are. . . . We may now fairly call you rich people, for if God preserve your husband's health what should hinder him from going on as he has begun; another subject will surely arise when he has finished his present work."

Writing, or at least publishing, was never that easy for Wordsworth. Amid this success, it is not surprising to find Dorothy lamenting the scant rewards of her brother's verse:

I wish I could give you like histories of the flowing in of wealth from our literary concerns, but alas! poetry is a bad trade; and William's works sell slowly; yet we do hope that in the course of a twelvemonth the present Editions will be sold off, and then there will be two hundred pounds more, which we shall greatly need.[3]

Wordsworth had earned a total of fifty pounds from the editions of the *Lyrical Ballads* published in 1800, 1802 and 1805. It was a small sum and overall a small sale, since the three editions together did not number two thousand copies.[4] The continuing demand, however, must have encouraged Wordsworth to hope that he had found appreciative readers, for when in June 1806 Longman had offered him no more than forty pounds for a proposed new collection of poems he was sufficiently undaunted to have considered printing the volume at his own expense, thinking that "in the present state of my reputation there can be no risk with a 1000 copies."[5] By November the single volume had become the pair to appear in 1807 as *Poems, in Two Volumes,* and Longman had agreed to a hundred guineas for a thousand copies. The increased remuneration and the size of the edition must have been further evidence to Wordsworth that he was at last winning recognition. His hopes were shortly undeceived. *Poems, in Two Volumes* appeared at the end of April, and by late May Wordsworth had already to insist to Lady Beaumont that he was not dismayed by the hostile reception given them (*LMY,* 145–51; quoted in part below). The reversal was nonetheless severe. Dorothy's letter, just quoted, reveals the disappointment in the family, and by July Wordsworth was enlisting Francis Wrangham's aid in trying to forestall a harsh notice in the *Critical Review,* "chiefly because the immediate sale of the books is more under the influence of reviews than is generally supposed, and the sale of this work is of some consequence to me" (*LMY,* 155).

It is just in the period when Wordsworth's earlier confidence had been undone but before Jeffrey's severe and influential handling of *Poems, in Two Volumes* appeared in the October *Edinburgh Review* that *The White Doe* originates, in a tour the Wordsworths made with the Marshalls from New Grange—at the period, that is, when Wordsworth might still have felt that popularity was possible, despite his divergence from common taste, and before his attitude to the actual reading public had settled into bitter contempt.

On July 6, Dorothy, William, and the Marshall party left New

Grange for a tour "up the Wharf as far as Bolton Abbey." Dorothy's praise of "the most beautiful valley that ever was seen" reveals how inescapable awareness of the changes that were elsewhere transforming the English landscape and economy had become. Her description reads almost like a diminished prose echo of the calling-up of "the din of towns and cities" by the serenity of the Wye valley in *Tintern Abbey* years before:

> the Ruin is greatly inferior to Kirkstall; but the situation infinitely more beautiful, a retired woody winding valley, with steep banks and rocky scars, no manufactories—no horrible Forges and yet the Forge near Kirkstall has often a very grand effect. (*LMY*, 158)

The visit planted the seeds of *The White Doe*. During the "very pleasant day" passed in the neighborhood, Wordsworth probably met the Reverend William Carr, who superintended the grounds, and learned the tradition of the founding of the abbey. His imagination engaged, he sought further materials by requesting Thomas Whitaker's recent *History and Antiquities of the Deanery of Craven* from the Marshalls. On October 18 Dorothy wrote Jane to say that Wordsworth had been "greedily devouring" the books in the two days they had been in his possession, and "(what is of more importance) he has found all the information which he wanted for the prosecution of his plan" (*LMY*, 167). This enthusiasm had already led to composition of "The Force of Prayer," the brief poem on the founding of the abbey published with *The White Doe* in 1815, which Dorothy copied out for Jane and asked to have read to Dr. Whitaker.

Wordsworth had finished *The Prelude* in May 1805, but it was not to be published; *The Recluse* had proceeded as far as the not entirely satisfying completion of *Home at Grasmere* in 1806, and then stalled in the shock of Coleridge's broken state on his return from Malta. However gratifying it may have been to Wordsworth to have put out his first new collection in seven years with *Poems, in Two Volumes,* he deprecated short pieces and aspired to the stature to be achieved only as the author of a major work. The new project was revivifying; by December 2, Wordsworth had written more than five hundred lines; a month later the total exceeded twelve hundred; by January 18, 1808, Wordsworth told Scott that the poem was seventeen hundred lines and completed (*LMY*, 179, 187, 191).

Ominously, the letter to Scott also contained an indignant re-

sponse to Jeffrey's review of *Poems, in Two Volumes,* but that Wordsworth had not been utterly dashed is evident from Dorothy's announcement in February that *The White Doe* "will probably be sent
to the press in less than a month. . . . It is to be published in
Quarto. He means to demand 100 guineas for 1,000 copies" (*LMY,*
192). More than a decade later Wordsworth was to declare that he
had published *The White Doe* in quarto "to show the world my own
opinion of it" (cited in Comparetti, p. 277), but that characteristically prideful remark should not obscure the significance of the gesture. The quarto was the most prestigious format of the book trade,
employed, to choose germane examples, for such best-sellers as Sir
Walter Scott's *Lay of the Last Minstrel* (1805), *Marmion* (1808),
and his subsequent romances. In Canto III of *Don Juan,* Byron,
typifying in the trimmer poet the production of careerist authors in
different nations, remarks: "In France, for instance, he would write
a chanson; / In England, a six canto quarto tale" (st. 86)—exactly
the plan of the original *White Doe.* The format, the engraved frontispiece, the fee, the nature of the materials, the fact that the genre of
narrative was free of the charges of egotistical system that Wordsworth's lyrics provoked all suggest that *The White Doe* was a bid for
a fashionable audience. Defending *The Idiot Boy* to John Wilson in
1802, Wordsworth had denied that "[g]entlemen, persons of fortune,
professional men, ladies persons who can afford to buy or can easily
procure books of half a guinea price, hot-pressed, and printed upon
superfine paper," were the most qualified judges of "human nature"
and hence of poetry; now he seemed prepared to address that very
audience.[6] Though he insisted through Dorothy that *The White Doe*
had "nothing" of the character of a romance, he had contemplated
calling it "a Tale" (the term Byron was to employ for such works as
The Corsair and *Lara*), and readers could surely be forgiven who
inferred from these signs that the poem was meant to compete in a
commercial market.

Speaking of *Peter Bell* in February 1808 Wordsworth cautioned
Sir George Beaumont that "no Poem of mine will ever be popular"
(*LMY,* 194), but the statement is offset by his actions at the same
time. Drawn to London by anxiety over Coleridge's health, he deter-
mined "to push the printing, and to correct the press himself" of
The White Doe (*LMY,* 198). This decisiveness does not suggest a
poet afraid that he has no audience, and had *The White Doe* taken,
Wordsworth intended to follow it with *Peter Bell* and *The Waggoner*

(*LMY,* 325). At the very least, *The White Doe* appears as a bid to enlarge the range of poetry associated with his name.

Immersion in the London literary world, however, unpleasantly intensified Wordsworth's consciousness of the disparity between his mode and the taste of the public he fantasized reaching. Apprised no doubt of the slow sales of *Poems, in Two Volumes,* surrounded by fashionable readers who kept abreast of the reviews and the swings of reputation, Wordsworth lost confidence. By the end of March, Dorothy was telling Mrs. Clarkson that she was sure to be *"enraptured"* by *The White Doe* and hoping that she might have

> some influence in persuading him to publish it, which he very much dislikes now that it comes to the point, though he left us fully determined. I can never expect that poem, or any which he may write to be immediately popular, like The Lay of the Last Minstrel; but I think the story will help out those parts which are above the common level of taste and knowledge, and that it will have a better sale than his former works, and perhaps help them off. (*LMY,* 203)

Dorothy's keen sense of the harm done to his popularity by Wordsworth's career-long reservations about narrative—what he stigmatized in the *Preface* to the *Lyrical Ballads* as "deluges of idle and extravagant stories in verse"—shows that at stake was not a single poem but the public perception of her brother.[7] It was the "system" defensively proclaimed in the *Preface* which provoked the attacks on *Poems, in Two Volumes;* the suspicion that Wordsworth was claiming merit exclusively for his kind of poetry, aggravated by a notion that around his principles a definable "Lakist school" had come into being, had been waiting for Wordsworth's next publication to vent itself. Concerned to denounce a schismatic movement, the literary establishment represented by the reviews largely overlooked the stylistic diversity and numerous signs of accommodation with tradition in the new collection.

Dorothy's hope that by presenting himself as the writer of an adventurous Elizabethan narrative Wordsworth would help his other works shows an acute grasp of the dynamics of a career, and she was fearless in reminding her brother of the material necessities of their existence:

> We are exceedingly concerned, to hear that you, William! have given up all thoughts of publishing your Poem. As to the Outcry

against you, I would defy it—what matter, if you get your 100 guineas in your pocket? Besides it is like as if they had run you down, when it is known you have a poem ready for publishing, and keep it back. It is our belief, and that of all who have heard it read, that the *Tale* would bear it up—and without money what *can* we do? New House! new furniture! such a large family! two servants and little Sally! we *cannot* go on so another half-year. . . . (*LMY*, 207)

This extraordinary mixture of pleading, cajoling, and shaming measures the crisis in Wordsworth's relation to his audience. If the motto on the title page of the second volume of the *Lyrical Ballads* (1800)— "Quam nihil ad genium, Papiniane, tuum!"—boasted Wordsworth's innovations, the *Preface* itself as late as the 1802 additions affirmed the bond of poet and ordinary readers; poets, Wordsworth there maintained, "do not write for Poets alone, but for men" (261). Succeeding years fulfilled the bleakest aspects of Dorothy's analysis: the consequence of withholding *The White Doe* was to hasten Wordsworth's distinction between "the People" and "the Public" (*LMY*, 194). If "the People" was a projection of an ideal audience uncorrupted by literary prejudice that nourished Wordsworth, a vision of a community of best selves, "the Public" was an index of his withdrawal from actual readers.[8]

Opinion of *The White Doe* among Wordsworth's friends divided on the issue of action. De Quincey said he was "delighted" by it, and Southey called it "masterful," telling Scott that the story "affected me more deeply than I wish to be affected."[9] Wordsworth read one book to Charles and Mary Lamb, who subsequently also read the poem through; he said that he "knew it could not please them," but the conclusion of his account to Coleridge betrays his disappointment: "Lamb has not a reasoning mind, therefore cannot have a comprehensive mind, and, least of all, has he an imaginative one" (*LMY*, 221–23). To his lengthy defense of the "victories in the world of the spirit," Coleridge replied by acknowledging that he too felt "a disproportion of the Accidents to the spiritual Incidents" in the poem as it then stood. He told Wordsworth that he had "conceived two little Incidents, the introduction of which, joined to a little abridgement," would "bring to a finer Balance the *Business* with the *Action* of the Tale," but Wordsworth's vehement scorn of Lamb's criticism daunted him: "I felt my courage fail—and that what I deemed a harmonizing would disgust you, as a *materialization* of the Plan, & appear to you like insensibility to the power of the history in the mind."[10]

Notwithstanding these reservations, Coleridge had been busy with Longman advancing the publication of *The White Doe,* hoping to have printing of the first two books under way even before revisions had been completed in the subsequent ones. The seriocomic sequence in which Wordsworth countermanded Coleridge's authority with his publisher, withdrew the poem, and yielded to the suggestions for revision is set forth by Kristine Dugas. The story therefore need not be retold, but two points are worth underscoring. The first—that despite his lofty insistence on the superior value of interiority over action, Wordsworth did substantially alter his work in the light of the criticisms voiced by its original audiences—argues that he continued to seek success even as he scornfully insisted on his indifference. The second is intertwined with the first: the poet who both in this poem and in his comments on it celebrated the power of the imagination to transcend circumstance remained vividly conscious of the financial necessity of publication.

Wordsworth left London on April 3, 1808; on April 20, Dorothy announced to Lady Beaumont that the "Poem is to be published. Longman has consented, in spite of the odium under which my Brother labours as a poet, to give him 100 guineas for 1,000 copies, according to his Demand" (*LMY,* 225). The terms match those for *Poems, in Two Volumes,* and the publishers would scarcely have offered as much for one 1700-line poem as for an entire collection were they not expecting to profit. Nothing shook Dorothy's conviction that "the Story will bear it up in spite of that spirit that is above the common level." "We Females have been very anxious" that *The White Doe* be *"speedily"* published, she wrote, for economic reasons, and so that "William may get it out of his head"; if alterations were necessary, she trusted that they would "not be of a difficult or troublesome kind." As before, she showed a shrewd eye for commerce: she told Coleridge that "we think that it is of the *utmost importance,* that it should come out before the Buz of your Lectures is settled" (*LMY,* 228, 230–31). By May, Dorothy was less sanguine, telling Jane Marshall that her brother's "sole object for publishing this poem at present would be for the sake of the money" (*LMY,* 236); by June, the date had been put off "till next winter" (*LMY,* 253). None of it was to be: Coleridge's lectures, begun on January 15, 1808, and designed to cover the English poets from Chaucer to current times, broke off before reaching those on Wordsworth's "System & Compositions"; Wordsworth, his spirits ebbing in the face of his readers, abandoned the idea of publication and, by undercutting his efforts with Longman, offended Coleridge.

But questions about the merits of *The White Doe* itself were not the only reason for this action. At the end of September 1808, Wordsworth wrote to Richard Sharp, a prominent Whig and Member of Parliament: "We are all here cut to the heart by the conduct of Sir Hew and his Brother Knight in Portugal—for myself, I have not suffered so much upon any public occasion these many years" (*LMY*, 267). The occasion was the signing of the Convention of Cintra. The year before, Napoleon's armies had invaded the Iberian Peninsula, forcing the Portuguese court to flee to Brazil and over-throwing the Spanish monarchy. The Spanish people revolted, and in the summer Britain sent in aid an expeditionary force under Sir Arthur Wellesley, later Duke of Wellington. On August 21, Wellesley signally defeated the French forces under Marshal Junot at Vimiero but was prevented from pursuing his victory by those appointed to succeed him in command, Sir Harry Burrard, who arrived the next day, and Sir Hew Dalrymple. In place of the triumph the initial mili-tary success had led the British people to expect, the generals at the end of August negotiated a convention in which they agreed to con-voy the defeated troops and their booty back to France, whence they would be free to resume fighting.

Wordsworth's disgust at what he saw as a betrayal of English advantage and Portuguese sovereignty was widely shared. Protest broke out across the country, and by mid-October 1808, Wordsworth was agitating to call a county meeting. "If anything is done in Cum-berland here it will originate with Wordsworth," Southey reported, and the documents presented in the Owen-Smyser edition of Words-worth's prose works reveal the degree of Wordsworth's anger and activity.[11]

This passionate response needs to be understood in the terms Wordsworth ultimately developed in his pamphlet on the conven-tion. Like many English radicals who had been inspired by the early days of the French Revolution and disaffected from their own gov-ernment, Wordsworth recoiled from Napoleon's imperial ambitions into the qualified chauvinism recorded in the sonnets on national in-dependence and liberty of 1803. Napoleon's brutal invasion of the Peninsula, enacting what had only been feared then in England, offered a welcome clarifying of sympathies. British assistance to the spontaneous uprising of the Iberian peoples made it possible once again to see Britain as the champion of liberty, France as expansionist and tyrannical, and a nation's eruption into violence as noble. The Peninsular War, in short, was a purified repetition of the revolution, a moment in which Wordsworth's patriotism was renewed and aligned with his countrymen.

In seeking a county meeting to publicize the indignity of the convention, Wordsworth indeed made common cause with those whose politics were otherwise anathema to him. He knew, for instance, that on October 12, Robert Waithman, the London alderman active in the movement for parliamentary reform, had carried a petition from the city to the king requesting that he institute "an inquiry into this dishonourable and unprecedented transaction" (I, 389). Throughout these weeks, the reformers mounted demands for an investigation from one county meeting after another: from Berkshire, from Essex, and, most tumultuously, from Hampshire. There William Cobbett gleefully seized upon the Convention of Cintra not merely to insist upon an inquiry but also to excoriate the 23,000 pounds in sinecures held by the Wellesley family, the 254,000 pounds paid annually to the 291 generals of the British army, and an entire catalogue of government abuses.[12]

Such established North Country figures of different political persuasions as William Calvert (the older brother of Wordsworth's benefactor Raisley Calvert), Humphry Senhouse, Robert Southey, John Spedding, and John Christian Curwen joined with Wordsworth and Coleridge in their campaign "to set the business in its true light in the county newspapers,—& frame the resolutions, to be brought forward by some weighty persons." "Wordsworth will speak at the meeting," wrote Southey, and a fragmentary draft of his intended address survives (I, 197, 367).

Those who controlled politics in Westmorland and Cumberland were alarmed at the prospect of a forceful critique of the government emerging in their backyard. At the end of October, Southey acknowledged that "Lord Lonsdale will do all he can to prevent a meeting, or oppose any thing that may be done at once" (I, 197); his allegiance to an administration that had elevated him to an earldom less than two years before was to be expected, but perhaps not his bluntness. By the end of November, Southey confessed to his brother:

Our projected county meeting came to nothing. Lord Lonsdale set his face against it, & upon consultation with Curwen, we

were convinced that it was hopeless to muster force against his
merry men, who would have bellowed as loud against us at the
meeting, as they would have done against the cursed Convention
before they were under orders of mum. (I, 197)

To Walter Savage Landor, he added a few days later: "Lord Lonsdale had received Mum as the word of command from those who
move his strings, & he moves the puppets of two Counties!" (I, 197).

Bitterly disappointed, Wordsworth "went home," in Southey's
phrase, "to ease his heart in a pamphlett, which I daily expect to
hear he has completed" (I, 197). The pamphlet, *The Convention of
Cintra*, or, to give its full name, *Concerning the Relations of Great
Britain, Spain, and Portugal, to each other, and to the common
enemy, at this crisis; and specifically as affected by The Convention
of Cintra: The whole brought to the test of those Principles, by which
alone the Independence and Freedom of Nations can be Preserved or
Recovered*, was, however, no speedier to appear than this sonorous
title—"less a Title than a Table of Contents," Wordsworth admitted
(*LMY*, 312)—suggests, not reaching publication until May 1809.

In *The Prelude*, Wordsworth recalls the effect on him of Britain's entry into the war against France in 1793:

> Not in my single self alone I found,
> But in the minds of all ingenuous youth,
> Change and subversion from this hour. No shock
> Given to my moral nature had I known—
> Down to that very moment—neither lapse
> Nor turn of sentiment—that might be named
> A revolution, save at this one time:
>
> . . . .
> I felt
> The ravage of this most unnatural strife
> In my own heart; there lay it like a weight,
> At enmity with all the tenderest springs
> Of my enjoyments. I, who with the breeze
> Had played, a green leaf on the blessed tree
> Of my beloved country—nor had wished
> For happier fortune than to wither there—
> Now from my pleasant station was cut off,
> And tossed about in whirlwinds.
>
>   (1805, X, 231–58) [13]

This passage conveys how intensely dissonance between his political ideals and the conduct of the government could disturb Wordsworth. He appropriates the language of "revolution" from the actual events in France which he had witnessed to his psychological response to British policy, transforming "change" and "subversion" from the goals of radical commitment to conditions imposed on him by the course of others. Wordsworth then rewrites political disagreement as "unnatural strife" and, drawing upon the Burkean image of the nation as rooted tree, figures its effect on him as an organic violation, cutting him off from the body politic. He deftly obscures his radicalism in the 1790s by presenting himself as an innocent, harmonious part of nature and, in a neat reversal, casts the blame for disruption on the government; the consequence of this tactic, however, is the affect of seeing himself as the passive victim of the whirlwinds of contention.

The crisis this sequence records occurred in 1793, but it was written only four years before the Cintra episode. If British reinforcement of the Iberian revolt against the invading French offered Wordsworth the occasion for a healing reunion with his country, Lonsdale's quashing of the proposed county meeting once again threw him into opposition. The clash between his principles and his patron revived the alienation of fifteen years before. Three years later, Byron could scornfully proclaim in Canto I of *Childe Harold's Pilgrimage* (st. 25), "Convention is the dwarfish demon styl'd / That foil'd the knights in Marialva's dome," but such aristocratic satire was beyond Wordsworth, for whom the national urgency was loaned particular force by the repetition.[14] In March 1809 Wordsworth wrote Francis Wrangham, a Cambridge contemporary excluded from a fellowship in 1793 because of sympathy with the French Revolution, to announce the publication of his pamphlet and forecast its reception: "I am aware it will create me a world of enemies, and call forth the old yell of Jacobinism" (*LMY,* 312). The link with the past underlies also his fears of libel; he revised and delayed production until De Quincey, who was supervising printing in London, could ascertain that no expression "would render me liable to a prosecution, either from the Government or the Individuals concerned" (*LMY,* 340). As a means of gaining the widest possible audience for his views, Wordsworth had begun to publish the tract in *The Courier,* the first installment appearing on December 27, 1808. De Quincey humorously reassured him that, according to its editor, Daniel Stuart, "there is no hope of

Newgate."[15] If Wordsworth's anxiety seems exaggerated, Lonsdale's antagonism gave him cause.[16]

These events are not unfamiliar, as my reliance on standard sources in these pages betrays. The connection between them and *The White Doe of Rylstone,* however, has remained unexamined. During the period when Wordsworth was furiously composing *The Convention of Cintra*—October 1808–May 1809—he continued work on *The White Doe.* A letter of Dorothy to De Quincey on May 1, just two days before Wordsworth wrote to Stuart begging him to make sure the pamphlet "may not be made a handle for exercising upon my Person a[n] act of injustice" (*LMY,* 327), illustrates the convergence of Wordsworth's poetic and political projects:

> My Brother has begun to correct and add to the poem of the White Doe, and has been tolerably successful. He intends to finish it before he begins with any other work, and has made up his mind, if he can satisfy himself in the alterations he intends to make, to publish it next winter, and to follow the publication by that of Peter Bell and the Waggoner. He has also made a resolution to write upon publick affairs in the *Courier,* or some other newspaper, for the sake of getting money; not wholly however on that account for unless he were animated by the importance of his subject and the hope of being of use he could do nothing in that way. (*LMY,* 325)

Dorothy's frankness manifests the imperative of commercial success that shadows both the poetic and political projects. Writing to Thomas Poole in March 1809 to urge him to "promote" the circulation of *The Convention of Cintra,* Wordsworth immediately disclaimed financial interest: "I speak this not from any paltry consideration of gain, for I do not expect a farthing from it, nor even wish for the least emolument of that kind, but for Truth's sake and liberty's." A few lines later he added: "Poetry you know well and Patriotism are not mines very affluent in gold ore—at least I do not find them so" (*LMY,* 310–11). The distinction, however, like his insistence upon the separation of *The White Doe* from worldly concerns, was false: the two projects were intrinsically one, and both depended on the world of actual readers and unfolding history Wordsworth denigrated.

It had been so from the beginning. Wordsworth's lament to Richard Sharp that the Convention of Cintra had cut him to the heart, quoted above, is only a postscript in a letter chiefly devoted to influencing Sharp's participation in the upcoming discussions of copyright in Parliament. Though Wordsworth genteelly cloaks his interest as "service to Literature," he argues straightforwardly that the proposed extension of copyright from fourteen years after the author's death to twenty-eight is "far too short a period . . . that the authors, in the Persons of their Heirs or posterity, can in any degree be benefited, I mean in a pecuniary point of view, for the trouble they must have taken to produce the works" (*LMY,* 266). When he then closes, "We are all here cut to the heart by the conduct of Sir Hew and his *Brother Knight* in Portugal" (*LMY,* 267; emphasis added), his usage unwittingly establishes the intimate connection between chivalric romance, current events, and the conditions of the market he disavowed.

The description of the officers of the British expeditionary force in chivalric terms was wholly unremarkable, and therefore the more significant. It was just this representation that Byron was to expose by treating both French and British combatants in the Peninsular War as "Ambition's honour'd fools!" who "fertilize the field that each pretends to gain" (I, sts. 42, 41). But his very title, *Childe Harold's Pilgrimage, A Romaunt,* and the pseudo-Spenserianisms of his diction show how thoroughly the seemingly arcane revival of romance and the language of contemporary British policy saturated each other: without the romance norm within which it thrived, Byron's anti-romance would have been impossible. No account of the avidity with which early-nineteenth-century readers devoured romance, bestowing upon it a generic pre-eminence that gave their very name to the Romantics, is possible apart from the wider questions this shared framework raises.[17]

As specimen, we may take Scott's *Marmion,* published in 1808, the year in which *The White Doe* might have appeared, and, like it, set in the sixteenth century. *Marmion* concludes with the decisive defeat of the Scots under James IV by the armies of Henry VIII at Flodden Field in Northumberland in September 1513. Each of the six cantos is preceded by an epistle, of which the first is addressed to W. S. Rose, the friend of Byron and fosterer of his interest in the Italian romances. Scott immediately sets his tale of former British glory into relation with the present, saddened by the recent deaths of Pitt and Nelson: "Deep grav'd in every British heart, / O never let those names depart!" (90).[18] Each is eulogized for his contributions to empire, Nelson as the one who triumphed "Where'er his country's foes were found" (90), and Pitt as the one who "bade the conqueror go forth, / And launch'd that thunderbolt of war / On Egypt, Hafnia, Trafalgar" (90). In this patriotic celebration, even Charles James Fox, who until his last years had led the Whig opposition to war with France, is lauded: "Record, that Fox a Briton died! / . . . Stood for his country's glory fast, / And nail'd her colours to the mast!" (91). "But oh! my country's wintry state / What second spring shall renovate," Scott had begun by lamenting, and the answer is evident:

> Warm'd by such names, well may we then
> Though dwindled sons of little men,
> Essay to break a feeble lance
> In the fair fields of old romance
>
> (93)

The "knightly tale of Albion's elder day" (93) functions to produce a rejuvenated national unity in the war against France.

Behind Scott's language lies perhaps the most notorious rhetorical tour de force of the era, Burke's depiction in *Reflections on the Revolution in France* (1790) of the fall of Marie Antoinette as the end of chivalry:

> little did I dream that I should live to see such disasters fallen upon her in a nation of gallant men, in a nation of men of honour and of cavaliers. I thought ten thousand swords must have leaped from their scabbards to avenge even a look that threatened her with insult.—But the age of chivalry is gone.— That of sophisters, oeconomists, and calculators, has succeeded; and the glory of Europe is extinguished for ever. Never, never more, shall we behold that generous loyalty to rank and sex, that proud submission, that dignified obedience, that subordination of the heart, which kept alive, even in servitude itself, the spirit of an exalted freedom. The unbought grace of life, the cheap defence of nations, the nurse of manly sentiment and heroic enterprize is gone! It is gone, that sensibility of principle, that chastity of honour, which felt a stain like a wound, which inspired courage whilst it mitigated ferocity, which ennobled whatever it touched, and under which vice itself lost half its evil, by losing all its grossness.[19]

The revival of romance was inseparable from this ideology. The overt jingoism against France in Scott's epistle contained within it a defense of the hierarchies of *ancien régime*, pre-Reform Bill England as well.

The contradictions that surround *The White Doe of Rylstone* thus reveal themselves. As Dorothy's realistic evaluations reiterated, Wordsworth's chivalric story was potentially well suited for the tastes of the reading public; though he refused to acknowledge that the writer had become dependent on the market, she could and did. In the entanglement of *The White Doe* with the bourgeois process of production, copyright, publicity, sale, and review, Wordsworth's experience testifies to the accuracy of Marlon Ross's formulation: "It is appropriate . . . though it is ironic, that romance, the genre that celebrates chivalry, should be the genre that solidifies the ascendence of market publishing" (276). Scott had been offered a thousand guineas by his publisher for *Marmion,* sight unseen, and the bargain was a good one on both sides: the first edition of two thousand copies, quarto, priced at one and a half guineas, sold out in two months; eight thousand copies total sold in the three months after publication, six thousand more in 1809, five thousand in 1810, and a further nine thousand in 1811. The phenomenal popularity of romance, even as it sang the world of chivalry, made literature the very trade of "oeconomists, and calculators" that it disguised. That Wordsworth should have conceived *The White Doe* in the presence of John Marshall, the new man of the industrial middle classes, and developed it with materials borrowed from him, therefore seems not fortuitous but paradigmatic: if the world of chivalry was Wordsworth's subject, the question of his relation to the world of manufacture and commerce (and readers and reviewers) was his dilemma. And if Wordsworth's alternative to commercial publishing was reliance on a patron, the Earl of Lonsdale's blocking of the county meeting was a further complication, because *The White Doe of Rylstone* is a poem about a rebellion, and it had been overtaken by the events growing out of the Peninsular War.

II

At the core of both the materials of *The White Doe* and the political situation on the Peninsula is the struggle of a native Catholic population against a powerful central authority. To contemporary observers, sixteenth-century England and nineteenth-century Spain fell into a widespread analogy. When his friend John Rickman told Southey,

"You know I reckon the state of Spain to be about like that of England under Elizabeth and James the First," Southey, an authority
on the Peninsula, concurred in the parallel between the periods:
"Your estimate of Spain is right."[20] Coleridge reached for the same
illustration to describe years later in the *Biographia Literaria* the
"national unanimity unexampled in our history since the reign of
Elizabeth" which prevailed at the time: "providence, never wanting
to a good work when men have done their parts, soon provided a
common focus in the cause of Spain, which made us all once more
Englishmen by at once gratifying and correcting the predilections of
both parties."[21]

Wordsworth unreservedly supported the insurgents on the Peninsula, yet the eruption and its aftermath in England had the power to
unsettle conflicts long past. The Rising of the North of 1569 upon
which *The White Doe* is based was the last battle of feudal England
against the modern state that the Tudors instituted. It was not merely
the most serious challenge to her authority that Elizabeth faced, but
was also, in the words of S. T. Bindoff, "a mass-denunciation of the
new way of life and the new technique of government."[22] As A. F.
Pollard argues, it brought to a head Catholic resentments against a
national church subject to the sovereign, the grievances of those who
had seen their medieval franchises absorbed into a uniform system,
and the resistance of the great lords to a monarchy served by upstarts
like Cecil independent of their influence. To Pollard these are the
forces of reaction, but in his account one hears the themes that run
through Wordsworth's critique of capitalist society in the nineteenth
century:

> The simple souls of the rank and file rose above the nicely-
> calculated lore of politics and warfare. They were making the
> last armed protest in England against the secular spirit; and they
> breathed the aspirations of a bygone age. They wore on their
> coats the red cross of the crusaders; they bore on their banners
> the five wounds of Christ and that homely supplication of all
> peasants in revolt, "God speed the plough"; and they demanded
> that England should turn again to the ancient ways of faith and
> governance. The catholic religion should be restored; the council
> purged of its new, and filled with its old, noble members. . . .[23]

All Wordsworth's local and nostalgic sympathies should have
been with the rebels, as they were with the oppressed Spaniards and
Portuguese. The Advertisement to his pamphlet begins by declaring:

"The following pages originated in the opposition which was made by his Majesty's ministers to the expression, in public meetings and otherwise, of the opinions and feelings of the people concerning the Convention of Cintra" (I, 223). If the rhetoric cleverly places the administration into a defensive posture, it was in fact Wordsworth who had gone into opposition. The contrast he developed in Spain between "a high-minded nation" and "the real decrepitude of its Government" (I, 228) mirrored his situation at home; he knew that he risked "the old yell of Jacobinism" by charging that the reprimand the ministers dealt the City of London for petitioning against the convention and the "menaces" thrown out in Parliament foreshadowed "a league . . . for the purpose of laying further restraints upon freedom of speech and of the press" in "contempt of the rights of the nation" (I, 284). In asserting that "in cases where the nation feels itself aggrieved, *itself* being the judge (and who else ought to be, or can be?) . . . the privilege of complaint and petition" is "established by the most grave and authentic charters of Englishmen" (I, 285), Wordsworth displays the emergent nationalism that colors his defense from precedent. His justification of his own dissent echoes the exaltation of the "PEOPLE" (I, 237) he eloquently proclaimed for Spain, and on both fronts the argument shed a complicating light on his account of the Rising of the North.

For Wordsworth to support a revolt abroad against a French invasion might have been out of harmony with the government, but it was patriotic. To write favorably in time of war about a rebellion, even a safely distant one, against a British government was a more ambiguous act; yet if "the people" were the source of right, the Rising gained authority. Reviewing in his pamphlet the conditions in which a weaker country may be beneficially incorporated into a stronger with which it forms a natural geographical unit, in order to deny that they exist in the case of Spain and France, Wordsworth demands: "Who does not rejoice that former partitions have disappeared,—and that England, Scotland, and Wales, are under one legislative and executive authority; and that Ireland (would that she had been more justly dealt with!) follows the same destiny?" (I, 323). Even without memories of Flodden Field and Culloden, the antagonisms he had recorded in *The White Doe* gave the lie to this tendentious question; the implicit rewriting of northern history here is of a piece with that discussed in the chapter on *The Solitary Reaper*. Similarly, the Spenser invoked by the prefatory poem "In trellis'd

shed," and hovering throughout *The White Doe,* had been secretary
to Lord Grey during his brutal suppression of the Irish, and de-
fended his chief's reform "by the sword" in *A View of the Present
State of Ireland.* Actions and arguments that Wordsworth praised
when referred to the Continent became problematic when located at
home, but events had brought the two sites uncannily close.

Consider, for example, the last words of Richard Norton in *The
White Doe.* In prison after his defeat, Norton asks Francis, the son
who refused to join his rebellion, to fulfill the promise he had made
to carry the banner which is its emblem to Bolton Priory:

> Might this our enterprize have sped,
> Change wide and deep the Land had seen,
> A renovation from the dead,
> A spring-tide of immortal green:
> The darksome Altars would have blazed
> Like stars when clouds are rolled away;
> Salvation to all eyes that gazed,
> Once more the Rood had been upraised
> To spread its arms, and stand for aye.
> . . . .
> This banner (for such vow I made)
> Should on the consecrated breast
> Of that same Temple have found rest:
> I would myself have hung it high,
> Glad offering of glad victory!
>   (1277–95)

This sacramental rite was enacted in a celebrated exploit of the
Peninsular War which Wordsworth retells in *The Convention of
Cintra:*

> When the Boy of Saragossa (as we have been told), too imma-
> ture in growth and unconfirmed in strength to be admitted by
> his Fellow-citizens into their ranks, too tender of age for them
> to bear the sight of him in arms—when this Boy, forgetful or
> unmindful of the restrictions which had been put upon him,
> rushed into the field where his countrymen were engaged in bat-
> tle, and, fighting with the sinew and courage of an unripe Hero,
> won a standard from the enemy, and bore his acquisition to the
> Church, and laid it with his own hands on the altar of the Vir-
> gin;—surely there was not less to be hoped for his Country from

this Act, than if the banner, taken from his grasp, had, without any such intermediation, been hung up in the place of worship—a direct offering to the incorporeal and supreme Being. (I, 293)

It is possible that Wordsworth composed the scene in *The White Doe* after retrieving his manuscript from London at the end of March 1809, which would mean that the Boy of Saragossa inspired Wordsworth's revision rather than repeated the fiction, but gaps in the manuscripts leave the sequence uncertain. The differing treatment accorded the paired moments is nonetheless evident. "Surely there is here," Wordsworth exclaims of the Boy, "an object which the most meditative and most elevated minds may contemplate with absolute delight"; "Who does not recognise," he concludes, with the same assumption of universality noted above, "in this presentation a visible affinity with deliverance, with patriotism, with hatred of oppression, and with human means put forth to the height for accomplishing, under divine countenance, the worthiest ends?" (I, 293). The significance of the gesture was altered by the temporal and geographical spacing between the two occurrences. Though Wordsworth invented the episode of Francis's flight with the standard and calls him "the noble Francis" (1511), he describes the banner itself as an "unblessed work" (350) and would not permit Francis's mission to succeed. The aura Wordsworth granted in the Spanish instance he would not bestow on the sign of a domestic rebellion.[24]

The different role of the Catholicism common to both situations underlies these different outcomes. His devotion distinguishes Richard Norton, but his faith challenges the recently founded Anglican church to whose supremacy the poet was committed. Because Catholicism abroad stood apart from considerations of national destiny, Wordsworth could remark that "bigotry among the Spaniards leaves much to be lamented" (I, 332) but conclude that "in the Catholic religion" there is "a source of animation and fortitude in desperate struggles,—which may be relied upon as one of the best hopes of the cause" (I, 337). Out of England, Wordsworth could enlist Catholicism as a bulwark against the encroachments of liberalism and materialism:

Spain has nothing to dread from Jacobinism. Manufactures and Commerce have there in far less degree than elsewhere—by unnaturally clustering the people together—enfeebled their bodies, inflamed their passions by intemperance, vitiated from childhood their moral affections, and destroyed their imaginations. Madrid

is no enormous city, like Paris; overgrown, and disproportion-
ate; sickening and bowing down, by its corrupt humours, the
frame of the body politic. Nor has the pestilential philosophism
of France made any progress in Spain. . . . A Spanish understanding is a hold too strong to give way to the meagre tactics
of the "Système de la Nature. . . . The Spaniards are a people
with imagination: and the paradoxical reveries of Rousseau, and
the flippancies of Voltaire, are plants which will not naturalise
in the country of Calderon and Cervantes. (I, 332)

This passage suggests the degree to which the Spain Wordsworth
drew in this pamphlet was a transposition of the rural ideal of the
Preface to the *Lyrical Ballads* and elaborated in the sonnets on national independence and liberty in *Poems, in Two Volumes* (discussed in the chapter on *The Solitary Reaper*). Coleridge captured
the quality when he remarked that "the effect of national enthusiasm
in the Spanish people is somewhat too much *idealized*."[25] The themes
are familiar: that worldly politicians cannot understand "natural and
social man; the deeper emotions; the simpler feelings; the spacious
range of the disinterested imagination; the pride in country for country's sake" (I, 305); that "the Peasant, and he who lives by the fair
reward of his manual labour, has ordinarily a larger proportion of
his gratifications dependent upon" this instinctive patriotism than do
the upper classes (I, 328); that advances that have made the mass
of the population *"better off* (as the phrase in conversation is)" have
been purchased by the fading of Imagination (I, 324–25); that what
is wanted is that "the Government and the higher orders of society
should deal sincerely toward the middle class and the lower" (I, 321).

To read *The White Doe of Rylstone* and *The Convention of
Cintra* together is to realize how closely the two works converge. The
purpose of the pamphlet was to "move and teach, and be consolatory
to him who looks upon it" (I, 230); its end to persuade that superior
to "the blaze and explosion of animal courage" stands "the vital and
sustaining warmth of fortitude" (I, 236) and to demonstrate that
"calamity . . . ever brings wisdom along with it; and, whatever outward agitation it may cause, does inwardly rectify the will" (I, 299);
its final testimony that "all knowledge of human nature leads ultimately to repose" (I, 237). To move from the poem to the pamphlet—that is, to Wordsworth's counsels for victory in the war against
France and to his passionate convictions about the degeneracy of
English public life—is to see the language surrounding Emily acquire

vivid political force. The moral qualities of his heroine are those that
will sustain the Spanish people and restore the English to their principles. An associational slide illuminates the relationship of the
imagination Emily exemplifies, the account of the French Revolution
in *The Prelude,* and *The Convention of Cintra.* In apostrophizing the
imagination in Book VI of *The Prelude,* Wordsworth deliberately
counters its imperial tendencies: "The mind beneath such banners
militant / Thinks not of spoils or trophies, nor of aught / That may
attest its prowess, blest in thoughts / That are their own perfection
and reward— / Strong in itself, and in the access of joy / Which
hides it like the overflowing Nile" (1805, VI, 543–48). The same
image, however, surfaces in *The Convention of Cintra* to describe the
entire Spanish people rising into an army: "A military spirit should
be there, and a military action, not confined like an ordinary river in
one channel, but spreading like the Nile over the whole face of the
land" (234). One might read *The White Doe* as Wordsworth's
attempt to tame the spirit of insurrection by transforming it into
chastened imagination.

The conjunction of poem and pamphlet simultaneously discloses
a contradiction in the project. R. J. White observes of *The Convention of Cintra* that "Wordsworth could not bring himself to apply his
principle of nationality to the French people. . . . The idea that the
French might have beaten, and might for long continue to beat, their
enemies by reason of a burning faith in a superior social system
brought to birth under the banner of Liberty, Equality and Fraternity,
seems to have eluded him."[26] "Eluded" is unfair to Wordsworth, but
White's critique, that Wordsworth branded Napoleon as satanic rather
than sought to understand the appeal that led him from success to
success, points to the revulsion from historical actuality his experience of the French Revolution produced in Wordsworth.

The same deflection shapes *The White Doe.* Wordsworth introduces the Rising in the second canto:

> It was the time when England's Queen
> Twelve years had reigned, a sovereign dread;
> Nor yet the restless crown had been
> Disturbed upon her virgin head;
> But now the inly-working North
> Was ripe to send its thousands forth,
> A potent vassalage, to fight
> In Percy's and in Neville's right,—

> Two earls fast leagued in discontent,
> Who gave their wishes open vent;
> And boldly urged a general plea,
> The rites of ancient piety
> To be by force of arms renewed;
> Glad prospect for the multitude!
>
> (361–74)

Wordsworth's "now" elides causation; the various motives for the rebellion sketched by the modern historians cited above, which Wordsworth knew from his sources, are bypassed, and explanation reduced to the "discontent" of the earls. This indifference is the more striking because the values endorsed by *The Convention of Cintra* suggest that Wordsworth, himself a northerner suspicious of the urban concentration of power, might well have been thought to sympathize with the rebels. He is equally uninterested in vindicating or condemning Elizabeth, who, in the words of the ballad, vowed to "ordayne them such a breakfast, / As never was in the North before," and reasserted her control with a cruel series of executions and appropriations. Wordsworth instead closes his poem with an apotheosis of Emily which detaches her from all political context:

> Distress and desolation spread
> Through human hearts, and pleasure dead,—
> Dead—but to live again on Earth,
> A second and a nobler birth;
> Dire overthrow, and yet how high
> The re-ascent in sanctity!
>
> . . . .
>
> At length, thus faintly, faintly tied
> To earth, she was set free, and died.
> Thy soul, exalted Emily,
> Maid of the blasted Family,
> Rose to the God from whom it came!
>
> (1861–87)

We are now in a position to reconsider Wordsworth's failure to publish *The White Doe* in 1808–09. The subordination of action to spiritual growth to which Wordsworth attributed the poor reception of the poem is an effect, not a cause. The lyric suspension of the action reflects a deeper dilemma: his uncertainty about how to treat a story of revolution. The question, muted but already troubling his ability to shape the events of 1569 into compelling poetic form, was rendered critical by the uprisings on the Peninsula. In his heated determination to protest the Convention of Cintra, Wordsworth recovered the political energies of his radical youth, but such commitments were inevitably conflicted, as the opposition of his patron made unmistakably clear. To see himself seen by others as a Jacobin was disturbing, but indeed Wordsworth's reliance on "the people" pointed toward conclusions that he would have found intolerable. "The people," yes, in Spain, but not in a rebellion in England, even in 1569, or if their leaders should be Cobbett or Orator Hunt, and their ends reform and democracy.

Francis's great prophecy of the downfall of the Nortons is charged by the echoes of the bewilderment the French Revolution caused Wordsworth. In Francis's prohibition of hope to Emily the narrative of 1569 appears as a repetition of the 1790s:

> Farewell all wishes, all debate,
> All prayers for this cause, or for that!
> Weep, if that aid thee; but depend
> Upon no help of outward friend;
> Espouse thy doom at once, and cleave
> To fortitude without reprieve.
> For we must fall, both we and ours,—
> This Mansion and these pleasant bowers;
> Walks, pools and arbours, homestead, hall,
> Our fate is theirs, will reach them all;
> The young Horse must forsake his manger,
> And learn to glory in a Stranger;
> The Hawk forget his perch,—the Hound
> Be parted from his ancient ground:
> The blast will sweep us all away,
> One desolation, one decay!
>
> (544–59)

Just so had Wordsworth recorded in *The Prelude* the apocalyptic vision triggered by the September massacres:

> "The horse is taught his manage, and the wind
> Of heaven wheels round and treads in his own steps;
> Year follows year, the tide returns again,
> Day follows day, all things have second birth;
> The earthquake is not satisfied at once"—
>
> (1805, X, 70–74)

Wordsworth's image of himself in the passage from *The Prelude* quoted above as "a green leaf on the blessed tree / Of my beloved country" who was "cut off / And tossed about in whirlwinds" likewise recurs in Francis's apostrophe of Emily as "The last leaf which by heaven's decree / Must hang upon a blasted tree" (571–72).

The unresolved tensions in his political position which produced this helplessness in the face of events determined Wordsworth's focus in *The White Doe* not on the origins or justice of the Rising of 1569 but on the sphere of the family. Francis and Emily are Protestant anomalies in a Catholic community, and their faith is the badge of their isolation. Francis's admonition to Emily to forgo "all wishes, all debate, / All prayers for this cause, or for that!" repeats Wordsworth's own baffled withdrawal a decade and a half earlier: "I lost / All feeling of conviction, and, in fine, / Sick, wearied out with contrarieties, / Yielded up moral questions in despair" (1805 *Prelude,* X, 897–900). But whereas Wordsworth could write that he had been restored to nature and imagination by Dorothy, who "Maintained for me a saving intercourse / With my true self" (1805, X, 914–15), the pathos of *The White Doe* grows from the breaking of the bond between brother and sister: Francis is murdered, and Emily survives alone. The poem maps a double displacement from history: from the Rising to the family, from the family to Emily's otherworldly ascent.

The doe who gives the poem its title guides Emily from the fatalism of Francis through nature to transcendence. From this final vantage, questions of causation and of right and wrong sink to nothingness. Wordsworth seems to underline his indifference to origin by accompanying *The White Doe* with *The Force of Prayer; or The Founding of Bolton Priory*. In the chief poem, the animal is the agent of redemption; in the tradition narrated in the shorter, young Romilly drowns because his greyhound hangs back and impairs his leap across the river Wharf. "What is good for a bootless bene?" asks the messenger who brings the news to the boy's mother; "endless sorrow," she replies. *The White Doe* derives its power from a kindred representation of history as the record of almost arbitrary pain. Wordsworth's repudiation of Scott's offer of information about the actual fate of the Nortons epitomizes his retreat from explanation: "a plague upon your industrious Antiquarianism that has put my fine story to confusion" (*LMY,* 237). Emily is the more affecting because she is passive: to fill in the ellipsis from my earlier quotation from *The*

Convention of Cintra, her course witnesses that "calamity (that is suffering, individual or national, when it has been inflicted by one to whom no injury has been done or provocation given) ever brings wisdom along with it." History evaded, the lesson of fortitude remains: like the ruined buildings Wordsworth saw on the tour which provoked *The White Doe,* Emily signifies but is silent.

Two difficulties thus blocked *The White Doe* in 1808–09: no more than Lonsdale would have permitted a county meeting to protest the government would readers have anticipated from a genre devoted to fostering national unity in time of war a poem based on a rebellion, still less a work devoted to supplanting martial values with martyrly ones. The lack of action in *The White Doe* complained of by the poem's first audiences is not a question of formal properties alone; the genre and the times both supported the expectation that an Elizabethan romance would celebrate English glory. It was the unsettled question of revolution that motivated Wordsworth's transfer of his story to another plane. "The people" in Spain he could idealize apart from their leaders; "the People" in England were too threatening. The separation between "People" and "Public" to which the poor reception given his poetry drove Wordsworth mirrored the split between "the people" and actual forms of expression in his political imagination: the problem of representation occupies both fields.

By its oblique connections to the French Revolution and to the Peninsular War *The White Doe* stands within history while claiming to rise above it. In the Fenwick note to *The Force of Prayer* Wordsworth lamented that "the spread of manufactories" had destroyed the rural peace he remembered in the Yorkshire and Lancashire valleys. "Alas, if these evils grow, how are they to be checked, and where is the remedy to be found," he asked, and answered: "Political economy will not supply it; that is certain, we must look to something deeper, purer, and higher" (quoted in Dugas, p. 147). That "something" was the spiritual resolve of Emily and the abstractly conceived Spanish populace; one wonders whether Wordsworth articulated for John Marshall the antithetical relation between Emily and the mercantilism he embodied. One thing was certain: Wordsworth could not both produce a "higher" value by a divorce from circumstance and hope for a marketplace success. The imagination *The White Doe* exemplifies is born from the foreclosure of history, and Wordsworth's inability to publish the poem is the sign of the larger crisis.

The appearance of *The White Doe* in 1815 provides a final twist to the poetic and political irresolution that haunts the poem. After years without mention of *The White Doe,* Dorothy wrote Catherine Clarkson on April 24, 1814, that it was to be published at last.[27] The letter shows Wordsworth fixing his canon, scheduling *The White Doe* to follow the long-awaited *Excursion* and the two-volume collected *Poems,* but there were important external developments as well. In October 1813, Napoleon had been decisively defeated at Leipzig; his brilliant last-ditch campaign could not prevent the Allies from entering Paris at the end of March 1814, and on April 13 the emperor abdicated at Fontainebleau. *The White Doe* headed to press in February 1815, with the Bourbons again seated on the throne of France and the long turmoil of the revolution seemingly ended. If this climate made it possible for Wordsworth to venture publication, one irony remained: *The White Doe* appeared in June in the midst of Napoleon's Hundred Days.

These conjunctions had no part in the conception of *The White Doe,* but the contradictions to which they point had much to do with its suppression in 1808–09. The interplay between poem and war, past and present, traditional loyalties and revolution, Catholicism and liberalism, allegiance and integrity, made *The White Doe* a node of contention for Wordsworth. The political conflicts resulted in the withholding of the poem and produced further complications. Holding back *The White Doe* and in consequence *Peter Bell* and *The Waggoner,* Wordsworth smothered a substantial portion of his output. Dorothy knew that a poet cannot create the taste by which he is enjoyed if he does not publish, but the consciousness that he was the author of those works, and *The Prelude* too, intensified Wordsworth's sense of being unappreciated and aggravated his contempt for the reading public.[28] Our accounts of *The White Doe* have in effect read back into the affair the lofty disdain for popularity that, rather, the matter and then the delay of the poem caused.

The literary environment in which *The White Doe* and its companions eventually reached print was already inhabited by radicals like Byron and Shelley. The pawky humor of *Peter Bell* and *The Waggoner* had become old-fashioned amid the postwar disillusionment; moreover, the poet who had set himself up as a grave spokesman with *The Excursion* could scarcely expect a return to his earlier manner to go unmocked. By 1815, the image of the late Wordsworth was already set, to react upon whatever he might publish.[29] But as this narrative of the interrupted publication of *The White Doe* implies, a characterization like "the late Wordsworth" depends on an entire horizon of forces beyond the words he wrote and yet intrinsic to them.

Notes

1. William Wordsworth, *The White Doe of Rylstone; or The Fate of the Nortons,* ed. Kristine Dugas (Ithaca: Cornell University Press, 1988). All quotations of the poem are from this edition, hereafter cited parenthetically in the text as Dugas. I have also made use of *The White Doe of Rylstone,* ed. A. P. Comparetti (Ithaca: Cornell University Press, 1940), cited parenthetically as Comparetti.

2. This account of Marshall is derived from W. G. Rimmer, *Marshalls of Leeds: Flax Spinners 1788–1886* (Cambridge: Cambridge University Press, 1960).

3. Letter of July 19, 1807. *The Letters of William and Dorothy Wordsworth, The Middle Years, Part I, 1806–1811,* ed. Ernest de Selincourt, 2d ed., rev. by Mary Moorman (Oxford: Clarendon, 1969), pp. 156–57. Hereafter cited in the text as *LMY.*

4. W. J. B. Owen, "Costs, Sales, and Profits of Longman's Editions of Wordsworth," *The Library,* n.s., 12 (1957): 93–107.

5. Quoted by Jared Curtis in his edition of *Poems, in Two Volumes* (Ithaca: Cornell University Press, 1983), p. 11.

6. *The Letters of William and Dorothy Wordsworth, The Early Years 1787–1805,* ed. Ernest de Selincourt, 2d ed. rev. by Chester L. Shaver (Oxford: Clarendon, 1967), p. 355.

7. *Lyrical Ballads,* ed. R. L. Brett and A. R. Jones (London: Methuen, 1968), p. 249. On this theme, see Andrew L. Griffin, "Wordsworth and the Problem of Imaginative Story: The Case of 'Simon Lee,'" *Publications of the Modern Language Association* 92 (1977): 392–409. All quotations are from this edition.

8. See on this subject Patrick Cruttwell, "Wordsworth, the Public, and the People," *Sewanee Review* 64 (1956): 71–80; and the impressive study by Jonathan Klancher, *The Making of English Reading Audiences 1790–1832* (Madison: University of Wisconsin Press, 1987).

9. Southey's opinion is quoted in Comparetti, p. 264; De Quincey's in John E. Jordan, *De Quincey to Wordsworth: A Biography of a Relationship* (Berkeley: University of California Press, 1963), pp. 89–90.

10. *Collected Letters of Samuel Taylor Coleridge,* 6 vols., ed. E. L. Griggs (Oxford: Clarendon, 1956–1971), III, 107–8.

11. *The Prose Works of William Wordsworth,* 3 vols., ed. W. J. B. Owen and Jane Worthington Smyser (Oxford: Clarendon, 1974), I, 196–98. My account of the aborted county meeting is a précis of Owen and Smyser; Gordon Kent Thomas, *Wordsworth's Dirge and Promise: Napoleon, Wellington and the Convention of Cintra* (Lincoln: University of Nebraska Press, 1971), par-

ticularly Chapter 2; Mary Moorman, *William Wordsworth: A Biography, The Later Years 1803–1850* (Oxford: Clarendon, 1965), pp. 136–38; and R. D. Havens, "A Project of Wordsworth's," *Review of English Studies* 5 (1929): 320–22. All quotations from *The Convention of Cintra* are taken from the Owen-Smyser edition and will be cited hereafter parenthetically by page number in the text.

12. I follow closely here George Spater, *William Cobbett: The Poor Man's Friend*, 2 vols. (Cambridge: Cambridge University Press, 1982), I, 212–14.

13. Text from *The Prelude, 1799, 1805, 1850*, ed. Jonathan Wordsworth, M. H. Abrams, and Stephen Gill (New York: Norton, 1979), pp. 370–72.

14. Text from *Lord Byron: The Complete Poetical Works*, ed. Jerome J. McGann, Vol. II (Oxford: Clarendon, 1980), p. 20.

15. *De Quincey to Wordsworth*, p. 163. Jordan provides the fullest account of De Quincey's beleaguered assistance with *The Convention of Cintra*.

16. When the pamphlet finally appeared at the end of May 1809, Wordsworth sent a copy to Lonsdale, respectfully affirming his trust "that it will be thoughtfully and candidly judged by you. . . . [T]he principles which I have endeavoured to uphold must have the sanction of a mind distinguished like that of your Lordship for regard to morality, and the true dignity and honour of your Country" (*LMY*, 346). What Lonsdale thought of the work I do not know, but to a politician timing would have been all: a dense, difficult, and comparatively expensive (5 shillings) pamphlet published eight months after the crisis, and which a year later had only sold 238 copies, would have been of considerably less concern than a county address to the king in the midst of the turmoil. He could afford to be gracious.

17. On the popularity and significance of romance, see Stuart Curran, *Poetic Form and British Romanticism* (New York: Oxford University Press, 1986), Chapter 6; and Marlon Ross, "Scott's Chivalric Pose: The Function of Metrical Romance in the Romantic Period," *Genre* 18 (1986): 267–97.

18. All quotations from J. Logie Robertson, ed., *The Poetical Works of Sir Walter Scott* (London: Oxford University Press, 1960). As this edition lacks line numbers, I give page references.

19. Edmund Burke, *Reflections on the Revolution in France*, and Thomas Paine, *The Rights of Man* (Garden City, N.Y.: Anchor Press/Doubleday, 1973), p. 89.

20. *The Life and Correspondence of Robert Southey*, 6 vols., ed. Charles Cuthbert Southey (London: Longman, 1849), III, 69.

21. *Biographia Literaria*, ed. James Engell and Walter Jackson Bate, *Collected Works of Samuel Taylor Coleridge*, series 7, 2 vols. (Princeton: Princeton University Press, 1983), I, 189.

22. S. T. Bindoff, *Tudor England* (Harmondsworth: Penguin, 1950), pp. 209–10.

23. A. F. Pollard, *The History of England from the Accession of Edward VI to the Death of Elizabeth (1547–1603)* (London: Longmans, 1934), Chapter 15, "The Crisis of Elizabeth's Reign," p. 294.

24. In the 1808 version of the poem Francis seems to have appeared unsympathetically as the betrayer of his family; see Dugas, pp. 6, 34–37.

25. *Collected Letters of Coleridge*, ed. Griggs, III, 216.

26. R. J. White, ed., *Political Tracts of Wordsworth, Coleridge and Shelley* (Cambridge: Cambridge University Press, 1953), p. xxxii.

27. *The Letters of William and Dorothy Wordsworth, The Middle Years, Part II, 1812–1820*, ed. Ernest de Selincourt, 2d ed., rev. by Mary Moorman and Alan G. Hill (Oxford: Clarendon, 1970), p. 140.

28. For Geoffrey Hartman, Wordsworth's holding back of his greatest poem "in the light of which we *now* read everything else" is a sign of strength: "Keeping *The Prelude* in reserve, almost like God his own Son, Wordsworth reposed on a text-experience whose life remained with God." "Words, Wish, Worth," rpt. in his *The Unremarkable Wordsworth*, Theory and History of Literature, ed. Wlad Godzich and Jochen Schulten-Sasse (Minneapolis: University of Minnesota Press, 1987), Vol. 34, p. 116. Hartman's characteristically sacralizing language smooths away the daily consequences such conviction produces.

29. For the reception of *The White Doe*, see Chapter 9, "Tales and Politics." On the formation of the image of Wordsworth, see the penetrating essay by James K. Chandler, " 'Wordsworth' after Waterloo," in *The Age of William Wordsworth*, ed. Kenneth R. Johnston and Gene W. Ruoff (New Brunswick: Rutgers University Press, 1987), pp. 84–111.

9

Tales and Politics:
The Corsair, Lara, and
The White Doe of Rylstone

The phrase *poetry and politics* evokes two immediate and more or less obvious meanings: the political milieu in which poems are written and published, and the political attitudes explicitly or tacitly evinced in poems. But there is another politics of poems, one that is usually lost to later generations of readers. It is a politics of physical presentation, of dedications, appendices, prices and sizes of volumes, illustrations, and other contextual matters. When we come to the same poems in collected works, anthologies, or whatever forms of subsequent publication we meet with, that original aspect has become invisible.

The first purpose of this chapter is to recreate that politics for two of Byron's tales, *The Corsair* and *Lara,* and one of Wordsworth's, *The White Doe of Rylstone,* which will reveal an apparently more thoroughgoing contrast than even the popular images of the poets—rebel-hero and aging conservative—suggest. The second purpose is in a sense to undermine the first: to show that despite the polarity, which is real as well as apparent, a surprising likeness exists between the unannounced political attitudes of Byron's two poems and the credo of Wordsworth's. The root of the paradox lies in what is at once the ambivalence and the richness of Byron's tales.

The presentation of Byron's poems was consistent with the politics of the circles in which he moved. Byron returned to England in July 1811 to find an old challenge from the Irish poet Thomas Moore, who had been angered by an allusion in *English Bards and*

Scotch Reviewers. From this contretemps sprang two of Byron's most important friendships, for the awkwardness was resolved through Samuel Rogers, at whose house Byron met Moore on November 4. Rogers was a poet of reputation, a wealthy banker, a connoisseur, and, most germane to our purposes, a notable Whig.[1] Through him Byron gained entrée to the upper tiers of Whig society, including an introduction to its central figure, Lord Holland, leader of the parliamentary opposition.

When Parliament reconvened, Byron took his seat in the House of Lords on January 15, 1812. Despite the diffidence with which he habitually cloaked the projects closest to his heart, it is evident that Byron had long nurtured parliamentary ambitions. He attended the House frequently in January and February, and, after consulting with Lord Holland, who was Recorder of Nottingham, made his maiden speech, on February 27, on the subject of the Luddite riots in Nottingham, site of Newstead Abbey. His powerful plea for sympathy toward the misery of the workers, joined with an ironic, radical attack on the Tory bill to impose the death penalty on the rioters, was widely reported in the papers.[2] Byron filled his letters with the praises won by his oratory. Years later, Holland wrote in his *Memoirs* that it was "not at all suited to our common notions of Parliamentary eloquence," but, Holland continued, "his speech and his verses on Princess Charlotte's tears fixed his politics, and he was upon system invariably attached to the party and principles of the Whigs."[3] Byron was not the man to be attached "upon system" to any principle or party, and his growing impatience with the discipline of everyday party politics soon cooled his parliamentary hopes, yet Holland's opinion points to the political image that Byron established for himself in the public eye.[4]

That image would have been even more sharply delineated had the authorship of Byron's anonymous political verses been known. In a lampoon *Ode to the Framers of the Frame Bill,* published anonymously in the *Morning Chronicle* on March 2, he vilified the Tory ministers "Who, when asked for a *remedy,* sent down a *rope.*" On March 7, the *Morning Chronicle* printed a second political squib, the *Sympathetic Address to a Young Lady:*

> Weep, daughter of a royal line,
>   A Sire's disgrace, a realm's decay;
> Ah! happy if each tear of thine

> Could wash a Father's fault away!
> Weep—for thy tears are Virtue's tears—
> Auspicious to these suffering Isles;
> And be each drop in future years
> Repaid thee by thy People's smiles!

These lines, which Holland thought decisive in fixing Byron's politics, were occasioned by a notorious scene.

When increased authority was granted the Prince Regent in early 1812, the Whigs assumed that as the fruit of their long alliance with him they would be brought into power. The Prince instead proposed a coalition of some of the old-guard Whigs and their Tory enemies. When the Whigs refused, he bitterly denounced them for their ingratitude at a banquet at Carlton House on February 22. His sixteen-year-old daughter, Princess Charlotte, burst into tears over the betrayal and was ordered from the room. Charlotte had already become a central figure in the political battles of the day. After her birth in 1796, the Prince had broken with her mother, Princess Caroline, and his subsequent treatment of her, which included separating her from her daughter, provided a convenient, popular rallying point for the opposition to him. These two stanzas, to which I will return, had an effect on Byron's contemporary reputation out of all proportion to their length.

I have rehearsed these well-known events because it is necessary to remember that Byron had already become visibly involved in party politics *before* the publication of *Childe Harold's Pilgrimage,* which did not appear until March 10, 1812. Musing afterward in his journal, Byron remembered that the response to his first speech was "not discouraging":

> but just after it my poem of C[hild]e H[arol]d was published—& nobody ever thought about my prose afterwards, nor indeed did I—it became to me a secondary and neglected object, though I sometimes wonder to myself *if* I should have succeeded?— (*BLJ,* IX, 16)

Byron's memory, insofar as it suggests that the immense and immediate success of *Childe Harold* simply swept away all traces of his parliamentary activity, is misleading. The earlier, if brief, fame colored the later and wider one.[5] The *Gentleman's Magazine,* for example, greeted *Childe Harold* by linking its praise for Byron's poetry to notice of his oratory:

we now congratulate his Lordship and the Public on this maturer demonstration of poetical genius—(and we will add, though foreign to the present purpose, on the fair promise of excelling in the British Senate, evinced by his eloquent Maiden Speech).[6]

The politics of the poem were consonant with those of the speech. In the attack on the Tory Lord Elgin for removing from Greece the marbles that bear his name, Byron made them, in William St. Clair's words, "a symbol—of Greece's slavery, of Europe's failure to help her, and of Britain's overweening pride."[7] The most evidently partisan lines in the poem were those on the Peninsular Campaign and the Convention of Cintra, which restated and intensified the Whig opposition to the conduct of the war. The Whig *Edinburgh Review* observed that Byron's speaking "in a very slighting and sarcastic manner of wars, and victories, and military heroes in general . . . we should have thought very little likely to attract popularity, in the present temper of this country" (Reiman, B, 2:837). At the other end of the political spectrum, the reactionary *Antijacobin Review* fulminated against "the unpatriotic defects" of this "bastard of the imagination," and the Tory *Quarterly Review* likewise denounced Byron's deflation of martial glory: "When we read the preceding sarcasms on the 'bravo's trade,' we are induced to ask, not without some anxiety and alarm, whether such are the opinions which a British peer entertains of a British army" (Reiman, B, 1:11 and B, 5:1992). This jingoism is even more virulently—if comically—displayed in the *Satirist,* which was provoked by the lines on "Ambition's honored fools" to exclaim: "For shame! For shame! my Lord" (Reiman, B, 5:2113). The *Eclectic Review,* struck by the notes to the poem in which Byron called the Irish our "Irish helots," described Byron as having become "an advocate of Catholic emancipation, and an adherent (if we are not mistaken) of a political party. The distributors of fame and popularity may, perhaps, have been influenced, in their eulogiums on the noble author's poetry, by adverting, unconsciously it may be, to his senatorial character" (Reiman, B, 2:705). Indeed, the co-ordination of Byron's poetic and political efforts was demonstrated by his making Catholic emancipation the topic of his second speech in Parliament on April 21.

These reactions to the political views expressed by *Childe Harold* help explain why the first bookseller to whom the manuscript was offered should have declined it. When Murray accepted it, he urged

Byron to moderate the remarks on religion and on Spain and Portugal so as not to "deprive" him "of some customers among the *Orthodox*."[8] Byron was adamant:

> With regard to the political & metaphysical parts, I am afraid I can alter nothing, but I have high authority for my Errors in that point, for even the *Aeneid* was a *political* poem & written for a *political purpose* . . . (*BLJ*, II, 90–91)

That these very views made him the favorite of the opposition to the Tories and the Regent is shown by an anecdote recorded by R. C. Dallas:

> A gratifying compliment was paid him on the appearance of Childe Harold's Pilgrimage, by the order given by the Princess Charlotte for its being magnificently bound. It was displayed for some days in Ebers's shop, in Bond-street. Lord Byron was highly pleased when I described it to him.[9]

Such gestures identified Byron with the Whigs in the public mind as much as his parliamentary speeches had done. In June, he was elected to the Hampden Club, at the encouragement of Lady Oxford, who "always urged a man to usefulness or glory," as Byron recalled (*BLJ*, III, 229). By October, Byron was Lady Oxford's recognized cavalier, staying with her at Eywood.

A distinction should here be entered. Byron wrote to Lady Melbourne of his new liaison: "I know very little of the P[rincess Caroline]'s party . . . & am not at all in ye. secret. . . . M'amie thinks I agree with her in *all* her politics, but she will discover that this is a mistake" (*BLJ*, II, 263). Though Byron thus disclaims any explicit commitment to party politics, it is his public image as much as his personal beliefs that is the concern of this essay, and he was increasingly the cynosure of Whig society. Princess Charlotte wrote to her confidante Mercer Elphinstone (also a friend of Byron) on October 28, "I have seen a great deal of Lord Byron lately," and on January 27, 1813, she expressed her pique that he had not been invited to an opposition ball in her honor.[10] Through Lady Oxford, Byron also became a frequent guest at Princess Caroline's gatherings, and his name recurs throughout her correspondence for 1813 and 1814. "I flatter myself," Princess Caroline wrote, "I am rather a favourite with the great bard."[11]

On June 1, 1813, Byron made his final speech in Parliament, presenting the petition for reform of Major John Cartwright. Almost simultaneously with the newspaper accounts of this renewed evidence of Byron's radical sympathies came the publication of the first of Byron's tales, *The Giaour,* on June 5, 1813. The work was dedicated to Samuel Rogers. Rogers's *Voyage of Columbus* (1812) has been cited as an influence on the fragmentary form of Byron's poem, but the dedication had political implications too. Commenting on *The Voyage of Columbus,* Rogers's biographer commented that Rogers's "Whig principles came out in the opening to the sixth canto—written, it should be remembered, in the very height of the struggle against Napoleon—'War and the Great in War let others sing, / Havoc and spoil, and tears and triumphing.' "[12] Like the expression of similiar sentiments in *Childe Harold,* these lines fixed the poem in the political spectrum for contemporary readers, and Byron's dedication to Rogers, in "admiration of his genius, respect for his character, and gratitude for his friendship," carried through the eleven editions and more than 8,700 copies over the next two years, signaled the political milieu to which he was attached. *The Giaour* was succeeded by *The Bride of Abydos,* announced for November 29, 1813, and bearing an equally politically significant dedication, to Lord Holland. How closely Byron's works were followed by the royal opposition to the Regent may be seen in the opinion of Princess Charlotte already on December 1 that *The Bride of Abydos* was "quite equal to his *Giaour. It is not* a fragment, wh. makes it more interesting I think" (Aspinall, p. 88). *The Bride of Abydos* sold even more swiftly than *The Giaour:* 6,000 copies in a month, 12,500 copies by the end of 1814.

The dedication of Byron's next tale, *The Corsair,* to Thomas Moore is still more revealing. On January 2, 1814, Byron composed a dedicatory letter praising Moore as "among the firmest" of Ireland's "patriots." It casts an interesting light on the oblique relationship between Byron's own works and contemporary politics to read his prophecy that Moore's planned eastern tale would be congenial to him because "The wrongs of your own Country—the magnificent and fiery spirit of her sons—the beauty and feeling of her daughters may there be found" (*BLJ,* IV, 12–14). Moore's patriotism was not confined to Irish matters. Though he had earlier dedicated his translations to Anacreon to the Prince Regent, he had since become one of the most notorious satirists of the Regent and the ministry. From

1812 on, the *Morning Chronicle* published his "vollies of small shot," as it published Byron's; in the words of Howard Mumford Jones, "Moore, Byron, and Hunt [whom Byron visited during his imprisonment for lèse-majesté] were the light cavalry of the Whig assault."[13] Moore's newspaper squibs culminated in March 1813 with the appearance, under the pseudonym of "Thomas Brown the Younger," of *Intercepted Letters, or the Two-Penny Post Bag,* an enormously successful collection of verse satires on the government purporting to be letters dropped by the postman.

Under these circumstances, it is understandable that Murray should have objected that there was "too much about politics" (*BLJ,* IV, 18) in the dedication. Byron told Moore that Murray was "a damned Tory" (*BLJ,* IV, 18), but he composed an alternative, moderating the references to Irish politics and giving Moore the choice.[14] Two weeks later, Byron defiantly announced to Murray: "Mr. M[oor]e has seen and decidedly preferred the part your tory bile sickens at—if every syllable were a rattle-snake or every letter a pestilence—they should not be expunged—let those who cannot swallow chew the expressions on Ireland" (*BLJ,* IV, 32). And so *The Corsair* appeared on February 1, introduced by its inflammatory preface.

One of the most repeated *ana* of the Byron legend is that, as Murray hastened to inform Byron, he had "sold on the day of publication—a thing perfectly unprecedented—10,000 copies" of *The Corsair,* but it is a story whose implications have been imperfectly understood because of bibliographical confusion. Together with *The Corsair,* Byron printed six short poems, the first of which is the *Sympathetic Address to a Young Lady,* now retitled *To a Lady Weeping* T. J. Wise, whose bibliography of Byron is still widely consulted, declared, like Coleridge and Prothero before him, that these poems were added to the second edition, but this judgment has been persuasively challenged by later scholars, and the evidence indicates that the poems were included in the first edition.[15] On January 17 Byron had set out for Newstead with Augusta, leaving behind the corrected proofs of *The Corsair.* Murray requested that *To a Lady Weeping* be withdrawn, but Byron was insistent, replying from Newstead on January 22: "The lines 'to a Lady weeping' must go with the Corsair" (*BLJ,* IV, 37). Accordingly, *To a Lady Weeping* remained, and when it and *The Corsair* appeared there was a gigantic outcry: to reprint and acknowledge a poem decrying "A Sire's disgrace, a realm's decay" in the midst of the triumphs of the British forces on the Continent was to invite condemnation. On the very day of publication, Byron was denounced in the *Courier,* which was soon joined by the *Morning Post,* whose slavish loyalty was about to earn it the nickname "Fawning Post," and the *Sun,* where a parody of the lines accused Byron of being a "dabbler in dull party rhyme" (*LJ,* II, 492). Byron found himself declared "deformed in mind & *body*" (*BLJ,* 4:49). As he wrote to Moore: "You can have no conception of the uproar the eight lines on the little Royalty's weeping in 1812 (now republished) have occasioned" (*BLJ,* IV, 51).

Without asking Byron's permission, Murray removed *To a Lady Weeping* from the later editions of *The Corsair,* to insert it in a new edition of *Childe Harold.* Byron told Moore on February 10 that the reason was that "M[urray] is in a fright, and wanted to shuffle. . . ." Fear, however, was not Murray's motive.

On February 3, 1814, Murray had written to Byron:

> After printing the poems at the end of the first edition, I transplanted them to [the seventh edition of] *Childe Harold,* conceiving that your Lordship would have the goodness to pardon this *ruse* to give additional impetus to the poem. . . . I sent, previous to publication, copies to all your friends, containing the poems at the end,[16] and one of them has provoked a good deal of discussion, so much so that I expect to sell off the whole edition of "Childe Harold" just to get at it. You have no notion of the sensation which the publication has occasioned.[17]

Byron replied the next day:

> You are to do as you please about ye. smaller poems—but I think removing them *now* from ye. *Corsair*—looks like *fear*—& if so you must allow me not to be pleased—I should also suppose that after the *fuss* of these Newspaper Esquires—they would materially assist the circulation of the Corsair—an object I should imagine at *present* of more importance to *yourself*— than C[hild]e Harold's 7th. appearance. Do as you like—but don't allow the withdrawing that *poem*—to draw any imputations of *dismay*—upon me—I care about as much for the Courier as I do for the Prince— (*BLJ,* IV, 45)

This exchange makes clear that Murray's chief concern was his sales, an interest of which Byron, too, shows himself aware, and that it is Byron, alarmed for his honor, who raises the notion of fear. Further reflection increased his care for his reputation. On February 7 he wrote Murray firmly: "On second and third thoughts the withdrawing the small poems from the *Corsair* (even to add to C[hild]e H[arol]d) looks like shrinking and shuffling—after the fuss made upon one of them by the tories—pray replace them in the Corsair's appendix" (*BLJ,* IV, 46). Two days later he repeated the request, but Murray had already anticipated him:

> As soon as I perceived the fuss that was made about certain lines, I caused them to be immediately reinstated; and I wrote on Saturday [the fifth] to inform you that I had done so. A conviction of duty made me do this. I can assure you, with the most unreserved sincerity, that "Childe Harold" did not require the insertion of the lines which have made so much noise to assist its sale; but they made it still more attractive, and my sordid propensities got the better of me. I sold at once nearly a thousand copies, of this new edition. (Smiles, I, 225)

Murray, in short, was determined to ensure that a political furor became a commercial success. In two months, by the end of March, *The Corsair* had sold out seven editions totaling twenty-five thousand copies, and the eighth edition, published in March, was gone by the end of the year.

As the print run for the first edition of *The Corsair* is likely to have been about two thousand copies, it is obvious that the ten thousand copies sold on the day of publication represent several editions.[18] Many of the purchasers no doubt had had their appetites whetted by the scandal attaching to *To a Lady Weeping* already spread by that morning's papers, so that it was in no small measure the short poem, found in the first edition and by February 5 reinstated in all subsequent editions, that stimulated the "unprecedented" demand. Hobhouse's journal entry for February 18 neatly analyzes the causes of the phenomenal popularity of *The Corsair:*

> I have read his "Corsair," which, although it has not such brilliant passages as the "Childe," is, on the whole, better. Its success has been astonishing, 13,000 copies sold in a month. The abuse showered upon Byron for the "Weep, Daughter of a Royal Line," helped it along.

Hobhouse, who had initially judged Byron to have "incautiously inserted" the lines in *The Corsair,* had soon to acknowledge that his own welcome at Murray's drawing room depended on his being the friend of Byron, "whose works are Murray's income."[19]

And what of the princess at the center of the controversy? It was the Tory tactic in 1814, as it had been in 1812, to pretend that Byron's *To a Lady Weeping* was an attempt to make Princess Charlotte "view the Prince Regent her father as an object of suspicion and Disgrace" (*LJ*, II, 463). But Charlotte remained Byron's fervent admirer. She wrote to Mercer Elphinstone on February 2, 1814:

> Lord Byron's new & best poem, as he says, was out yesterday, & I had the *first* that was issued & *devour'd* it twice in the course of the day. . . . I am quite sure you will say there are passages that would admit of being written in gold. (Aspinall, p. 108)

No doubt the substance of this letter was soon relayed to Byron. As for Princess Caroline, she let it be known that she "had requested Fuseli to paint from 'the Corsair'—leaving to him the choice of any passage for the subject," as Byron learned on March 22 (*BLJ*, III, 255). Certainly readers who first encountered *The Corsair* in this climate, placed between the dedication to Moore and *To a Lady Weeping*, apprehended the poem as modern readers by and large do not. It is one of the great strengths of Jerome McGann's new Clarendon edition of Byron's poetry to recover this context, although it must be reconstructed from the annotation rather than felt immediately in the shape of a volume.

Byron plainly relished the political celebrity earned by *To a Lady Weeping*. In March, he offered the poem in response to Moore's request for contributions to *The Two-Penny Post Bag:*

> I have nothing of the sort you mention but *the lines* (the Weepers), if you like to have them in the Bag. I wish to give them all possible circulation. The *Vault* reflection is downright actionable, and to print it would be peril to the publisher; but I think the Tears have a natural right to be bagged. . . . I cannot conceive how the *Vault* has got about,—but so it is. (*BLJ*, IV, 80)

The "Vault reflection" was the lines later titled *Windsor Poetics*, Byron's 1813 attack on the Regent, who had entered the tomb at Windsor to stand between the coffins of "heartless Henry and headless Charles." Byron was disingenuous in denying knowledge of how the poem had "got about"; he had sent it to Lady Melbourne on April

7, 1813, asking her to "give Ld. Holland or anybody you like or dislike a copy" (*BLJ*, III, 38). Within two weeks, the poem reached Princess Caroline, who passed it on to her lady-in-waiting: "as you like sometimes high treason, I send you a copy of the verses written by Lord Byron. . . . [Y]ou may communicate it to any of your friends you please" (Bury, II, 389). Though widely circulated,[20] these lines remained unpublished; others of Byron's political broadsides found their way into the papers in the months following publication of *To a Lady Weeping* and *The Corsair*. The *Condolatory Address* which Byron had sent to the beautiful Whig Lady Jersey on May 29, 1814, on the occasion of the Regent's returning her picture, appeared with Byron's name in the *Champion* on July 31, 1814, and was quoted in the *Morning Chronicle* the next day. These lines, depicting the Regent as a "vain old man" with a "corrupted eye and wither'd heart," were yet more savage than *To a Lady Weeping*. In April, Byron had published the *Ode to Napoleon Buonaparte,* anonymous but known to be his well before his name appeared on the title page of the tenth edition later in the year; Princess Caroline, in her odd English, charmingly called it "the Decadence of Bonaparte" (Bury, I, 399).

Lara appeared in this environment in August 1814. Byron remembered writing it "amidst balls and fooleries, and after coming home from masquerades and routs, in the summer of the sovereigns" (*BLJ*, IX, 170–71). His distaste for the conservative rulers whose victories were being celebrated by the lavish state visits deepened the "darkness and dismay" (*BLJ,* IV, 133) of his new poem; the story of sullen rebellion contrasts strongly with the general rejoicing. Of the mode of publication, Byron wrote Moore on July 8: "Rogers and I have almost coalesced into a joint invasion of the public" (*BLJ,* IV, 138). Even without Moore, who declined to make a third, the military metaphor was not unapt: the union of Rogers and Byron announced the quarter from which the volume proceeded. On August 6, 1814, Murray published *Lara* together with Rogers's *Jacqueline.* The writers' names were not to be seen in the first edition, but the authorship was no secret, and an advertisement informing the reader that he might "regard it as a sequel to *The Corsair"* removed any doubt that *Lara* was Byron's.

The Corsair, with its freedom-loving band of pirates led by the noble Conrad defying Turkish rule, had been markedly anti-authoritarian. Gulnare's explanation of her inability to love Seyd witnesses the evils of his tyranny as powerfully as his plan to torture Conrad: "I felt—I feel—Love dwells with—with the free" (1108). The paean to Greece that opens the third canto (taken from the unpublished *Curse of Minerva,* a continuation of Byron's denunciation of Lord Elgin) drew out the political implications, as in this apostrophe to Athens: "His Corsair's isle was once thine own domain— / Would that with freedom it were thine again!" (1232–33). In the second canto of *Lara,* the hero, who, unlike his fellow nobles, is "stainless of Oppression's crime" (816), liberates the serfs to aid him against Otho's vengeance.

David Erdman has found a telling example of how such acts led Byron's contemporaries to associate "him and his wild Giaours and Corsairs with the violent aspects of British Jacobinism": at the trial for high treason in June 1817 of Jeremiah Brandreth, a Nottingham Luddite, the defense attorney compared Brandreth to Conrad and quoted thirty lines of *The Corsair,* saying "he was sure the . . . jury would . . . concur with him in thinking that the noble poet must have taken for his model some striking resemblance to the 'Nottingham Captain.' "[21] No wonder, then, that Francis Jeffrey, reviewing *The Bride of Abydos* and *The Corsair* for the *Edinburgh Review,* saw Byron as exemplifying the "strong passions" of the current age:

> This is the stage of society in which fanaticism has its second birth, and *political enthusiasm its first true development*—when plans of visionary reform, and schemes of boundless ambition are conceived, and almost realized by the energy with which they are pursued—*the era of revolutions and projects*—of vast performances and infinite expectations. (Reiman, B, 2:849; emphasis added)

All of this suggests just how clearly *Lara,* of which Byron said the setting was only "the Moon" (*BLJ,* IV, 146), existed, and was perceived as existing, in a political context. What Byron could mean to his readers is shown by a reminiscence of William Hale White ("Mark Rutherford"), who, in an essay entitled "The Morality of Byron's Poetry: 'The Corsair,' " recalled how his father (a staunch Whig), and "a compositor in a dingy printing office, repeated verses from 'Childe Harold' at the case." In Rutherford's novel *The Revolution in Tanner's Lane,* a character comments: "Not to the prosperous man, a dweller in beautiful scenery, well married to an intelligent wife, is Byron precious, but to the poor wretch, say some City clerk, with an aspiration beyond his desk."[22] Just as the treatment of Princesses Caroline and Charlotte provided an issue that united upper- and lower-class opposition to the Regent, so the appeal of Byron's poetry cut across class boundaries to find a receptive audience among the working classes.

That Byron attained such wide readership points to an important feature of his works—their prices. When Hobhouse brought out his *Miscellany* for ten shillings sixpence, Byron advised:

> But dont ask half a guinea for your next book, consider half a guinea carries a man to the opera, and if he goes to Hookham's [a bookseller who also sold opera tickets] tis odds but he buys more tickets than books, aye and cheaper too, try seven shillings, Mr. Hobhouse, seven shillings, Sir, stick to that . . . (*BLJ*, II, 16)

Byron repeatedly attributed the failure of the volume to its cost. Hence the *Satirist* touched a tender nerve when it complained of the price asked for his own *Giaour:* "The noble lord appears to have an aristocratical solicitude to be read only by the opulent. Four shillings and sixpence for forty-one octavo pages of poetry!" (Reiman, B, 5:2134) Byron agreed, and rebuked Murray: "it is unconscionable— but you have *no conscience*" (*BLJ*, III, 70). The later, expanded editions of *The Giaour* rose to five shillings sixpence, the same price asked for *The Bride of Abydos* and *The Corsair,* whereas the *Ode to Napoleon Buonaparte,* a pamphlet made from a single sheet, cost only one shilling sixpence. *Lara* and *Jacqueline* together cost seven shillings sixpence, but it was a larger volume than its predecessors. These prices were high but not exorbitant. What Murray may have sacrificed in the profit of each book sold he more than made up in volume.

To all of these features—content, dedications, prices, readership—Wordsworth's *The White Doe of Rylstone* forms an instructive contrast. On May 5, 1814, three months after the appearance of *The Corsair,* Wordsworth wrote rather enviously to Rogers to announce *The Excursion:* "I shall be content if the publication pays its expenses, for Mr. Scott and your friend Lord B. flourishing at the rate they do, how can an honest *Poet* hope to thrive?"[23]

Although Wordsworth had completed a version of *The White Doe* by 1808 and originally intended to publish it then, he kept it back, at least in part from apprehension of hostile reviews like those received by his *Poems, in Two Volumes* in 1807. The poem was re-submitted to the publishers in 1814, and on August 5, just before the appearance of *Lara,* the firm wrote that "Mr. Longman has perused [the manuscript] with exceeding pleasure." The final terms were confirmed in a letter of January 28, 1815, in which Longman offered to print the poem "in any form that shall be agreeable to yourself or we will print 750 in 4to paying you 100 Gs on publication by Bill at 6 Mths with the condition that no new edition be published till our own books are sold."[24] That Longman shouid have purchased the poem outright from Wordsworth was unusual in their dealings and suggests his admiration for it. The 105 pounds that he paid, while not despicable, pale beside the 700 pounds Byron received for *Lara.* Most important, Wordsworth chose to print in quarto, to show the world, as he later defiantly told Humphry Davy, his opinion of the poem.[25] Though Wordsworth may have judged *The White Doe* "in conception, the highest work he had ever produced" (Comparetti, p. 251), such a decision could only have an adverse effect on sales, as Byron, who advised Hunt the same year about *The Story of Rimini,* well knew: "don't let your bookseller publish in *Quarto* it is the worst size possible for circulation" (*BLJ,* IV, 326). But Wordsworth, who in 1802 had defined the poet broadly as "a man speaking to men," had been sufficiently stung by the reviewers to declare that he hoped that *The White Doe* would "be acceptable to the intelligent, for whom alone it is written" (Comparetti, p. 250). When the volume appeared on June 2, 1815, its price of twenty-one shillings was a clear indication that Wordsworth no longer aimed for a large popular audience. To ask a guinea for a poem of under two thousand lines, no matter how handsomely printed, a poem Longman had already computed "only makes half what we expected,"[26] was guaranteed to provoke resentment. Jeffrey, in the *Edinburgh Review,* observed that "the story of the poem, though not capable of furnishing out matter for a quarto volume, might yet have made an interesting ballad," especially, he continued, had it been treated by Byron, but nothing in the body of the notice could have been more forceful than the opening sentence: "This, we think, has the merit of being the very worst poem we ever saw imprinted in a quarto volume" (Reiman, A, 2:454–55). *The White Doe* is not that, of course, or it would not justify discussion. Jeffrey's attack on the format and attendant price of the poem is a response to a deliberate artistic gesture on Wordsworth's part. Other readers followed suit: the edition of seven hundred fifty was not exhausted sixteen years later. *Lara,* in contrast, had sold with *Jacqueline* three editions totaling six thousand copies in a month, and four editions totaling three thousand more by the end of the year when issued separately. No wonder Wordsworth was bitter.

A few weeks after the publication of *The White Doe,* on June 18, 1815, the Sunday of the Battle of Waterloo, Byron and Wordsworth dined together at the home of Samuel Rogers. The poets were to meet only twice, and their political differences that momentous evening were predictable. According to his nephew, Wordsworth maintained that Napoleon "had no chance whatever if the allies kept together," whereas Byron "seemed to wish Buonaparte wd. be victorious."[27]

Wordsworth's conservatism showed itself in other ways in the actual volume of *The White Doe.* The frontispiece is an engraving of the doe by Sir George Beaumont, artist, patron, and friend of the Wordsworths, already praised in the *Elegiac Stanzas Suggested by a Picture of Peele Castle*—and a high Tory. After the "advertisement" appears the sonnet "Weak is the will of man," which defines the task of imagination as "to pluck the amaranthine Flower / Of faith, and round the Sufferer's temples bind / Wreaths that endure affliction's heaviest shower"; the second epigraph is taken from Bacon, and affirms the strength to be obtained from trusting in "Divine protection and favour." This note is reiterated by the short poem that closes the volume, *The Force of Prayer.* The dedication is an eight-stanza poem to Wordsworth's wife, characterizing the poem that follows as a "moral strain" and testfying that the story "of female patience winning firm repose" had solaced the "wedded life" of the Wordsworths after the loss of two of their children in 1812. These prefatory materials, which give initial shape to the volume, seem remote from the political challenges of Byron's dedications or the titanic wills and tumultuous passions of his narratives. Wordsworth's account of the ill-fated Rising of the North against Queen Elizabeth in 1569 could scarcely escape analogy, in the year of Waterloo, to the turmoil of the French Revolution and its aftermath, and this tableau of grave domestic tranquillity and these declarations of faith established a political position.

The story of *The White Doe of Rylstone,* which Wordsworth assembled from traditional materials, may be quickly told. Richard Norton and eight of his sons join the revolt of Neville and Percy, under a banner symbolizing "the old and holy church" (660) reluctantly wrought by Norton's Protestant daughter, Emily. Though

Wordsworth depicts the personal dignity of Norton, he unambiguously judges the banner and the rebellion it inspirits as "an unblessed work" (350). Wordsworth's portrayal of the Catholics was not without contemporary resonance, and his presentation differs markedly from Byron's favoring of Catholic emancipation. The tale focuses on the two of Norton's children who stand apart from the rising, the eldest son Francis and Emily. Though he opposes his father's politics, Francis also feels the "sympathy of Sire and Sons" (475), and follows his father and brothers on their expedition to "See, hear, obstruct, or mitigate" (518). Before he leaves Rylstone, he prophesies to Emily: "Hope nothing, I repeat, for we / Are doomed to perish utterly. . . Espouse thy doom at once, and cleave / To fortitude without reprieve" (534–49). Francis witnesses the defeat and execution of his kin and is himself slain in seeking to fulfill his father's last request, to bear the banner to Bolton Priory. In a reversal of Wordsworth's own revolutionary youth which contrasts strongly with Byron's concern for the fate of the rebellious son (Selim, Alp, and others, as I have argued elsewhere), the act of rebellion is thus placed at the father's door: it is he who destroys the family. Whether Francis dies because in not rebelling he refused to "obey a natural lord" (468) or because in carrying the banner he participated minimally in the rebellion (as does Emily, in making the banner), rebellion of any sort is condemned. His sister, brought back from despair by sympathetic exchange with the doe who gives the poem its name, attains "a soft spring-day of holy, / Mild, delicious melancholy" (1776–77). "By sorrow lifted tow'rds her God," Emily reaches "the purest sky / Of undisturbed mortality," and is at last "set free" from earth (1870–84).

Byron mockingly dismissed Wordsworth's poem in a bit of doggerel: "I look'd at Wordsworth's milk-white 'Rylstone Doe': / Hillo!" (*BLJ*, V, 187). So severe a rejection of the dramatic possibilities inherent in the historical materials, such principled cultivation of quietism as *The White Doe* exhibits, must have seemed the antipodes of Byron's adventurousness.[28] Considered more closely, however, the distance diminishes. Byron's heroes are caught in the same dilemma as the doomed Francis, who loves the father he tries to resist: they too are usually defeated by stern but emulated older figures, the possessors of dominant paternal authority. And perhaps it is not so far from the devotion of Emily and the domestic vision of the dedicatory verses of *The White Doe* to the fidelity of Medora and the loyalty of

Gulnare/Khaled, or from all of them to the Victorian pieties of the hearth. In *The Revolution in Tanner's Lane,* the novel quoted above, what speaks to Rutherford's character from *The Corsair,* even more than its lofty, scornful daring, is the picture of "Love": "The vision of Medora will not intensify the shadow over Rosoman Street, Clerkenwell, but will soften it."[29]

That Byron's tale could have a softening effect as well as a revolutionary one is less surprising than it first seems. The exaggerated individualism of the Byronic hero is the antithesis of the annulment of self in *The White Doe,* but this individualism withdraws the Byronic hero from any concerted political involvement. Lara leads a popular insurrection only to protect himself: "By mingling with his own the cause of all, / E'en if he failed he still delayed his fall" (II, 240–41). Byron reiterates Lara's indifference to others: "What cared he for the freedom of the crowd? / He raised the humble but to bend the proud" (II, 252–53). In statements like these, politics retreats before psychology. The reader's attention is fixed on the hero, who exists in magnificent isolation. Defeat nourishes such a figure as much as victory: all gestures, whatever their content, in the end function chiefly to augment his grandiose self. For Lara even death, the final removal from the sphere of social action, is converted to the crowning act of self-aggrandizement, the theatrically noble end. In his flamboyance the Byronic hero is as alien to any genuine political engagement as his opposite, the martyred Emily. This narcissistic self-concentration makes "Byronism" an attitude rather than an agenda and cuts against the social and political sentiments with which the tales are filled. Their overall effect is less radical than the stirring phrases suggest when detached from context.[30]

This tension between their expressed political views and their underlying psychological configuration precludes any narrowly political interpretation of the tales and also explains some of their wide success. Readers of diverse persuasions could find themselves reflected in the tales; the rebelliousness of Conrad or his somewhat incongruous gentlemanliness, the passion of Gulnare or the devotion of Medora, exert very different appeals. If the tales do not place the stuff of politics at their imaginative center (as Byron's later historical dramas do), that limitation, from one perspective, enlarges their range of interest. Princess Charlotte, avidly admiring what she found a *"loving & loveable"* print of Byron, or crying "like a *fool"* over his verses to Annabella, behaved like many another young girl in England, seeing in Byron not only a poet aligned with her cause but also, more powerfully, a romantic ideal (Aspinall, pp. 233, 241). The conservative Murray, founder of *The Quarterly Review* and publisher to the Admiralty, was happy to publish *The Corsair* and *Lara,* but when, after the theological scandal of *Cain,* Byron turned in the later cantos of *Don Juan* to explicit political satire and prophecy, Murray abandoned what had been an immensely lucrative relationship. Appearing under the radical auspices of John Hunt, *Don Juan* was ignored or attacked in the reviews but sold by tens of thousands, in editions priced as low as one shilling. The tales evaded such polarization, because their portrayal of character modified the political categories from which they emerged, gaining from this enriching complication their continuing affective power. Fully to appreciate the tales we must incorporate into our understanding of them their political materials, both the political themes intrinsic to them and the circumstances in which they came into being, which have become part of the history of their meaning. Such a contextual approach adds dimensions to Byron's poems, provided it is not taken as itself exhausting their interest. As the surprising affinities with *The White Doe of Rylstone* reveal, it is through their refusal to be limited by the very kinds of explanation needed to recover their full meaning that the tales retain their fascination.

Notes

1. On Rogers's intimacy with Wilkes, Fox, Sheridan, Tooke, and Sharp, see P. W. Clayden, *The Early Life of Samuel Rogers* (London: Smith Elder, 1887). For the friendship of Rogers and Byron, see also Ernest Giddey, "Byron and Samuel Rogers," *The Byron Journal* 7 (1979): 4–19.

2. Byron made a partial list of the papers reporting the speech in his letters. See *Byron's Letters and Journals,* ed. Leslie A. Marchand (Cambridge, Mass.: Harvard University Press, 1973–), II, 166–67. Hereafter cited in the text as *BLJ.*

3. Henry Richard Vassall, 3d Lord Holland, *Further Memoirs of the Whig Party,* ed. Lord Stavordale (London: John Murray, 1905), p. 123.

4. In *Byron's Politics* (Brighton: Harvester, 1987), Malcolm Kelsall argues that Byron remained within the discourse of the aristocratic Whig opposition and thus increasingly out of touch with the evolving political realities of postwar Britain. As the remainder of this chapter and Chapter 10 suggest, Byron's work appealed to groups beyond his own undeniable class allegiances.

5. Frank Peel's *The Rising of the Luddites* (1880, rpt. 1968, 4th ed. rev.,

with intro. by E. P. Thompson [New York: Augustus Kelley]) gives a dramatized view of the comparative fame of speech and poem: "The effect of this impassioned harangue on the noble lords who listened to it was, we may well believe, sufficiently startling, and the political opinions of Lord Byron almost caused as much sensation for a time as his wonderful poem" (p. 76). See also Byron's shrewd comment, remembered by R. C. Dallas, to whom he had donated the copyright of *Childe Harold:* "He concluded with saying, that he had, by his speech, given me the best advertisement for Childe Harold's Pilgrimage." *Recollections of the Life of Lord Byron* (London: Knight, 1824), p. 204.

6. Reprinted in *The Romantics Reviewed*, ed. Donald H. Reiman (New York: Garland, 1972), Part B, 3:1079. Hereafter cited in the text as Reiman.

7. *Lord Elgin and the Marbles* (London: Oxford University Press, 1967), p. 189.

8. *The Works of Lord Byron, Letters and Journals*, ed. R. E. Prothero, Vol. II (London: John Murray, 1898), p. 25n. Hereafter cited in the text as *LJ.*

9. *Recollections*, p. 236.

10. *Letters of the Princess Charlotte 1811–17*, ed. A. Aspinall (London: Home & Van Thal, 1949), pp. 35, 50. Hereafter cited in the text as Aspinall.

11. Lady Charlotte Bury, *The Diary of a Lady-in-Waiting* (London: Lane, 1908), II, 280. Hereafter cited in the text as Bury.

12. P. W. Clayden, *Rogers and His Contemporaries* (London: Smith Elder, 1889), I, 70.

13. *The Harp That Once* (New York: Holt, 1937), p. 140.

14. The alternative is printed in *Lord Byron: Complete Poetical Works*, ed. Jerome J. McGann, Vol. III (Oxford: Clarendon, 1981), p. 446. All quotations of Byron's poetry are taken from this edition.

15. Wise's reconstruction of the textual history of the volume is found in his *A Bibliography of the Writings in Verse and Prose of George Gordon Noel, Baron Byron* . . . (1933, rpt. 1963 London: Dawson's), I, 92–98. It was persuasively disputed by William H. McCarthy, Jr., "The First Edition of Byron's 'Corsair,' " *The Colophon*, n.s., 2, no. 1 (Autumn 1936): 51–59; and dismissed as "fantastic" by Francis Lewis Randolph, *Studies for a Byron Bibliography* (Lititz, Pa.: Sutter House, 1979), p. 33. Carl Woodring is led astray by Wise's error; the account by Leslie Marchand, on which I have drawn throughout, is accurate, although, as I try to show, it was not merely Murray's "Tory associations and publisher's fears" that led him to shift *To a Lady Weeping* (*Byron: A Biography* [New York: Knopf, 1957], p. 434). See also McGann, III, 444–45.

16. This explains how the newspapers were able to condemn *To a Lady Weeping* on the very day it appeared.

17. Samuel Smiles, *A Publisher and His Friends: Memoir and Correspondence of the Late John Murray*, 2d ed. (London: John Murray, 1891), I, 224. Hereafter cited in the text as Smiles.

18. See Randolph, *Studies*, p. 2.

19. John Cam Hobhouse, *Recollections of a Long Life 1786–1816*, ed. Lady Dorchester (London: John Murray, 1909), I, 86, 83, 99. Byron's unease

about this commercial success is acutely examined by Robert Escarpit, *Lord Byron: Un tempérament littéraire* (Paris: Le Cercle du Livre, 1957), I, 96–102.

20. The *Antijacobin Review*, for example, alludes to them as Byron's in its review of *The Bride of Abydos* and *The Corsair* (Reiman, B, 1:49).

21. David Erdman, "Byron and Revolt in England," *Science and Society* 11 (1947): 234–48. This chapter is indebted as well to three other essays by Erdman: "Lord Byron and the Genteel Reformers," *Publications of the Modern Language Association* 56 (1941): 1065–94; "Lord Byron as Rinaldo," *PMLA* 57 (1942): 189–231; and "Byron and 'The New Force of the People,'" *Keats-Shelley Journal* 11 (1962): 47–64. I have also learned greatly from Carl Woodring's *Politics in English Romantic Poetry* (Cambridge, Mass.: Harvard University Press, 1970).

22. The quotations from William Hale White are taken from *Byron: The Critical Heritage*, ed. Andrew Rutherford (New York: Barnes & Noble, 1970), pp. 369–72. On White's father, see Irvin Stock, *William Hale White* (London: Allen & Unwin, 1956), p. 33.

23. *The Letters of William and Dorothy Wordsworth, The Middle Years, Part II, 1812–1820,* ed. E. de Selincourt, rev. by Chester L. Shaver (Oxford: Clarendon, 1970), p. 148.

24. W. J. B. Owen, "Letters of Longman & Co. to Wordsworth, 1814–36," *The Library,* 5th series, 9 (March 1954): 25–34. See also Owen's "Costs, Sales, and Profits of Longman's Editions of Wordsworth," *The Library,* n.s. 12 (June 1957): 93–107.

25. Alice Pattee Comparetti, *The White Doe of Rylstone by William Wordsworth: A Critical Edition,* Cornell Studies in English, No. 29 (Ithaca: Cornell University Press, 1940), p. 277. Hereafter cited in the text as Comparetti. Quotations from *The White Doe* in the text are from *The White Doe of Rylstone; or The Fate of the Nortons,* ed. Kristine Dugas (Ithaca: Cornell University Press, 1988).

26. Letter of August 5, 1814.

27. Mark L. Reed, *Wordsworth: The Chronology of the Middle Years 1800–1815* (Cambridge, Mass.: Harvard University Press, 1975), pp. 498–99. If Wordsworth's memory of having met Byron only twice is correct, this is presumably the same evening of which Rogers recalled that "Wordsworth tried to talk his best and talked too much—he did not appear to advantage" (*Henry Crabb Robinson on Books and Their Writers,* ed. E. J. Morley [London: 1938], I, 436), but of which Byron responded to Annabella's question "Well, how did the young poet get on with the old one?" by declaring, "I had but one feeling from the beginning of the visit to the end—reverence!" (*Diary, Reminiscences, and Correspondence of Henry Crabb Robinson,* ed. Thomas Sadler [London: Macmillan, 1869] III, 488).

28. The contrast may be epitomized by the lines from *The Borderers* that after 1837 formed the motto to *The White Doe:* "Action is transitory— a step, a blow, / The motion of a muscle—this way or that— / 'Tis done; and in the after-vacancy / We wonder at ourselves like men betrayed: / Suffering is permanent, obscure and dark, / And has the nature of infinity"; and Byron's journal entry of November 24, 1813: " 'Action—action—action'—said Demos-

thenes: 'Actions—actions,' I say, and not writing,—least of all, rhyme" (*BLJ*, III, 220).

29. *Byron: The Critical Heritage*, p. 371.

30. Without seeking to analyze it further, Andrew Rutherford has commented with some asperity on the "formula [of the tales] of exciting without radically disturbing" ("Byron the Best-Seller," *Byron Foundation Lecture* [Nottingham: University of Nottingham, 1964], p. 20). Though more persuasive in outline than in detail, *Social Relations in Byron's Eastern Tales* (Rutherford, N.J.: Fairleigh Dickinson University Press, 1987), by Daniel P. Watkins, provocatively reads the specious autonomy of the Byronic hero as itself the sign of Byron's liberal bourgeois individualism.

10

The Hone-ing of Byron's *Corsair*

Attention to the technology of reproduction reveals, as does scarcely any other line of inquiry, the decisive importance of reception; it thereby allows the correction, within limits, of the process of reification undergone by the work of art. Consideration of mass art leads to a revision of the concept of genius; it is a reminder not to overlook the invoice which alone allows the inspiration involved in the genius of a work of art to become fruitful.[1]

"You should not let those fellows publish false 'Don Juans,' " Byron protested to his publisher, John Murray, on learning that William Hone had brought out a spurious third canto of his poem.[2] Hone's connection with the publication of *Don Juan* is a comparatively well-studied affair, but it was not the first occasion on which the names of the poor, dissenting, radical publisher and the aristocratic poet were linked. In April 1816, Byron's *Fare Thee Well* and *A Sketch from Private Life,* originally set up in an edition of fifty copies for private circulation, had been reprinted in John Scott's *Champion* and then repeatedly pirated.[3] The most widely known of these editions of Byron were assembled by Hone, who entitled them *Poems on His Domestic Circumstances.* His first edition also contained *Napoleon's Farewell,* the ode on Waterloo, putatively "from the French," *On the Star of the Legion of Honor,* and two spurious poems, an ode (*Oh Shame to Thee*), and *Madame Lavallette.* By Hone's sixth edi-

216

tion, still in 1816, the total had grown to nine poems by the addition of Byron's *Adieu to Malta* and 112 lines of *The Curse of Minerva*. These pirated editions have a twofold significance. Most of the poems are not domestic but political, marks of Byron's sympathy with Napoleon against the reactionary monarchies that had defeated him. The juxtaposition of the two kinds of poems points up the degree to which Byron's separation from Annabella became a political issue: criticism of his private morality formed a large part of the Whig attack on the Regent, and the Tories were only too ready to reciprocate by exploiting the scandals now surrounding one of his prominent opponents. Both admirers and detractors of Byron were fascinated by the *Poems on His Domestic Circumstances,* and Hone's compilations alone, moderately priced at one shilling, reached a twenty-third edition by 1817.[4] These sales are the second important feature, because they show, in the words of Graham Pollard, that the works that "in Byron's lifetime . . . had a vastly greater circulation than anything else he wrote"[5] owed much of their fame to Hone and other pirates.

Between his publication of these poems in 1816 and his responses to *Don Juan* in 1819, Hone brought out in 1817 an unauthorized adaptation of Byron's *Corsair.* This text is noted in Samuel Chew's *Byron in England* and the bibliographies, but it has never attracted attention. This is not surprising, perhaps, because in strictly literary terms it is not very good, but it throws into relief facets of Byron's original volume otherwise less visible.[6] The appearance of Byron's work under Hone's imprint, moreover, precisely focuses aspects of Byron's contemporary reputation obscured by the merely internal relations of the accepted canon of English literature, and these in turn suggest some larger questions about the modes of existence of literary works in their own time.[7]

The first question Hone's adaptation raises is why it should have appeared in 1817. After the immense success of *The Corsair* in 1814—seven editions totaling tens of thousands of copies—sales of the poem naturally slowed; an eighth and ninth edition appeared in 1815, from which point the poem was available in Murray's collected editions. There had been no separate issue of the poem for at least a year, therefore, when Hone's adaptation appeared, and it was followed in 1818 by a reset version from Murray, the tenth edition. Although I cannot offer a certain explanation for this renewed interest in *The Corsair,* some evidence of what the poem may have meant to its audience in 1817 and of the activities of William Hone in that year may illuminate the subject.

On January 28, 1817, the Regent's carriage was surrounded by a hostile crowd and stoned as he returned from the opening of Parliament. The government, alarmed, or at least seizing upon the incident to fabricate an alarm, pushed through the so-called Gagging Acts and eventually obtained the suspension of habeas corpus. Hone, since 1796 a member of the London Corresponding Society, the working-class wing of the reform movement, replied by founding a two-penny weekly journal, the *Reformists' Register,* in which he was aided first by Francis Place, the radical tailor, and then by Jeremy Bentham. Modeled on Cobbett's famed "twopenny trash," the *Political Register,* Hone's paper took up some of the slack created when Cobbett, afraid like other radicals of arrest, fled to America.

The *Reformists' Register* did not encompass all of Hone's radical publishing in 1817, and I pass over his numerous satiric pamphlets to concentrate on the main events. On February 13, 1817, Sherwood, Neely, and Jones published for the first time Southey's youthful drama *Wat Tyler* (1794). Embarrassed by the sudden unauthorized appearance of this memento of his Jacobinical sympathies, Southey sought an injunction to halt publication.[8] The decision of the Lord Chancellor was a landmark in the tangled history of copyright, to which I will return. Lord Eldon ruled that according to precedent "a person cannot recover in damages for a work which is, in its nature, calculated to do injury to the public." Precisely because *Wat Tyler* was seditious, therefore, the Court of Chancery could not stop its distribution, a paradoxical conclusion which Eldon adhered to in full recognition that its effect might be "to multiply copies of mischievous publications." Sherwood, Neely, and Jones nonetheless withdrew their edition, perhaps, as they said, "in deference to the Lord Chancellor's opinion of its mischievous tendency," perhaps because they feared that the opinion left them vulnerable to the graver charge of seditious libel. Hone stepped into the breach, quickly bringing out an edition of *Wat Tyler* at the same price of three shillings sixpence, and adding a preface attacking Southey as an apostate to liberty, charges that were to receive their most damning expression in Byron's *Vision of Judgment* (1822). The radical campaign to discomfit the laureate and the ministers for whom he spoke continued with ever cheaper editions, some of which sold for as little as twopence. Sales were rumored to have reached as high as sixty thousand copies, far exceeding the success of any of Southey's legitimate poems.

In February 1817 Hone also published the works with which his name has ever since been associated: *The Late John Wilkes's Catechism of a Ministerial Member, The Political Litany,* and *The Sinecurist's Creed.*[9] These twopenny pamphlets put crude parodies of the liturgy to forceful satiric use, as a sample of the *Catechism* demonstrates:

Q. Rehearse the Articles of thy Belief.
A. I believe in George, the Regent Almighty, Maker of New Streets, and Knights of the Bath.

    And in the present Ministry, his only choice, who were conceived of Toryism, brought forth of William Pitt, suffered loss of place under Charles James Fox, were execrated, dead, and buried. In a few months they rose again from their minority; they re-ascended to the Treasury benches, and sit at the right hand of a little man with a large wig; from whence they laugh at the Petitions of the People who may pray for Reform, and that the sweat of their brow may procure them Bread.

Hone issued the parodies on February 14; informed that they had been found blasphemous, he stopped their sale on February 22. In that week they sold more than three thousand copies, and their notoriety was such that the still more radical publisher Richard Carlile soon released another edition of them. Despite his having withdrawn the pamphlets, Hone found himself the target of three ex officio informations filed by the Attorney General, each charging him with blasphemous libel. Such an instrument enabled the Attorney General to file a complaint without convening a grand jury, and thus operated as a general weapon of intimidation. On May 3, Hone was arrested; unable to post bond and sureties, he remained until July 5 in prison, whence he edited the *Reformists' Register.*

The first case, that of the *Catechism,* came to trial in the Court of King's Bench on December 18. The impoverished Hone elected to defend himself, rebutting charges of blasphemy by courageously insisting on his true intentions. "From the beginning to the end of the production in question," he asserted, "the subject and the object were political." "It was essential to him that the jury should also understand," he reiterated, "that had he been a publisher of Ministerial parodies, he should not now be defending himself on the floor of the Court." To prove his point, Hone read one after another a series of parodies that had never been prosecuted, including some by

Canning, currently a cabinet minister, in the *Anti-Jacobin,* others from *Blackwood's,* and going back through his wonderfully eclectic reading to Martin Luther and several eminent churchmen. Hone read for hours, his comic materials regularly producing bursts of laughter in the courtroom. In less than a quarter of an hour's deliberation the jury acquitted him. The anomaly of English law that permitted the very pamphlets the government was trying to suppress to be reproduced in the transcripts and newspaper accounts of the trials once they had been entered in testimony exposed the prosecution to ridicule.

The reverse only increased the government's determination. Though ill, Lord Chief Justice Ellenborough replaced Justice Abbott as the presiding judge at the next trial. The second day was much like the first, but one aspect of the bill against Hone deserves to be stressed. The Attorney General had argued that the low price of the pamphlets placed them in the hands of "the lower classes of society, which are not fit to cope with the sort of topics which are artfully raised for them," and had inveighed against "such publications [being] cheaply thrown among this class of people." Hone now replied that twopence was merely the customary price for half a sheet, on which he could make an adequate profit, and that he knew that the wealthy as well as the poor had purchased the pamphlets. A day's fencing between Hone and Ellenborough, greatly displeased by the amusement provoked by Hone's selections, ended as before with Hone's acquittal. It was widely expected that the government would abandon its course; an editorial in the *Times* warned that the verdicts indicated the temper of the people. Ellenborough, however, persisted, and on December 20 Hone was acquitted for the third time, in twenty minutes.

It was a humiliating setback for Ellenborough, who soon retired, dying shortly afterward, and for Tory prestige. The Wordsworths, deeply committed to the "House of Lonsdale," were in London at the time of the trials, and Dorothy no doubt conveyed her brother's sentiments when she wrote Thomas Monkhouse: "The acquittal of Hone is enough to make one out of love with English Juries."[10] To others, the verdicts were a landmark in the fight for freedom of the press; twenty thousand people cheered Hone outside the hall on the third day, and an ample subscription was raised on his behalf. He quickly published the three trials, which were available separately at one shilling each or together with additional materials at four shillings, and they ran into many editions. Buyers of these documents of radical triumph would have found Byron's *Poems on His Domestic Circumstances* and a shilling portrait of the poet listed among Hone's publications, which included such titles as the *Addresses* of Charles Phillips, a flamboyant Irish radical, and the *Letters to the Lord Mayor* by Major Cartwright, whose petition for reform Byron had presented at his last speech in Parliament in 1813.

One other important perspective needs to be outlined in order to suggest the aura of an edition of *The Corsair* from Hone in 1817. In June, there had been an uprising at Pentridge, fomented in part by government *agents provocateurs* and quickly crushed.[11] The leaders, respectable workingmen, were harshly indicted for high treason in July and brought to trial at the Derby Assizes in the middle of October. Jeremiah Brandreth, the "Nottingham Captain," who in the course of the rising had killed a man, was found guilty on the 18th, as was William Turner on the 21st. Faced with these convictions, the defense sought to exonerate the third man charged, Isaac Ludlam, by arguing that he had only "yielded to the overpowering force of their extraordinary leader." No doubt remembering Byron's maiden speech in Parliament in 1812 against the death penalty for this very same class of rioting Nottingham weavers, Thomas Denman, a Whig, attempted to establish the irresistible magentism of Brandreth by comparing him to Byron's Corsair. "I may spare the Court the trouble of hearing a second time, my own observations upon him," Denman began, "because I have since found him so wonderfully depicted by a noble poet of our own time, and one of the greatest geniusses of any age, that I shall take the liberty of now reading that prophetic description. It will perfectly bring before you his character, and even his appearance, the commanding qualities of his powerful but uncultivated mind, and the nature of his influence over those that he seduced to outrage." Denman then read some thirty lines of *The Corsair,* including the famous description of Conrad's mysterious power:

> What is that spell that thus his lawless train
> Confess and envy, yet oppose in vain;
> What should it be that thus their faith can bind,
> The power, the nerve, the magic of the mind.[12]

Unfortunately, Denman's exculpatory tactic failed, and Ludlam, too, was found guilty. The moment is nonetheless provocative, for if it shows Byron's poem invoked in an effort to shape history, it also shows how history shaped the significance of Byron's poem. It was one thing for Jeffrey to find *The Corsair* in 1814 the epitome of an age of "visionary reform" and "boundless ambition," of "the era of revolutions and projects";[13] it was another to have Conrad seemingly made actual in a domestic insurrection. The poem acquired a meaning not referable solely to Byron. Brandreth became a radical martyr, and his name carried far beyond radical circles.

The interweaving of these names would have been apparent to any Londoner reading the newspapers at the end of 1817. From mid-October on, the *Times* was filled with the trials of Brandreth and his associates; Denman's quotation from *The Corsair* and his reported statement that "the noble poet could not have drawn a truer picture if he had actually contemplated Jeremiah Brandreth" appeared on the front page on October 27. The prisoners were executed on November 7, the day after the death of Princess Charlotte, a rallying point of the Whigs to whom Byron had addressed his celebrated *To a Lady Weeping,* and particulars of their last days continued to appear until November 10. On November 14, the *Times* printed an account of the prosecution of Carlile for the publishing of Hone's parodies, and on the same day a transcript of Brandreth's trials was advertised. On the 22nd, the trial of T. J. Wooler, the publisher of the radical *Black Dwarf,* was reported; and on the 25th, there was a summary of the case of another bookseller charged with selling the parodies. These matters extended into December, when the trial of Hone himself filled the paper.[14]

These links between Hone, Byron, and Brandreth enable us to see some of the context of Hone's adaptation of *The Corsair*. If Denman's quotation was not in itself the occasion for its appearance—and I have been unable to fix the exact date of publication—still this network of radical connections best discloses the implications of Hone's title page:

Hone's
Lord Byron's Corsair
Conrad,
The Corsair;
or,
The Pirate's Isle.
A Tale.
Adapted as a Romance.
[vignette]

London:
Printed By and For William Hone,
Reformists' Register Office, 67, Old Bailey.
1817.
Price Four-pence.

Hone's proud advertisement of his address attests the co-opting of Byron, long since departed from England, by the radical cause: an adaptation of *The Corsair* emanating from the *Reformists' Register* office stands in quite another light than did the original, issued by the Tory John Murray from Albemarle Street. The price is no less significant: as the testimony in Hone's trials reveals, the authorities were fearful of the dissemination of potentially inflammatory literature among the lower classes. At Murray's price of five shillings sixpence, a standard figure for volumes of poetry from the established houses, *The Corsair* was well beyond the reach of many readers: at fourpence, less than a sixteenth the cost, it became available for a new and different audience. When in 1816 Cobbett had dropped the price of his *Political Register* to twopence and thus raised its circulation to forty thousand copies, he commented: "Two or three journeymen or labourers cannot spare a shilling and a halfpenny [the former price] a week; but they can spare a halfpenny or three farthings each, which is what they pay for a good large quid of tobacco."[15] Hone brought Byron, or at least his version of Byron, to this working-class but literate populace.

Fully a third of Hone's title page is taken up with a picture of the dramatic incident in *The Corsair* when Conrad throws off his disguise as a dervish and stands revealed in Seyd's palace. The picture is unsigned, but the Harvard copy, from which I am working, bears a laconic inscription by George Cruikshank: "Badly engraved from a drawing by me."[16] The prominent illustration seems consonant with the popular audience Hone wooed, for it certainly makes a more immediate and sensational appeal than did Murray's volume, which had no plates.[17] Hone's daughter remembered that Cruikshank had first come to Hone's attention when recommended by Sherwood (of the Sherwood, Neely, and Jones who pirated *Wat Tyler*) to touch up a plate of either "Napoleon or Byron."[18] *The Corsair* is a relatively early instance of the collaboration that was to produce the brilliant and enormously popular satires on the Regent and his ministers, the pamphlets running from *The Political House That Jack Built* (1819) through the racy commentaries on the trial of Caroline to *The Political Showman—at Home!* (1821).

Hone described his adaptation of *The Corsair* as "a romance." Whether the term had exact generic connotations for Hone's audience I doubt, but it does point to two characteristics of the text. Byron's narrative is not firmly placed in time, and the indefiniteness brings its turbulence closer to the reader. From the outset, Hone locates his story in a comfortably distant past: "In the beginning of the seventeenth century, a powerful band of Italian pirates seized upon one of the small rocky but beautiful Islands of the Grecian Archipelago, and made it their headquarters and home." This flat opening gives Hone's version that remote quality suggested in Johnson's definition of romance as "a military fable of the middle ages." It contrasts strongly with the original, in which Byron plunges the reader directly into the pirates' celebration of the superiority of their free life to the existences of the "luxurious slave" and the "vain lord of wantonness and ease." A large measure of Byron's appeal for his middle-class and aristocratic readers stemmed from the fascination the exotic holds for the perhaps overcivilized: words like *ease* and *luxury* would have been irrelevant to the audience at whom Hone aimed, but in adapting Byron to his circumstances Hone lost the paradoxical qualities that held the poet's audience.

The most important characteristic of Hone's transformation of *The Corsair* into "romance" is already apparent in the excerpt just quoted: except for a few lines from the original at the head of each of the four chapters into which Hone divides the story and two verses of Medora's song, his adaptation is in prose. This, too, seems a sign of Hone's assessment of his market, for not only does he sacrifice the rapidity and variety of Byron's couplets, he makes some predictable lexical alterations as well. To a query from Murray about the propriety of putting the name of Cain in the mouth of a Muslim in *The Bride of Abydos,* Byron had angrily replied: "I don't care one lump of Sugar for my *poetry*—but for my *costume*—and my *correctness* on those points . . . I will combat lustily" (*BLJ,* III, 165). As one might expect, Hone eliminates most (but not all) of the exotic words that gave Byron's poems their air of authenticity. *Sirocco, capote, pilaff, almah, saick, afrit,* and *serai* all disappear from his text, although most of these would have been familiar to educated English readers from the vogue of orientalism begun by Beckford's *Vathek* (1786) and reinforced by the popularity of travel literature. Hone's

Conrad speaks like a bluff Englishman; it is somewhat disappointing to find the gloomy, commanding Byronic hero asking his companions for assistance in accents like these:

> "Friends and fellow-warriors, you are aware that I am not a man of words; and you will acquit me of unmeaning vanity, when I ask you to say if you regard me as an able and disinterested leader?"

This speech arises from one of the changes Hone makes in the structure of *The Corsair*. His additions to the plot help to define by contrast the disjunctive qualities from which Byron's narratives gain power. Hone recognizes, for example, that the secret past of the Byronic hero is intrinsic to his effect, and so he writes that "of the origin of this their commander, none of the pirates knew anything." Yet Hone cannot resist filling in the gaps that Byron tantalizingly leaves in his poem, and so invents a prehistory that has no warrant in the original. Conrad is made "by birth . . . a noble Venetian" who "had fallen in love, during his prosperity, with the young and beautiful daughter of another magnifico of Venice, who had encouraged his addresses until the result of his imprudence became apparent, when he abruptly dismissed him." Conrad persuades his beloved to elope with him, but they are discovered, and Conrad is banished. "From this moment, the character of Conrad was determined; and he solemnly dedicated himself to a life of rapine and revenge." Hone seems to have cribbed this twist from *The Siege of Corinth* (1816), of which the hero, Alp, is a Venetian who turns renegade when Francesca's stern father denies him Francesca's hand. The conflation of two of Byron's tales suggests that the Byronic hero is no mere product of later criticism: Byron and his heroes formed one composite myth, overstepping the particularities of any one tale. Hone thus tells the reader what the pirates don't know, and this all too conventional story strips the glamour from the Byronic hero, replacing the artful vagueness that stimulates the imagination with a reductive explanation of Conrad's character. "My narration may have suggested," to use the phrase Byron employs in *Don Juan* (I, 59) to mock just such expectations as Hone patly fulfills, that Conrad's beloved is Medora. In *The Corsair,* Conrad's love for Medora is a given of the text: Byron offers no account of its beginning or development, and the reader accepts her presence in the story without inquiring further. Hone diminishes the absolute primacy of Conrad's passion for Medora by the very details he adds in order to establish it.

I have argued elsewhere that the plot of *The Corsair* is founded on the splitting and duplication of the heroine in Medora and Gulnare, and Hone responds to this logic of repetition by generating a structure still more schematic than Byron's own.[19] As in the second part of the tale Conrad, disguised as a dervish, raids Seyd's palace and attempts to rescue Gulnare, so in the new materials added before the commencement of the story proper, Conrad, disguised as a Turk, raids the convent in which Medora has been immured by her father, rescues her, and brings her to the pirates' island. I expected when first taking up his adaptation that Hone would have deepened the radical emphases of the original, but this denunciation of "parental tyranny" and brief glimpse of antimonasticism is the only instance in which Hone might be said to exceed Byron. In fact, Hone moralizes relentlessly, and his desire to compass Byron's tale within the bounds of decency leads him into some unintentionally funny contradictions. "Nature triumphed," Hone proclaims when Medora agrees to leave the convent with her lover, but Nature is not permitted to rule alone:

> Conrad and Medora were united by a captive friar the moment they reached the island, but some time elapsed before Medora clearly comprehended the lawless occupation of her husband. When gradually informed of the fatal truth, her heart died within her; and though nothing could estrange her affections from her lord, a secret consciousness of their mutual degradation continually haunted her.

The narrow morality of Hone's *Corsair* highlights the equivocation in Byron's portrait of his dazzling hero. Hone came from a strict nonconformist family and ended a member of a Congregational chapel; a radical he may be, but he sees the pirates only as "ruthless spoilers," never as champions of liberty. Though Byron's Conrad, exhorting his comrades to free the women trapped in Seyd's burning seraglio, lectures them "wrong not on your lives / One female form—remember—*we* have wives" (II, 202–3), Hone's depiction of the marriage of Conrad and Medora bespeaks an even greater propriety, and indicates the distance between Byron's aristocratic nonchalance about sexual matters and the *mores* of the working-class radicals with whom he shared political ground.

Hone's unwillingness to palliate Conrad's reputation is visible in the conclusion of his adaptation. Byron's poem closes with the death of Medora and the disappearance of Conrad:

> Long mourned his band whom none could mourn beside;
> And fair the monument they gave his bride;
> For him they raise not the recording stone—
> His death yet dubious, deeds too widely known;
> He left a Corsair's name to other times,
> Linked with one virtue, and a thousand crimes.

Although in Hone's version the original rhymes are still disconcertingly audible beneath the prose, the detail of the prolonged mourning and the final epigrammatic summary of the Corsair's fame have been omitted:

> The band raised a fair tomb to Medora; but the death of Conrad dubious, and his exploits too well known, they forebore to record them on perishable stone. The fate of Gulnare remains in obscurity.

The sentence about Gulnare that Hone substitutes for the most memorable couplet of Byron's poem witnesses a need to tie up every thread of a story, even when there is nothing to be said, and this conventional closure again foregrounds Byron's experiments with narrative form in the tales.

Thus far I have been proceeding from Hone's adaptation; it is perhaps even more instructive to examine Byron's work from the perspective of its bastard offspring. To turn from Hone's closely printed sixteen-page pamphlet to Murray's fine paper and generous margins is to encounter a conception of the book as a handsome cultural artifact rather than merely as a means of cheap mechanical reproduction. The exalted cultural position occupied by *The Corsair* is displayed in several signs of the original editions dropped by Hone. The title page, for example, contains a motto from "Tasso, Canto decimo, Gerusalemma Liberata," and each canto of the poem is headed by similarly untranslated epigraphs from Dante's *Inferno*. Within the poem there are allusions to Ariadne and Cleopatra and, in the lines on Athens which Byron took from his unpublished *Curse of Minerva* to open Canto III, to Socrates and to Greek place names known from myth and history. This presumption of a traditionally educated audience is apparent in the notes as well, where Byron refers the reader to *Orlando Furioso* and supports the verisimilitude of Conrad's entering Seyd's palace in disguise by citing analogies from Gibbon and from Sismondi (in French and Latin). All these are cut by Hone, no doubt as not germane to the story and inappropriate for his audience, but it is these markers that together define the milieu of Byron's work.

As the notes are not integrally part of *The Corsair* it might seem that lopping them off would be a trivial matter, but they contribute surprisingly to the overall effect of the poem. The notes establish the presence of Byron himself, whether in the knowledgeable glosses on the poem's esoteric vocabulary and the length of Greek twilights, the irony with which he dismisses his own sensationalism, as in the blasé remark upon Seyd's tearing his beard that it is "a common and not very novel effect of Mussulman anger," or the worldly observation on gallows humor that "During one part of the French Revolution, it became a fashion to leave some 'mot' as a legacy; and the quantity of facetious last words spoken during that period would form a melancholy jest-book of considerable size." Byron's lordly insouciance stands out most vividly in the paragraph he appended to the passage from *The Curse of Minerva:*

> The opening lines as far as section II have, perhaps, little business here, and were annexed to an unpublished (though printed) poem; but they were written on the spot in the Spring of 1811, and—I scarce know why—the reader must excuse their appearance here if he can.

The careless and negligent ease of a man of quality could scarcely be carried further.

The witty authorial figure of the notes nicely offsets the melodramatic intensity of *The Corsair* itself, and this speaker is the one initially heard in the volume. The reader first meets a seven-page dedication to Thomas Moore, printed in larger type than the following poem, which from its opening, "My dear Moore," establishes a tone of gentlemanly intercourse. The Byron who modestly asks, "May I add a few words on a subject on which all men are supposed to be fluent, and none agreeable?—Self," who discourses on the heroic couplet and Spenser, Scott, Milton, and Thomson, and who good-naturedly agrees that Childe Harold is "a very repulsive personage" is not finally to be confused with his wild Giaours and Corsairs.

The urbane frame of the notes and dedication subtly influences our perception of *The Corsair*. In its flatness, Hone's adaptation has

virtually no narrator; nothing in the text tempts the reader to speculate about a personal source for the story. A reader of the original
editions of *The Corsair,* in contrast, strongly feels the personality of
Byron in the volume, and consequently refers the unidentified narrative voice of the poem to him. Consider, for example, the following
generalizations of a sort that studs the texture of *The Corsair:*

> There is a war, a chaos of the mind,
> When all its elements convulsed—combined—
> Lie dark and jarring with perturbed force,
> And gnashing with impenitent Remorse;
> That juggling fiend—who never spake before—
> But cries, "I warned thee!" when the deed is o'er.
> (II, 328–33)

or

> Strange though it seem—yet with extremest grief
> Is linked a mirth—it does not bring relief—
> That playfulness of Sorrow ne'er beguiles,
> And smiles in bitterness—but still it smiles;
> And sometimes with the wisest and the best,
> Till even the scaffold echoes with their jest!
> (II, 446–51)

or this last, rather different from the rebelliousness usually thought to
typify *The Corsair:*

> Oh, what can sanctify the joys of home,
> Like Hope's gay glance from Ocean's troubled foam?
> (III, 565–66)

Such sentiments are what Barthes called *doxa,* unexamined common-
places about human behavior, tacitly ideological assumptions. Their
expression forms an unspoken bond between the poet and his reader,
reassuring him that however anarchic the Byronic hero may be, Byron and he inhabit the same moral universe.

The comforting familiarity of moments like these is extended in
the six supplementary poems that compose the remainder of the early
editions of *The Corsair,* also disregarded by Hone. The first of these,
To a Lady Weeping, originally printed in 1812, locates the volume
within the world of recent domestic politics. Scandalous though the

verses were, they grew from Byron's life as a Whig favorite, and point to an area of experience as immediate for the contemporary reader as the venue of the tale is remote.[20] The beautiful lyric entitled *From the Turkish* ("The chain I gave") and the two rather pallid sonnets *To Ginevra* pose no challenges to the tastes and habits of a Regency audience. These are followed by an *Inscription on the Monument of a Newfoundland Dog,* a eulogy on Byron's cherished Boatswain in a common eighteenth-century mode, as Leslie Marchand observes.[21] These verses are dated from Newstead Abbey and thus attest the status as well as the sympathetic spirit of the author. The volume ends fittingly with a passionate but conventional lyric, "Farewell! if ever fondest prayer."

Taken as a whole, then, the *Corsair* volume does not stray far from the decorum of genteel poetry of the day. The ensemble creates an untroubling impression which contains the more daring sallies Byron makes within it: the reprinting of *To a Lady Weeping* which thereby acknowledged the verses as his,[22] and the notes which suggest an archbishop of York might once have been a pirate and compare Conrad to a "brother buccaneer," Jean Lafitte, who was then playing a major role in the British defeat at the Battle of New Orleans. These gestures gave Byron's volume contemporary political applications that Hone's volume lacks, but the timing of Hone's publication and the announcements of his title page chimed with the radical resonances of *The Corsair,* whereas the cumulative effect of Byron's collection was to damp them.

In the imaginary dialogue between Byron and "Odoherty" that constitutes the fourth of the *Noctes Ambrosianae,* "Christopher North" makes the poet remark: "But I do confess—for I was born an aristocrat—that I was a good deal pained when I saw my books, in consequence of [Eldon's] decree, degraded to be published in sixpenny numbers by Benbow, with Lawrence's Lectures—Southey's Wat Tyler—Paine's Age of Reason—and the Chevalier de Faublas."[23] This presumably double objection suggests the conclusions of this essay. The first concerns price, or rather price and class. For the noble poet who gave away his copyrights, it was essential that relations with his publisher should seem an affair of gentlemen rather than a business proposition. Murray, who Hone declared was "known to be the most loyal and . . . reported to be the most opulent bookseller in the United Kingdom,"[24] calculated his sales shrewdly, and both he and

Byron did well from their partnership. As Thilo von Bremen has suggested, however, Murray may not fully have realized the possibility of increasing sales—and hence profits—by lowering the prices of his editions (p. 155). To do so, however, would have meant forsaking the respectable book trade for the popular market, and Byron, as John Wilson saw, would have keenly regretted the loss of cachet.[25] His mockery of Hobhouse for having gone beyond the gentlemen reformers, his contempt for lower-class radicals like Carlile, and his ambivalence at finding himself engaged with Cockneys like Leigh and John Hunt show the gulf Byron's consciousness of his rank put between himself and those who claimed him as an ally. I do not know the sales of Hone's adaptation of *The Corsair,* but in 1821 Byron might still have found it among the advertisements in Hone's *The Political Showman—At Home!* in what to him would have been the uncongenial company of Hazlitt's *Political Essays.*[26] It was not until the outcries caused by *Don Juan, Cain,* and *The Vision of Judgment* that Byron was to abandon Murray's elegant editions for the cheap printings of John Hunt.

The second aspect is the nature of piratical publication itself. The entwining of Byron's career with Hone culminated with the anonymous publication of *Don Juan* (1819), in an expensive quarto format designed to forestall prosecution for libel.[27] Within four days of the appearance of Byron's poem, Hone produced *Don John, or Don Juan Unmasked,* a pamphlet in which he noted with heavy irony that Murray, "Publisher to the Board of Longitude, and of the Quarterly Review—the Bookseller to the Admiralty, and a strenuous supporter of orthodoxy and the Bible Society" (p. 30), was shielded by his respectability from the reprisals Hone had incurred by his parodies. Murray, Hone charged, "actually publishes a Parody on the Ten Commandments of God [*Don Juan,* I, 205–6], whilst this prosecution is pending against Russell, for a Parody on the Litany, which is entirely a human composition" (p. 37n).[28] Hone concluded the pamphlet with a fine rhetorical flourish:

Q. Why did not Mr. Murray suppress Lord Byron's *Parody* on the Ten Commandments?
A. Because it contains nothing in ridicule of Ministers, and therefore nothing that *they* could suppose, would be to the displeasure of Almighty God. (p. 50)

The accusations were not confined to Hone's pamphlet. Aspland, the editor of the Unitarian magazine the *Monthly Repository,* had helped Hone during his trial, and the journal broadcast his contentions:

> If parodies of Scripture, *as well as of the Liturgy,* be blasphemous, even-handed justice requires that poor parodists alone should not be punished. The grossest parody of modern times is one upon The Ten Commandments in Lord Byron's *Don Juan,* published and republished within a few months, by *Murray,* of Albemarle Street, the publisher of the *Quarterly Review,* and of other "orthodox" and "loyal" works. In truth the offence is not turning the Scriptures into ridicule, but making ministers of state ridiculous.[29]

Shortly afterward, Hone came out with his spurious third canto of *Don Juan,* in which Byron's hero is tellingly metamorphosed into a radical publisher.

This controversy had its effect on Byron, who was carefully watching the fortunes of his poem from Italy. Mindful that it was likely to fall under Eldon's decree that seditious and blasphemous works could not be protected by copyright, he wrote Murray on December 4: "The third Canto of 'Don Juan' is completed in about two hundred stanzas—very decent—I believe—but do not know—& it is useless to discuss it until it can be ascertained if [it] may or may not be a property" (*BLJ,* VI, 253). Whether and in what sense an author's work was his property was precisely what was at stake. The terms of Eldon's decision made clear that the connection of author and work was not a natural one of producer and product, but a complex issue involving the reigning values of society. What was not a property if it offended prevailing norms became one if judged differently. Three years before, when James Johnston published spurious poems under his name, Byron had sought to establish his texts by fixing their publisher as the badge of authenticity. He had written Murray: "To prevent the recurrence of similar falsifications you may state—that I consider myself responsible for no publication from the year 1812 up to the present date which is not from your press" (*BLJ,* V, 139). A similar attempt to limit Hone's *Poems on His Domestic Circumstances,* however, was met by a cheeky reply:

> A paragraph in the Morning Papers notices W. Hone's Advertisement of all Lord Byron's New Poems being published by him,

> and concludes by declaring that no Poems are *"to be consid-
> ered"* as Lord Byron's or as *"being sanctioned"* by him, unless
> published by his Lordship's Bookseller, Mr. Murray, Albemarle-
> street. W. Hone thinks Mr. Murray must be aware, that though
> it may be quite expeditious that the Poems published by W. Hone
> should not be "considered" as Lord Byron's, or as being "sanc-
> tioned" by Lord Byron, yet that the public, without any effort of
> logic, will still inquire—if they are not Lord Byron's? W. Hone
> therefore presents his respectful compliments to Mr. Murray,
> and will thank him to oblige the public by stating which of the
> Seven Poems on his Domestic Circumstances, in Mr. Hone's
> Publication is not written by Lord Byron.

As Hugh J. Luke remarks, Murray might well have answered that
two of the poems in the collection were not in fact by Byron, but
there is no evidence that he did so, and Hone continued to publish.[30]
Authentic texts could not be restricted to those issued by the offi-
cially sanctioned publisher.

Hone's piracies thus bring into prominence the ways in which a
text, once written, separates from its author and enters an economy
of production and distribution, to be acted upon by forces beyond
the writer's prevision or control. Byron might well have wished to
explain *The Corsair* by the poetics of Romantic genius, but comprehension of it requires that we take into account the mundane matters
of circumstance and presentation, of price and surrounding materials.
It was by these, as much as by his clumsy refitting of the text itself,
that Hone made *The Corsair* suit his readers as it had suited Murray's very different ones. The current standard editions of Byron
disperse the poems that once appeared together, and so mask important elements of the impression the *Corsair* volume originally made.
For example, though most of the poems may be found in Volume 3
of the E. H. Coleridge edition (the *Inscription* is in Volume 1), the
format separates the tale from the *Poems 1809–13* where the shorter
pieces are located. The single-volume editions by Houghton Mifflin
and in the Oxford Standard Authors series follow generic principles
which similarly break up the contiguity of the poems, and even the
admirable new Oxford edition by Jerome McGann is forced by its
chronological ordering to place *To a Lady Weeping* in Volume 1
and *The Corsair* in Volume 3. The honing of *The Corsair* is an amus-
ing anecdote of literary history, but it is more: the adaptation directs
us to the relations between the literary text and its imagined audi-

ence, and to the influences that shape the significance of a text once published. It thus invites us to reconsider our notions of what constitutes a text and how it should be preserved and interpreted.

Notes

1. Walter Benjamin, "Edward Fuchs, Collector and Historian," *One-Way Street and Other Writings,* trans. Edmund Jephcott and Kingsley Shorter (London: NLB, 1979), p. 362.

2. *Byron's Letters and Journals,* 12 vols., ed. Leslie Marchand (London: John Murray, 1973–82), VI, 236. Hereafter cited in the text as *BLJ.*

3. For an account of this brouhaha, see David V. Erdman, " 'Fare Thee Well'—Byron's Last Days in England," *Shelley and His Circle,* ed. Kenneth Cameron, Vol. IV (Cambridge, Mass.: Harvard University Press, 1970), pp. 638–64.

4. Jerome McGann has plausibly suggested that Hone's declaration of a twenty-third edition may reflect puffery rather than the actual publication record.

5. Graham Pollard, "Pirated Collections of Byron," *London Times Literary Supplement* 1863, October 16, 1937, p. 764.

6. Samuel C. Chew, *Byron in England* (London: John Murray, 1924), p. 12n; and, for example, Oscar J. Santucho, *George Gordon, Lord Byron,* Scarecrow Author Bibliographies, No. 30 (Metuchen, N.J.: Scarecrow Press, 1977), p. 588. In the same year as this essay was first delivered, however, Marina Vitale published "The Domesticated Heroine in Byron's *Corsair* and William Hone's Prose Adaptation," *History and Literature* 10 (1984): 72–94. I did not see Vitale's study until after mine was published; she offers a more thoroughgoing ideological examination of "the two images of women built up in the two texts" (p. 74).

7. The unpublished dissertation of Hugh J. Luke, Jr., "Drams for the Vulgar: A Study of Some Radical Publishers and Publications in Early Nineteenth-Century London" (University of Texas, 1963), is an invaluable introduction to this context. See also *For the Cause of Truth: Radicalism in London 1796–1821* (Oxford: Clarendon, 1982), by J. Ann Hone, which appeared after this essay was completed.

8. The history given by Frank T. Hoadley, "The Controversy over Southey's *Wat Tyler,*" *Studies in Philology* 38 (1941): 81–96, is amplified by Luke, pp. 202–19.

9. The subsequent account draws chiefly upon *The Three Trials of William Hone . . . with the Proceedings of the Public Meeting* (London: 1818). The only biography, *William Hone: His Life and Times,* by F. W. Hackwood (London: T. F. Unwin, 1912), is incomplete and unreliable. There is a good short study by J. Ann Hone, "William Hone (1780–1842), Publisher and Bookseller: An Approach to Early 19th Century London Radicalism," *Historical Studies* (University of Melbourne) 16 (1974): 55–70. On Hone's caricatures and their background, see M. Dorothy George, *English Political Cari-*

cature: A Study of Opinion and Propaganda, 2 vols. (Oxford: Clarendon, 1959); Edgell Rickword, *Radical Squibs and Loyal Ripostes* (Bath: Adams and Dart, 1971); and John Wardroper, *Kings, Lords and Wicked Libellers: Satire and Protest 1760–1837* (London: John Murray, 1973).

10. *The Letters of William and Dorothy Wordsworth, The Middle Years, Part II, 1812–1820,* ed. Ernest de Selincourt, 2d ed., rev. by Mary Moorman and Alan G. Hill (Oxford: Clarendon, 1970), p. 410. For the response of Keats and his circle, see Aileen Ward, "Keats's Sonnet, 'Nebuchadnezzar's Dream,' " *Philological Quarterly* 34 (1955): 177–88.

11. R. J. White confesses in the preface to his *Waterloo to Peterloo* (London: Heinemann, 1957) that "This book was begun many years ago in an attempt to lay the ghost of" Jeremiah Brandreth (p. ix). Chapter 14, "The Pentrich Revolution," gives a terse account of the rising and notes the invocation of Byron at Brandreth's trial. See also David Erdman, "Byron and Revolt in England," *Science and Society* 11 (1947): 234–48.

12. Misquoted from *The Corsair,* I, 179–82. Denman, who went on to become Lord Chief Justice in the post–Reform Bill administration in 1832, had reviewed *Childe Harold's Pilgrimage I–II* for the *Monthly Review* in 1812. See *The Romantics Reviewed,* ed. Donald H. Reiman (New York: Garland, 1972), Part B, 4:1730–35. I follow *The Trials of Jeremiah Brandreth, William Turner, Isaac Ludlam . . . Taken in Shorthand by William Brodie Gurney* (London: 1817). Because the defense did not allude to the part played by *agents provocateurs,* for motives still hotly debated, this transcript must be supplemented by the materials cited in n. 14 below.

13. Francis Jeffrey, unsigned review of *The Corsair* and *The Bride of Abydos, Edinburgh Review* 23 (1814): 198–229. Quoted in *Byron: The Critical Heritage,* ed. Andrew Rutherford (New York: Barnes and Noble, 1970), p. 54.

14. The *Examiner* printed highly critical reports of the Derby trials on October 26, November 2, November 9, and December 14; on December 21, it celebrated Hone's acquittal and observed that "people will at the utmost conclude that the notions of the pious and the impious wait upon their political notions" (pp. 805–6). The description of the Derby execution printed on November 9 reveals the same mixture of religion and politics that characterized the trial of Hone: "Turner came out next and advanced with unusual firmness of step. While the executioner was putting the rope round his neck he exclaimed loudly and distinctly, 'This is all Oliver [the spy] and the government.' The Chaplain at this moment came in front of these two and *prevented any further observations"* (pp. 715–17). Quoted in the same issue is the *Chester Guardian,* which commented on the thin line separating mere misdemeanour from high treason and, doubting that there had been any real possibility of a general rising, questioned the government's stern measures: "We are not disrespectful, because one of the Counsel discovered Brandreth to be a man of *great* qualities, and has drawn a parallel, after the manner of Plutarch, between him and Lord Byron's *Corsair!*—To be sure, we thought the comparison *facetious,* but we are told that it is *fine"* (pp. 717–18). R. J. White argues that the outbreak was "revolution as Lords Liverpool and Sidmouth understood it," however "old-fashioned" and short-lived, owing nothing to the "ex-

traordinary ineptitude" of Oliver. E. P. Thompson presents Brandreth and his fellows in a more heroic light and stresses the role of Oliver in *The Making of the English Working Class* (1963; rpt. New York: Vintage, 1966), pp. 649–69.

15. Quoted in William H. Wickwar, *The Struggle for the Freedom of the Press 1819–32* (London: George Allen and Unwin, 1928), p. 54.

16. I quote from a photocopy provided me by the courtesy of the Houghton Library, Harvard University. Cruikshank later illustrated George Clinton's *Memoirs of the Life and Writings of Lord Byron* (1827), and his forty plates were sold separately for six shillings. Interestingly, he did not then repeat this scene; the two plates for *The Corsair* are of Gulnare visiting Conrad in prison and Conrad mourning Medora.

17. In 1814, however, Murray published a dozen engravings from designs by Stothard to illustrate Byron's works: two of these are for *The Corsair*. Prices of the set ranged from eighteen to forty-two shillings, making it a not inexpensive nicety. Publication of illustrations for a purchaser of Byron's poems to bind into his copies flourished. In 1814, for example, Thomas Tegg published six plates for *The Corsair*. The artist was John Thurston, a successful book illustrator, and the engraver Cosmo Armstrong, who also engraved the celebrated Phillips portrait of Byron. The price was five shillings sixpence "or Proofs, on India Paper, Ten Shillings and Sixpence."

18. Hackwood, *William Hone*, p. 189.

19. *Byron and His Fictions* (Detroit: Wayne State University Press), pp. 46–49.

20. On this poem, see Chapter 9. Jerome McGann untangles the complex publishing history of the supplementary poems in his *Lord Byron: The Complete Poetical Works* (Oxford: Clarendon, 1981), III, 444–45. Carl Woodring's *Politics in English Romantic Poetry* (Cambridge, Mass.: Harvard University Press, 1970) has a masterly chapter on Byron.

21. Leslie Marchand, *Byron: A Biography*, 3 vols. (New York: Knopf, 1957), I, 161n.

22. In *Lord Byron als Erfolgsautor*, Athenaion Literaturwissenschaft, Band 6 (Wiesbaden: Athenaion, 1977), Thilo von Bremen contrasts the furor aroused by *To a Lady Weeping* in 1814 with its having passed unnoticed in 1812 in order to show how great a difference an author's name makes to a text (p. 41).

23. John Wilson, *Noctes Ambrosianae*, rev. ed., 5 vols., ed. R. Shelton Mackenzie (New York: Widdleton, 1880), I, 205. Quoted in part in A. S. Collins, *The Profession of Letters* (New York: Dutton, 1929), p. 184.

24. I quote from a photocopy of Hone's *Don John, or, Don Juan Unmasked* (p. 37n), kindly provided by the Houghton Library, Harvard University.

25. Murray did, however, sell editions after the first at reduced prices. The three-volume *Complete Works* (1819, octavo) contained all of *Childe Harold*, the tales, *Manfred, Hebrew Melodies,* etc. for forty-two shillings; an ongoing *Collected Works* had reached Volume 7 by that year, each volume selling for seven shillings (small octavo). These sets represented a substantial

saving over the original prices—though scarcely comparable to Hone's four-penny and two-shilling productions.

26. A volume initiated as well as published by Hone.

27. See the analysis of this episode by Hugh J. Luke, Jr., "The Publishing of Byron's *Don Juan,*" *Publications of the Modern Language Association* 80 (1965): 199–209.

28. Russell, as Hone passionately explained (pp. 36–37), was a Birmingham bookseller tried and convicted in 1819 for selling Hone's parodies, despite Hone's acquittal in London in 1817. See also Wickwar, *The Struggle,* p. 108.

29. *Monthly Repository* 14 (1819): 716.

30. I follow Luke here, who quotes Hone's reply from "an unidentified and undated newspaper clipping in a scrapbook of contemporary Byroniana owned by Professor Willis W. Pratt." *Drams for the Vulgar,* pp. 224–25.

IV
Texts and History

11

"Will No One Tell Me What She Sings?": *The Solitary Reaper* and the Contexts of Criticism

I

Wordsworth once told an acquaintance that "although he was known to the world only as a poet, he had given twelve hours of thought to the conditions and prospects of society, for one to poetry."[1] Despite such an important study as Carl Woodring's *Politics in English Romantic Poetry* (Cambridge, Mass.: Harvard University Press, 1970), criticism of Wordsworth until fairly recently often read as if he were imagined to possess a bicameral mind, with one chamber for society and another, walled apart, for poetry, as if, that is, Wordsworth's lyrics stood apart from the recognized political aspirations of *The Prelude* and the conservatism of his later years. The forceful historical criticism of a new generation of critics, solidly grounded and theoretically assertive, has done much to reintegrate Wordsworth and recover the manifold bearings of his representations.[2] The following pages both participate in this critical shift and position it by taking as their starting point the dominant study these critics inherited: Geoffrey Hartman's *Wordsworth's Poetry 1787–1814*.

The continuing vitality of Hartman's book can be inferred from its publishing history. First brought out by Yale University Press in 1964 and reprinted several times in paperback thereafter, it reappeared in 1971 with a "Retrospect" standing as an introduction, and was taken up in this form by Harvard University Press in 1987. *The Solitary Reaper* is the first poem Hartman considers in his first chapter, forthrightly entitled "Thesis," and this spotlit status makes the poem a significant test case for any competing critical method. The preface to *Wordsworth's Poetry 1787–1814* announces Hartman's interests: "The view of Wordsworth presented in this book covers three things: the individual poem, the sequence of the poems, and the generic relation of poetry to the mind. Since Wordsworth is directly concerned with the growth of the individual mind, a study of the first two subjects connects easily and fruitfully with the last."[3]

These sentences provoke as much by what they leave out as by what they specify. Especially noticeable in the first is the gap between individual poems and the sequence they form, and the *generic* relation of poetry to the mind. As Hartman engagingly concedes in his "Retrospect," "I . . . was more interested, I now see, in the integrity of the mind than in that of the single poem" (xvii). The development of single poems is not all that is subordinated in this formulation: the leap from particular poems to *mind* also skips over the actual historical life of the writer. Hartman traces an evolving pattern in Wordsworth's imagination; he is comparatively uninterested in the wider social and political forces to which the pattern speaks.

By "sequence of the poems," moreover, Hartman does not mean either the order of the poems Wordsworth designed in his collections or the order of composition. He develops his argument by succes..vely discussing *The Solitary Reaper,* written in 1805; *The Boy of Winander,* written in 1799, *Strange Fits of Passion,* also of 1799; and *Tintern Abbey,* from 1798. Chapter III of *Wordsworth's Poetry,* entitled "The Chronological Pattern," follows Wordsworth's poetry from *The Vale of Esthwaite* beyond *The Excursion,* and it is here, more than two hundred pages later, that Hartman considers the poems surrounding *The Solitary Reaper* on its first publication. His concern, however, as the subheading declares, is "The Major Lyrics," and this restriction forecloses attention to the intricate interrelationships Wordsworth had created in deploying his texts.

This essay explores the two fields Hartman's concentration upon Wordsworth's "consciousness of consciousness," as the Retrospect puts it (xii), scants: Wordsworth's deliberate placement of *The Solitary Reaper* amid other works on its first appearance in *Poems, in Two Volumes* (1807), and the less definable place of the poem within a contemporary sociopolitical field. Wordsworth gave substantial care to the effect sequences of short pieces induce in their readers; the rhythms his arrangements generate are intrinsic to his intention.[4] Yet once generated, the exchanges among poems in a collection set off resonances beyond conscious design and so shade into larger issues of the social relationships that inextricably entwine the very vocabulary and procedures of a text and reach out toward the world of events in which it is embedded. In trying to recover this world, I will seem to talk around *The Solitary Reaper* but not about it, but that is the distinction the essay questions. I have deliberately shifted attention from the unchanging natural order *in* the poem to the conditions of production *of* the poem. Hartman's richly interior narrative exalts *The Solitary Reaper* but deprives the poem of its living historical force; recovering its moment and milieu with the thickness of detail I hope pardonable in a specimen demonstration draws into view further dimensions of the poem and the political implications of the imagination Hartman tracks.

The question of context in Hartman's discussion of *The Solitary Reaper* is of special interest because its ambiguity is not readily apparent. Hartman begins: "Wordsworth records in 'The Solitary Reaper' his reaction to an ordinary incident" (3). A few pages later he adds:

> It was on reading a sentence in a friend's manuscript (Wilkinson's "Tour in Scotland") that the two-year-old memory of the solitary reaper returned to him; and though the poem does not record this directly, it reflects an analogous fact, that the imagination was revived from an unexpected source. (5)

The first quotation suggests that Wordsworth's encounter with the solitary reaper actually took place on the tour he and Dorothy made of Scotland in 1803. The second, though making plain that the impetus for Wordsworth's poem was Wilkinson's *Tours to the British Mountains,* unpublished until 1824 but known to his friends in manuscript, reduces it to the status of an intermediary, a prompting that revived the memory of a specific incident. Wordsworth's own note to the poem, however, printed with it on the poem's first publication, is unusual in not citing any incident in Wordsworth's own experience: "This poem was suggested by a beautiful sentence in a MS. Tour in Scotland written by a friend, the last line being taken from it *verbatim."*

The puzzle to consider is the relation between Wilkinson's narrative, Wordsworth's tour of Scotland in 1803, and the composition of *The Solitary Reaper* in 1805. Wordsworth thought highly enough of Wilkinson's "beautiful sentence" also to transcribe it in a commonplace book, DC MS. 26: "Passed by a Female who was reaping alone, she sung in Erse as she bended over her sickle, the sweetest human Voice I ever heard. Her strains were tenderly melancholy & felt delicious long after they were heard no more." The issue is not a single poignant phrase but the network of ideas that inform Wordsworth's vision of Scotland: did Wordsworth see Scotland from the start through Wilkinson's eyes? There is a vast difference between having one's memory jogged by an outside stimulus and an original experience shaped by a previous writer, and on this the transcription offers no help, because it was almost certainly made *after* the writing of the poem.[5] Nonetheless, the possibility that Wilkinson's *Tour* underlies *The Solitary Reaper* as well as providing its memorable conclusion warrants a more extensive look than has yet been given. The perspective lays bare the filiations of *The Solitary Reaper* within *Poems, in Two Volumes* and opens to analysis the motifs of the collection. To the degree that the shift from the present-tense imperatives of the first stanza of *The Solitary Reaper* ("Behold . . . Stop . . . listen!") to the past tense of the last has been seen as the paradigm of "emotion recollected in tranquillity," the siting of the poem affects our entire sense of Wordsworth's poetry.

II

Thomas Wilkinson touches the Wordsworth circle at many points. He had been born in 1751 at Yanwath, where he continued to reside, so close to Penrith that after an 1801 visit from Wordsworth he could characterize him as "a young Poet . . . who sprung originally from the next village."[6] De Quincey, who was particularly envious that Wordsworth had addressed a poem to Wilkinson while he himself was "never honoured with one line, one allusion, from his pen," declared that Wilkinson, "for some reason that I could never fathom . . . was a sort of pet with Wordsworth," but his description conveys the basis of the affection: "he was a Quaker, of elegant habits, rustic simplicity, and with tastes, as Wordsworth affirms, 'too pure to be refined.' "[7] Despite the retirement in which he lived, Wilkinson's membership in the Society of Friends brought him into several larger ambits. Charles Lloyd was staying with him in 1795 when he published his *Poems on Various Subjects,* and he was also active in the antislavery campaign. His longest poem was *An Appeal to England on Behalf of the Abused Africans* (1795), and Thomas Clarkson began his history of the slave trade in Wilkinson's house. It was through Wilkinson that Clarkson settled a few miles away in Eusemere. Wilkinson supervised the building of his house and arranged for its sale to Lord Lowther when the Clarksons subsequently moved south (Carr, pp. 54–55). Clarkson was also a good friend of Wordsworth, who celebrated the final passage of the bill abolishing the slave trade in a sonnet to Clarkson included in the second volume of the 1807 collection.

Like the sonnet to Clarkson, the poem describing Wilkinson from which De Quincey quotes, *To the Spade of a Friend,* illustrates how in *Poems, in Two Volumes* Wordsworth cites his private circle as instances of public virtue. The apostrophe to the spade enables Wordsworth to praise Wilkinson indirectly:

> Rare Master hath it been thy lot to know;
> Long hast Thou serv'd a Man to reason true;
> Whose life combines the best of high and low,
> The toiling many and the resting few;
>
> Health, quiet, meekness, ardour, hope secure,
> And industry of body and of mind;
> And elegant enjoyments, that are pure
> As Nature is; too pure to be refined.
>   (5–12)[8]

At the beginning of the poem, Wordsworth himself takes up the humble spade "with pride," pronouncing it "a tool of honour in my hands"; at the conclusion, he imagines it inherited after Wilkinson's death, "consecrate[d]" as a "trophy," "More noble than the noblest Warrior's sword," past service but cherished by its recipient:

> His thrift thy uselessness will never scorn;
> An *Heir-loom* in his cottage wilt thou be:—
> High will be hang thee up, and will adorn
> His rustic chimney with the last of Thee!
>   (29–32)

It is all too obvious that Wordsworth has made of the personified spade the very emblem of a traditional ideal, a life close to the land, industrious, thrifty, yet elegant, reasonable, pure. The poem is a compact treasury of all the virtues ascribed to retirement from the Latin writers onward, Wordsworth's republican plainness at its most direct. Wilkinson appears as a type of the character Wordsworth celebrates elsewhere in the collection: in Clarkson, who is said to possess "a good Man's calm, / A great Man's happiness"; in *Resolution and Independence* and the *Ode to Duty,* poems Jared Curtis establishes would have been near to this one in Wordsworth's initial plan for a one-volume publication (Curtis, pp. 12–17); and most fully in the *Character of the Happy Warrior.*

In the Fenwick note to the poem Wordsworth observed of Wilkinson: "Persons of his religious persuasion do now, in a far greater degree than formerly, attach themselves to trade and commerce. He kept the old track." Wordsworth continued: "Through his connexion with the family in which Edmund Burke was educated, he became acquainted with the great man, who used to receive him with great kindness and condescension: and many times have I heard Wilkinson speak of those interesting interviews" (quoted in Curtis, p. 424). One could scarcely ask a more complete exemplum of the virtues of "the old track" than that given by this portrait of Wilkinson living "in beautiful retirement"[9] on his ancestral estate.

The opposition between "trade and commerce" and Wilkinson's adherence to the land has an evident ideological purpose signaled by the name of Burke, and also visible in the full title under which Wordsworth published his poem: "To the Spade of a Friend, / (An Agriculturist). / Composed while we were labouring together in his Pleasure-Ground." The term *agriculturist* carried in Wordsworth's day the overtones of the "improvers," those gentlemen farmers who were experimentally and scientifically transforming English agriculture. But the final phrase defines Wilkinson's social position more clearly, for Wilkinson is at work not on a farm at all but on a "Pleasure-Ground," and his tool is a spade to shape "pleasant walks" (2), not a plow to produce crops. It is important to note how consistently the "monument of peaceful happiness" (24) Wordsworth is here engaged in building cleanses "labour" of "toil" (cf. 8, 25) even while employing its vocabulary. *To the Spade of a Friend* is less a paean to "rustic" (32) existence than an image of *otium.*

The Solitary Reaper comes into being through this complex of associations. It was Wilkinson who brought Wordsworth into contact with the man who was to be his patron, Lord Lowther (soon to be Earl of Lonsdale). During a short tour of Ullswater with Dorothy in November 1805, Wordsworth saw a spot that appealed to him for their long-meditated home. He put negotiations for purchase into the hands of Wilkinson, who, when the price was raised above what

Wordsworth was willing to pay, turned without consulting him to Lord Lowther, by whom he was employed, as Dorothy put it, "to regulate the improvments in [Lowther's] grounds."[10] The design by Robert Smirke to which Lowther Castle was rebuilt in 1806 was the very image of Tory authority: to oversee its grounds was to serve at the very center of aristocratic display.[11] Lowther advanced the difference demanded by the seller, enabling Wilkinson to conclude an agreement. Wordsworth, to his embarrassment, learned of Lowther's generous action only afterward, when Wilkinson recounted his conversation with the lord: "he was personally unknown to [Wordsworth]: but he wished to be acquainted with him, and desired me to bring him to Lowther when he again came to see me."[12] The incident upon which *To the Spade of a Friend* is based occurred during his August visit to thank Wilkinson and to inspect the property. Wilkinson remembered that he duly took Wordsworth to call at the castle, but Lowther "was gone to shoot moor-game" (Carr, p. 69), enacting the aristocrat's rather than the farmer's relation to nature.

To the Spade of a Friend thus coincides with Wordsworth's becoming a freeholder of Westmoreland, and with his shift in allegiance from small farmers like the protagonist of *Michael* to the landed interest. His first letter to Lord Lowther was an acknowledgment of obligation:

> Sensible as I am of your Lordship's delicacy of mind, I cannot employ many words on this occasion; I must however be permitted to say that I am deeply impressed by this proof of your favorable opinion of me; and I cannot help adding that a Place which its own Beauty first recommended to me will be greatly endeared by being connected in my mind with so pleasing a remembrance of your particular kindness towards me, and of your general benevolence. (*LMY*, 74–75)

In his biography of his uncle, Christopher Wordsworth asserted that Lowther's intercession made a profound impact on the poet's attitudes:

> It removed every remnant of painful feeling that might still have lingered there, in connection with a name recently borne by one who had debarred him, his brothers, and sister, from the enjoyment of their patrimony for nineteen years. The name of Lonsdale, rendered more illustrious as it now was, by the private and public virtues of its noble possessor, became henceforth an object of affectionate respect to the household at Grasmere.[13]

The evolution to which Christopher Wordsworth points was more subtle, long-standing, and overdetermined than this analysis of a single gesture suggests; its marker is rather the writing of *The Solitary Reaper* than the orthodox biography. The first mention of the poem occurs in a letter from Dorothy Wordsworth, probably written on November 7, 1805, the same day as Wordsworth saw the estate at Broadhow he wished to purchase (*EY*, 636–40). Dorothy tells Lady Beaumont that the "object" of the letter is "to transcribe for you a poem which my Brother wrote the day before yesterday," but enthusiasm for the beauties of Ullswater leads her into a relevant dilation. The causes underlying the Wordsworths' interest in finding a new residence appear in the contrast Dorothy mournfully draws between "[t]his Dale . . . not yet . . . intruded upon by any of the Fancybuilders" and "poor Grasmere," its former sanctity corrupted by "the white-washing of the church," and by other enormities such as "a trim Box . . . erected on a hill-side, surrounded with fir and Larch plantations, that look like a blotch or scar on the fair surface of the mountain," "Mr. Crump's newly-erected large mansion," and one new proprietor's glaringly visible *"sunk Fence."* To these offenses Dorothy adds apprehensions of deforestation, as well as the building of picturesque pavilions and obelisks, in the vale. When at the end of the letter she finally transcribes the poem, the "lamentations for the fate of Grasmere" throw a suggestive light on Wordsworth's composition of it at this time, two years after the Scots tour. Wordsworth had in 1800 celebrated Grasmere as a holy spot, "Perfect Contentment, Unity entire"; in the sequence of Dorothy's letter, the vision of a serenely traditional way of life offered by *The Solitary Reaper* springs as if in response to the invasion of that peace by Liverpool merchants and attorneys like Mr. Crump and a nameless "dashing man from Manchester" eager to have a *"fine place."* The idealization of Scotland, more remote and more primitive, succeeds the failure of Wordsworth's hopes to find in Grasmere a "termination and a last retreat."[14]

Nor should we ignore how Dorothy's contempt for the entrepreneurial middle class is accompanied by an alliance implicitly formed between the agricultural laborer in *The Solitary Reaper* and the aristocratic world celebrated in and by the letter. It is addressed to Lady Beaumont, in whose house at Coleorton the Wordsworths were to pass the winter and spring of 1806, and invokes Lord Lowther. In a single sentence, Dorothy here acknowledges that the poem is indebted to Wilkinson and indicates that William has already mentioned him to Sir George as the supervisor of Lowther's grounds. Beaumont, whose gardens Wordsworth helped to plan, Wilkinson, and Lowther thus collectively represent the proper use of landscape which the "Fancy-builders" have violated. Kelliher suggests that Wilkinson's initialed autograph copy of *The Solitary Reaper* must have been presented at the time Wordsworth enlisted his aid in negotiating purchase of the Broadhow estate (157); though Kelliher does not comment, nothing could better manifest the submerged property relations of the poem. In the context of the letter, the vision enshrined by *The Solitary Reaper* reflects the antagonism of the old land-based society of patrons and dependents to the new commercial elements that were disrupting it.

These associations map the specific ideal of community in which *The Solitary Reaper* participates, and they are more visible still in its acknowledged occasion, Wilkinson's *Tours to the British Mountains.* In November 1806, Wordsworth wrote to Wilkinson from Coleorton to explain not having returned the still-unpublished manuscript of the *Tours:*

> what shall I say in apology for your Journal, which is locked up with my manuscripts at Grasmere. . . . On the other page you will find a copy of verses addressed to an implement of yours, they are supposed to have been composed that afternoon when you and I were labouring together in your pleasure ground, an afternoon I often think of with pleasure; as indeed I do of your beautiful retirement there. (*LMY*, 104–5)

As Susan Wolfson has commented to me, "locked up with my manuscripts" is explanation, metaphor, and *précis* of the argument of this essay. Mark Reed speculates that Wordsworth may have taken the journal away with him when he visited his new property in August (Reed, 331), but that explanation does not square with the verbatim echo of the journal in the last line of *The Solitary Reaper,* written the previous November. Though Wordsworth might have taken a copy of the unpublished journal again in August, he evidently knew the passage well, or even had it to hand, when he wrote the poem. Moreover, on November 5, 1805, the date at which Dorothy's letter fixes the composition of the poem, the Wordsworths were still in Grasmere, so that the conventional explanation of the genesis of the poem—in Hartman's words, "It was on reading a sentence in a friend's manuscript . . . that the two-year-old memory of the solitary reaper returned to him"—cannot be quite right either, unless we assume that Wordsworth had the manuscript with him before going to Ullswater.

The question thus arises of when Wordsworth became acquainted with the journal of Wilkinson's 1787 travels. Mary Carr, Thomas Wilkinson's great-niece and biographer, asserted in 1905 that it had been known for some time:

> The poet Wordsworth and his sister, were familiar with the manuscript of this tour long before it was published, which was not done until 1823 [*sic:* 1824]. They set out to follow, partly in the same route, in 1803. (Carr, p. 29)

Since Wilkinson knew Wordsworth at least since 1801, this statement is not improbable. H. D. Rawnsley, who relied on Carr but who, as a devoted Wordsworthian living in Westmorland, was in an excellent position to have independent knowledge, went further:

> This same Wilkinson wrote, in 1789, a journal of a tour to the Highlands, which Wordsworth borrowed when he, Dorothy, and Coleridge followed the same track in 1803. Wordsworth was so much struck by a passage in that journal—which they used as a kind of guide—that, inspired by it, he wrote the exquisite poem *The Solitary Highland Reaper*.[15]

These statements are not discoveries, but their significance has scarcely been fully pondered. If Wordsworth had the journal with him in 1803, then in place of an "imagination . . . revived from an unexpected source," stimulated by the encounter with Wilkinson's manuscript to recover a "two-year-old memory" (see above), we should think of an experience already ideologically tinged.

His accompaniment in 1787 of the American John Pemberton on a preaching tour of Scotland was the one extensive piece of Quaker service that Wilkinson undertook. In arranging meetings he was often disconcerted by local suspicion of the Quaker ministry, but he was nonetheless a curious and engaged traveler. He concludes his narrative by reflecting on the contrast between the "modern magnificence" of Edinburgh and the poverty of the Highlanders:

> The natural result of this is a wish, that the lowest classes in the Highlands were taken by the hand, and led to an industry tending to something of permanent comfort. There is a tendency in

> man to better his condition; but I do not see how these people
> can better theirs, without help at starting.

The passage typifies Wilkinson's compassion and common sense but
reveals also his unashamed paternalism. This attitude, typical of many
travelers in Scotland, underwrites Wordsworth's response. Wilkinson
continues with a brief vignette of natural innocence:

> I would not by any means be understood as describing them
> comfortless: they enjoy the pure air and the breezes of health
> on their native mountains. They drink at the clear spring, climb
> their rugged rocks, and bound over their wastes, with a vigour
> that our citizens cannot equal; and perhaps these simple feelings
> of our nature, the foundation of our enjoyments, are as lively in
> them as in the rest of mankind.[16]

It is easy to see why the writer of this passage commended himself to the author of the *Lyrical Ballads;* it is equally easy to see how
such sentiments could occlude the real poverty of the Highlanders.
Wilkinson strikes a nice balance; he does not fail to note the hardships of those he sees as "the poor but happy Highlanders" (13).
Faced with the disparity between "the two extremities of human habi-
tations—the palace and the hovel," Wilkinson reminds himself that
the dwellers in each are equally his "brethren" and takes refuge in the
myth of aristocratic solicitude: "I already know, that those who inhabit the most princely mansion, feel for the poverty and cheerfully
relieve the suffering of the cot, the hut, and the hovel" (25–26).
Throughout his tour, Wilkinson weighs his regret that the cottagers
are "poorly accommodated" against his faith that they "are in some
degree contented, and in a great degree innocent" (27). Even the
question of the relative merits of factory and agricultural work is set
within the pastoral motif. Wilkinson praises the manufactories he sees
for creating jobs but adds: "I conceive employment in the field is full
as much on the side of contentment and health; therefore it should
stand as high in our approbation" (10).

Wilkinson is most interesting when he gives way to his "prying
disposition" and joins the life before him: "I got into a Highland hay-
field; and off went my coat, and to work I fell" (28). As he later
records,

> it was, indeed, customary with me to go into the harvest field
> and hold conversation with the amiable Highlanders: I generally

found one at least that understood English, and he was my inter-
preter. I would often try their sickles, and reap and talk with
them. (53–54)

A detailed discussion of the Highland scythe and the unhandy Highland rakes leads to a brief demonstration of agricultural improving,
comically told:

> Captain MacLauchlane said they were pleased with my exhibi-
> tion; but I found they knew nothing of either foot-cock or great-
> cock with the rake, so I shewed them that method, and found
> myself rising into consequence in coming to the Highlands of
> Scotland and teaching them to make hay. (28–29)

Traveling fifteen years after Wilkinson, the Wordsworths are
similarly struck by the "wretchedly poor families"[17] they encounter;
their landscape is more marked than was Wilkinson's, however, by
signs of industrialism. Of the village of Galashiels, for instance, Dorothy records in her journal: "a pretty place it once has been, but a
manufactory is established there; and a townish bustle and ugly stone
houses are fast taking the place of the brown-roofed thatched cot-
tages" (I, 394). Elsewhere she observes mines and machinery, and
sights like "the Carron Ironworks, seen at a distance;—the sky above
them was red with a fiery light" (I, 384). The towns often seemed to
Dorothy "doleful example[s] of Scotch filth" (I, 295), and the countryside "naked" (I, 217) and giving an effect of "barrenness, of what
was not altogether genial" even when not actually barren (I, 232).
The "Duke of Athol's gardens and pleasure-grounds" (I, 349) and
those of the improving, "modern" Duke of Argyll (I, 297) offset such
impressions. Her description of the latter discloses the ideology that
colors Dorothy's response to nature:

> There is in the natural endowments of Inverary something akin
> to every feature of the general character of the county; yet even
> the very mountains and the lake itself have a kind of princely
> festivity in their appearance; I do not know how to communi-
> cate the feeling, but it seemed as if it were no insult to the hills
> to look on them as the shield and enclosure of the ducal domain,
> to which the water might delight in bearing its tribute. (I, 297)

The hospitality of the Highlanders also aroused Dorothy's ap-
preciation, but her warmth is that of an outsider aware of the differ-

ences that separate her from her hosts. Unsure near Tarbet of their route, Wordsworth goes into a field to ask directions: "He addressed himself to one who appeared like a master, and all drew near him, staring at Wm. as nobody could have stared but out of sheer rudeness, except in such a lonely place" (I, 265). The initial diffidence is soon replaced by a "courteous" invitation to lodge for the night, but the distance between the Wordsworths and the Highlanders remains. Dorothy continues:

> After tea Wm. and I walked out; we amused ourselves with watching the Highlanders at work: they went leisurely about everything, and whatever was to be done, all followed, old men, and young, and little children. We were driven into the house by a shower, which came on with the evening darkness, and the people leaving their work paused at the same time. I was pleased to see them a while after sitting round a blazing fire in the kitchen, father and son-in-law, master and man, and the mother with a little child on her knee. . . . We heard the company laughing and talking long after we were in bed; indeed I believe they never work till they are tired. (I, 266)

Like Wilkinson, Dorothy lapses into idyll, but his plunging in to help shows up the condescension of the Wordsworths' amusement at the laborers, as it does Dorothy's faintly censorious remarks on their lack of diligence. Dorothy, however, is too honest a writer to absorb the family into a vision of domestic happiness. "In talking of the French and the present times," she notes,

> their language was what most people would call Jacobinical. They spoke much of the oppressions endured by the Highlanders further up, of the absolute impossibility of their living in any comfort, and of the cruelty of laying so many restraints on emigration.

Though the family laments the decline of loyalties, they do not hesitate to criticize the aristocrats for their abdication of responsibility:

> Speaking of another neighbouring laird, they said he had gone, like the rest of them, to Edinburgh, left his lands and his own people, spending his money where it brought him not any esteem, so that he was of no value either at home or abroad. (I, 267–68)

Such politically charged sentiments, voiced in the tangy idioms of popular speech, are eliminated from the Scotland of *The Solitary Reaper*.

III

For Hartman, the disturbing undertones that deepen the encounter of reaper and poet swell from the intimations of death in the *"consciousness of self raised to apocalyptic pitch"* (17) into which the poet has been surprised. The counterpoint to Hartman's emphasis on *self*-consciousness has been delicately restored by Michael Cooke:

> A cluster of words—"single," "solitary," "by herself," and "alone"—suggests in the form of physical solitude (which the speaker seems careful not to disrupt) a character of independence and uniqueness that Frederick Garber has justly emphasized. And yet the two things the Highland Lass does, reaping and singing, have distinctly social overtones in this context of solitude. What is the interaction between society and its antithesis, uniqueness and independence? What troubled forces congregate and are resolved around the solitary reaper?[18]

Cooke pursues these questions by linking the kinship her singing establishes between the reaper and the poet, and the relation the poem projects with its audience. He shrewdly comments that even if the poem narrates (in Hartman's phrase) an isolated "self-acquired revelation" (5), its speaker presumes a responsive audience: "This can but suggest the presence of a cryptic community of response, or something infallibly efficacious in the object to which the response is made. The origin or character of this community of response is what needs further attention, especially since it is *not* based on a consensus, on a reliable orthodoxy, but rather on spontaneous evocation" (233). "Spontaneous evocation" and the notion of an "infallibly efficacious object," however, are really two aspects of the same abstraction: both assume that reactions to experiences or texts are universal and unmediated. In the end, then, Cooke accords with Hartman (and Garber) and virtually cancels before it could begin the project of investigating the actual "community of response" that *Poems, in Two Volumes* creates for *The Solitary Reaper*.

The markers that regulate the distance between the speaker and the reaper enable one to move beyond the idea of community or the phenomenology of encounter to the particular historical structure the poem represents. "Will no one tell me what she sings?" the speaker of *The Solitary Reaper* inquires (17). Hartman characterizes the question as "a sociable gesture" (8), but there is no one in the landscape to whom the question might be addressed, and the reaper, singing in Erse, inhabits a separate linguistic universe. The diction of the poem manifests the speaker's superiority to the laborer before him, with her "humble" (21), "familiar" (22) song. "Lass," by which the poem characterizes her (2), signals a social hierarchy: Johnson's *Dictionary* said of the word that it is "used now only of mean girls."

To adopt the term whose richness for the study of Wordsworth Hartman's work shows, the surmises on which the remainder of the stanza are built diminish present actuality:

> Perhaps the plaintive numbers flow
> For old, unhappy, far-off things,
> And battles long ago:
> Or is it some more humble lay,
> Familiar matter of today?
> Some natural sorrow, loss, or pain,
> That has been, and may be again!
> (17–24)

The misery the Wordsworths saw on their journey is elided into "far-off things," and specific social ills are softened into cyclical "natural sorrow[s]." In this dissolving of the particular, the "farthest Hebrides" and the "Arabian sands" become interchangeable (12–16). With no chance to speak, the girl cannot intrude into the poem the discontent—and perhaps even the Jacobinical sympathies—of Wordsworth's interlocutors. Her song is expressive but not communicative; Wordsworth appropriates it without needing to understand it. The uncrossed barrier between the speaker and the girl is replicated in time by the two-year gap between the Scots tour and the writing of the poem; along both dimensions the press of human concerns is subdued.

If Wordsworth eliminated the particularity of the reaper, it was to invest her with the aura of mythic timelessness; and aura, as Walter Benjamin insisted, is a property dependent on the maintenance of distance.[19] Hartman emphasizes the *halting* of the traveler, but equally important is his freedom to move on, because the distinction between the unconstrained spectator and the worker at her task reveals the contemporary charge of this renewing of the traditional image of the peasant.[20]

IV

"When we were travelling in Scotland," Dorothy wrote toward the end of her journal, "an invasion was hourly looked for" (I, 356), and a week after their return Wordsworth joined the Grasmere Volunteers, with whom he continued to drill throughout the fall. "[S]urely there never was a more determined hater of the French nor one more willing to do his utmost to destroy them if they really do come" (*LEY*, 403), Dorothy told Catherine Clarkson. The volunteers, however, were perhaps less important as defense against the French, who never invaded, than as "a major police force for the preservation of internal order" and "instrument of propaganda," as H. T. Dickinson argues:

> It demonstrated the willingness of the propertied classes to fight to preserve their privileged position. . . . The willingness to serve at any level became a test of loyalty to the existing regime. The parades, the military exercises and the patriotic speeches at celebration dinners were all designed to demonstrate the strength and commitment of the propertied classes.[21]

The complex of values underlying Wordsworth's patriotism operates also within *The Solitary Reaper*. The Scots tour seems a microcosm of Wordsworth's career: begun with a visit to the grave of the Jacobin Robert Burns, it ended in a meeting with the Tory Sir Walter Scott.

Wordsworth's passionate enmity to the French deepened as the Napoleonic wars extended. On November 4, 1805, the day before the composition of *The Solitary Reaper*, Wordsworth stayed over at Ambleside on the way back from Patterdale "to see the Newspapers, in the hope that they might bring more authentic details of the event of the great Battle." "There was nothing," Dorothy continued to Lady Beaumont, "but a confirmation of the general belief that it was as bad as possible." Dorothy reported herself as "quite overwhelmed with the disastrous tidings" of the capitulation of General Mack and twenty-three thousand Austrians to Napoleon at Ulm, but William, she wrote, "still hopes that it will not prove so" (*LEY*, 635). Three weeks after having sent her *The Solitary Reaper*, Dorothy responded to Lady Beaumont's praise of the poem, and this later letter displays the mixture of private and public concerns touched by the work. Dorothy passes from memories of John Wordsworth, drowned on February 5, to another "blow" at sea, the death of Nelson at Trafalgar, a loss that in her account outweighs his victory: "bitterly did we lament for him and our Country." It is in this sequence that she turns to the lyric:

> I was sure that you would be pleased with the Stanzas on the Solitary Reaper. There is something inexpressibly soothing to me in the sound of those two Lines
>
>> Oh listen! for the Vale profound
>> Is overflowing with the sound—
>
> I often catch myself repeating them in disconnection with any thought, or even, I may say, recollection of the Poem. (*LEY*, 649–50)

Dorothy's comment points to the critical problem explored in this essay: she at once embeds the poem in a web of experience, offers it as an escape from experience, and asserts its autonomy from experience. If poems may be shrunk when reduced to their biographical elements, they are equally—if less obviously—impoverished when cut off from the circumstance of their engendering. The consolations of *The Solitary Reaper* arise from the griefs that run through the letter. Wordsworth blended private and public in drawing upon the character of his brother John for his poem on Nelson, *The Character of the Happy Warrior* (December 1805—January 1806), thus associating it with *Elegiac Stanzas Suggested by a Picture of Peele Castle* (May–June 1806). In turn, the final line of that poem, "Not without hope we suffer and we mourn," broadens from personal loss to general bereavement, including such widely shared sorrows as those occasioned by Nelson's death. The central trope of the poem, as Wordsworth declared in the title, is taken from a picture by Beaumont. By addressing him as one "who would have been the Friend, / If he had lived, of Him who I deplore" (41–42), Wordsworth further suggests how the place left by the lost brother is in part filled by the support of the patron. The letter concludes with Dorothy's brief summary of their journey to Ullswater and their "delightful day at Lowther" (*LEY*, 651).

It is not difficult to see why the Wordsworth of 1805, experiencing the corruption of Grasmere by the urban values he had thought to flee, bereaved in family, and believing his England threatened by foreign enemies, should have welcomed the support offered by Lowther and Beaumont. One aided in the purchase of land; the other, knowing of the poet's investment in the voyage of the *Earl of Abergavenny,* had on her sinking immediately extended financial help. It was not, however, the mere sums involved, as his detractors were to charge, but the vision of stability held out by the landed aristocracy at a moment of converging crises that powerfully appealed to Wordsworth. With *The Prelude* behind him, he was embarked in this period on a process of psychic consolidation, mourning his losses and reintegrating with his origins as the son of Lord Lowther's agent. As the filiations between those poems suggest, however, Wordsworth makes his private journey continuous with public concerns.

These implications are those created by reading *The Solitary Reaper* within the context Wordsworth gave it in *Poems, in Two Volumes.* Jared Curtis's scrupulous reconstruction of the making of the collection demonstrates how Wordsworth "deliberately shaped" his book; seeking to "aid the reader's response" and to "harmonize" a potentially miscellaneous gathering into a "single work," Wordsworth clustered the short poems into "individual groups [which] define meaningful contexts that support and widen the range of each individual poem" (Curtis, Introduction; see also note 4). *The Solitary Reaper* appeared in a group entitled "Poems Written During a Tour in Scotland," but the poems were largely not written during the tour: the title was a fiction, presenting as a spontaneous record a subsequent, carefully ordered collection.[22] In 1815, Wordsworth moved *The Solitary Reaper* to the heading "Poems of the Imagination," devised for that edition. After 1820, however, he returned the poem to its original surroundings, and so reaffirmed its dialogue with the great national events of the day and its place within the half-century-long debate on the landed ideal and England's declining peasantry.

The first volume of *Poems, in Two Volumes* anticipates in several places the Scots materials of the second. The opening section contains the balladlike *The Seven Sisters, or The Solitude of Binnorie,* a tale of seven maidens who together throw themselves into the ocean rather than endure dishonor. The second section, "Poems, Composed During a Tour, Chiefly on Foot," balances "Poems Written During a Tour, in Scotland" in the second volume, and its carefully placed climactic poem, *Resolution and Independence,* emphasizes the admonitory force of the leech gatherer by comparing him to "grave

Livers . . . in Scotland . . . / Religious men, who give to God and Man their dues" (104–5). These hints contribute to the chief task of the volume, the elaboration of a nationalist myth. The opening stanza of the last of the Lucy poems is representative:

> I travell'd among unknown Men,
>   In Lands beyond the Sea;
> Nor England! did I know till then
>   What love I bore to thee.

The England invoked acquires particular shape in the sonnets that make up the remainder of the first volume. The vision of a London revealed as beautiful by the cessation of its usual commercial activity in *Composed upon Westminster Bridge* introduces an attitude sharpened in succeeding sonnets, like the scorn shown "money'd Worldlings" in *October, 1803* and the lament for a culture devoted to "[g]etting and spending" in *The World Is Too Much With Us*. The sestet of that sonnet plays off interestingly against *The Solitary Reaper*:

> Great God! I'd rather be
> A Pagan suckled in a creed outworn;
> So might I, standing on this pleasant lea,
> Have glimpses that would make me less forlorn;
> Have sight of Proteus coming from the sea;
> Or hear old Triton blow his wreathed horn.
>
> (9–14)

For the lost harmonies of Greek mythology glimpsed in the sonnet Wordsworth substitutes in *The Solitary Reaper* a vision of agrarian serenity, removed in space to Scotland but presented as contemporary. If the tone of the poem is elegiac, the effect, in Dorothy's phrase, is nonetheless "inexpressively soothing"; the ideal of rural constancies *The Solitary Reaper* preserves purposefully functions in context to make one "less forlorn" about the current state of England.

Writing to Lady Beaumont on May 21, 1807, to assure her of his indifference to the reception of *Poems, in Two Volumes* among "London wits and witlings," Wordsworth insisted that his works could not be understood by those "who live, or wish to live, in the broad light of the world":

The things which I have taken, whether from within or without,—what have they to do with routs, dinners, morning calls,

> hurry from door to door, from street to street, on foot or in
> Carriage; with Mr. Pitt or Mr. Fox, Mr. Paul or Sir Francis Bur-
> dett, the Westminster Election or the Borough of Honiton . . .

As his defensiveness betrays, however, exactly the reverse of this
aloofness from politics was true. *Poems, in Two Volumes* was intimately connected with matters such as the Westminster election, as
Wordsworth acknowledged in making a claim for the cumulative importance of the "Sonnets Dedicated to Liberty" which conclude the
first volume:

> I would boldly say at once, that these Sonnets, while they each
> fix the attention upon some important sentiment separately con-
> sidered, do at the same time collectively make a Poem on the
> subject of civil Liberty and national independence, which, either
> for simplicity of style or grandeur of moral sentiment, is, alas!
> likely to have few parallels in the Poetry of the present day.
> (*LMY*, 145–47)

Wordsworth's vaunt asks us to read the sonnets as a sequence,
alert to their interactions and thematic developments. Wordsworth
strengthened their interrelations by consecutive numbering and emphasized their air of spontaneous response to crisis by dating several
between August and November 1803; together they compose a conservative mythmaking narrative. The sequence begins with the poet
gazing from France on the "Star of my Country" and sighing that he
must "[a]mong men who do not love her linger here" (sonnet no.
1); he invidiously compares the France of 1802 to the revolutionary
promise he felt when last there (nos. 3 and 5). Later sonnets contrast British freedom with the French extinction of the Venetian
republic and subjugation of Switzerland (nos. 6 and 12), and celebrate the familiar sensations of return (*Composed in the Valley, Near
Dover, on the Day of Landing*):

> Dear fellow Traveller! here we are once more.
> The Cock that crows, the Smoke that curls, that sound
> Of Bells, those Boys that in yon meadow-ground
> In white sleev'd shirts are playing by the score,
> And even this little River's gentle roar,
> All, all are English. Oft have I look'd round
> With joy in Kent's green vales but never found
> Myself so satisfied in heart before.
>
>   (1–8)

The rural English peace that Wordsworth opposed to French super-ficiality and tyranny is an ideological image, the antithesis of com-mercial London and the frame in which *The Solitary Reaper* is placed. The battle of values Wordsworth was fighting within England is even more prominent than this jingoism against the French. If France is characterized by "unceasing change" (no. 15), in England too "[o]ld things have been unsettled" (no. 21), and the "[p]lain living and high thinking" Wordsworth advocates is the rallying cry of the aristocracy against entrepreneurs who believe that "[t]he wealthiest man among us is the best" (no. 13):

> When I have borne in memory what has tamed
> Great Nations, how ennobling thoughts depart
> When Men change Swords for Ledgers, and desert
> The Student's bower for gold, some fears unnamed
> I had, my Country!
>
> (no. 17)

The Miltonism of these sonnets is not simply formal but part and parcel of Wordsworth's effort to seize for the conservative cause his radical, middle-class, Puritan precursor and the revolution of which he was a spokesman. For many of their first readers, the son-nets were the noblest part of the *Poems, in Two Volumes.*[23] The warm response they earned is a measure of how directly they spoke to an England threatened from within by the specter of the French Revolution and still at war with France itself from without. Because the French had taken inspiration from seventeenth-century English republican thought, the pressing contemporary situation made inter-pretation of England's own revolution a subject of renewed debate; Wordsworth's brother Christopher, for example, published in 1824 a monograph on that piece of royalist propaganda, the *Eikon Basil-ike,* which earned the poet's praise.

Wordsworth's Milton, whose "soul was like a Star and dwelt apart," a Milton whom Hartman absorbs into his own critical voice,[24] is the product of an interpretation designed to cleanse Milton of his regicide associations and claim him for the established order. The memorable phrase from the sonnet *London, 1802* (no. 4) blurs Mil-ton's engagement in the fierce political struggles of the revolution and the protectorate, calming the passion of his commitments and evading their content. The former radicals who elevated English republicanism over French excess drew on Milton's prophetic stature

while gingerly handling his politics. Wordsworth employs him to en-
force his appeal for a return to morality in politics and to duty as a
guiding principle. Earlier lines in the same sonnet make Wordsworth's
values clear:

> altar, sword, and pen,
> Fireside, the heroic wealth of hall and bower,
> Have forfeited their ancient English dower
> Of inward happiness. We are selfish men
>
> (3–6)

This vision transforms the turmoil of a seventeenth-century revolution into a glorified picture of the Middle Ages. The "ancient English
dower" here invoked perpetuates national religion and feudal obligation: not for Wordsworth the radical vision of an unfinished revolution, betrayed even before the Restoration by the men of property.[25]
Milton is coupled with the trappings of chivalry:

> In our Halls is hung
> Armoury of the invincible Knights of old:
> We must be free or die, who speak the tongue
> That Shakespeare spake; the faith and morals hold
> Which Milton held.
>
> (no. 16)

As the repetition "hold"/"held" insinuates the identity of 1640 and
1803, only familiarity prevents us from recognizing how cannily
Wordsworth reverses Milton's historical position, and how thoroughly
what presents itself as the language of nationalism is in fact the language of class.

In this reconfiguration of history Scotland plays a salient role.
In *To the Men of Kent. October 1803,* Wordsworth draws on Norman legend to present the militia awaiting the expected invasion as if
they were medieval warriors sending "words of invitation" to single
combat, awing the enemy by their "glittering lance" (5–7). Immediately following this piece of patriotic propaganda and also headed
October, 1803 comes a sonnet inspired by the Scots tour:

> Six thousand Veterans practis'd in War's game,
> Tried Men, at Killicranky were array'd
> Against an equal Host that wore the Plaid,

> Shepherds and Herdsmen.—Like a whirlwind came
> The Highlanders, the slaughter spread like flame;
> And Garry thundering down his mountain-road
> Was stopp'd, and could not breathe beneath the load
> Of the dead bodies. 'Twas a day of shame
> For them whom precept and pedantry
> Of cold mechanic battle do enslave.
> Oh! for a single hour of that Dundee
> Who on that day the word of onset gave!
> Like conquest would the Men of England see;
> And her Foes find a like inglorious Grave.
>
> (no. 24)

The Battle of Killiecrankie, fought July 17, 1689, between royalist forces under General MacKay and Jacobites led by Viscount Dundee, looms large among the events that seated William and Mary on the English throne. Though, as Wordsworth recounts, his Highlanders triumphed, the death of Dundee ended all chances of a Stuart succession. Wordsworth thus transforms the Highlanders from the dangerous enemies of English order into the epitome of English courage. The jubilant prophecy of victory over the French in the very next sonnet, and the penultimate poem in the first volume, *Anticipation, October, 1803,* is made to grow from the heroic deeds of this one.

The revisionism Wordsworth achieves here is worth contemplating. Until their final defeat in 1745, the Jacobites had been a perpetual threat to English stability; George III's minister, the Earl of Bute, provoked continuing acrimony by being a Scot; and the distrust aroused by the Scots was still vividly felt in many quarters at the end of the eighteenth century. Johnson's well-known antipathy to the Scots represented widely held sentiments, and the Highlanders in particular were reviled as backward and feared as outlaws. Wordsworth's Scots poems constitute a significant contribution to that movement to incorporate and domesticate Scots tradition associated with Sir Walter Scott.[26]

Whatever the poetic merits of *In the Pass of Killicranky,* the cultural reversal implied by its political program is clear, as is the close linkage between the "Sonnets Dedicated to Liberty" which close the first volume of *Poems, in Two Volumes* and the "Poems Written During a Tour in Scotland" which open the second. The initial poem of the gathering is *Rob Roy's Grave,* where Wordsworth bends folk materials into contemporary nationalism. Rob Roy adheres to "the simple Plan, / That they should take who have the power, / And they should keep who can" (38–40). But if his exploits suggest comparison with the "present Boast" of France, Wordsworth no sooner suggests the parallel with Napoleon than he retracts it:

> For Thou, although with some wild thoughts,
> Wild Chieftain of a Savage Clan!
> Hadst this to boast of; thou didst love
>   The *Liberty* of Man.
>
> And, had it been thy lot to live
> With us who now behold the light,
> Thou would'st have nobly stirred thyself,
>   And battled for the Right.
>
> (101–8)

In Wordsworth's rhyme, "the Right" appropriates the "light" of an Enlightenment rationalism exposed by the wisdom of experience. The strain of political thought that takes back the radical's term *liberty* for traditional society is a familiar one; Wordsworth goes it one better by making the Highland rebels into champions of English empire against the French, their customary allies.

The Solitary Reaper is the second poem of "Poems Written During a Tour in Scotland." If the surmise that relates the maiden's pensiveness to "battles long ago" appears to remove the poem from immediate political concerns, the context suggests another interpretation. The poem's timelessness is a gesture, like the appeal to a Milton whose "soul was like a Star and dwelt apart," toward invulnerable affirmations. Swerves like these are withdrawals not from engagement but into a rhetorical mode that is effective precisely because it does not appear, to put the charge against Wordsworth's didacticism as Keats put it, "to have a palpable design upon us."[27] Wordsworth is no less didactic for being indirect: the *"heavenly* destiny" (11) evoked by the "very sound of courtesy" (20) in the Highland greeting of the next poem, *Stepping Westward,* is the pledge of a world where the old values endure. "Nothing is left which I can venerate," Wordsworth had despaired of contemporary England ("Sonnets Dedicated to Liberty," no. 22), and he made of Scotland a repository of antique virtue. *Stepping Westward* is followed by *Glen-Almain,* a reflection inspired by the burying place ascribed by custom to Ossian, the bard whose fraudulent invention by James Macpherson marks the inception of the Scotch tradition Wordsworth joins.

The counterpoint between "Sonnets Dedicated to Liberty" and "Poems Written During a Tour in Scotland" continues in the succeeding poems. The lost "household laws" lamented in the first sequence (no. 13) are exemplified in the fidelity of *The Matron of Jedborough and Her Husband.* "Thou wear'st upon thy forehead clear / The freedom of a Mountaineer" (30–31), Wordsworth says of the subject of *To a Highland Girl;* his comparison of her to "a wave / Of the wild sea" (53–54) further echoes the declaration in *Thought of a Briton on the Subjugation of Switzerland* in the first sequence (no. 12) that the Mountains and the Sea are Liberty's chosen homes. The Highland girl is the embodiment of the personified Liberty in the sonnet: with the fall of Switzerland, Scotland is implicitly her remaining fastness.

Carl Woodring has commented that the love of liberty Wordsworth celebrates in the political sonnets also "instigates and suffuses" *The Solitary Reaper,* but, taking the collection as a whole, one comes to question whether the liberty Wordsworth endorses is merely that "of a calm, subjective, indolent sense of freedom and independence," just as one wonders whether *The Solitary Reaper* is really no more than a poem of "relaxed personal experience."[28] Several accents heard before are renewed in the last stanza of *To a Highland Girl:*

> Now thanks to Heaven! that of its grace
> Hath led me to this lonely place.
> Joy have I had; and going hence
> I bear away my recompence.
>
> (60–63)

This apostrophe casts all the way back to the inspiriting encounter with the leech gatherer in *Resolution and Independence;* it catches up the conclusion of *The Solitary Reaper*—"The music in my heart I bore / Long after it was heard no more"—into a network in which the virtues of Scotland are the bulwark against English commercialism and foreign aggressors. The final poem of the Scots sequence, *Yarrow Unvisited,* is conventionally taken as expressing the romantic poet's preference for the realms of imagination, but Wordsworth's imagination is a critique of this world and not a mere flight from it. "We have a vision of our own; / Ah! why should we undo it?" (51–52), he rhetorically demands of Dorothy, and that vision was meant not simply to "soothe us in our sorrow" (62) but also to stand in powerful opposition to the spirit of the times.

The Blind Highland Boy gives its title to the final division of *Poems, in Two Volumes*. The narrative of a child who gleefully goes adventuring on the "perilous Deep" in a washtub is largely comic, but its concluding moral resonates widely in the volume: "though his fancies had been wild, / Yet he was pleased, and reconciled / To live in peace on shore" (201–5). The final poems of the volume reiterate the Wordsworthian values of integrity, perseverance, and acceptance. In the *Song, at the Feast of Brougham Castle, Upon the Restoration of Lord Clifford, the Shepherd, to the Estates and Honours of His Ancestors,* the aristocratic ideal flourishes again. *To the Spade of a Friend* is followed by the *Lines Composed at Grasmere,* inspired by news of the imminent death of Charles James Fox, the aristocratic "Friend of the People," recently appointed to the Cabinet, to whom Wordsworth had sent a copy of the 1800 *Lyrical Ballads* with a plea to help preserve the agricultural way of life represented in poems like *Michael (LEY,* 312–15). The opening of the poem—"Loud is the Vale! the Voice is up / With which she speaks when storms are gone"—looks back to *The Solitary Reaper*—"O listen! for the Vale profound / Is overflowing with the sound"—while its elegiac matter and invocation of "the Comforter" (11) looks to the next poem, *Elegiac Stanzas Suggested by a Picture of Peele Castle,* and the last, the *Intimations Ode*. The pairing suggested between this ode and the only other ode in the collection, the *Ode to Duty* in the first volume, colors Wordsworth's austere climactic affirmations (see Chapter 4). The "habitual sway" of nature in the final poem inevitably recalls the submission to duty in the former; indeed, Wordsworth's description of his youthful radicalism as an exhausting whirligig of "uncharter'd freedom" (37) is the epitome of British constitutionalism. The resignation of the *Intimations Ode* is closely linked to the calls to "plain living and high thinking" in Wordsworth's stern patriotism, and the "soothing thoughts that spring / Out of human suffering" (186–87) include, even if they are not to be limited to, the sacrifices of public responsibility. The "I" of the *Intimations Ode* synthesizes the voices heard in the two volumes.

V

Amid this company, Wordsworth's reaper is not at all solitary. Wordsworth's poem came into being in a wartime England, divided by momentous questions of foreign policy and by shifts of economic power that disrupted the traditional alignment of the classes; the notion of class itself, social historians have argued, took shape in these years.[29] To focus on the "poet's reaction to the solitary reaper," as Hartman does (14), is deceptive, for the poem raises the issue not of a reaction but of a representation. Written out of Wilkinson's prior representation, the poem belongs to its moment of composition two years after the Scots tour and its publication two years after that, rather than to the private sphere of a poet's reaction to an event.

Hartman permits biography to enter his discussion of *The Solitary Reaper* "in a limited way":

> The original incident stems from a tour made in 1803: this tour elicited a number of poems gathered later under the title of "Memorials," most of which are elegiac in mood, memorials in more than one sense. . . . The North Country, it appears, associated with Burns and the bards and ballad singers of old, was to Wordsworth a poetic ground as sacred as the "South Country" (the Mediterranean) to other Romantics. . . . It should also be noted that "The Solitary Reaper" was not written until 1805, the year Wordsworth lost his brother, and the year preceding the "Elegiac Stanzas" on Peele Castle, with the darkest lines, perhaps, that Wordsworth ever wrote. . . . (13–14)

Sacred is here a heavily loaded word: the invocation of the sacred slides over the contemporary secular and political significance of the Romantics' allegiances to lands beyond England. The Hellenism of Shelley and Byron, for example, is inseparable from their revolutionary principles, and to speak of Wordsworth's employment of Scotland in terms of the sacred is to perpetuate an idealism that deflects scrutiny from its definable conservative significance. To suggest that the reason for the "intense opening" of *The Solitary Reaper* is "that the link between harvesting and joy—'they that sow in tears shall reap in joy'—is broken; that a natural order is reversed," falsely characterizes the poem as exclusively transcendental. Wordsworth sent the poem forth into a field of competing ideological appeals, and both the poem and its author speak within a specific sociohistorical matrix.

The final vision of Wordsworth—the last sentence—of *Wordsworth's Poetry 1787–1814* declares: "He is the most isolated figure among the great English poets" (338). This isolation is the artifact of a critical discourse that, by ignoring the connections of poems like

The Solitary Reaper to their wider horizons, has repressed their social and political significance. The actual Scotland Dorothy and William saw, blighted with poverty, oppressed by English reprisals for the Jacobite uprisings, already encroached upon by factories, marked by absentee landlords as well as improving grandees, and echoing with murmurs of radical discontent, does not figure in the poem. Instead, *The Solitary Reaper* proffers a picture of a timeless, self-subsistent, preindustrial way of life intimately harmonized with nature. The image is nostalgic, and its nostalgia is polemical.

To become conscious of the historically specific conservatism that inhabits *The Solitary Reaper* is not to reduce the poem to an outdated topicality but to apprehend the gesture the poem makes. That gesture is not simple; I have disengaged one series from *Poems, in Two Volumes,* and others invite attention. The erotic, for example: if the Scotland of *The Solitary Reaper* is founded not on social reality but on political desire, the repeated representation of appealing young women suggests that that desire is itself tinged by the indulgence of sexual fantasy the tour, less than two months after the birth of his first child, offered Wordsworth. If he exploited the image of the reaper, in this behaving uncomfortably like the *nouveaux riches* erecting their mansions in Grasmere, his return was the reverberating, laminating meanings his artfully planned collection of poems offers his readers: for her song, his polyphony.

The "halted traveller" of Hartman's criticism corresponds to one pole only of the act of reading *The Solitary Reaper*. The reader who apprehends the poem as a single lyric repeats the pause of the traveler, stopped for a moment of full contemplation. But just as the traveler moves on to the next incident of his tour, the reader proceeds to the next poem in the sequence, and that renewed movement represents the persistent aspiration of *Poems, in Two Volumes* toward Wordsworth's vision of himself as teacher and public figure, as he insisted in the letter to Lady Beaumont already quoted. The sequence was the formal means Wordsworth developed to manage the tension between lyric and the larger forms for which he strove, urged by Coleridge, between pastoral suspension and philosophic epic, private and public. It preserved the wealth and autonomy of the moment, while countering the charges the critics leveled of mere narcissistic self-absorption by incorporating the moments in contexts of general import. The reader, like the traveler, passes on, not to cancel the still moment but to supplement it, with all that Derrida has taught us about supplements. The world acknowledged and accumulated by the collection as a whole, though not represented in *The Solitary Reaper* itself, is present to the reader and suggests the complex of forces which make the moment cherishable for Wordsworth (and for us). If this perspective also conveys the uses to which Wordsworth puts it, the discontinuities of the sequence ensure that connections remain evocative rather than restrictive. The mediations from poem to poem together build up a representation of the social process in which Wordsworth acted. If we are not to divide Wordsworth's output, lessen his achievements, and blind ourselves to the sources of our own enchantments, our criticism must confront "surmise" as a gesture to be examined, and recover the critique implicit in Wordsworth's richest withdrawals.[30]

Notes

1. Wordsworth to Orville Dewey in 1833, quoted by F. M. Todd, *Politics and the Poet* (London: Methuen, 1957), p. 11. Todd admirably met his aim, "to fill in some of the background essential" (p. 11) to an understanding of Wordsworth, but his formulation leaves unstudied the implicit "foreground" of the poems themselves. *The Solitary Reaper* is understandably absent from Todd's index. In contrast, I seek to unpack how Wordsworth's changing political beliefs saturate and shape the verbal surface of his lyrics.

2. A brief roster of significant actors in this "movement" might begin with two students of Jerome McGann (whose own work is cited in Chapter 13), James K. Chandler, *Wordsworth's Second Nature* (Chicago: University of Chicago Press, 1984), and Marjorie Levinson, *Wordsworth's Great Period Poems* (Cambridge: Cambridge University Press, 1986); and go on to include Kenneth R. Johnston, particularly "The Politics of 'Tintern Abbey,'" *The Wordsworth Circle* 14 (1983): 6–14, and "Philanthropy or Treason? Wordsworth as 'Active Partisan,'" *Studies in Romanticism* 25 (1986): 371–409; Alan Liu, *Wordsworth: The Sense of History* (Stanford: Stanford University Press, 1989); and David Simpson, particularly "Criticism, Politics, and Style in Wordsworth's Poetry," *Critical Inquiry* 11 (1984): 52–81, and *Wordsworth's Historical Imagination* (New York: Methuen, 1987). Liu takes the occasion of reviewing Simpson's book to meditate upon the unresolved philosophical issues of the New Historicism in *The Wordsworth Circle* 19 (1988): 172–81.

3. Geoffrey H. Hartman, *Wordsworth's Poetry 1787–1814* (Cambridge, Mass.: Harvard University Press, 1987), p. xxi. All references are to this edition, hereafter cited parenthetically in the text.

4. On the "complex interior balancing" of this collection in particular, see Stuart Curran, "Multum in Parvo: Wordsworth's *Poems, in Two Volumes* of 1807," in *Poems in Their Place: The Intertextuality and Order of Poetic Collections*, ed. Neil Fraistat (Chapel Hill: University of North Carolina Press,

1986), pp. 234–53. On the general question, see Fraistat's own study, *The Poem and the Book: Interpreting Collections of Romantic Poetry* (Chapel Hill: University of North Carolina Press, 1985).

5. On DC MS. 26, see Mary Moorman, "Wordsworth's Commonplace Book," *Notes and Queries*, n.s., 4 (1957): 400–405; Paul F. Betz, *Blake Newsletter* 3 (1970): 84–89; and Mark L. Reed, *Wordsworth: The Chronology of the Middle Years* (Cambridge, Mass.: Harvard University Press, 1975), Appendix IX. Reed (hereafter cited parenthetically in the text) follows Betz in dating the entry circa July–August 1807. The notebook contains a number of Scottish materials, such as extracts from Robert Heron's *Journey through the Western Countries of Scotland* (1793), Thomas Pennant's *A Tour in Scotland, 1769* (1771), and J. L. Buchanan's *Travels in the Western Hebrides* (1793), as well as poems copied by Wilkinson.

6. My account of Wilkinson is based on *Thomas Wilkinson: A Friend of Wordsworth*, by his great-niece, Mary Carr (London: Headley Brothers, 1905); and on Hilton Kelliher, "Thomas Wilkinson of Yanwath, Friend of Wordsworth and Coleridge," *British Library Journal* 8 (1982): 147–67, which supplements and corrects Carr. This quotation is from Kelliher, p. 152. They are cited hereafter parenthetically in the text.

7. Thomas De Quincey, *Reminiscences of the English Lake Poets*, ed. John E. Jordan (London: Dent, 1961), p. 300. On the artificiality of this and kindred compilations of De Quincey's recollections, see Mark Schoenfield, "The Shifting Relic: Thomas De Quincey's 'Samuel Taylor Coleridge,' " *Nineteenth-Century Contexts* 12 (1988): 105–21.

8. All quotations are from the edition of Jared Curtis, *Poems, in Two Volumes* (Ithaca: Cornell University Press, 1983), hereafter cited parenthetically in the text.

9. *The Letters of William and Dorothy Wordsworth, The Middle Years, Part I, 1806–1811*, ed. Ernest de Selincourt, 2d ed., rev. by Mary Moorman (Oxford: Clarendon, 1969), p. 105. Hereafter cited in the text as *LMY*.

10. *The Letters of William and Dorothy Wordsworth, The Early Years, 1787–1805*, ed. Ernest de Selincourt, 2d ed., rev. by Chester L. Shaver (Oxford: Clarendon, 1967), p. 639. Hereafter cited parenthetically in the text as *LEY*.

11. On Smirke and the antidemocratic, anti–French Revolution symbolism of contemporary castle building, see Mark Girouard, *The Return to Camelot* (New Haven: Yale University Press, 1981), p. 49.

12. Quoted in Mary Moorman, *William Wordsworth: A Biography, The Later Years 1803–1850* (Oxford: Clarendon, 1965), p. 60.

13. *Memoirs of William Wordsworth*, 2 vols., ed. Henry Reed (Boston: Ticknor, Reed, and Fields, 1851), I, 319–20.

14. The poem quoted is *Home at Grasmere*, ed. Beth. Darlington (Ithaca: Cornell University Press, 1977), MS. B, ll. 170, 166.

15. *Literary Associations of the English Lakes*, 3d ed., 2 vols. (Glasgow: MacLehose and Sons, 1906), II, 22. Rawnsley also records that Edmund Burke had invited Wilkinson to accompany him to the trial of Warren Hastings in 1791 (II, 32), and when the Tory statesman William Canning came to visit Wilkinson in 1825, he found a biography of Burke in the parlour (II, 34).

16. *Tours to the British Mountains* (London: Taylor and Hessey, 1824), p. 89. Hereafter cited parenthetically in the text.

17. *Journals of Dorothy Wordsworth,* 2 vols., ed. Ernest de Selincourt (London: Macmillan, 1941), I, 279. Hereafter cited parenthetically in the text.

18. *The Romantic Will* (New Haven: Yale University Press, 1976), p. 44, hereafter cited parenthetically in the text. I have suppressed Cooke's note to Frederick Garber's valuable *Wordsworth and the Poetry of Encounter* (Urbana: University of Illinois Press, 1971). I am indebted to Don Bialostosky for emphasizing the importance of Cooke's divergence from Hartman.

19. Walter Benjamin, "The Work of Art in the Age of Mechanical Reproduction," *Illuminations,* tr. Harry Zohn, ed. Hannah Arendt (New York: Schocken, 1969), pp. 217–51.

20. My colleague Paul Alkon points out that comparison with the pragmatic observations on work songs that Scots reapers provoked in Samuel Johnson throws into relief the idealizing of Wordsworth's poem: "I saw the harvest of a small field. The women reaped the corn, and the men bound up the sheaves. The strokes of the sickle were timed by the modulation of the harvest song, in which all their voices were united. They accompany in the Highlands every action, which can be done in equal time, with an appropriated strain, which has, they say, not much meaning; but its effects are regularity and cheerfulness." *A Tour to the Hebrides,* Samuel Johnson and James Boswell, ed. R. W. Chapman (London: Oxford University Press, 1924), pp. 55–56.

21. *British Radicalism and the French Revolution* (Oxford: Blackwell, 1985), p. 36.

22. On the "extraordinary coherence" of this group, see the perceptive essay by Jeffrey C. Robinson, "The Structure of Wordsworth's *Memorials of a Tour in Scotland, 1803,"* *Papers in Language and Literature* 13 (1977): 54–70.

23. In the *Annual Review,* Lucy Aikin commented that the sonnets "hold a severe and manly tone which cannot be in times like these too much listened to." James Montgomery in the *Eclectic Review* judged the sonnets "in point of imagery and sentiment, perhaps the most poetical" of a collection he found mostly trivial. In the course of his censorious notice in the *Edinburgh Review,* Francis Jeffrey declared that Wordsworth's "sonnets are as much superior to the greater part of his other poems, as Milton's sonnets are superior to his." All quotations from *The Romantics Reviewed,* ed. Donald H. Reiman (New York: Garland, 1972), Part A, 1:19, 1:336, 2:437.

24. Note, for instance, Hartman's paraphrase of the image of Milton in Wordsworth's sonnets "Dedicated to Liberty": "Here was a man whose soul dwelt apart like a star, yet with an ideal of service that informed both poetry and life" (279). The fusion precludes critical distance on Wordsworth's use of Milton.

25. It is revealing to read *Wordsworth's Poetry 1787–1814* against Christopher Hill's *Milton and the English Revolution* (Harmondsworth: Penguin, 1979).

26. On the fabrication of the image of Scotland in the Romantic period, see the fascinating essay by Hugh Trevor-Roper, "The Invention of Tradition:

The Highland Tradition of Scotland," *The Invention of Tradition,* ed. Eric Hobsbawm and Terence Ranger (Cambridge: Cambridge University Press, 1983), pp. 15–41.

27. *The Letters of John Keats,* 2 vols., ed. Hyder Edward Rollins (Cambridge, Mass.: Harvard University Press, 1958), I, 224.

28. *The Solitary Reaper* is only mentioned in Woodring's *Politics in English Romantic Poetry.* I quote here from Woodring's "On Liberty in the Poetry of Wordsworth," *Publications of the Modern Language Association* 70 (1955): 1033–48.

29. See, for example, Harold Perkin, *Origins of Modern English Society* (1969; rpt. London: Ark, 1985), pp. 26–32.

30. I am grateful to Paul Alpers for an astute reading of an earlier version of this chapter.

12

Wordsworth at St. Bees: Scandals, Sisterhoods, and Wordsworth's Later Poetry

I

Anyone seeking to direct attention to Wordsworth's later poetry must acknowledge the general lack of interest in the subject. The image of Wordsworth the lost leader, living on in decline and withdrawal, seems as firmly fixed now as it has been for a century. If one points out that Wordsworth's poetry after 1807 is, if anything, more politically engaged and more topical than what went before, the notorious conservatism of the later years remains a stumbling block. But merely to invoke this conservatism is not to understand how it functions in particular poems. Distaste for Wordsworth's views has thus far largely precluded asking what kinds of poetry he evolved to convey them and what sorts of interest such poems might repay. The late poems deliberately no longer offer the richly represented self of, say, *The Prelude,* but once understood within their historical situation, their contexts steadily widen and their procedures gain meaning. By revealing the unexpected conjunction of Anglican idealism and Tory scandal underlying one of Wordsworth's neglected poems, I hope to suggest the considerable, if oblique, force possessed by much of his late work; these wider implications will emerge at the end of the chapter.

II

Stanzas Suggested in a Steam-Boat off St. Bees Heads, on the Coast of Cumberland is a poem ignored by modern criticism of Wordsworth.

Mary Moorman's verdict that "Poetically, it may be said to have as little merit as any poem he ever wrote" is more mention than it receives elsewhere.[1] One's first response to the poem is likely to be surprise at the image it conjures of the poet of nature incongruously seated aboard a steamer. The nine-line stanza form, each stanza ending with the repetition of "St. Bees," has, too, a formal playfulness that one does not usually associate with Wordsworth,[2] and Wordsworth's own wonder at his mode of travel is fundamental to the theme of the poem, his reaction to a new age.

The poem begins magnificently:

> If Life were slumber on a bed of down,
> Toil unimposed, vicissitude unknown,
> Sad were our lot: no Hunter of the Hare
> Exults like him whose javelin from the lair
> Has roused the Lion; no one plucks the Rose,
> Whose proffered beauty in safe shelter blows
> 'Mid a trim garden's summer luxuries,
> With joy like his who climbs on hands and knees,
> For some rare Plant, yon Headland of St. Bees.
>
> This independence upon oar and sail,
> This new indifference to breeze or gale,
> This straight-lined progress, furrowing a flat lea,
> And regular as if locked in certainty,
> Depress the hours. Up, Spirit of the Storm!
> That courage may find something to perform;
> That Fortitude, whose blood disdains to freeze
> At Danger's bidding, may confront the seas,
> Firm as the towering Headlands of St. Bees.[3]

The third stanza retracts that "wild wish," and one's sense of the discipline Wordsworth characteristically imposed upon himself is confirmed in the discovery from the manuscripts that the recantation was added at a comparatively late stage in the composition of the work. Such spiritual discipline is consonant with the theme of the poem, which places against the "useful Art" of the nineteenth century the Christian wisdom of a monastic community. Wordsworth concludes:

> Alas! the Genius of our age from Schools
> Less humble draws her lessons, aims and rules.
> To Prowess guided by her insight keen
> Matter and Spirit are as one Machine;

> Boastful idolatress of formal skill
> She in her own would merge the eternal will:
> Expert to move in paths that Newton trod,
> From Newton's Universe would banish God.
> Better, if Reason's triumphs match with these,
> Her flight before the bold credulities
> That furthered the first teaching of St. Bees.

At the center of Wordsworth's poem is the legend of St. Bega, Englished as St. Bees, the daughter of a seventh-Century Irish king, who reputedly became the first nun in Cumberland. The convent she founded was burnt by the Danes but reborn in the twelfth century as an abbey which endured until the dissolution of the monasteries under Henry VIII.[4] These materials Wordsworth makes the vehicle of an argument driven home in the opening and concluding stanzas against his contemporaries' faith in scientific progress and utilitarian values. The monks are praised throughout for their civilizing force; the "humanizing Virtues" (st. 6) of Bega and her descendants are praised for having guided the mariner and succored the traveler, cultivated the fields and fed the poor, taught the sacraments and softened the relation between lord and vassal. Wordsworth formulates his appeal carefully, for these are socially useful achievements. The monks are not depicted as withdrawn from the world but as exemplars of a society grounded in spirituality, figures to counter the increasingly materialist world Wordsworth saw around him.

Though it appears a long way from the poet of the *Lyrical Ballads* to this celebration of monastic institutions, it is easy to grasp the attraction of such a life for Wordsworth. The monks sung in *St. Bees* live solitary but in a community, in the world but not of it, halfway between religious and secular. They are just such creatures as the poet of *The Recluse* would have wished. Wordsworth's engagement with the monastic ideal was of long standing: the sonnet *Nuns Fret Not* dates from 1802; *The Tuft of Primroses* of 1806–1808 blends Sts. Basil and Gregory with Wordsworth's own life at Grasmere and is followed by the passage on the Grande Chartreuse added to the sixth book of *The Prelude,* the poems lamenting the dissolution of the monasteries in the *Ecclesiastical Sketches,* and other works.

These continuities suggest that *St. Bees* is more than a tourist's momentary effusion, but to sketch its historical significance requires a longer look at the contemporary ideology of monasticism.[5] In 1795 or 1796 the Reverend Thomas Dudley Fosbrooke, whose expanded edition of Gilpin's *Wye Tour* (1818) Wordsworth owned, published a poem entitled *The Economy of Monastic Life* (*as it existed in England*).[6] The verse is undistinguished, but the poem nonetheless intrigues. In its last part, Fosbrooke urges that "Commerce" should be "courteous" to the monks for advancing trade; the similarly personified "Learning" is asked to respect the monks for having transmitted legends, rhetoric, and philosophy. "The preservation of learning, and a beneficial operation on the savage, warlike temper of the feudal ages," Fosbrooke writes, "may be tributes now rendered to a system, which still interests the fancy" (16). Fosbrooke illustrates the mixture of attitudes that was to characterize the revival of interest in monasticism in the nineteenth century: an Anglican clergyman with ten children and a Freemason, he was antipathetic to clerical celibacy and suspicious of papistry; he condemned "monkery," as he called it, as "puerile," yet he was fascinated by its rules and practices.[7] The copious notes with which he surrounded his poem anticipated his publication in 1802 of *British Monachism; or, Manners and Customs of the Monks and Nuns of England*. This antiquarian survey was a sizable popular success, and when in 1817 Fosbrooke brought out a long-awaited "new edition, very much enlarged and embellished with numerous plates," he proudly noted in the preface that the first edition had "been so honoured by the public approbation as to be advertised in sale-catalogues at twice the original price" (v).[8]

This second edition also proved a best-seller and earned a forty-page discussion by Southey in the *Quarterly Review* of July 1819.[9] Southey penetrated Fosbrooke's scorn and pedantry to reveal the potential stimulus of the monastic ideal. What in Fosbrooke is only a curiosity becomes in Southey a weapon in contemporary disputes. He begins his essay by attacking the "portentous abortions" of "Jeremy-benthamism" (59), setting against the impoverished notions of utility he attributes to his antagonists the more generous conceptions of usefulness epitomized by the monasteries. Though as a fervid anti-Catholic he insists that the monasteries began in superstition and ended in corruption, he maintains that they were valuable as centers of a true education, as a respectable career for the younger branches of good families, and as asylums far better than contemporary madhouses.

The core of the essay is Southey's argument that the monasteries answered a need that had, if anything, become greater amid the upheavals of his own day. "The difficulty which continually presses upon civilized society," he wrote, "is that of finding fit occupation and adequate maintenance for all its members according to their respective classes, and this increases precisely in proportion with the general improvement of the country" (59). Southey saw with impressive clarity that this general problem fell with particular weight upon the lot of contemporary women. Though women of the lower classes were overworked, a convergence of circumstances and attitudes had deprived those in the middle classes of their social role. Southey recognized that what he called English "reserve" and what a social historian today might call the new norms of femininity and respectability prevented woman from entering business, while "improvements in machinery" had made inroads into occupations once their province—weaving and the like. Only marriage remained, but the protracted wars had diminished the supply of men, widowing many women and dooming numerous others to spinsterhood. Southey powerfully clinches his argument:

> All these changes have had an unfavorable effect upon the condition of women. They also, throughout the intermediate classes, have been educated for refined life. But it is in refined life that the moral checks to population operate with full force—with such force indeed as to make celibacy the lot of far the greater number of females who have little or no fortune. . . . All the circumstances and prejudices of society are against them. Of the few employments which are left for them, there is not one to which they can betake themselves without a certain degree of degradation, and all are overstocked. They are fallen from the rank in which they have grown up, and they wither on the stalk, not in single blessedness but in forlorn desertion. (92)

One has only to think of Jane Eyre, Lucy Snowe, and their sisters in the Victorian novel to feel the justice of Southey's portrait, and it is this reality that makes his proposed remedy of establishing Protestant nunneries, none of which had existed in England since the dissolution, less implausible. In the closing pages of his article he rehearses Samuel Richardson's suggestion that such nunneries be founded in every county, traces English plans for such houses, and reports that in 1816 the Queen and Princess Charlotte had actually created a Ladies Association near Bath. He ends by lobbying for its support and reiterating "the great and certain good" such institutions would achieve.

Southey's piece is an early instance of this High Church feminism, and enough has perhaps been said to make clear that when Wordsworth lauded a seventh-century nun he was contributing to a lively issue. In 1824 Southey wrote that his publisher, Murray, understood the popular interest in his projected history of the monastic orders, and he hoped to obtain five hundred pounds a volume for a six-volume study.[10] Nothing came of this scheme, but in 1824 he published what he once described as a "running commentary" on Wordsworth's *Ecclesiastical Sketches,*[11] the immensely successful history of Anglicanism entitled *The Book of the Church,* and, in 1826, in response to criticism on that work, the *Vindiciae Ecclesiae Anglicanae,* which Wordsworth's nephew Christopher thought "made up chiefly of [Wordsworth's] conversation."[12] During these years, others pressed the idea of sisterhoods. In the December 1825 issue of *Blackwood's Magazine,* Southey's friend the doctor Robert Gooch wrote on the life and work of the Beguines in Belgium and pleaded that "all serious Christians . . . join and found an order of women like the Sisters of Charity in Catholic countries . . . let them be placed both as nurses and pupils in the hospitals of Edinburgh and London, or in the county hospitals." Traveling Englishmen had witnessed on the Continent the care given by Roman Catholic nuns to the poor and the war-wounded, and they were eager for their somnolent church to awaken and combat with similar means the wretchedness at home. The following year, Byron's cousin the Reverend Alexander R. C. Dallas published an open letter to the Bishop of London advocating the development of Protestant Sisters of Charity in order to improve medical aid among the poor.[13] These counsels blend spirituality with the practical necessities of ameliorating the distress swelling in the cities. As Owen Chadwick observes: "Beyond other ages early Victorians knew that gentle ladies could only work in Stepney or nurse cholera if sustained by grace beyond the common lot."[14]

In 1829 Southey returned to the subject in his *Sir Thomas More: or, Colloquies on the Progress and Prospects of Society.* In the thirteenth of the imaginary dialogues between himself as "Montesinos" and More, Southey amplified the points he had made years before in the review of Fosbrooke. Where, More asks, are the institutions that might shelter the women thrown into want by the "commercial earthquakes" or "your hard-headed society," where the institutions that might channel their religious impulses and provide them a function? "But where," More demands, "is the woman who shall be the Clara or the Teresa of Protestant England?"[15] In that cry one hears the George Eliot of more than forty years later, meditating in the preface to *Middlemarch* upon the difficulties besetting woman's search for a vocation. Wordsworth declared himself "greatly interested with much of the" *Colloquies* and told a correspondent that "there is perhaps not a page of them that [Southey] did not read me in M:S and several of the Dialogues are upon subjects which we have often discussed";[16] indeed, Southey's critique of industrial society spelled out his own position. The immediate consequence of the *Colloquies,* however, was a devastating reply by Thomas Macaulay in the January 1830 issue of the *Edinburgh Review*. Although the notoriety it ensured helped to draw the *Colloquies* into a second edition in 1831, Southey's reasoned exposition of the usefulness of colleges of women, bound by no vow but dedicated to service, was not to be acted upon until after his death.

A greater mind than Southey's was soon involved in the discussion of reviving the conventual life, and once again the links with Wordsworth are strong. In 1833, the same year that Wordsworth visited St. Bees, John Henry Newman began to publish in the *British Magazine* a series of essays entitled *The Church of the Fathers*. The *British Magazine* was the organ of those High Churchmen opposed to the reforms looming over the Church of England; it was edited by H. J. Rose, the Cambridge theologian who had been Christopher Wordsworth's curate in 1819 and a prominent figure in the Tractarian movement. Wordsworth had been corresponding with him since 1828, and informed an acquaintance who inquired about the *British Magazine* that Rose was "a particular friend of Dr. Wordsworth's and I may say with pride and gratitude, of myself" (*LY,* II, 713). Newman's essays sketched the heroes of the fourth-century church, expatiating gracefully upon Antony, Augustine, Basil, and Gregory, those founders of monasticism for whom Wordsworth had long before demonstrated his affinity. Monasticism, Newman suggested, was a natural outgrowth of intense spirituality, and he contrasted its sobering discipline "with the sort of religion into which the unhappy enthusiast of the present day is precipitated by the high and dry system of the establishment." The writing is ingratiating but unremittingly polemical, and everywhere Newman's point is the same: the aridity of the existing church has driven the desire for holiness once expressed in such forms as monasticism into the perversions of "methodism and dissent." *The Church of the Fathers* was a sortie in Newman's campaign to restore Anglicanism to its Catholic heritage. The essays were reprinted in an anonymous volume in 1840 and reached four editions by 1868.

"I know not any more distressing development of the cruel temper of Protestantism," Newman wrote,

> than the determined, bitter, and scoffing spirit in which it has set itself against institutions which give dignity and independence to the position of women in society. As matters stand, marriage is almost the only shelter which a defenseless portion of the community has against the rude world;—a maiden life, that holy estate, is not only left in desolateness, but oppressed with heartless ridicule and insult;—whereas foundations for single women, under proper precautions, at once hold out protection to those who avail themselves of them, and give dignity to the single state itself, and thus save numbers from the temptation of throwing themselves rashly away upon unworthy objects, thereby transgressing their own sense of propriety, and embittering their future life. . . . And if women have themselves lost so much by the established state of things, what has been the loss of the poor, sick, and aged, to whose service they might consecrate that life which they refuse to shackle by the marriage vow?[17]

These aspirations were soon to be realized. In 1840, after reading Newman, Marian Hughes took a vow of celibacy in Christ from Pusey, becoming the first Anglican woman to do so since the Reformation. In 1845, Lord John Manners, a leading member of the Young England party in Parliament, heading a committee of which Gladstone was secretary, founded the first community of nursing sisters as a memorial to Southey. Other communities quickly followed. In 1848, for example, Wordsworth's nephew Christopher, then a canon of Westminster, was instrumental in establishing the Commuity of Nursing Sisters of St. John the Divine, devoted to tending the sick and poor of London; the first Lady Superintendent was his sister-in-law, and the President and Visitor was C. J. Blomfield, the Bishop of London and Wordsworth's correspondent (Overton, p. 124). In 1861 there were eighty-six sisters in the Church of England; in 1878 approximately seven hundred; and by the end of the century probably between two and three thousand (Allchin, p. 120). Considering the deep distrust of anything that looked like Roman Catholic influence, this growth is remarkable. These conservative writers were no promoters of equal rights for women like the contemporary Saint-

Simonians, but so long as its spiritual heart commanded respect, the ideal of service was not demeaning. For many women, such as Priscilla Lydia Sellon, about whom there exists an approving sonnet in Wordsworth's hand,[18] the sisterhoods were a step toward independence and even power despite their perpetuation of the old sexual stereotypes.

The connection between *St. Bees* and the High Church revival is even closer than I have suggested thus far. In 1843 a third edition of Fosbrooke's *British Monachism* appeared, an indication of the widening interest in its subject. The text's hostility to Roman Catholicism prompted Newman to undertake a series of *Lives of the English Saints,* written by a team of Tractarians. St. Bega fell to F. W. Faber, an enthusiastic Wordsworthian who had first visited Ambleside in 1837 and charmed everyone, particularly Mary, who thought him "a perfect *model* of what a deacon of our church ought to be."[19] Even Henry Crabb Robinson, who judged him a "flaming zealot" on religious matters, confessed that he was "very amiable and interesting."[20] Wordsworth had given Faber a signed copy of his poems in 1841, and Faber went abroad clutching *The Excursion*. The record of that trip, *Sights and Thoughts in Foreign Churches and Among Foreign Peoples,* published in 1842, is dedicated to Wordsworth "in affectionate remembrance of much personal kindness, and many thoughtful conversations on the rites, prerogatives, and doctrines of the holy church." When Faber asked for permission to include Wordsworth's poem in his life of Bega, Wordsworth consented, and even profited from the occasion to make some improvements in his text.[21] The poem concludes Volume 3 of the *Lives,* where it was introduced by Faber's note pointing out that Wordsworth had written the verses "so long ago as 1833":

> The date is noticed as giving a fresh instance of the remarkable way in which his poems did in divers places anticipate the revival of catholic doctrines among us. When any one considers the tone of sneering which was almost universal in English authors when treating of a religious past with which they did not sympathize, the tone of these verses is very striking indeed, the more striking since Mr. Wordsworth's works prove him to be very little in sympathy with Roman doctrine on the whole.[22]

Wordsworth's breadth of understanding is indeed impressive when compared to the condescension of Fosbrooke, but a modern reader

has difficulty in comprehending just how remarkable was Wordsworth's giving of the poem to Faber. To write warmly of an Irish
saint at a time when there was no more violently debated issue than
the status of the Anglican church in predominantly Catholic Ireland
was generous, but for Wordsworth to permit the poem to be republished in a virtual manifesto of the Catholic-leaning party in the
church when he bitterly fought Catholic emancipation and all other
steps of accommodation suggests his capacity to rise above contention. Even after the defection of many of its members to Roman
Catholicism, Wordsworth maintained that the whole tendency of the
Oxford movement had been for good.[23] Although his note on the
corruption of requiems reveals how cautious Wordsworth could be to
avoid any hint that he approved of Romanism, the catholicity—in
both senses—of *St. Bees* did not escape censure. In 1847, Christopher
Wordsworth, hoping to draw from his uncle further verses on the
Church of England, remonstrated: "You have, I think, done justice—
perhaps I may be allowed to say *more* than justice—to the *better* elements of Romanism in your lines on St. Bees" (Overton, pp. 126–
27). Christopher, however, later Bishop of Lincoln, was generally in
accord with the ideals espoused in *St. Bees;* four years later, he cited
the poem first among Wordsworth's works in a passage of *The
Memoirs of William Wordsworth* designed to prove the poet's aver-
sion to Puritan theology and polity.[24] From the other side of this
major Victorian divide, criticism was inevitable. Reviewing *Yarrow
Revisited,* the Unitarian magazine the *Monthly Repository* singled out
St. Bees as an example of the disturbance of Wordsworth's genius by
a misguided and mischievous philosophy.[25] Thus, in our day a poem
that seems bland and lacking in urgency was in its own the center of
no trivial controversy. From our perspective, the honorary degree
conferred on Wordsworth in 1839 by the University of Oxford may
seem merely the due recognition of a lifetime's achievement, but it
was not without partisan implications. Keble, Wordsworth's champion, was a Tractarian, and the values embodied in *St. Bees,* and still
more the political position to which they were allied, played a part
in his nomination. The Creweian oration, in which Keble hailed
Wordsworth as the poet of honorable poverty, suggests how he could
be enlisted in the service of an ideology favoring moral regeneration
over social change.[26] And so, too, at Cambridge: in 1844, Thomas
Thorpe, the president of the Camden Society, that body which did so
much to foster the increased ritualism of the period, declared that

Wordsworth "might be considered one of the founders of the society."[27] The poet of a universal benevolence in the 1790s had become in the 1830s the favorite of a particular faction.

That the late Wordsworth cannot be restricted by the disputes of contemporary party politics, though he cannot be understood without reference to them, is, however, also evident from *St. Bees.* Here I must briefly retrace ground just covered in order to reach new territory. The arguments for sisterhoods were repeated more forcefully and with the same combination of fervor and practicality in regard to communities of men. In the same year as *St. Bees* Richard Hurrell Froude's passionate *Remains,* prefaced by Newman, struck the common chord:

> It has lately come into my head that the present state of things in England makes an opening for reviving the monastic system. I think of putting the view forward under the title of "Project for Reviving Religion in great Towns." Certainly colleges of unmarried priests, (who might of course retire to a living, when they could and liked) would be the cheapest possible way of providing for the spiritual wants of a large population.[28]

Faber argued that "a sturdier weapon than a married clergy can alone hope to convert (for we may not use a milder word) the crowded multitudes of modern England," and Lord John Manners was only speaking more bluntly when he announced that monastic institutions were "the only means of Christianizing Manchester" (quoted in Allchin, p. 43). The parochial system was entirely inadequate to cope with the new industrial cities, where the poor, and not only the poor, were without religious instruction and places of worship or, what for these writers was as bad, were abandoned to dissenting preachers, often itinerant and unable to provide the stability of a parish.

It was to meet this problem, although by a less radical measure, that George Henry Law, Bishop of Chester, founded in 1817 a Theological College at St. Bees. Law, the descendant of a line of Westmorland "statesmen" and brother of Chief Justice Ellenborough, was a firm conservative who once defined the duty of a bishop as "to stop the wild progress of enthusiasm" (quoted in Chadwick, II, 293). But to stop enthusiasm meant also to revitalize the Church of England so that the church might be a fit receptacle for it; Law was an evangelical. The purpose of the college was to train youths desirous of entering the ministry but too poor to attend Oxford or Cambridge. Law hoped thereby to meet the church's deficiencies, to produce clergymen willing to serve in what a recent church historian has characterized as "the more remote and disagreeable northern and midland parishes."[29] The college filled the need and succeeded: by the end of the century it had supplied hundreds of candidates for orders.

Wordsworth alludes to the founding of the college in the penultimate stanza of his poem, which begins with the dissolution of the ancient monastery:

> But all availed not; by a mandate given
> Through lawless will the Brotherhood was driven
> Forth from their cells;—their ancient House laid low
> In Reformation's sweeping overthrow.
> But now once more the local Heart revives,
> The inextinguishable Spirit strives.
> Oh may that Power who hushed the stormy seas,
> And cleared a way for the first Votaries,
> Prosper the new-born College of St. Bees!

It is one index of Wordsworth's range of sympathy that a poem congenial to Tractarians should celebrate an evangelical foundation, but it is worth remembering that the Oxford movement and evangelicalism sprang initially from the same desire to lead a more fervent life than was possible within the everyday practice of the Church of England. Wordsworth saw no difficulty in the transition from the Catholic convent to the evangelical college. His enthusiastic endorsement of the missionary commitment of the college is attested by a canceled stanza of *St. Bees,* surviving in the Dove Cottage Papers and never printed in any edition:[30]

> Giver of light mayst thou withholding not
> Thy ancient fervor from this hallowed spot
> M̸a̸y̸s̸t̸ ̸t̸h̸o̸u̸ inspire t̸h̸e̸ little band of Student Youth
> And send them forth for Messengers of Truth
>   upon streets and lane
> So where for want of nurture thousands pine
>   on streets and allies
> Yet yet a few more sparks of grace divine
> Shall fall   & huts of wandering savages
> And armed canoes in Polynesian seas
> Draw peace and concord from remote St. Bees.

The variants to the fifth line show Wordsworth more responsive to urban conditions than he is often given credit for being, and I rather regret the excision of the Polynesian canoes; they would have added an exotic—if culturally imperialist—note to the canon.

The introductory note to *St. Bees* describing the college, however, turns discussion from the lofty realm of Anglican idealism to that of political scandal. The relevant portion should be quoted:

> After the dissolution of the monasteries, Archbishop Grindal founded a free school at St. Bees, from which the counties of Cumberland and Westmorland have derived great benefit; and recently, under the patronage of the Earl of Lonsdale, a college has been established there for the education of ministers for the English Church.

The grammar school, founded in 1583 by letters patent from Queen Elizabeth confirming the bequest of Edmund Grindal, her archbishop successively of York and Canterbury, was the most famous institution of learning in the town of St. Bees. Its omission from Wordsworth's poem is therefore suprising, but the omission is in a sense the key to the function of the whole.

Within the ancient parish of St. Bees lay the prosperous port of Whitehaven, developed in the seventeenth and eighteenth centuries by the Lowthers, the ancestors of Wordsworth's patron, the Earl of Lonsdale, and vast stretches of the Cumberland coalfield that was a major source of Lowther wealth.[31] Coal had been worked in the area since the thirteenth century, and the mineral rights to the land Grindal left to support his school were already in the sixteenth century quite valuable. His will had provided that his school be administered by a board of seven governors, and by 1742 Sir James Lowther and his steward were members of the board. What follows is a classic case of interlocking directorates and economic self-interest, and it is *not* surprising that no record of it exists in the school register. The board leased all the collieries and coal mines belonging to the school to Sir James Lowther, one of its own members, for a term of 867 years at an annual rent of three pounds ten shillings. Whatever the value of this lease might have been in 1742, the terms were extremely disadvantageous to the school, and by the early nineteenth century improvements in mining had rendered the disparity between the rent received by the school and the worth of the coal extracted from the land enormous. In 1814, a new schoolmaster, William Wilson, began to investigate the peculiar conditions of the lease and brought the matter to the attention of the current governors, who were statutorily charged with protecting the interests of the school. The seven, however, included the Earl of Lonsdale, the beneficiary of the lease, and various of his dependents: his superintendent and clergymen holding livings in his gift. Against the largest landowner in the county the schoolmaster could do little. For his pains the governors reduced his salary from seventy pounds a year to fifty pounds, and Bishop Law refused to confirm him in the incumbency of the parish church of St. Bees because the governors were dissatisfied with him. Under the circumstances Wilson was virtually forced to resign the mastership in 1816.

The matter might have rested there, an unpleasant but not exceptional testimony to the power of the aristocracy, were it not for one thing: Henry Brougham's contest against the Lowther interests in the Westmorland parliamentary elections of 1818. In 1816 Brougham had chaired a parliamentary committee to inquire into the education of the poor in London, and his dedication soon led to an expanded study of the abuse of charities throughout the kingdom. In May of 1818 Wilson gave evidence to Brougham's committee in the House of Commons about the situation at St. Bees, and it does not exaggerate to say that the case became infamous.

Wordsworth's activity in the 1818 election has been well enough described not to need repeating here.[32] Keats, hoping to visit Wordsworth at Rydal Mount, was saddened to discover the poet out canvassing for the Lowthers when he called, and Wordsworth's tireless campaigning did more than anything else to fix the image of him as a turncoat. But it is hard, perhaps, to recapture at this date the full brightness of the publicity attendant upon Brougham's challenge. "Since 1774," Arthur Aspinall writes, "no one had ever dared to challenge Lord Lonsdale's right to select two members for the county, the political destinies of which he controlled as absolutely as did any petty German Tyrant those of his hereditary domain."[33] The prescriptive authority with which the family regarded the parliamentary seats can be seen in their two candidates for 1818, both the earl's sons. In Brougham's challenge the case of St. Bees played no small part. The contest opened in January 1818, but the voting was not till June. The letters written during this period and preserved in the Records Office at Carlisle from Lord Lowther, one of the candidates, to his father the earl betray the vulnerability the Lowthers felt before Brougham's charges of peculation—and how deeply Wordsworth was involved in their deliberations.[34] The novelty of the contest, moreover, ensured national attention: no other provincial election was covered as thoroughly in the London papers, and the *Morning Chronicle* and the *Times* ran lengthy accounts. The parliamentary reports of the Commission on the Abuse of Charities were also published and then scrutinized in the great journals, so that St. Bees developed into a focus of charge and countercharge. In July 1818 the Tory *Quarterly Review* made a weak attempt to refute what it dismissed as Brougham's effort to "inflict a wound" on the "Earl of Lonsdale, one of the governors of St. Bees school, in Cumberland," ascribing the investigation to low political opportunism.[35] Although Brougham had been defeated at the poll, the St. Bees case was only beginning to gather steam. In October 1818 Brougham published a pamphlet in which he reiterated the injustice of the lease and accused Lonsdale, "who sustains in his own person the double character of trustee and lessee," of suppressing attempts to right the wrong.[36] Within a year the pamphlet had gone through twelve editions, helped no doubt by a series of articles in the *Edinburgh Review* (to which Brougham was a key contributor) in 1819 and 1820 scathingly exposing the profits the Lowthers continued to make out of St. Bees and gleefully reporting the Attorney General's decision at last to bring suit.[37] Brougham's decision to contest Westmorland (again unsuccessfully) in 1820 kept the pot boiling.

What were the actual rights of the St. Bees case? The Attorney General's suit charged that the presence of the earl and his steward on the Board of Governors in 1742 invalidated the original lease, and in 1827 it was thrown out in Chancery. The earl was ordered to pay five thousand pounds to the school, as penalty for coal taken between 1742 and 1821, and after examining the amounts of coal actually mined, a payment of eight thousand, three hundred pounds was asked for the years 1821 through 1826. A new lease of only forty-two years was granted the earl, at rates to vary according to prevailing prices, and under these terms coal for which he had been paying three pounds, ten shillings a year earned the school for the rest of the century an average of seven hundred pounds a year. The school became rich, and it thrives still today.

In writing on St. Bees, then, Wordsworth was touching upon one of the flagrant scandals of his time, and memory of that scandal was still fresh in 1833, when Wordsworth wrote his poem, and in 1835, when he published it. In 1827 Brougham contested Westmorland a third time, and his popularity once more guaranteed extensive cover-age in the newspapers. Though he again lost, the continued electoral success of the Lowthers was a product rather of the unreformed system of representation than of wide popularity. For those who resented Lowther domination, St. Bees was a handy stick. In July 1830, for example, the *Carlisle Journal* addressed an open letter to Brougham, saying that the people did not know how the case had been settled, asking what had happened to the "Large funds locked up in Chancery," and excoriating the Lowthers (July 10, 1830). That autumn the paper denounced the donation of prizes by the Lowthers at the Carlisle races, saying that the money "smells of St. Bees": "It is too bad, however, to fob thousands and then boast of a beggarly twenty pounds, given as a sort of charity. Bah!" (October 9, 1830). In 1832 the same independent paper published a list of the current governors of St. Bees School, noting how many of them were Lowther clients and insisting on "the propriety of keeping the names of these persons constantly before the public eye." Six months later, grossly overestimating the Lowther revenues during the years of the original lease, the paper cited the misappropriation of funds as an instance of the "public plunder pocketed by this one cormorant family" (March 31 and September 29, 1832).

In 1832 the Reform Bill changed the electorate of the county, and the Lowther hold was immediately broken. If Wordsworth did not mention the Grammar School at St. Bees in his poem, and only circumspectly in his note, these anecdotes show exactly what he was being circumspect about. They show us, too, the kind of poem *Stanzas Suggested in a Steam-Boat off St. Bees Heads* is, a kind easily recognized in a Renaissance or Restoration text: it is in part a writer's compliment to his patron. When Wordsworth says that the theological college was established "under the patronage of the Earl of Lonsdale," he expresses one view of the situation, the Lowther view. Such patronage was the responsibility of the enlightened aristocracy the Lowthers saw themselves as being. To perform the patronage was to demonstrate one's benevolence and hence one's fitness to rule. When the family had repaired the school in 1809, the account that found its way into *The Monthly Magazine* reflected this traditional ideology of hierarchy and obligation: "Through the munificence of the Earl of Lonsdale, this long-respected seminary is now put into complete order, and made more suitable to the purpose intended by the pious founder, than it has been at any time since its erection."[38] Wordsworth was justified in describing as "patronage" the earl's having underwritten the expense of roofing the choir of the priory church and fitting out the lecture rooms for the new theological college; to this day, Lonsdale's generosity is acknowledged in the materials offered to visitors. But there is another view of the case, that suggested by the attack of the *Carlisle Journal* on the money the Lowthers donated for race prizes. While it would be mean-spirited to stigmatize the earl's benefactions to the college as conscience money for the sums obtained from the lease, it is true that the college stood across the street from the school; school, church, and college were inseparably entwined, and some of the Lowther wealth enabling the grand acts of patronage stemmed from such questionable transactions as that of the lease. To a radical, the sums returned to the college seem a paltry offset to the injustice of the lease. An 1829 guidebook to Cumberland and West-morland baldly states the matter: "The revenue of this school is now very considerable, the Earl of Lonsdale having lately given up certain possessions, &c, which had been withheld for many years, till the late parliamentary inquiry into the state of this and other charities."[39]

In suggesting, then, a connection between the virtuous Bega and the founding of the college, Wordsworth was presenting his patron as the restorer of a lost harmony, repeating in the nineteenth century the pious actions of the Normans who founded the abbey in the twelfth. Wordsworth is here the apologist of a particular vision of Christian Natural Law, one that accommodates the realities of capi-talism within the traditional social order of the landed aristocracy.[40] As one can see in Fosbrooke's plea that commerce respect the monks, they stand in all the works we have considered not only as spiritual figures and guardians of learning but also as "useful" men, prototypes of a sincerely Christian capitalism. The blandness of Wordsworth's poem can be appreciated in context as a specific political gesture, an embodiment of the ideal relation of lord, land, and labor that Words-worth recommended against the cash nexus and class divisions devel-oping in his day.[41]

It would be easier to grasp the significance of *St. Bees* did we read it not in editions guided by Wordsworth's subsequent arrange-ments or by chronological principles but in the volume he initially organized so carefully. Just as some of the poem's point is obscured when it is not headed by its original note, so its proximity to other poems alters its effect, and Wordsworth's adamant instructions to the printer reveal the care he exercised in making his groupings.[42] The modern reader, should he come upon the poem at all, finds it as the eleventh among the "Poems Composed or Suggested During a Tour, in the Summer of 1833," the category into which it was incorporated in 1845. In the *Yarrow Revisited* volume, however, *St. Bees* is more prominent: in the table of contents the title is marked off from its neighbors by spaces and capital letters, and the text stands with its own title page in a fairly emphatic position toward the end of the book. The notes on the verso of the title page and on a fresh page at the end of the poem further encourage one to treat the work as a substantial unit rather than to slide through it as part of a sequence. In the 1835 volume, *St. Bees* is followed by three sonnets the author says are meant to be included among the *Ecclesiastical Sketches,* and not far in front of it are two sonnets on the Lowthers. In one of these Wordsworth praises the earl's magistracy, and in the other he points to the union in the newly rebuilt Lowther Castle of "cathedral pomp and grace" with "the baronial castle's sterner mien": the architectural detail reflects the ideal coalescence of temporal and spiritual power. These sonnets frame *St. Bees,* amplifying and clarifying the structure of allegiances implicit in it, and this inner frame of ideals proclaimed in short poems is itself contained in an outer one, for they are preceded by *The Warning* and followed by *Humanity,* two of Wordsworth's most extended and bitter jeremiads against the demagoguery he saw everywhere triumphant. Most important in appreciating *St. Bees* is the postscript of the volume, where Wordsworth brings together a defense of the church and a heated critique of the Utilitarian Poor Law of 1834, a bill of which Brougham was a powerful supporter. In arguing against a system that confined the able-bodied poor to a workhouse and in effect blamed the poor for their own poverty, Wordsworth reveals the essential continuity of his beliefs since *The Old Cumberland Beggar* long before. The conjunction of poem and postscript, placing the humane care of the monks against the punitive relief of the reformers, enforces the application of *St. Bees* to contemporary politics. Wordsworth's medievalism was a testimony to the public virtues he thought were required to save the country, and *Yarrow Revisited* was one of the most popular of his individual publications. Appearing in April 1835, in what was for Wordsworth a rather large first edition of fifteen hundred copies, it was widely reviewed and sold out by the end of the year, a success that led immediately to a second edition in 1836.[43] If part of this acclaim is attributable to the general growth of Wordsworth's reputation after the *Works* of 1827, much was doubtless a response to the new volume itself.

III

Current criticism, when it considers Wordsworth's later career at all, continues to envision it as a falling-off from the poet's glorious revolutionary years. But from the vantage of poems like *St. Bees* and the materials surrounding it, one is more likely to see Wordsworth's revolutionary ardors as an aberration from a pattern of family service to the Lowthers. His father and grandfather both had been their agents, and in his activities in the 1818 election Wordsworth was doing no more for them than his forebears had habitually done. From this perspective, Wordsworth's radicalism in the 1790s and the isolation of Dove Cottage appear as interruptions caused by the death of his parents and the hardships visited upon the children by the refusal of the first Earl of Lonsdale to pay his debts to the family, a grievance then acted upon by the general enthusiasm of the times. I purposely oversimplify and exaggerate in order to suggest that when Wordsworth became the squire of Rydal Mount he was fulfilling a destiny predicted by his beginnings in that fine, comfortably bourgeois house in Cockermouth—a destiny expected by his relatives, achieved by his brothers Christopher and Richard, and denied John only by his early death. The order Wordsworth celebrates in *St. Bees* was passing away in 1835, if it had ever really been. The Reform Bill dealt a blow to its political base, and the expanding reading audience turned authors away from patrons and toward the public for reward. Wordsworth deplored these changes, and his recognition of them makes *St. Bees* seem the more fragile, perhaps even desperate. In adhering to this vision, however, which flowers so strongly just because it seemed to be dissolving, Wordsworth was remaining true to the loyalties of his origins.

I want to suggest, therefore, that one advantage of giving more serious consideration to the poems Wordsworth wrote after 1807, or 1814, or wherever critical opinion draws the line, will be a more fruitful understanding of the works written before that boundary. I want it both ways, however. I want also to argue that a poet's final period should not be held in thrall to his earlier one, just because that earlier is more appealing. Wordsworth had the misfortune, spared most of his Romantic contemporaries, of outliving the period in which we place him. Our accounts of Wordsworth's decline, moreover, depend on a view of literary production still bound by a nineteenth-century fascination with the single author. Perhaps the phenomenon we approach through the changes in Wordsworth's personal life—increased comfort, rationalization of the terrors that animate his greatest verse, or whatever explanations are advanced for his loss of poetic power—would look different if approached in historical terms. If, for instance, instead of reading *The Egyptian Maid,* Wordsworth's venture into Arthuriana in the *Yarrow Revisited* volume, retrospectively against the *Lyrical Ballads,* we read it laterally against Tennyson's *Lady of Shalott* (1832), some of its oddity would disappear, and our notions of periodization generally might undergo salutary revision.

In such a context the problem of Wordsworth's "decline"—and I would now place the word in quotation marks to question it—appears not idiosyncratic but as part of a cultural shift. The works Wordsworth was writing in the 1830s share several characteristics with their contemporaries. Literary historians usually treat the decade as the decade saw itself: in Mill's phrase, as an age of transition. Patrick Brantlinger notes that "The number of literary works from the 1830s which are still much read is small: *Sartor Resartus* and *The French Revolution;* Tennyson's first volume; Macaulay's essays; and *Sketches by Boz, Pickwick Papers,* and *Oliver Twist.* Certainly many contemporaries felt that history had reached a crisis point in the 1830s and that the arts were not cultivated as they had been in the past."[44] Brantlinger quotes Bulwer-Lytton's diagnosis from the midst of the crisis in 1833: from the time of the Reform Bill, Bulwer-Lytton commented, "the intellectual spirit hitherto partially directed to, became *wholly* absorbed in, politics."[45] To the poet who rooted poetry in emotion recollected in tranquillity the furious debates of the 1830s were more unsettling than to most, but Brantlinger's list of remembered works shows how literature generally shifted from concern with individual psychology to broader, or more topical, or more analytic forms. Understanding late Wordsworth requires crossing some customary barriers, pedagogical as well as theoretical, between poetry and prose, Romantic and Victorian, literature and politics.

Wordsworth's contemporaries were closer to the diverse resonances of Wordsworth's late style. Commenting on *Yarrow Revisited,* Hartley Coleridge, that unabashed observer of his elders, wryly confessed: "I do wish, however, that there had been a little less of Lowther Castle, and that he had not call'd poor old Lady Lonsdale a *Nymph.*" Though Hartley Coleridge was alert to the absurdity of Wordsworth's hyperbole, the qualification comes after praise: "This is, indeed, nothing like the Ode on Immortality, or the finer parts of the Excursion, there is neither the same profundity of thought nor the same solar warmth of feeling—but there is a vein of tenderness, sweetness, and beauty which is almost new."[46] Six months later he refined his estimate:

> I think I perceive in Wordsworth's last volume, a decided in-clination to the playful, the elegant, and the beautiful; with an almost studied exclusion of the profound feeling and severe thought which characterized the offspring of his middle age. This can be the only reason why Derwent thinks these poems *poor* and *degenerate;* for they are as perfect, perhaps more per-fect, in their kind than any of their predecessors: but the kind is less intense, and therefore, incapable of that unique excellence which the disciples adore. (196)

In the years since, Derwent's view has largely prevailed, but Hartley's recognition that the issue was not one of lessening power but of differing kind is more fertile. As the title poem of the *Yarrow Re-visited* volume makes clear, these are works of the fancy, not of the sublime imagination, self-consciously minor poetry, as it were. In slyly proposing that his "taste is more Catholic" than his brother's, Hartley Coleridge exemplifies the spirit he found in the collection, for the adjective plays on the specific tendency of poems like *St. Bees* as well as on the reader's breadth of sympathy. A similar quiet joke in-habits the last line of *St. Bees.* When in 1823 Walter Savage Landor attacked the epithet "second birth" in *Laodamia* as "stinking and reeking of the conventicle" Wordsworth demurred, but altered it.[47] His sensitivity to such religious overtones suggests that when he char-acterized the College of St. Bees as "new-born" he was not only re-ferring to its recent foundation but also glancing at its evangelical bias. The line makes for a tactful and witty conclusion unseen be-cause unexpected from Wordsworth.

The last word may be Wordsworth's own, and his description of *Yarrow Revisited* makes Hartley Coleridge's appear too concessive. The connection between the poems and contemporary politics is evi-dent in a letter Wordsworth wrote to a Tory MP, Henry Thomas Liddell, during the debate on the Irish church. "This day," Wordsworth begins, "I am told, is to decide the fate of the Ministers, and with them that of the Nation. . . . [T]he scenes that I witnessed during the earlier years of the French Revolution, when I was resident in France, come back on me with appalling violence." And he continues:

> Pray be so kind as to tell me how my little vol: of Poems must be sent to you. . . . You will find in it some political verses, which highflying critics will not allow to be poetry—enough for me, if they be admitted to be good rhetoric and enlightened patriotism, which the Whigs will, of course, be slow to consent to. (*LY*, II, 39)

Rhetoric as *Yarrow Revisited* conceives it is not our current preoccupation with the endless figurative play of language, but rather the older and larger concept of ethics and persuasion. If Wordsworth's doctrines were not victorious in the 1830s, neither were they irrelevant; his medievalism was in part a romance, but it was also a standard. The Reform Bill had been carried by popular agitation, but it was soon captured by middle-class economic interests; the debates on limiting factory working hours soon showed that the people were as badly off under Whig *laissez-faire* as they had been under Tory *noblesse oblige*.

In the case of St. Bees Wordsworth connived at an injustice, to put the matter no more harshly than that. Paradoxically, the prejudices—to use the word in its full Burkean sense—that led him astray in the particular instance were inextricable from humane principles. The episode exposes the difficulties of Wordsworth's position, for the exploiter here was no upstart Manchester industrialist but the very representative of that landed aristocracy to whom he looked for relief. The values cherished in *St. Bees* found a similarly equivocal monument in the Gothic country houses the new rich (in this like the Lowthers) erected as the symbols of their legitimacy, as well as in churches and public buildings across the land. Less equivocally, they flowed into the campaigns of Carlyle, Ruskin, Morris, and the Christian Socialists, just as Wordsworth's opposition to the Poor Law brought him into unacknowledged conjunction with Dickens, whose *Oliver Twist* remains the most famous denunciation of the law. Wordsworth's celebration of monasticism grew from a coherent social vision; as the terrors of the French Revolution came back upon him like those unbidden visitations that had always been the source of his inspiration, he turned to a body of thought more exigent and more modest than the rationalist political theory that had failed him in the 1790s. Where once he had sought in his personal past for renewal, so now he turned to an earlier period of history. The bold "credulities" of *St. Bees*—and Newman used the same word—he recognized as a permanent form of the supernatural intimations his poetry had always spoken to. If the discipline of monasticism forfeited the openness to accident that had been important to the young Wordsworth, perhaps it was also more reliable than chance revelation, a bracing necessary to preserve the sense of mystery in a positivist age. The picture of the monastery reasserted the religious base of education, obliquely answering such secular institutions as the recently founded London University, another of Brougham's causes. Monasticism was for Wordsworth personally an ideal that reconciled the impulses to solitude and to community which had warred throughout his career. The figure of the nun was the final modulation of that pure, maternal image the Blessed Babe of *The Prelude* centers upon: the "one beloved presence" as she might be realized in an iron time.[48] The praise of the monks' liturgy in *St. Bees* shows, too, how Wordsworth had learned that the losses that had animated much of his verse could find expression and solace in impersonal tradition:

> Were not, in sooth, their Requiems sacred ties
> Woven out of passion's sharpest agonies,
> Subdued, composed, and formalized by art,
> To fix a wiser sorrow in the heart?

These verses measure the journey Wordsworth had taken since he wrote of the Pedlar's youthful communion on the mountaintops: "Such hour by prayer or praise was unprofan'd; / He neither pray'd, nor offer'd thanks or praise."[49] "Subdued, composed, and formalized by art" might stand as an epigraph for Wordsworth's late style. "Playful," "elegant," "beautiful"—Hartley Coleridge's terms—are not for late Wordsworth incompatible with intensity and indignation.[50] When we come to appreciate such complexly situated rhetoric as that of *St. Bees,* we shall find the corpus of Wordsworth's late work not entirely a corpse, the desiccation not entirely complete.

Notes

1. Mary Moorman, *William Wordsworth: A Biography* (Oxford: Clarendon, 1957–65), II, 481.

2. Moorman finds that Wordsworth's "determination to adopt the stanza of Charlotte Smith's *St. Monica* . . . was not a happy one" (481), but in choosing a model already associated with a monastic subject, as he told his readers, Wordsworth was exploiting the expressive powers of form itself. In contrast to Moorman, Bernard Groom, in *The Unity of Wordsworth's Poetry* (London: Macmillan, 1966), adduces *St. Bees* as an instance of the "new nimbleness" of Wordsworth's late metrical experiments (182).

3. The text is that of the first edition, *Yarrow Revisited, and Other Poems* (London: Longman, 1835).

4. The monastery and the legends associated with it are the subject of numerous contributions to the *Transactions of the Cumberland and Westmorland Antiquarian and Archaeological Society* [hereafter CWAAS], n.s. 25 (1925), n.s. 28 (1928), n.s. 52 (1952). See also n.s. 4 (1904), and *CWAAS* Tract Series no. 2 (1887). *The Registry of the Priory of St. Bees* was edited by James Wilson as Vol. 126 of the Publications of the Surtees Society (Durham: Andrews, 1915).

5. The following account is not a full discussion of Wordsworth's knowledge of monasticism; he had, for example, the works of St. Gregory Nazianzen in his library. See Chester L. Shaver and Alice C. Shaver, *Wordsworth's Library: A Catalogue* (New York: Garland, 1979), p. 109. I wish only to trace a line bearing upon *St. Bees*. In *A Dream of Order* (Lincoln: University of Nebraska Press, 1970), Alice Chandler surveys the complex of ideas that composed Victorian medievalism. In her witty and detailed study *Reversing the Conquest,* forthcoming from Rutgers University Press, Clare Simmons traces the shifting relations of Saxon and Norman in nineteenth-century literature, history, and popular culture.

6. Thomas Dudley Fosbrooke, *The Economy of Monastic Life* (*as it existed in England*), *A Poem, with Philosophical and Archaeological Illustrations* (Glocester: Raikes, n.d.).

7. On Fosbrooke, see Peter F. Anson, *Building Up the Waste Places* (Leighton Buzzard: Faith Press, 1973), p. 16. I am heavily indebted to this work and to Anson's companion volume, *The Call of the Cloister,* rev. and ed. by A. W. Campbell (London: SPCK, 1964).

8. Thomas Dudley Fosbrooke, *British Monachism, A New Edition* (London: Nichols, Son, and Bentley, 1817).

9. *Quarterly Review* 22, 43 (July 1819), art. 3, pp. 59–102.

10. *The Life and Correspondence of Robert Southey,* 6 vols. (London: Longman, 1850), V, 186–87.

11. Southey, V, 65.

12. John Henry Overton and Elizabeth Wordsworth, *Christopher Wordsworth: Bishop of Lincoln* (London: Rivingtons, 1888), p. 38. Hereafter cited in the text as Overton.

13. See Anson, *Call of the Cloister,* pp. 25–26; Michael Hill, *The Religious Order* (London: Heinemann, 1958); R. W. Sockman, *The Revival of the Conventual Life in the Church of England in the Nineteenth Century* (New York: W. D. Gray, 1917); and A. M. Allchin, *The Silent Rebellion: Anglican Religious Communities 1845–1900* (London: SCM Press, 1958), hereafter cited in the text as Allchin. Susan P. Casteras, "Virgin Vows: The Early Vic-

torian Artists' Portrayal of Nuns and Novices," *Victorian Studies* 24 (1981): 157–84, reveals the ambivalences in the public response to the sisterhoods; and Nina Auerbach touches briefly upon the relation between them and the novels she studies in the introduction to her *Communities of Women: An Idea in Fiction* (Cambridge, Mass.: Harvard University Press, 1978).

14. Owen Chadwick, *The Victorian Church*, 3d ed. (London: Adam and Charles Black, 1971), Part 1, 506; hereafter cited in the text as Chadwick.

15. Robert Southey, *Sir Thomas More: or, Colloquies on the Progress and Prospects of Society*, 2d ed., 2 vols. (London: Murray, 1831), II, 214.

16. *The Letters of William and Dorothy Wordsworth, The Later Years, Part II, 1829–1834*, 2d ed., ed. Alan G. Hill (Oxford: Clarendon, 1979), p. 79. This volume and its successor, *The Later Years, Part III, 1835–1839*, ed. Alan G. Hill (Oxford: Clarendon, 1982), are hereafter cited in the text as *LY*.

17. I quote from the revised text in John Henry Cardinal Newman, *Historical Sketches* (London: Longmans, 1917), II, 165–66.

18. The sonnet was printed in his edition of the *Poetical Works* (London: Macmillan, 1896) by W. A. Knight, who conjectured that Wordsworth's son-in-law, Edward Quillinan, was the author (VIII, 325).

19. *The Letters of Mary Wordsworth 1800–1855*, selected and ed. by Mary E. Burton (Oxford: Clarendon, 1958), p. 188.

20. *The Correspondence of Henry Crabb Robinson with the Wordsworth Circle*, 2 vols, ed. Edith J. Morley (Oxford: Clarendon, 1927), I, 472–73.

21. See Helen Darbishire, *Some Variants in Wordsworth's Text in the Volumes of 1836–37 in the King's Library* (Oxford: Roxburghe Club, 1949), pp. 14–15, 28, 45–46; and the textual apparatus and notes to *St. Bees* in *The Poetical Works of William Wordsworth*, 5 vols., ed. E. de Selincourt and Helen Darbishire (Oxford: Clarendon, 1940–49), IV, 25–30, 402–4. This edition is hereafter cited as *PW*.

22. *Lives of the English Saints* (London: James Toovey, 1844), III, 181–82. The catalogue of Wordsworth's library lists the volume devoted to the Cistercian saints in this series, as well as the six volumes of Newman's *Parochial Sermons* (Shaver and Shaver, 185). In 1842, Wordsworth permitted a selection of his verse to be published, entitled *Contributions of William Wordsworth to the Revival of Catholic Truths;* see Moorman, II, 480. Crabb Robinson admitted that Wordsworth praised the "Oxford School" for "inspir[ing] the age with deeper reverence for antiquity And a more cordial conformity with ritual observances—As well as a warmer piety" but insisted that "he goes no further." He noted disapprovingly: "Nevertheless he is claimed by them as their poet. And they have published a selection from his works with a dishonest preface from which one might infer he went all lengths with them." Crabb Robinson, *Correspondence*. I, 427.

23. See Edith C. Batho, *The Later Wordsworth* (Cambridge: Cambridge University Press, 1933), p. 301.

24. Christopher Wordsworth, *Memoirs of William Wordsworth*, 2 vols. (London: Moxon, 1851), II, 150.

25. *Monthly Repository*, 2d series, 9 (1835): 430–34, rpt. in *The Romantics Reviewed*, ed. Donald H. Reiman (New York: Garland, 1972), Part A, 699–703.

26. See Stephen Prickett, *Romanticism and Religion* (Cambridge: Cambridge University Press, 1976), Chapter 4; and G. B. Tennyson, *Victorian Devotional Poetry: The Tractarian Mode* (Cambridge, Mass.: Harvard University Press, 1981), Chapter 2.

27. Quoted in Michael Bright, "English Literary Romanticism and the Oxford Movement," *Journal of the History of Ideas* 40 (1979): 385–404.

28. Quoted in Anson, *Building Up the Waste Places,* p. 19.

29. R. A. Soloway, *Prelates and People* (London: Routledge Kegan Paul, 1969), p. 319. For the college, see F. W. B. Bullock, *A History of Training for the Ministry of the Church of England* (St. Leonards-on-Sea: Budd and Gillatt, 1955).

30. DC MS. 128, quoted by permission of the Trustees of Dove Cottage.

31. The following account has been compiled chiefly from William Jackson, "Archbishop Grindal and His Grammar School of St. Bees," *Papers and Pedigrees Mainly Relating to Cumberland and Westmorland, CWAAS,* extra series, 6 (London: Bemrose, 1892), pp. 186–255; *The Victoria History of the Countries of England,* ed. James Wilson (Westminster: Constable, 1905), Vol. 2; and William Rollinson, *A History of Cumberland and Westmorland* (London: Phillimore, 1978).

32. See John Edwin Wells, "Wordsworth and De Quincey in Westmorland Politics 1818," *Publications of the Modern Language Association* 55 (1940): 1080–1128; and W. W. Douglas, "Wordsworth in Politics: The Westmorland Election of 1818," *Modern Language Notes* 58 (1948): 437–49.

33. Arthur Aspinall, *Lord Brougham and the Whig Party,* University of Manchester Historical Series No. 47 (Manchester: Manchester University Press, 1927), p. 86.

34. Bundle 78 (1818), D/Lons/L1/2. On October 3, for example, Lord Lowther forwards to his father a pamphlet in reply to Brougham's charges, telling him that "the same post will carry one to Wordsworth."

35. *Quarterly Review* 20, 38 (July 1818), art. 14, p. 535.

36. *Letter to Sir Samuel Romilly, M. P. upon the Abuse of Charities,* rpt. *Speeches of Henry Lord Brougham,* 2 vols. (Philadelphia: Lea and Blanchard, 1841), II, 74.

37. *Edinburgh Review* 31, 62 (March 1819), art. 7, pp. 497–549; 32, 63 (July 1819), art. 5, pp. 89–110; 33, 65 (January 1820), art. 6, pp. 109–31.

38. *The Monthly Magazine* 28 (1809): 223.

39. William Parson and William White, *A History, Directory, and Gazetteer of Cumberland and Westmorland* (1829; rpt. Beckermet, Cumbria: Michael Moon, 1976), pp. 236–37.

40. In this he follows Edmund Burke; see C. B. Macpherson, *Burke* (New York: Hill and Wang, 1980).

41. Note the letter to Daniel Stuart of April 7, 1817:

I see clearly that the principal ties which kept the different classes of society in a vital and harmonious dependence upon each other have, within these 30 years either been greatly impaired or wholly dissolved. Everything has been put up to market, and sold for the highest price it would bring. Farmers used formerly to be attached to their

Landlords, and labourers to their Farmers who employed them. All that kind of feeling has vanished—in like manner, the connexion between the trading and landed interests of country towns undergoes no modification whatsoever from personal feeling, whereas within my memory it was almost wholly governed by it. A country squire, or substantial yeoman, used formerly to resort to the same shops which his father had frequented before him, and nothing but a serious injury real or supposed would have appeared to him a justification for breaking up a connexion which was attended with substantial amity and interchanges of hospitality from generation to generation. All this moral cement is dissolved, habits and prejudices are broken and rooted up; nothing being substituted in their place but a quickened selfinterest.

The Letters of William and Dorothy Wordsworth, The Middle Years, Part II, 1812–1820, ed. Ernest de Selincourt, 2d ed., rev. by Mary Moorman and Alan G. Hill (Oxford: Clarendon, 1970), pp. 375–76.

42. The corrected proofs for *Yarrow Revisited* which make up DC MS. 137 are covered with complaints about the misordering of the texts. For example, *"Again* Mr. W has to repeat that these Poems are not arranged according to his direction—these Lines are to follow the series of Sonnets 1822 *to be followed* by the Somnambulist," and "This Poem to be placed the *first* of the 3 which are to conclude the Volume viz *Humanity, Lines to a Portrait,* & The Power of Sound—this direction, as many others have been *repeatedly* given."

43. See W. J. B. Owen, "Costs, Sales, and Profits of Longman's Editions of Wordsworth," *The Library,* n.s., 12 (1957): 93–107.

44. Patrick Brantlinger, *The Spirit of Reform: British Literature and Politics, 1832–67* (Cambridge, Mass.: Harvard University Press, 1977), p. 11.

45. Quoted from *England and the English,* on p. 14 of Brantlinger, *The Spirit of Reform.*

46. *Letters of Hartley Coleridge,* ed. Grace Evelyn Griggs and Earl Leslie Griggs (London: Oxford University Press, 1937), pp. 186–87.

47. *PW,* II, 519. Similarly in sonnet 40 of the *Ecclesiastical Sonnets* (part 2), on the Anglican reformers, where Wordsworth changed "new-born Church" to "Their church reformed" in order to avoid what his nephew Christopher called "the invidious inferences that would be drawn from this epithet by the enemies of the English Church" (*Memoirs,* p. 113).

48. If Wordsworth admired the serene but active compassion of the religious, he remained wary of the vows to which they were "captive"; see "Incident at Bruges" in the *Memorials of a Tour on the Continent,* 1820.

49. Quoted from MS E, *THE RUINED COTTAGE and THE PEDLAR,* ed. James Butler (Ithaca: Cornell University Press, 1979), p. 400.

50. His concern to get right his critique of the age in the last stanza of *St. Bees* led him to overlook through many revisions the presence of the two extra lines that stand in the first edition.

13

Placing Poor Susan: Wordsworth
and the New Historicism

The New Historicism has invigorated the study of English romantic poetry, renewing our sense of the depth, particularity, and strength of the poets' engagement with their world, and underwriting a healthily critical engagement with their values.[1] But the approach has perils too, chiefly those of restricting the meanings of the poetic text to the generalized ideological matrix to which it is declared to belong. One might avoid these pitfalls by recognizing that the historical situation of the text can only be reached along the treacherous, badly signposted byways of representation, and taking the circuitous route such recognition implies. ("Those that travel on turnpike roads," Cobbett insisted, "know nothing of England." "A road smooth as a die, a real stock-jobber's road," provoked his anger: "my object was, not to see inns and turnpike-roads, but to see the *country.*")[2] Wordsworth's *Poor Susan* provides a useful test case for this proposition. No poem from the 1800 *Lyrical Ballads* can be said to have been ignored, but if reprinting and anthologizing are measures of a poem's standing, neither in its own day nor in ours has *Poor Susan* been central to the presentation of Wordsworth.[3] Jack Stillinger, for example, included it in his Riverside edition, *William Wordsworth: Selected Poems and Prefaces,* but neither the Norton Anthology nor the recent admirable Oxford Authors edition of Wordsworth by Stephen Gill does so. *Poor Susan,* though marginal to the canon, poses important questions of the relation of poems to the historical circumstances from which they emerge and, because the body of critical discussion is less ample than for other poems, permits the assumptions governing critical procedure to be examined with particular clarity. My aim in doing so is not to reject the New Historicism, querulous as some of these pages may seem, but to refine its approach.

Poor Susan centers on a vision of Susan's rural past that the song of a bird triggers one London morning:

> At the corner of Wood-Street, when day-light appears,
> There's a Thrush that sings loud, it has sung for three years:
> Poor Susan has pass'd by the spot and has heard
> In the silence of morning the song of the bird.
>
> 'Tis a note of enchantment; what ails her? She sees
> A mountain ascending, a vision of trees;
> Bright volumes of vapour through Lothbury glide,
> And a river flows on through the vale of Cheapside.[4]

As Julian Boyd and Zelda Boyd have shown, the present perfect tense which marks Wordsworth's verbs in these stanzas indicates a past action continuing into the present: "has sung," "has pass'd," "has heard."[5] This tense is rapidly succeeded by the simple, declarative present: Susan "sees" a mountain ascending, volumes of vapour "glide" through Lothbury, a river "flows" through Cheapside. The reiterated emphasis on sight in the speaker's formulation that Susan *sees a vision* of trees (rather than actual trees) is the only indication that what she sees may be an illusion, but this qualification is offset by the force of the remainder of the passage. Wordsworth's syntax operates characteristically here, to blur the division between vision and ordinary reality: the last two lines of the second stanza, beyond the semicolon, stand as assertions independent of Susan's perspective.

In the third stanza Susan seems almost to enter the world she sees:

> Green pastures she views in the midst of the dale,
> Down which she so often has tripp'd with her pail,
> And a single small cottage, a nest like a dove's
> The only one dwelling on earth that she loves.

This stanza demonstrates the links between imagination and memory in Wordsworth, for her vision restores Susan's past; indeed, from the reader's perspective, it gives Susan a past. The momentary encounter in the middle of the city between Susan and the song of the thrush opens backward first to a three-year continuing action and then into an indefinite but enduring past. The present perfect verb—"has tripp'd"—carries with it the unvarying rhythms of Susan's rural life, and carries that life into the present. Vision and memory are one because in the post-Lockean world it is the capacity to reflect upon one's experience that constitutes the self. Since it is continuity of consciousness, and not merely of lived experience, that grounds the self, imagination must become narrative. The virtually anonymous "Poor Susan" of the first stanza acquires a particular history: the "single small cottage," "The only one dwelling on earth that she loves," is not so much a metonymic substitution for her unique individuality as it is its cause. The claim that Wordsworth made in his letter to Charles James Fox accompanying a presentation copy of the 1800 *Lyrical Ballads* is germane here. In reminding Fox of the connection between identity and property in the lives of the Lake Country smallholders, Wordsworth was recalling him to Burkean principles: "Their little tract of land serves as a kind of permanent rallying point for their domestic feelings, as a tablet upon which they are written which makes them objects of memory in a thousand instances when they would otherwise be forgotten."[6] The power of imagination in the poem is inseparable from the permanence of these domestic affections. The bird's song stimulates a train of associations which enable Susan to write her past onto the London scene: the "volumes," in their secondary sense like the "tablets" of Wordsworth's letter to Fox, contain her life history.

The streets mentioned in the poem place Susan in the midst of the City, the financial heart of London east of St. Paul's. The geographical detail is worth considering for a moment. "Wood-Street" contributes to the figurative contrast the poem implicitly draws between city and country; the etymology that derives the name of the street from its function as the place where wood was sold in the Middle Ages nicely epitomizes the historical processes in which Susan has been caught up and at which Wordsworth obliquely hints. "Cheapside" (from the Anglo-Saxon *chepe,* a market) had been a famous market street since before Elizabethan times, and Lothbury runs along the northern side of the Bank of England. For the poem's first London readers in 1800 these names would have suggested an entire world of mercantile activity, and they would have recognized the contrast, as in Wordsworth's later sonnet *Composed upon Westminster Bridge,* between "the silence of morning" and the bustle and noise that characterized the area during the day. In his commentary to Isabella Fenwick, Wordsworth cited the unexpected tranquillity as the origin of the poem: "this arose out of my observation of the affecting music of these birds hanging in this way in the London streets in the freshness and stillness of the Spring morning" (Brett and Jones, p. 302).

Susan's vision thus not only restores her personal past; it also undoes the accelerating growth of London that struck every eighteenth-century visitor to the capital. The ascending mountain and the trees she superimposes on the city, the vision that returns Cheapside to a vale, precisely reverses the contemporary eating-up of the country by the sprawling metropolis, and serves as critique of the commercial values on which the city is built. "Green pastures she views in the midst of the dale," the speaker reports, and the ambiguity of the verb (strengthened by the rhyme of "dale" with "vale" in the previous stanza) fuses the landscape of Susan's past with a vision of Cheapside already miraculously transformed into bucolic. Wordsworth's simply declarative verbs ("glide," "flows") animate the vision and make pastoral appear not as a lost past, elsewhere, but as a present brought into being by the intensity of desire. Together with the perfect verbs, with their implications of continuous action, they halt the process of historical change which was destroying the countryside.

In the fourth stanza the vision ends:

> She looks, and her heart is in Heaven, but they fade,
> The mist and the river, the hill and the shade;
> The stream will not flow, and the hill will not rise,
> And the colours have all pass'd away from her eyes.

Despite its air of finality, the last line sustains uncertainty. The locution leaves unsettled whether the colors have faded from the world that is seen or from the eyes that see. Moreover, if the series of subtractions of this stanza ("they fade . . . The stream will not flow . . . the hill will not rise") thwart the continuities of the first three stanzas, the present perfect of the last verb retains its force: the colors have passed away, but implicitly something remains.

Readers of Wordsworth will be familiar with such ambiguities of perception inherent in notions of creative imagination, and I do not claim neglected merits for *Poor Susan*. The poem nonetheless tantalizes because of the very explicitness with which it stages a contest between two orders of reality: the reality of Susan's vision and the reality of ordinary perception and of what we might crudely call historical actuality. The problem of critical discourse, how we see Susan, mirrors and reduplicates the problem of how Susan sees.

Some twenty-five years ago, in *The Simple Wordsworth,* John F. Danby wrote of *Poor Susan:*

> The river "flows on through the vale" only to come up against the external reality (to which the poet is really more attentive) of Cheapside. The last verse is a clever fusion of the two voices, that of poor Susan herself, recognizing the hallucination for what it is, and that of the poet inexorably overlaying the girl's: all such hallucinations are transitory and unreal, it is the cage and Cheapside that must be lived with. . . . The poem is in fact not nostalgic, but an appreciation of what nostalgia means. It is about the thrush and the cage, and the country girl in London. It is about how poor servant-girls have their moments of home-sickness and impossible day-dream but must always come back to their poor servant-girls' lives. Wordsworth is not sentimental.[7]

Danby values Wordsworth's compassion, and *The Simple Wordsworth* demonstrated to many for the first time the complexities of Wordsworth's plain manner, yet in praising *Poor Susan* Danby misses the careful ambiguities of its representation: the poem does not make the general assertion that "all such hallucinations are transitory and unreal." Danby's reduction of the vision to the status of "impossible day-dream" and his concomitant granting of a greater reality to "the cage and Cheapside" perpetuate the ordinary definitions of reality the poem's language tests. Though Danby insists that Wordsworth is not sentimental, he is: his definitions deny the validity of Susan's imaginative experience and so impose upon her a bleak existence from which there is no escape.

This critique of Danby's premises I owe to F. H. Langman, who acutely argues that the transitoriness of Susan's vision does not prove that it is not real; for Langman, her loss in her inability to sustain her imaginative state.[8] Langman reads more sensitively than Danby does the declarative verbs through which Susan's vision is given to us, as it is given to her, its status unquestioned. In contrast to Danby's insistence that social circumstance is the true reality, Langman emphasizes the religious language of the poem and the affirmative statements by which it, too, is marked: "She looks, and her heart is in Heaven." He lays particular stress on the last stanza:

> Poor Outcast! return—to receive thee once more
> The house of thy Father will open its door,
> And thou once again, in thy plain russet gown,
> May'st hear the thrush sing from a tree of its own.

Langman interprets Susan's vision in the light of Wordsworth's echo-ing of scripture: her vision is a glimpse of a timeless pastoral para-dise, not so much a nostalgic return to a life once lived as a perma-nent possibility, and a future, an image of the end of exile in a welcome in the house of the Father.

In this debate between Danby and Langman one recognizes a variation of the once prominent division among critics of the English romantics into idealists and tough-minded ironists. Take, for exam-ple, the disagreement between those who saw Keats's nightingale or Grecian urn as emblems of a higher realm and those who saw them as cheats which Keats heroically renounces. These debates dominated critical discussion in the 1950s and 1960s, and in seeking to focus at-tention rather on the oppositions of language which by holding both possibilities open without resolving them makes possible such debate, I am conscious of responding to the deconstructive impulses of the 1970s. The questions the Danby-Langman debate pose about the na-ture of reality within *Poor Susan* point to questions now being raised about the relations of poems to their social and ideological context by the New Historicism, and to these I now turn.

Heather Glen devotes several pages to *Poor Susan* in her recent powerful study, *Vision and Disenchantment: Blake's Songs and Words-worth's LYRICAL BALLADS.*[9] Glen's title is an act of homage to E. P. Thompson, whose famous description of Wordsworth's and Coleridge's loss of the radical confidence of the 1790s, "Disenchant-ment or Default? A Lay Sermon," underlies her historical and critical method.[10] The acknowledgments to the book declare a second influ-ence as well, that of L. C. Knights, "under whose guidance I began to work on Blake and Wordsworth" (p. viii); Knight's best-known work, *Drama and Society in the Age of Jonson,* as its title suggests, prac-tices an engaged historical criticism that is a model for Glen's own. When, in a pairing that has become familiar, Glen links *Poor Susan* to Blake's *The Chimney Sweeper* from *Songs of Innocence,* the pro-cedure is paradigmatic of the book as a whole. Of her two subjects, Glen's bias inclines toward Blake's more direct radical denunciations; throughout her study she does not so much allow the different modes of the two writers mutually to criticize each other as set Blake as the standard against which to measure Wordsworth. *Vision and Disenchantment* is nonetheless one of the most important studies of the *Lyrical Ballads* to have been published in recent years. I quarrel with it here not to diminish Glen's achievement but because the difficulties even she fails to resolve are those that any historically oriented criticism faces as it moves from the ambiguities of poetic language to assertions about historical context and ideology.

Glen focuses on the "conventional narrative standpoint" from which Wordsworth presents Susan:

> She is seen as a person, with a personal history in which the speaker is sympathetically interested, and a fantasy-life which he finds imaginatively compelling. " 'Tis a note of enchantment"; the polite observer's conventional rhapsody lightly acknowledges that he, too, is moved. But to him, Susan's more profound emotional response—a genuine and quite unconventional surrender to "enchantment"—is an "ailment." . . . Like the subjects described by [Erasmus] Darwin, Susan is suffering from an aberration which the observer regards with sympathetic interest. This poem is, of course, very different from Darwin's case histories. Susan's "reverie" is, to some extent, seen from her point of view: as an irresistible force whose present potency is compellingly realized. . . . But the perspective of polite rationality remains, counterpointing the evocation of her vision, and registering it as hallucinatory even at its most powerful. Always implicit in the description is the speaker's sense of another, more "accepted" reality than that which she sees. (pp. 103–4)

I have ventured such a lengthy quotation in order to show Glen's attempt to do justice to Wordsworth's ambiguities. Not much is wrong with this paraphrase—except that in her delineation of the speaker as the embodiment of polite rationality Glen ignores the possibility that the two viewpoints of the poem—epitomized by the way line 6 poses the "note of enchantment" against "what ails her?"—are equally weighted and left in suspended juxtaposition. Though Glen speaks of the counterpoint between the two perspectives, she gradually comes to occupy a position identical to the one she rightly criticizes. If to the speaker Susan's passionate involvement is merely an "ailment," the energy and declarative verbal force with which the poem presents her vision intimate that his failure to appreciate its power is as much an issue for Wordsworth as are doubts of its truth.

In the *Preface* to the *Lyrical Ballads,* Wordsworth cited *Poor Susan* as an instance that would make "perfectly intelligible" what he intended by poems in which "the feeling therein developed gives importance to the action and situation and not the action and situation to the feeling" (248). The polarity between Susan's feelings and the speaker's diagnosis exemplifies a pattern prominent in the collection. Wordsworth repeatedly dramatizes the confrontation of mutually misunderstanding voices. To take just two examples in which the limitations of the uncomprehending adult, rational perspective are exposed, consider the obtuse questioner and the little girl of *We Are Seven* and the bullying parent and his intuitive son in *Anecdote for Fathers.* In these poems, as in *Simon Lee,* where the speaker's humanitarian gesture does not escape hints of self-aggrandizement and insufficient tact, Wordsworth's didactic technique depends on presenting a speaker as the embodiment of the inadequate responses he would teach us to move beyond. This characteristic strategy led to charges of simple-mindedness in Wordsworth's own time, and seems to have produced a more sophisticated form of the same misreading in Glen. She comments: "Susan is seen from the single perspective of a liberal humanitarianism that is responsive to and takes seriously modes of experience other than its own, but finds its own categories unquestioned by them" (p. 107). This summary betrays Glen's failure to grasp Wordsworth's dramatic method: because the *speaker* does not question other modes of experience, she assumes that the *poem* fails to do so. In short, she identifies the speaker with Wordsworth himself. For Glen *Poor Susan* contains "no unsettling shifts of register or conflicting possibilities of meaning" (p. 107). Wordsworth, however, works not by jarring discords but by subtle suggestion, by a play of partial truths teasing the reader to seek for larger meanings beyond the words. Such a mode is inevitably a problem for a criticism concerned to understand poetic language within the pre-existing categories of social discourse.

To put this in a different way, I would argue that Glen moves to unpack the ideological freight poetic language bears before she fully meditates on the slipperiness of its terms. For her, Blake's poetry is superior to Wordsworth's because it embodies the "many different contemporary 'languages' " (p. 106) which correspond to the actual divisions of society; Wordsworth's she sees as committed to a "common language of men" which is in fact belied by the tension-laden class structure. Glen's notion of "common language" is, as we have seen, more monologic than Wordsworth's actual practice: the realms betokened by "enchantment" and "ailment" remain discrete. She also neglects the religious overtones Wordsworth's phrasing evokes and the complicating effect they have on the meaning of the poem. Glen dismisses the pastoral imagery of the third stanza as "static and conventional":

> There is little imaginative pressure behind these generalized pastoral images or these tripping rhythms. This is a remembered landscape—not, like that of the little sweep, a place of present activity—and it is landscape already simplified into cliché. (p. 105)

As the contrast between this judgment and Langman's unfolding of the ideals represented by the conventional imagery of the stanza confirms, one critic's cliché is another's participation in a vital tradition. Though the vision fades, is it any the less the core of Susan's character, the "permanent rallying point" of her self? "This is a remembered landscape," Glen declares, but is it only a remembered one and not also the emblem of an ideal by which London may be judged? Unavailing fictions are not valueless.

Glen consistently interprets Susan's vision as if it had only autobiographical reference, and in consequence she is particularly severe on the last stanza:

> The final effect of the poem is one of diminuendo: of a human reassurance, a return to community, which involves both loss and retreat—"Poor Outcast! return. . . ." It is a closing off very different from the disconcerting opening out into a world of present and contradictory possibilities with which Blake's poem concludes. . . . Wordsworth assumes a social community from which Susan is an "outcast" and to which she may potentially "return." Yet that community is, significantly, a distanced one—and distanced not merely in that to be part of it involves a retreat to the country and the past. (pp. 106–7)

A reader alert to the scriptural echoes, as Langman is, will hear in Susan's father the Father, and in her return the return of the forgiven Prodigal not merely the return of Susan to her country origins. As the community is not a merely human community, so is its location not simply past ("her heart is in Heaven").

Cutting off the religious registers of the language in which it is represented inevitably impoverishes the experience granted Susan and tips the scales of Glen's concluding comparison of the way "each poem [Blake's and Wordsworth's] sees and values vision":

> Susan's "reverie," however compelling, is essentially private: antithetical to rather than operative within a society composed of different interacting subjectivities. And hence it must inevitably fade. . . . [T]he satisfaction proposed for Susan [the "regressive nostalgia" of her return] is a satisfaction for her alone, not for "all": and it is much less immediate and potent than that proposed by her imagination. . . . "Vision" for Wordsworth is a private faculty, which may bring joy to the individual, but which must ultimately "fade into the light of common day." (pp. 107–8)

This use of *private* is arguable on two levels. A vision expressed in traditional religious language can scarcely be said to be private: the weight of centuries of communal spiritual experience endures, however transitory Susan's own experience may be. The perfect verbs, moreover, suggest the continuing availability of these values, not for Susan alone, but for Susan as representative of all those now living in the city, exiled from their spiritual home. A more profound objection concerns the notion of reading inherent in this judgment. Glen's reduction of the unresolved drama of perspectives in Wordsworth's language correspondingly restricts the activity of the reader: where language becomes monologic, reading can only be the decoding or reception of unproblematic messages. In the summarizing paragraphs from which these quotations are excerpted Glen conceives of a reader who understands no more than Susan; because her vision is said to be private and fades, vision itself is said to be a mere withdrawal. Wordsworth scorned poems that allowed such a passive reduplication of meanings declared by the text and bent his efforts to arousing his readers' imaginations. "Vision" is private in *Poor Susan* only if we exclude the mental action the poem inspires in them. *Poor Susan* generates in meditative readers a vision wider than Susan's and warned by her example of the threat the deracinating city poses to pastoral values. To excise all registers of language but that of represented "social fact" leads to overlooking the community the poem creates among its readers, a community that has no specific historical location but exists as the forever renewable potential of poetic response itself. The transition from "Susan's 'reverie,' however compelling, is essentially private," to " 'Vision' *for Wordsworth* is a private faculty" (emphasis added) is the consequence of a failure to understand the mode of virtual existence that is the property of imagination in such dramatic poems as *Poor Susan.* (I shall return to this point in concluding.)

The paradox of Glen's reading is that her reduction of Susan is made in the name of a radical concern for social improvement. The polyphony she prefers in Blake to the monology she imputes to Wordsworth is partly specious, because a plurality of languages is no different from a common language if in either case one understands language(s) to be transparent to a given ideology or "social fact." By treating language as wholly referable to social reality, Glen herself undoes the carefully maintained ambiguities that surround the status of Susan's vision. The authoritarian discourse she attributes to the polite observer of Wordsworth's poem is replicated in her own procedures; like him, she also judges Susan's vision "private," the mere product of an interesting "fantasy-life," of no final importance to those concerned with the actual world. Glen's humanitarian but materialist perspective strips away Susan's imaginative life and leaves her enmeshed in the web of circumstance.

Glen's charges fall heavily on the last stanza of *Poor Susan,* a stanza Wordsworth removed from all printings of the poem subsequent to the edition of 1800. The debate between Danby and Langman can also be reformulated as a debate over texts (Danby uses the later version, Langman the earlier), although one not explicitly conducted as such. If we make this textual history part of our understanding of *Poor Susan* we make possible a criticism that would take as its province the history in and of poems, a criticism that would read the shifts in form manifested in a poet's career as the best entry into questions of the relationships between texts and historical circumstance.

Commenting on Wordsworth's presentation of Susan amidst the city in the first stanza, Glen notes:

> "Poor Susan," out before others are awake, is clearly a victim of this environment, but her present situation is only obliquely registered. Wordsworth does not explore the reasons for her predicament: he shows none of Blake's interest in the exploitative dynamics of the society. (p. 103)

Taken together with the last stanza, however, there is rather more information about Susan than this statement would lead one to expect.

The country lass come up to London is a familiar figure, and the in-herited stock of popular literature and contemporary awareness of population movements fill in the story. Susan is the rural girl trans-planted to the city, perhaps to seek employment after economic hard-ship in the village or on the farm, perhaps (if we register the hints of a transgression needing forgiveness in the final stanza) to hide her shame after a sexual misadventure. Erotic, rather than economic, mis-fortune may have brought her to London. The presentation may be oblique, but it is not bare: it merely refuses to label Susan ("victim," "exploitative dynamics") by a prior and conventional analysis.

For at least one of its early readers Susan was a typical but vivid presence:

> Susan stood for the representative of poor *Rus in Urbe.* There was quite enough to stamp the moral of the thing never to be forgotten. Fast volumes of vapour &c. The last verse of Susan was to be got rid of at all events. It threw a kind of dubiety upon Susan's moral conduct. Susan is a servant maid. I see her trundling her mop and contemplating the whirling phenomenon thro' blurred optics; but to term her a poor outcast seems as much as to say that poor Susan was no better than she should be, which I trust was not what you meant to express.[11]

I am struck by the way in which Wordsworth's declarative presenta-tion of Susan's vision prompts Lamb to a similarly seemingly uncom-plicated act of visualization: "Susan *is* a servant maid. . . . I *see* her trundling her mop" (emphasis added). But I am even more interested by Lamb's recognition that the poem may have signified something other than what Wordsworth meant to express; indeed, since Words-worth may have excised the last stanza because of Lamb's protest, the poem did suggest something other than what Wordsworth intended or, at any rate, something other than what he was willing to have it suggest two years later.[12]

The latter half of Lamb's commentary rather unsettles the cer-tainties of the first part. A reader would not be wholly unjustified who saw in Susan the country girl gone wrong, perhaps even become one of the many prostitutes to be found in the windings and alleys of the city in late-eighteenth-century London. One might approach the outcast Susan through the wronged women of the *Lyrical Ballads,* Ruth or Martha Ray of *The Thorn,* or the prostitutes whose shocking effect on him Wordsworth recounts in *The Prelude* (1805, VII, 348–435), perhaps even through such celebrated images as Hogarth's Harlot's

Progress. If the caged thrush to which she listens is a symbol for Susan's entrapment in the city, perhaps we might also think of the trope of the bird in the gilded cage; perhaps the "plain russet gown" in which the poet imagines the restored Susan is meant as a contrast to the traditionally more flaring garb of the streetwalker. Is it so certain that the wholly undescribed Susan *is* a servant maid?

By one of those coincidences that portend shifts in the critical weather, there appeared simultaneously with the first publication of this essay in 1986 the most detailed attempt yet to confront this question, David Simpson's "What Bothered Charles Lamb About Poor Susan?"[13] As the titles suggest, Simpson's essay and this chapter proceed from a similar curiosity about responses to "Wordsworth's abstraction from the exclusively particular," as Simpson puts it (p. 609), and converge in their overall conclusions. In seeking to reconstruct Susan's career, Simpson impressively assembles the contemporary data of prostitution in London and installs Susan within its ever-renewed population:

> As soon as the country girl set foot in London, she became a city girl, and one moreover at the unstable top of a very slippery slope. As soon as she descended from the stage coach, she would have to run the gauntlet of eager brothel-keepers who awaited at the inns, pretending to offer a "temporary place of lodging" but in fact looking for new girls. This was just the first hurdle, and perhaps the easiest. (p. 595)

And so on through the temptations of luxury and desire, pregnancy, and loss of place. "As we waver between seeing Susan as a servant and as a prostitute," Simpson sums up, "it is as if the poem captures the whole complex of the protagonist's social situation, whereby she is not servant or prostitute, but both, since one leads to the other in the lives of so many young girls in the city" (p. 609).

Simpson acknowledges that Wordsworth may have left unspoken this stock narrative of seduction and betrayal so as to preclude "the possible pitfall of an instant moral judgment or a prefabricated reaction," yet in "teas[ing] out" (we use the same verb) "allusions and implications," he maps it onto Susan (p. 608). The ambiguity of the text is conserved as "a true historical perception of Susan's position" (p. 609), but by a process of supplementing and projecting what the text ignores. Simpson's is an exemplary New Historicist interpretation, but such are the conundrums of reading silences. My use of

Lamb is somewhat different, to emphasize that Lamb's response to Susan is a fruitful instance of the gap between the power of language to suggest beyond the intentions even of the poet and the declarative statements readers make about poems. Susan cannot be referred to social reality as quickly and transparently as Lamb—or any other critic—would like. Lamb initially (if perhaps inadvertently) suggests a doubly figurative reading of Wordsworth's character: "Susan stood for the representative of poor *Rus in Urbe.*" Like the popular traditions to which I have been alluding in trying to place Susan, this phrase reminds us that if the poem "arose out of [Wordsworth's] observation," it was nonetheless mediated by a literary genealogy. Lamb's vignette recalls Swift's *Description of a City Shower* (1710), which is perhaps to say that Wordsworth's Susan reminded Lamb of Swift's:

> Brisk *Susan* whips her Linen from the Rope,
> While the first drizzling Show'r is born aslope,
> Such is that Sprinkling which some careless Quean
> Flirts on you from her Mop, but not so clean.
> You fly, invoke the Gods; then turning, stop
> To rail; she singing, still whirls on her Mop.

This intertextual dimension underscores the difficulty of assigning the signifiers of a poem a single referential content on which to rest analysis. The vast differences in tone and point of view between Swift and Wordsworth invite historical interpretation, but then it must be history passed through the changing genre of urban pastoral rather than the absorption of the poems into social history.

When Wordsworth republished the poem in his 1815 collection he also changed the title to *The Reverie of Poor Susan*. Lamb's comment on the subtitle added to the 1800 text of *The Ancient Mariner* may speak on this occasion too:

> I am sorry that Coleridge has christened his Ancient Marinere "a poet's Reverie"—it is as bad as Bottom the Weaver's declaration that *he is* not a Lion but only the scenical representation of a Lion. What new idea is gained by this Title, but one subversive of all credit, which the Tale should force upon us, of its truth?[14]

Like Wordsworth's publishing as *Resolution and Independence* the poem his circle had always referred to in manuscript as *The Leech-Gatherer,* or like expansion of the formal heading of *Ode,* as it was in 1807, to *Ode: Intimations of Immortality from Recollections of Earliest Childhood,* as it became in 1815 and all later editions, the new title predetermines interpretation of Susan's experience and lessens the ambiguities of status from which its richness came. At the same time, however, the title shifts emphasis from "poor Susan" to her psychological processes, from her external condition to her internal powers. In so doing, it discloses a range of meanings in the now no longer primary adjective *poor.* At least three possibilities seem present: that Susan is economically deprived, that she is pitiable because economically deprived and displaced, or that she is pitiable because she keenly feels the loss of her vision. The three meanings are interrelated, since her vision arises from the conditions of her life, but separating the meanings in this fashion reminds us that "poor Susan" in the economic sense is not an inclusive definition. As Max Byrd observes: "Susan's power of fantasy defeats, for a time at least, the realities of London. She is 'poor' in one sense, far from the mountains and streams she imagines; but rich in another, for the city yields to her human pressure before she at last yields to it."[15] Though brief, the passion of Susan's vision should warn that circumstances do not entirely define character.

The Reverie of Poor Susan brings another conundrum. R. L. Brett and A. R. Jones comment that the new title "is a translation of the title of Burger's poem *Des Arme Suschens Traum"* (302), and the same statement can be found in John Hayden's edition of Wordsworth.[16] Here again, a straightforward assertion obscures a critical problem. A translation presupposes an act of translating: did Wordsworth translate the title of Burger's 1773 ballad? Would he have translated the title if he weren't translating the poem? Or is the similarity merely coincidental? I am less concerned to resolve the question than to explore its implications, for to the degree that *Poor Susan* is meant to recall Burger it places the poem within Wordsworth's general literary project of revising the sensational materials of gothic romanticism. Wordsworth found Burger's personages lacking in the "character" he thought "absolutely necessary" to illustrate human nature, and judged Burger to rely for effect on those "incidents which are among the lowest allurements of poetry." Though he assented to Coleridge's praise of *Des Arme Suschens Traum* as "the most perfect and Shaksperian" of Burger's works, the poem witnesses the accuracy of his objections.[17] Burger's poem is narrated by a girl who tells how her false lover came to her in a dream: he takes her "Treuring" from her hand and breaks it; the myrtle in her garden, symbol of married peace, turns to rosemary, symbol of rue; and her pearls turn to tears. "The dream meant death," she exclaims, and it proves fateful: the rosemary becomes her funeral wreath. The connection with Wordsworth's poem is slight, but Suschen's vision, too, has an uncanny vividness: "Fast schwur'ich, dass ich hell gewacht, / So hell erblickt' ich ihn." If the new title is meant to bring the two works into conjunction, Burger's ballad, or "lyric Romance" as he later called it, offers further evidence for seeing erotic misfortune in Susan's past. The hints Wordsworth removed with the last stanza he reinstalled, as it were, in his allusive title. Though the diminutive form of Susan's name, her superstitious trust in the "Traumbuch," and the simplicity of the ballad form suggest that Burger's character is also an unsophisticated country girl, she is "arme" chiefly because her lover has betrayed her. The filiation with Burger adds one more consideration that needs to be weighed in understanding the resonances sounded by "poor Susan."

The new emphases of the title and the omission of the last stanza cooperate to lessen Susan's individuality. Her reverie, rather than her past life and possible future, fills the shortened poem. The different emphases of the two texts are reflected in the uncertainty about where to place the poem Wordsworth displayed when in 1809 he sketched the arrangement by categories that guided the subsequent editions of his works. The third class he outlines is "Poems relating to natural objects and their influence on the mind," and to this group he first assigns "poor Susan perhaps." One paragraph later, he amends his choice:

> Next might come the Naming of Places, as a Transition to the Poems relating to human life; which might be prettily connected, harmoniously I may say, by Poor Susan mentioned before, and better perhaps placed here, Beggars, Simon Lee, last of Flock, Goody Blake, etc. to ascend through a regular scale of imagination to the Thorn, the Highland Girl, The Leech-gatherer, Hartleap Well. This class of poems I suppose to consist chiefly of objects most interesting to the mind not by its personal feelings or a strong appeal to the instincts or natural affections, but to be interesting to a meditative and imaginative mind either from the moral importance of the pictures or from the employment they give to the understanding affected through the imagination and to the higher faculties.[18]

When Wordsworth republished the poem in 1815 it stood among the "Poems of the Imagination," and there it remained.

There are two ways of reading this history. One is to stress that the category of the imagination, or at least the placement of *Poor Susan* in that category, comes about with the suppression of detail in the revised text. To that degree, Wordsworth's imagination, and not just Susan's, might be seen as withdrawing from engagement into a consoling but delusory private realm, and accusations of default might stand. But I would vary this conclusion to suggest that the imagination consists in the poem's resistance to translation into social categories,[19] and that this resistance can be traced in the textual history of the poem.

The final version of *Poor Susan* ends abruptly: "and the colours have all passed away from her eyes!" Wordsworth offers us neither the sorrow of Suschen's amorous betrayal nor the promise of Susan's reconciliation. In place of these complete stories the final text offers us only the pathos of a loss without explanation, the pathos of a storylessness whose resistance to our powers of questioning and narrative calls them forth. What is resisted, however, has left its traces. In its original version, Susan's pastoral vision is succeeded by the speaker's reverie: the fantasy of forgiveness and return is his. Susan, enchanted by her vision, is herself a text for the (presumably) male speaker to write upon. Her voice is incorporated in his; her fixed silence becomes his imagining of her past, implicit judgment of her present, and assignment of her future. Glen's critique, as we have seen, depends on the identification of Wordsworth with his speaker. I would interpret the singsong anapests of the poem as a sign of Wordsworth's desire to distance himself from this spokesman, but that any such movement from poetic form to sign of character remains doubtful is attested by Glen's response.[20] In excising the original last stanza Wordsworth cut short the plot his speaker had written for Susan and in so doing diminished the characterization of him. By removing the speaker's fantasized story from the text, Wordsworth simultaneously removed himself from implication in it. Polite humanitarians write conventional happy endings, imaginative poets come into being by truncating such fictions. Yet Wordsworth's unease about the relation between male writer and female subject reflects a historically specifiable situation: the lyric that emerges is shaped by the absence of the story as first written.

The speaker's meeting with Susan occurs within that structure of social power in eighteenth-century London that makes girls in the streets in the early morning a subject for male explanation. The erotic and economic explanations I have thus far distinguished for purposes of argument can now be seen as complementary elements of this hierarchy of privilege. The difference between them, however, points to a significant contemporary issue, registered by Lamb: were the actual displaced women who crowded London's streets to be understood sociologically—that is, sympathetically—as the victims of economic change, or morally, as fallen women? The language of religious pastoral in the poem points to a similar dilemma. Though timeless, as I argued above, it is located in a particular historical milieu in which it was peculiarly susceptible to exploitation. Is the vision of religious consolation a genuine alternative to Susan's circumstances or a delusory palliative, self-serving when extended by polite speakers like that of *Poor Susan*? These questions, which animate the social debates of the 1790s, correspond precisely to the uncertainties in the representation of Susan's vision and underlie the unsettled relation to his speaker that Wordsworth revealed by the excision of the last stanza. The form of his poem, narrative apocopated into lyric, is the evidence of their disturbing irresolution. The questionable status of Susan and her vision is less the additive multiplicity of meaning cherished by the New Critics than it is the nodal point of a historically specifiable conflict between modes of understanding such figures as Susan represents.

A comparison will clarify this assertion. *Poor Susan* has the same form as *The Solitary Reaper:* both poems present a male speaker, arrested for a moment of erotically charged contemplation by the sight of a woman of a lower class. The speaker of *The Solitary Reaper* stands in a powerfully double relation to the figure before him: if he incorporates her song without understanding it, the Erse in which she sings protects her privacy. This simultaneous crossing and maintenance of the distance between them makes *The Solitary Reaper* a rich field for criticism. The poem has the mysterious inwardness of the reaper and the closure the speaker brings to his experiences as he moves on, the surmise of lyric and the satisfaction of completed narrative. The speaker of the first version of *Poor Susan,* in contrast, possesses Susan. The inwardness of her moment of contemplation becomes the narrative of his; the poet himself risks appearing as the exploiter of the female figure. His revision suggests that Wordsworth may have been uneasy with the invasive intimacy of this relationship; at any rate, he anticipated Glen's critique by himself rejecting the plot the speaker had written for Susan in the original last stanza. The abrupt ending is the trace that shows the inadequacy of the discourses through which Susan had been disposed of, which is to say that the historical situation of the poem manifests itself in a negative form, as an act of repudiation. What Wordsworth can represent he erases; what he cannot, a satisfyingly authoritative (I use the word deliberately) placing of Susan and her vision, persists, historically circumscribed but absent, as the enigma of the poem. In so doing, Wordsworth creates a tryst without a climax—and an instructive fable for critics.

Danby in the passage quoted above draws from *Poor Susan* the moral that "it is the cage and Cheapside that must be lived with." The cage is an unremarkable feature of other critics' discussions as well, but a return to the text quickly confirms that there is no cage in it. In the 1800 text the cage could be inferred only from the slight strangeness of the last line of the poem ("May'st hear the thrush sing from a tree of its own"); when Wordsworth dropped this stanza, he strengthened the hint of a cage by the change of "There's a Thrush" in the second line to "Hangs a Thrush." If that verb almost requires that the thrush be caged, still Wordsworth does not state as much, and readers of the *Preface* to the 1815 edition will remember how charged with metaphorical power the verb was for Wordsworth (quoted in Stillinger, pp. 483–84). If one argues from the historical fact of caged thrushes in eighteenth-century London, Wordsworth's reticence becomes the more significant. Tongue somewhat in cheek, I would read the cage that Danby reifies as the emblematic artifact of a critical method that denies the polysemy of poetic language, and I am fascinated by the grim comedy of critics who deplore Susan's condemnation to a cage of their own making, who see her as "imprisoned" (Stillinger, p. 499). The ambiguous status of Susan's vision eludes equation with social fact, even as Wordsworth's poem eludes the statements critical discourse makes about it ("Susan is a servant maid," "The title is a translation," etc.).

Susan's seeing in the poem is a microcosm of the reading process, and questions about the status of her vision play out questions of the status we accord texts. The truncated encounter places us in the position of the speaker: as he gazes at Susan, so we gaze at the poem, our certainties fading like her vision, and his comprehension, in the elisions and gaps of the text. The readings of *Poor Susan*— Danby's, Langman's, Glen's, Simpson's, mine—form a series that repeats the interpretive puzzles of the poem, each the record of a teasing encounter as much the "ailment" of the understanding as the "enchantment" of the imagination. Our differences one from another can be historically situated but not construed into progressive mastery of the text. The poem circulates among its readers, re-originating its problems for each and so provoking a renewed exchange of critical debate. The poem attracts our common gaze and throws us back on our differences, enacting both our desire to understand the mute figures before us and its frustration.

Notes

1. No name is more associated with this movement than that of Jerome McGann. I will cite here only his *The Romantic Ideology* (Chicago: University of Chicago Press, 1983) and the essays collected in *The Beauty of Inflections* (Oxford: Clarendon, 1985).

2. William Cobbett, *Rural Rides,* ed. George Woodcock (Baltimore: Penguin, 1967), pp. 240, 69, 31.

3. The poem was reprinted, unsigned, in *The Courier* of August 18, 1801 (see R. S. Woof, "Wordsworth's Poetry and Stuart's Newspapers: 1797–1803," *Studies in Bibliography* 15 [1962]: 149–89), but in only one of the more than forty contemporary collections surveyed by Stephen Bauer ("Wordsworth and the Early Anthologies: II," *The Library* 30 [1975]: 244–45).

4. Quotations of *Poor Susan* are from the text of the first edition as given in *Wordsworth and Coleridge: Lyrical Ballads,* ed. R. L. Brett and A. R. Jones (London: Methuen, 1968), p. 170.

5. Julian Boyd and Zelda Boyd, "The Perfect of Experience," *Studies in Romanticism* 16 (1977): 3–13.

6. *The Letters of William and Dorothy Wordsworth, The Early Years, 1787–1805,* ed. Ernest de Selincourt, 2d ed., rev. by Chester L. Shaver (Oxford: Clarendon, 1967), pp. 314–15.

7. John F. Danby, *The Simple Wordsworth* (London: Routledge, 1960), pp. 31–32.

8. F. H. Langman, "Two Wordsworth Poems," *Southern Review* (Adelaide) 11 (1978): 247–64.

9. Heather Glen, *Vision and Disenchantment* (Cambridge: Cambridge University Press, 1983).

10. Thompson's essay is in *Power and Consciousness,* ed. Conor Cruise O'Brien and William Dean Vanech (London: University of London Press, 1969), pp. 1–13.

11. *The Letters of Charles and Mary Anne Lamb,* ed. E. W. Marrs, Jr. (Ithaca: Cornell University Press, 1975–), III, 147.

12. Ernest de Selincourt noted that the fifth stanza "was probably dropped owing to a protest of Lamb's" (*Poetical Works of William Wordsworth,* 5 vols.

[Oxford: Clarendon, 1944–49], II, 507). Yet the stanza was omitted as early as the 1802 reprinting of the *Lyrical Ballads,* long before Lamb's comments, just quoted, which occur in a letter of 1815 responding to Wordsworth's present of the just-published two-volume edition of his works. Lamb may have been pleased to see that a criticism made years before had been taken up, but his responsibility for the revision remains undetermined.

13. *Studies in English Literature* 26 (1986): 589–612.

14. Lamb, *Letters,* I, 266.

15. Max Byrd, *London Transformed: Images of the City in the Eighteenth Century* (New Haven: Yale University Press, 1978), pp. 42–43.

16. *William Wordsworth: The Poems,* 2 vols., ed. John O. Hayden (Harmondsworth: Penguin, 1977), I, 942.

17. Quoted in *The Critical Opinions of William Wordsworth,* ed. Markham L. Peacock, Jr. (Baltimore: Johns Hopkins University Press, 1950), pp. 192–93.

18. *The Letters of William and Dorothy Wordsworth, The Middle Years, Part I, 1806–1811,* ed. Ernest de Selincourt, 2d ed., rev. by Mary Moorman (Oxford: Clarendon, 1969), p. 335.

19. Or natural ones, for the difference between the two categories in the 1809 schema is between "the influence of natural objects on the mind," a rubric that focuses on Susan's rural upbringing, and "objects interesting to a meditative and imaginative mind," which I take it points to the readers of a poem still more than to the characters in it. The poet teaches the reader "the moral importance of the pictures" poems present by developing his capacity to respond to the nuances their partial perspectives imply.

20. The same meter marks *The Farmer of Tilsbury Vale,* a poem Wordsworth asked his reader to compare with *Poor Susan* in the Fenwick note (quoted in Hayden, p. 942). Wordsworth's indulgent view of Old Adam, a once-prosperous farmer whose means run out and who decamps to London, plays interestingly against the view of Susan's plight elaborated by Danby and Glen. Adam's heart remains in Tilsbury Vale, as Susan's does in her past, but even in the city "Nature . . . Full ten times a day takes his heart by surprise" (ll. 63–64), and he thrives in his new environment: "He seems ten birthdays younger, is green and is stout; / Twice as fast as before does his blood run about" (53–54). Simpson ascribes the difference between Adam's continued sustenance by nature and the transience of Susan's vision to the farmer's having "lived most of his life in the country, so that his habits and experiences were fully formed before he came to London," whereas "Susan must have come as a young adult or girl, perhaps even in her middle teens. She simply has less recollected experience to draw upon" (p. 602). The contrast is persuasively developed, yet what interests me is the interpretive imperative that converts the poem's lack of specification of Susan's age into the certainty that she "must have come" to the city as a young adult.

Index